ENGLISH INN SIGNS

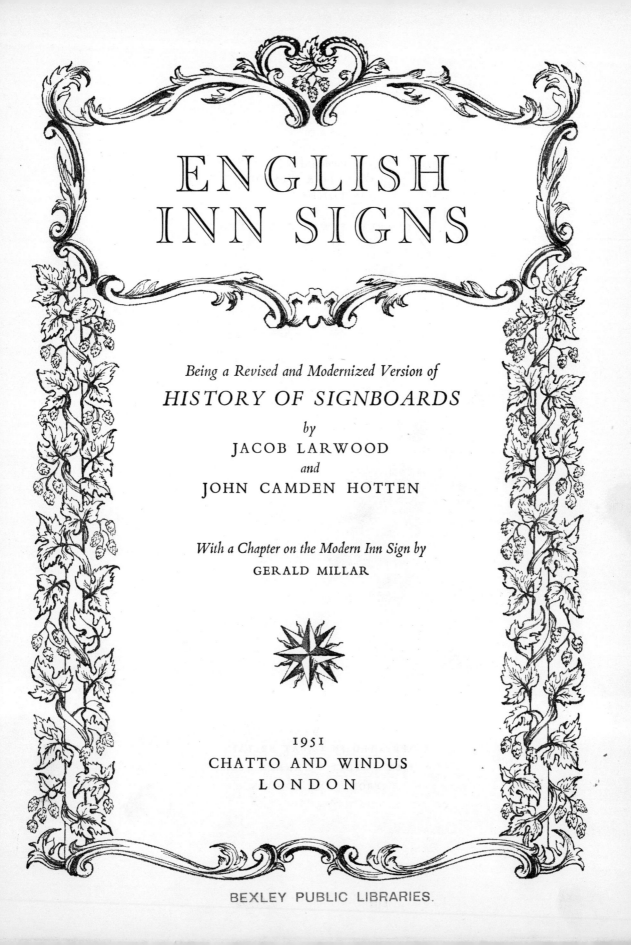

ENGLISH INN SIGNS

Being a Revised and Modernized Version of

HISTORY OF SIGNBOARDS

by

JACOB LARWOOD

and

JOHN CAMDEN HOTTEN

With a Chapter on the Modern Inn Sign by

GERALD MILLAR

1951

CHATTO AND WINDUS

LONDON

Published by
CHATTO & WINDUS
LONDON
★
CLARKE, IRWIN & CO. LTD
TORONTO

HISTORY OF SIGNBOARDS, of which
ENGLISH INN SIGNS is a revised and modernized
version, was first published in 1866.   The joint authors
of the book were Jacob Larwood and John Camden
Hotten, the latter of whom was also the publisher.
Hotten had founded his firm in 1853, and at his death
in 1874 it was acquired by Andrew Chatto, who
renamed the firm Chatto and Windus.   Apart from
a large paper edition, four editions in Cr. 8vo appeared
in the first year of publication, and eight further
editions followed, the twelfth and last
appearing in 1907.

Contents

Billheads

The above illustrations are reproduced by kind permission of Sir Ambrose Heal, from whose original collection of billheads these examples were selected

List of Inn Signs

	TITLE	LOCALITY	ARTIST	BREWER OR OWNER
	RED LION	Eye, Suffolk	*S. L. Webster*	Youngs, Crawshay & Youngs, Ltd.
27	CHEQUERS	Fareham	*Ralph Ellis*	Henty & Constable (Brewers), Ltd.
	BLUE ANCHOR	Trotton	*Ralph Ellis*	„ „
	LICENSEE B. ROWE	(Museum exhibit)	*E. M. Dinkel*	Victoria & Albert Museum
28	THE BROCKET ARMS	Ayot St Lawrence, Herts.	*E. M. Dinkel*	Lord Brocket
29	BEDFORD ARMS HOTEL	Woburn	*H. N. Easthaugh*	Trust Houses, Ltd.
	TANKERVILLE ARMS	Hounslow	*Ralph Ellis*	Watney, Combe, Reid & Co., Ltd.
30	THE GRAFTON ARMS	Barnham, Suffolk	*E. M. Dinkel*	Greene, King & Sons, Ltd.
31	THE CRAWSHAY ARMS	Philadelphia Lane, Norwich	*S. L. Webster*	Youngs, Crawshay & Youngs, Ltd.
32	BUCK	Earsham	*S. L. Webster*	„ „

Following page 272

	TITLE	LOCALITY	ARTIST	BREWER OR OWNER
33	BUCK	Thorpe, Norwich	*S. L. Webster*	„ „
	THE GRIFFIN	(Museum exhibit)	*Design only by E. M. Dinkel*	Victoria and Albert Museum
34	THE GOLDEN HIND	Plymouth	*Ralph Ellis*	Plymouth Breweries, Ltd.
35	THE SHIP INN	Thursby	*E. M. Dinkel*	Carlisle and District State Management Scheme
	THE ROYAL GEORGE	Worthing	*Ralph Ellis*	Henty & Constable (Brewers), Ltd.
36	THE LORD RODNEY	Church Green, Keighley	*H. R. Hosking*	S. M. Lund & Son
	THE LORD NELSON	—	*Design only by L. A. Husking*	'Brewing Trade Review'
37	KING'S HEAD	Drayton	*Ralph Ellis*	Henty & Constable (Brewers), Ltd.
	THE NELSON	Birmingham	*Ralph Ellis*	Frederick Smith, Ltd.
38	KING'S HEAD	Davey Place, Norwich	*S. L. Webster*	Youngs, Crawshay & Youngs, Ltd.
39	LEICESTER ARMS	Luton	*Ralph Ellis*	J. W. Green, Ltd.
	SOMERSET TAVERN	Luton	*Ralph Ellis*	„ „
40	THE KING'S HEAD	Gravesend	*Ralph Ellis*	Charrington & Co., Ltd.
	THE KING'S HEAD	Richmond, Yorks.	*Ralph Ellis*	Major H. Levin
41	THE SPOTTED COW	Littlehampton	*Ralph Ellis*	Henty & Constable (Brewers), Ltd.
	SHOULDER OF MUTTON AND CUCUMBERS	Yapton, Arundel	*Ralph Ellis*	„ „

	TITLE	LOCALITY	ARTIST	BREWER OR OWNER
42	THE GREYHOUND	—	E. M. Dinkel	Unknown
	THE OLD SPOTTED DOG	Neasdon	Ralph Ellis	Charrington & Co., Ltd.
43	THE GREYHOUND INN	Reepham, Norfolk	S. L. Webster	Youngs, Crawshay & Youngs, Ltd.
44	THE BLUE BOYS	Kipping's Cross, Kent	Ralph Ellis	Page & Overton's Brewery, Ltd.
45	THE PEACOCK	Bourneville	Ralph Ellis	Bourneville Village Trust
	THE SWAN	Tingrith	Ralph Ellis	J. W. Green, Ltd.
46	THE HAMPSHIRE HOG	Hammersmith	Ralph Ellis	Watney, Combe, Reid & Co., Ltd.
	THE SQUIRREL	Battle, Sussex	Ralph Ellis	Page & Overton's Brewery, Ltd.
47	THE BEAR INN	Amberley, Glos.	Keith Henderson	Free House
	THE RED COW HOTEL	Hammersmith	Cosmo Clark, A.R.A.	Fuller Smith & Turner, Ltd.
48	WAGON AND HORSES (Double sided)	Ridge Hill, nr. St Albans	Eric Newton	Trust Houses, Ltd.

Following page 304

	TITLE	LOCALITY	ARTIST	BREWER OR OWNER
49	THE WHITE HORSE HOTEL	Dorking, Surrey	E. N. Easthaugh	„ „
	THE PLOUGH	Redford	Ralph Ellis	Henty & Constable (Brewers), Ltd.
50	THE PIED HORSE	Slough, Bucks	Maurice Randall	Courage & Co., Ltd.
	THE FALCON	Eltham, S.E.9	Maurice Randall	„ „
51	THE ROSE & CROWN	Low Hesket	E. M. Dinkel	Carlisle & District State Management Scheme
	THE BLACK BOY	Sudbury	E. M. Dinkel	Greene, King & Sons, Ltd.
52	THE QUEEN	Corby	E. M. Dinkel	Carlisle & District State Management Scheme
	THE JACK OF TRUMPS	Barnham, Suffolk	E. M. Dinkel	Greene, King & Sons, Ltd.
53	KING'S ARMS	Ludham, Norfolk	S. L. Webster	Youngs, Crawshay & Youngs, Ltd.
	SHIP INN	Foulsham, Norfolk	S. L. Webster	„ „
	SHIP INN	King St., Norwich	S. L. Webster	„ „
54	THE COMET	Hatfield	Eric Kennington	Benskins Watford Brewery, Ltd.
55	THE NEW WELLINGTON	Newmarket	H. G. Theaker	Greene, King & Sons, Ltd.
	THE SARACEN'S HEAD	Margate	Miss Herry Perry	Truman, Hanbury, Buxton & Co., Ltd.
56	RIFLEMAN	St George's, Norwich	S. L. Webster	Youngs, Crawshay & Youngs, Ltd.

	TITLE	LOCALITY	ARTIST	BREWER OR OWNER
	THE HIGHLAND LADDIE	Glasson	*E. M. Dinkel*	Carlisle & District State Management Scheme
57	THE COGERS (Double sided)	Salisbury Court, Fleet Street	*Sir Edwin Lutyens, R.A.*	Barclay Perkins & Co., Ltd.
58	THE TALLY-HO	Barnet	*Cosmo Clark, A.R.A.*	Charrington & Co., Ltd.
59	DICK TURPIN (Double sided)	Village Sign of Gadshill, Kent	*Maxwell Ayrton*	
60	THE TWO BREWERS	Chipperfield	*Eric Newton*	Trust Houses, Ltd.
	THE BREWERY TAP	Ferneaux Pelham, Herts.	*E. M. Dinkel*	Rayment & Co., Ltd.
61	THE BLACK SWAN	Abingdon	*Birdwood Willcocks*	Watney, Combe, Reid & Co., Ltd.
	THE THREE MAGPIES	Sells Green, Seend	*E. M. Dinkel*	Wadworth & Co., Ltd.
62	MAP DIAGRAM	—	*H. J. T. Gowen and S. L. Webster*	Youngs, Crawshay & Youngs, Ltd.
63	GREENE KING TRADE SIGN	—	*Kruger Gray*	Made for Greene, King & Sons, Ltd., by Royal Doulton Potteries
64	THE JOLLY CAULKERS	Rotherhithe	*Cosmo Clark, A.R.A.*	Barclay Perkins & Co., Ltd.

Chapter I

GENERAL SURVEY OF SIGNBOARD HISTORY

THE first known reference to tradesmen's signs occurs with respect to the ancient Egyptians. Only occasionally however does an Egyptian shop appear to have had a sign with an inscription concerning it, and an emblem indicating it. Little more is known of signs amongst the Greeks, though Aristotle, Lucian, and some other writers refer to them.

Only with the Romans we begin to have distinct data. In Rome as in our mediæval towns some streets derived their names from signs. Such, for instance, was the vicus Ursi Pileati (the street of The Bear with the Hat on), in the Esquiliae. The nature of their signs is well known. The *Bush*, their tavern-sign, gave rise to the proverb ' *Vino vendibili suspensa hedera non opus est* ' ; and hence we derive our sign of the *Bush* and our proverb ' Good Wine needs no Bush '. An *ansa*, or handle of a pitcher, was the sign of their post-houses. It is clearly evident from various authors that they also had painted signs, or exterior decorations which served their purpose. Phaedrus speaks of a sign containing the story of the mice and the weasels, Horace admires the realism of the Roman tavern-signs, Cicero speaks of the sign of the *Cock* on the New Forum, and Pliny mentions the same sign, also that of the *Shepherd & Staff*.

We can learn a little more from an inspection of the Roman signs themselves as they have come down amongst the ruins of Herculaneum and Pompeii. A few were painted, but as a rule they appear to have been made in relief of stone or terra-cotta, and let into the pilasters at the side of the open shop-fronts. Thus there have been found a *Goat*, the sign of a dairy, and a *Mule* driving a mill, the sign of a baker. At the door of a schoolmaster was the not very tempting sign of a boy receiving a birching. Very similar to our *Two Jolly Brewers*, carrying a barrel slung on a long pole, a Pompeian publican had *Two Slaves* carrying an amphora represented above his door. Another wine merchant had a painting of *Bacchus* pressing a bunch of grapes. At a perfumer's shop in the street of Mercury were represented various items connected with the owner's profession, four men carrying a box with vases of perfume, men occupied in laying out and perfuming a corpse, etc. There was also a sign similar to the one mentioned by Horace, the *Two Gladiators*, under which, in the usual Pompeian cacography, was an imprecation upon those who should damage it. Besides these there were the signs of the *Anchor*, the *Ship* (perhaps a ship-chandler's), a sort of *Cross*, the *Chequers*, the *Phallus* on a baker's shop, whilst in Herculaneum there was a very cleverly painted *Cupid*, carrying a pair of ladies' shoes, one on his head and the other in his hand.

It is also probable that at a later period the various artificers of Rome had their tools as the signs of their houses, to indicate their professions. Since they sculptured

I

B

them on their tombs in the catacombs, we may perhaps conclude that they would do the same on their houses in the land of the living. Thus on the tomb of Diogenes the gravedigger there is a *pick-axe and a lamp*, Bauto and Maxima have the tools of carpenters, a *saw, an adze, and a chisel* ; Veneria, a tire-woman, has a *mirror and a comb*. There are others who have *wool-combers' implements* ; a physician, who has a *cupping-glass* ; a poulterer with a *case of poultry* ; a surveyor with a *measuring rule* ; a baker with a *bushel, a millstone, and ears of corn*. In fact, almost every trade had its symbolic implements. Even the cockney custom of punning on the name, still fairly common on signboards, finds its precedent. The grave of Dracontius bore a *dragon* ; Onager, a *wild ass* ; Umbricius, a *shady tree* ; Leon, a *lion* ; Doleus, father and son, *two casks* ; Herbacia, *two baskets of herbs*, and Porcula, a *pig*.

We may conclude that our forefathers adopted the signboard from the Romans. At first there were not so many shops as to require pictures for distinction, and the open shop-front needed no emblem to indicate the trade carried on within. Yet the inns by the roadside and in the towns undoubtedly had signs. There was the Roman bush of evergreens to indicate the sale of wine. The *Bush* certainly must be counted amongst the most ancient and popular of signs. Not only are traces of its use found among Roman and other remains, but during the middle ages also we have evidence of its display. Indications of it are to be seen in the Bayeux Tapestry, in that part where a house is set on fire, with the inscription : *Hic domus incenditur*. Next to this appears a large building from which projects something very like a pole and a bush, both at the front and the back of the building. Certain devices may have been adopted to attract the attention of the different classes of wayfarers, as the *Cross* for the Christian customer, and the *Sun* or the *Moon* for the pagan. In Caedmon's metrical paraphrase of Scripture history (*c*. A.D. 1000), in the drawings relating to the history of Abraham there are distinctly represented certain cruciform ornaments painted on the walls, which might serve the purpose of signs.★ Then we find various emblems or standards, to court respectively the custom of various classes of wayfarer. He who desired the patronage of soldiers might put up some weapon. Or if he sought his customers among the artificers there were the various implements of trade with which he could appeal to the different mechanics who frequented his neighbourhood.

Along with these very simple signs at a later period, coats of arms, crests, and badges gradually made their appearance at the doors of shops and inns. The reasons which dictated the choice of such subjects were various. Tradition has it that one of the principal was this. In the middle ages the houses of the nobility, both in town and country when the families were absent, were used as hostelries for travellers. The family arms hung in front of the house, and the most conspicuous charge in those arms gave a name to the establishment amongst passers-by. These, unacquainted with the mysteries of heraldry, e.g. called a lion *gules* or *azure* by the vernacular name of the *Red* or *Blue Lion*. Such coats of arms gradually became popular, and innkeepers began to adopt them, hanging out red lions and green dragons as the best way to

★ See upon this subject under ' Religious Signs '.

acquaint the public that they offered food and shelter. The palace of St Laurence Poulteney, the town residence of Charles Brandon, Duke of Suffolk and also of the Dukes of Buckingham, was called the *Rose* from that badge being hung up in front of the house. It is referred to in *King Henry VIII*.*

A house in the town of Lewes was formerly known as *The Three Pelicans,* the fact of those birds constituting the arms of Pelham having been lost sight of. Another is still called the *Cats,* these being nothing more than supporters of the arms of the (Sackville) Dorset family, two leopards *argent,* spotted *sable.*

So long as civilization was at a low ebb and competition trifling signs were of but little use. A few objects typical of the trade carried on would suffice. A *knife* for the cutler ; a *stocking* for the hosier ; a *hand* for the glover ; a pair of *scissors* for the tailor ; a *bunch of grapes* for the vintner fully answered public requirements. But as luxury increased and the number of houses or shops dealing in the same article multiplied, something more was wanted. Perhaps partly because trades continued to be confined to particular streets it became desirable to give to each shop a name or token by which it might be mentioned in conversation, so that it could be recommended and customers sent to it. Reading was still a rare acquirement, consequently to write up the owner's name would have been of little use. Those that could advertised their name by a rebus ; thus a hare and a bottle stood for Harebottle, and two cocks for Cox. Others, whose names no rebus could represent, adopted pictorial objects. As time went on new subjects were continually required. The animal kingdom was ransacked from the elephant to the bee, from the eagle to the sparrow ; the vegetable kingdom from the palm-tree and cedar to the marigold and daisy ; everything on the earth and in the firmament above it was put under contribution. Signs included portraits of the great men of all ages, and views of towns, both painted with a great deal more of fancy than of truth. Articles of dress, implements of trades, domestic utensils, things visible and invisible, things real and those imaginary were adopted in order to attract attention and to obtain publicity. Finally, as all signs in a town were generally painted by the same small number of persons, whose talents and powers of invention were limited, it followed that the same subjects were often repeated, introducing only a change in colour for a difference.

A modern writer classifies signs under four main heads : ' pagan and priestly ', ' historical and commemorative ', ' heraldic and sporting ', and ' punning and miscellaneous '. It will be seen however that the signs to be found to this day are so varied in their nature and origin as to defy a satisfactory classification.

Since all the pictures were of much the same quality rival tradesmen tried to outvie each other in the size of their signs, each one striving to obtrude his picture into public notice by putting it out farther in the street than his neighbour's. The London *Liber Albus* of 1419 names this subject amongst the inquisitions at the wardmotes : ' Item, if the ale-stake of any tavern is longer or extends further than ordinary '. It was ordained that none of the taverners in the Chepe and elsewhere in the City

* Act I, Sc. 2.

should in future have an ale-stake extending or lying over the King's highway of greater length than seven feet at most.

The booksellers generally had woodcuts of their signs for the colophons of their books, so that their shops might be known by the inspection of these cuts. Among these a sign was considered an heirloom, and descended from father to son like the coat of arms of the nobility. This was the case with the *Brazen Serpent*, the sign of Reynold Wolfe. His trade was continued after his death by his wife Joan, who 1 July 1574 made her will whereby she desired to be buried near her husband, in St Faith's church, and bequeathed to her son, Robert Wolfe, the chapel-house, the Brazen Serpent and all the prints, letters, furniture, etc.*

As soon as signboards were generally adopted, quaintness or less often costliness became desired. No doubt the signs were generally of little artistic value. Good artists were scarce, and in any case there was little security for such work, exposed to the sun, wind, rain, frost and the nightly attacks of revellers and roisterers. Great care, however, was bestowed upon the ornamentation of the ironwork by which the sign was suspended. This was perfectly in keeping with the taste of the times, when even the simplest lock or hinge bore its scrolls and strapwork.

The signs were in general suspended from an iron bar, fixed either in the wall of the house or in a post or obelisk standing in front of it. In either case the iron-work was shaped and ornamented with that taste so conspicuous in the metalwork of the Mediæval and Renaissance times. In provincial towns and villages where there was sufficient room in the streets, the sign was often suspended from a kind of small triumphal arch standing out in the road, partly wood, partly iron, and ornamented with all that carving, gilding and colouring could bestow upon it.† Some of the designs of this class of ironwork which have come down to us in the works of the old masters are indeed exquisite.

Painted signs then, suspended in that way, were perhaps more common than those of any other kind. Yet not a few shops simply suspended at their doors some prominent article of their trade. Actually this custom long outlived the use of the more elegant signboards. In Larwood's time it might be daily witnessed in the streets, where the ironmonger's frying-pan or dust-pan, the hardware-dealer's teapot, the grocer's tea-canister, the shoemaker's last or clog, the *Golden Boot*, and many similar objects bore witness to this old custom. There are, of course, not a few instances of this kind surviving to the present day (1950).

There was in London another class of houses that had a peculiar way of placing their signs—viz. the Stews upon the Bankside, which were by a proclamation of 1545-6 'whited and painted with signs on the front, for a token of the said houses'. Stow enumerates some of these symbols, such as the *Cross Keys*, the *Gun*, the *Castle*, the *Crane*, the *Cardinal's Hat*, the *Bell*, the *Swan*, etc.

An observer of James I's time jotted down in a document now among the Har-

* Of their printing-office.
† See description of *White Hart*, Scole, p. 15.

leian MSS.* the names of all the inns, taverns and side-streets in the line of road between Charing Cross and the Tower of London. In imagination we can walk with him through the metropolis :—

On the way from Whitehall to Charing Cross we pass : the *White Hart*, the *Red Lion*, the *Mairmade*, *iij Tuns*, *Salutation*, the *Graihound*, the *Bell*, the *Golden Lyon*. In sight of Charing Cross : the *Garter*, the *Crown*, the *Bear & Ragged Staffe*, the *Angel*, the *King Harry Head*. Then from Charing Cross towards yᵉ cittie : another *White Hart*, the *Eagle & Child*, the *Helmet*, the *Swan*, the *Bell*, *King Harry Head*, the *Flower-de-Luce*, *Angel*, the *Holy Lambe*, the *Bear & Harroe*, the *Plough*, the *Shippe*, the *Black Bell*, another *King Harry Head*, the *Bull Head*, the *Golden Bull*, ' a sixpenny ordinarye ', another *Flower-de-luce*, the *Red Lyon*, the *Horns*, the *White Hors*, the *Prince's Arms*, *Bell Savadge's In*, the *S. John the Baptist*, the *Talbot*, the *Shipp of War*, the *S. Dunstan*, the *Hercules* or the *Owld Man Tavern*, the *Mitar*, another *iij Tunnes Inn* and a *iij Tunnes Tavern*, and a *Graihound*, another *Mitar*, another *King Harry Head*, *iij Tunnes*, and the *iij Cranes*.

In the next reign we find the following enumerated by Taylor (the Water Poet) in one of his pamphlets :—5 *Angels*, 4 *Anchors*, 6 *Bells*, 5 *Bullsheads*, 4 *Black Bulls*, 4 *Bears*, 5 *Bears & Dolphins*, 10 *Castles*, 4 *Crosses* (red or white), 7 *Three Crowns*, 7 *Green Dragons*, 6 *Dogs*, 5 *Fountains*, 3 *Fleeces*, 8 *Globes*, 5 *Greyhounds*, 9 *White Harts*, 4 *White Horses*, 5 *Harrows*, 20 *King's Heads*, 7 *King's Arms*, 1 *Queen's Head*, 8 *Golden Lyons*, 6 *Red Lyons*, 7 *Halfmoons*, 10 *Mitres*, 33 *Maidenheads*, 10 *Mermaids*, 2 *Mouths*, 8 *Nagsheads*, 8 *Prince's Arms*, 4 *Pope's Heads*, 13 *Suns*, 8 *Stars*, etc. Besides these he mentions an *Adam & Eve*, an *Antwerp* Tavern, a *Cat*, a *Christopher*, a *Cooper's Hoop*, a *Garter*, a *Goat*, a *Hart's Horn* and a *Mitre*, etc. These were all taverns in London. In another work Taylor gives us the signs of the 686 or thereabouts taverns and alehouses in ten shires about London, all similar to those just enumerated. Amongst the number there is not one combination of two objects, except the *Eagle & Child*, and the *Bear & Ragged Staff*. In a black-letter tract entitled *News from Bartholomew Fayre* the following are named : the *Boreshead* near London Stone, the *Swan* at Dowgate, *The Mitre* in Cheap, the *Bullhead*, the *Boreshead* in Old Fish St., *Three Cranes* in the Vintree, *Saint Martin's* in the Centree, the *Windmill* in Lothbury, the *Ship* at the Exchange, the *King's Head* in New Fish St., the *Mermaid* in Cornhill, the *Red Lion* in the Strand, the *Three Tuns* in Newgate Market, and the *Swan* in Old Fish St. Drunken Barnaby in his work published in 1638 but probably written *c.* 1608–38, says that in his travels he called at several of the London taverns :—*The Axe* in Aldermanbury, the *Rose* in Holborn, the ' *Griffin* i' th' Old Bailey ', the *Three Cranes*, the *Cardinal's Hat*, and the *Hart's Horns*.

Thomas Heywood introduced a song on the London inn-signs, in his *Rape of Lucrece*, 1608 :—

> The Gintry to the *King's Head*,
> The Nobles to the *Crown*.
> The Knights unto the *Golden Fleese*,
> And to the *Plough*, Clowne.

---

* Harl. MS. 6580, 631.

The Churchmen to the *Mitre*,
　The Shepheard to the *Star*,
The Gardner hies him to the *Rose*,
　To the *Drum* the Man of War.

The Huntsmen to the *White Hart*,
　To the *Ship* the Merchants goe,
But you that doe the Muses love,
　The sign called *River Po*.

The Banquerout * to the *World's End*,
　The Fool to the *Fortune* hie,
Unto the *Mouth* the Oyster-Wife
　The Fiddler to the *Pie*.

The Punk † unto the *Cockatrice*,
　The Drunkard to the *Vine*,
The Beggar to the *Bush*, there meet,
　And with Duke Humphrey dine.

No doubt based on Heywood's work is this from the *Roxburgh Ballads* :—

London's Ordinarie, or Every Man in his Humour

Through the Royal Exchange as I walked,
　Where Gallants in sattin doe shine,
At midst of the day, they parted away,
　To severall places to dine.

The Gentrie went to the *King's Head*,
　The Nobles unto the *Crowne* :
The Knights went to the *Golden Fleece*,
　And the Ploughmen to the *Clowne*.

The Cleargie will dine at the *Miter*,
　The Vintners at the *Three Tunnes*,
The Usurers to the *Devill* will goe,
　And the Fryers to the *Nunnes*.

The Ladyes will dine at the *Feathers*,
　The Globe no Captains will scorne ;
The Huntsmen will goe to the *Grayhound* below,
　And some Townes-men to the *Horne*.

The Plummers will dine at the *Fountaine*,
　The Cookes at the *Holly Lambe*,
The Drunkards by noone, to the *Man in the Moone*,
　And the Cuckholdes to the *Ramme*.

---

* Bankrupt.　　　　　　　　　　　　　　　　　† Prostitute.

The Roarers will dine at the *Lyon*,
  The Waterman at the *Old Swan* ;
The Bawdes will to the *Negro* goe,
  And Whores to the *Naked Man*.

The Keepers will to the *White Hart*,
  The Marchants unto the *Shippe*,
The Beggars they must take their way,
  To the *Egg-shell* and the *Whippe*.

The Farryers will to the *Horse*,
  The Blacksmith unto the *Locke*,
The Butchers unto the *Bull* will goe,
  And the Carmen to *Bridewell Clocke*.

The Fishmongers unto the *Dolphin*,
  The Barbers to the *Cheat Loafe*,★
The Turners unto the *Ladle* will goe,
  Where they may merrylie quaffe.

The Taylors will dine at the *Sheeres*,
  The Shoemakers will to the *Boote*.
The Welshmen they will take their way,
  And dine at the sign of the *Gote*.

The Hosiers will dine at the *Legge*,
  The Drapers at the signe of the *Brush*,
The Fletchers to *Robin Hood* will goe,
  And the Spendthrift to *Begger's Bush*.

The Pewterers to the *Quarte Pot*,
  The Coopers will dine at the *Hoope*,
The Cobblers to the *Last* will goe,
  And the Bargemen to the *Sloope*.

The Carpenters will to the *Axe*,
  The Colliers will dine at the *Sacke*,
The Fruterer he to the *Cherry-Tree*,
  Good fellowes no liquor will lacke.

The Goldsmith will to the *Three Cups*,
  For money they hold it as drosse ;
Your Puritan to the *Pewter Canne*,
  And your Papists to the *Crosse*.

The Weavers will dine at the *Shuttle*,
  The Glovers will unto the *Glove*,
The Maydens all to the *Mayden Head*,
  And true Lovers unto the *Dove*.

★ i.e. a household loaf of wheaten seconds bread.

The Saddlers will dine at the *Saddle*,
   The Painters will to the *Greene Dragon*,
The Dutchmen will go to the *Froe*,*
   Where each man will drink his *Flagon*.

The Chandlers will dine at the *Skales*,
   The Salters at the signe of the *Bagge*,
The Porters take pain at the *Labour In Vain*,
   And the Horse-Courser to the *White Nagge*.

Thus every Man in his humour
   That comes from the North or the South,
But he that has no money in his purse,
   May dine at the signe of the *Mouth*.

The Swaggerers will dine at the *Fencers*,
   But those that have lost their wits,
With *Bedlam Tom* let that be their home,
   And the *Drumme* the Drummers best fits.

The Cheter will dine at the *Checker*,
   The Pickpockets in a blind alehouse,
Tel on and tride them up Holborne they ride
   And they there end at the *Gallowes*.

In very early times publicans were compelled by law to have a sign. In 1393 Florence North, a brewer of Chelsea, was 'presented' for not putting up the usual sign. In Cambridge the regulations were equally severe; by an Act of Parliament in 1430–1 † it was enacted:

> Whoever shall brew ale in the town of Cambridge with intention of selling it, must hang out a sign, otherwise he shall forfeit his ale.

But with the other trades it was always optional. Hence Charles I on his accession to the throne gave the inhabitants of London a charter by which amongst other favours he granted them the right to hang out signboards :—

> that it may and shall be lawful to the Citizens of the same city and any of them, for the time being, to expose and hang in and over the streets and ways, and alleys of the said city and suburbs of the same signs, and posts of signs, affixed to their houses and shops, for the better finding out such citizen's dwellings, shops, arts, or occupations.

Because of this close connection between the inn and the sign, the taking away of a publican's licence was accompanied by the pulling down of his sign. (Massinger has a reference to the fact in *A New Way to Pay Old Debts.‡*)

At the time of the great Civil War, the house-signs played no inconsiderable part in the changes and convulsions of the State, and took a prominent place in the politics

---

* i.e. *Vrouw*, woman.　　　　† 9 Hen. VI, c. x.　　　　‡ Act IV, Sc. 2.

of the day. An earlier example, possibly a mythical one, where a sign was made a matter of high treason, was that of an unfortunate fellow who kept the *Crown* in Cheapside in 1467. He is said to have lost his head for saying he would ' make his son heir to the Crown '. More examples are to be met with in the history of the Commonwealth troubles. On the death of Charles I John Taylor the Water-poet, a Royalist to the backbone, boldly showed his opinion by taking as a sign for his ale-house in Phoenix Alley, Long Acre, the *Mourning Crown*. He was, however, soon compelled to take it down. Richard Flecknoe,* tells us how many of the severe Puritans were shocked at anything smelling of Popery :—' As for the signs they have pretty well begun their reformation already, changing the sign of the *Salutation* of Our Lady into the *Souldier & Citizen*, and the *Catherine Wheel* into the *Cat & Wheel* ; such ridiculous work they make of this reformation and so jealous they are against all mirth and jollity, as they would pluck down the *Cat & Fiddle* too, if it durst but play so loud as they might hear it.' No doubt they invented very godly signs, but these have in general not come down to us.

At this time the fashion first prevailed which continued as long as the signboard was an important institution—that of using house-signs to symbolize political ideas. Imaginary signs as a part of secret imprints conveying most unmistakably the sentiments of the book were often used in the old days of political plots and violent lampoons. Instances are the imprints :—

> *Vox Borealis* printed by Margery Marprelate, in Thwack Coat Lane at the sign of the *Crab-Tree Cudgell*, without any privilege of the Catercaps, 1641.

> *Articles of High Treason* made and enacted by the late Halfquarter usurping Convention. Imprinted for Erasmus Thorogood and to be sold at the sign of the *Roasted Rump*, 1659.

> *A Catalogue of Books* of the Newest Fashion, to be sold by auction at the Whigs' Coffeehouse, at the sign of the *Jackanapes* in Prating Alley, near the Deanery of Saint Paul's.

> *The Censure of the Rota* upon Mr. Milton's book, entitled ' The Ready and Easy Way to Establish a Free Commonwealth etc.' Printed at London by Paul Giddy, Printer to the Rota at the sign of the *Windmill*, in Turn-again Lane, 1660.

In the newspapers of the 18th century we find that signs were constantly used as emblems of or as sharp hits at the politics of the day. Thus in the *Weekly Journal* for 17 August 1718 allusions were made by the opposition party to the sign of the *Salutation* in Newgate St., to which the *Original Weekly Journal* a week later retaliates by a description and explanation of an indelicate sign said to be in King St., Westminster.

On the morning of 28 September 1736 all the tavern-signs in London were in deep mourning ; no wonder, for it seemed their patron and friend gin was defunct—killed by the new Act against spirituous liquors ! They soon dropped their mourning, for gin had only been in a very brief slumber, and woke up much refreshed by his

---

* *AENigmatical Characters*, 1665.

sleep.   Fifteen years later, when Hogarth painted his ' Gin Lane ', royal gin was to be had cheaply enough if we may believe the signboard in that picture, which informs us that gentlemen and others could get drunk for a penny, and dead drunk for two-pence, with the provision of clean straw for nothing.

After the Great Fire many of the rebuilt houses adopted instead of the former wooden signboards projecting in the street, signs carved in stone, and generally painted or gilt.   These were let into the front of the houses beneath the first-floor windows. Many of these signs were still to be seen in Larwood's time, and a few still remain. A small collection of those removed is to be found in the Guildhall Museum.   In the streets not visited by the Fire things continued on the old footing, each shopkeeper being fired with an ambition to project his sign a few inches farther than his neigh-bour's.   The consequence was that what with the narrow streets, the penthouses, and the signboards, the air and light of the heavens were almost wholly intercepted from the luckless wayfarers through the streets of London.   We can picture to ourselves the unfortunate plumed, feathered, silken gallant of the period, walking in his low shoes and silk stockings through the ill-paved dirty streets on a stormy November day, when the weather included fog, sleet, snow and rain.   Flower-pots were blown from the penthouses, spouts sent down shower-baths from almost every house, and the streaming signs swung overhead on their rusty creaking hinges.   Certainly the evil was great, and demanded that redress which was given in 1667, when a new act ' ordered that in all the streets no signboard shall hang across, but that the sign shall be fixed against the balconies or some convenient part of the side of the house '.

Still, with all their faults, the signs had some advantages for the wayfarer.   Gay refers to them, and suggests that even their dissonant creaking, according to the old weather proverb, was not without its use :—

> But when the swinging signs your ears offend
> With creaking noise, then rainy floods impend.*

He points out another benefit to be derived from the signboards :—

> If drawn by Bus'ness to a street unknown,
> Let the sworn Porter point thee through the town ;
> Be sure observe the Signs, for Signs remain
> Like faithful Landmarks to the walking Train.

Besides, they offered constant matter of thought, speculation and amusement to the curious observer.   Even Dean Swift and the Lord High Treasurer Harley

> Would try to read the lines
> Writ underneath the country signs.

Certainly these productions are often highly entertaining.   Until Larwood's time they had never been extensively collected and preserved, although they form a not unimportant and quite characteristic part of our popular literature.

* *Trivia*, Canto 1.

Many of the odd combinations that often are displayed on signboards have frequently puzzled curious inquirers. Some dual signs of this kind are explicable, but others have arisen by a process of combining two different signs. Larwood following the *Spectator* ★ styled this 'quartering' (but he would be nearer the mark heraldically if he called it impaling, since such signs represent the union of two houses, not the descendants of such a union).

In the beginning of the 18th century we find named these signs, which so puzzled a person of an inquisitive turn of mind that he wrote to the *British Apollo* (the meagre *Notes and Queries* of those days) in 1706 in the hope of eliciting an explanation of their quaint combination :—

> I'm amazed at the Signs
> As I pass through the Town.
> To see the odd mixture ;
> A *Magpie & Crown*,
> The *Whale & the Crow*,
> The *Razor & Hen*,
> The *Leg & Seven Stars*,
> The *Axe & the Bottle*,
> The *Tun & the Lute*,
> The *Eagle & Child*,
> The *Shovel & Boot*.

All these signs are also named by Tom Brown in 1708 :—' The first amusements we encountered were the variety and contradictory language of the signs, enough to persuade a man there were no rules of concord among the citizens. Here we saw *Joseph's Dream*, the *Bull & Mouth*, the *Whale & Crow*, the *Shovel & Boot*, the *Leg & Star*, the *Bible & Swan*, the *Frying Pan & Drum*, the *Lute & Tun*, the *Hog in Armour*, and a thousand others that the wise men that put them there can give no reason for.'

From this enumeration we see that a century had worked great changes in the signs. Those at the beginning of the 17th century were almost all simple, and there were few combinations. Now we meet very heterogeneous objects joined together. Various reasons can be found to account for this. First it must be borne in mind that most of the London signs had no inscription to tell the public ' this is a lion ' or ' this is a bear '. Hence the populace could easily make mistakes, and call an object by a wrong name. This might give rise to an absurd combination, as with the *Leg & Star* which perhaps, was originally nothing but the two insignia of the Order of the Garter, the garter being represented in its natural place, on the leg, with the star of the Order beside it. Secondly, the name might be corrupted through faulty pronunciation, and when the sign was to be repainted or imitated in another street those objects would be represented by which it was best known. Thus the *Shovel & Boot* might have been a corruption of the *Shovel & Boat*. The *Ship & Shovel* is still a common sign in places where grain is carried by canal boats. The *Bull & Mouth* is *said* to be a corruption of the *Boulogne Mouth*—the Mouth of Boulogne Harbour.

★ Cf. pp. 12–13.

Finally, whimsical shopkeepers would frequently aim at the most odd combinations they could imagine for no other reason but to attract attention. Taking these premises into consideration, some of the signs which so puzzled Tom Brown might be easily accounted for : the *Axe & Bottle*, in this way might have been a corruption of the *Battle-axe*. The *Bible & Swan* was perhaps a sign in honour of Luther, who is generally represented by the symbol of a swan, a figure which many Lutheran Churches have on their steeple instead of a weathercock. The *Lute & Tun* was conceivably a pun on the name of Luton, similar to the *Bolt & Tun* of Prior Bolton, who adopted this devise as his rebus.

Often in recent years a sign has been compounded with the adjective *Royal* in order to commemorate a distinguished guest. Instances are the *Fountain*, Sheerness, now the *Royal Fountain*, the *Angel*, Grantham, now the *Angel & Royal*, and the *Bull*, Dartford, now the *Royal Victoria & Bull*.

Other causes of combinations, and many very amusing and instructive remarks about signs, are given in the *Spectator*.*

There is nothing like sound literature and good sense to be met with in those objects that are everywhere thrusting themselves out to the eye and endeavouring to become visible. Our streets are filled with *blue boars*, *black swans*, and *red lions*, not to mention *flying pigs* and *hogs in armour*, with many creatures more extraordinary than any in the deserts of Africa. Strange that one who has all the birds and beasts in nature to choose out of, should live at the sign of an *ens rationis*. My first task, therefore, should be like that of Hercules, to clear the city from monsters. In the second place, I should forbid that creatures of jarring and incongruous natures should be joined together in the same sign ; such as the *Bell & the Neat's Tongue*, the *Dog & the Gridiron*, the *Fox & the Goose* may be supposed to have met, but what has the *Fox & the Seven Stars* to do together ? And when did *Lamb & Dolphin* ever meet except upon a signpost ? As for the *Cat & Fiddle*, there is a conceit in it, and therefore I do not intend that anything I have here said should affect it.

I must, however, observe to you upon this subject, that it is usual for a young tradesman at his first setting up to add to his own sign that of the master whom he served, as the husband after marriage gives a place to his mistress's arms in his own coat. This I take to have given rise to many of those absurdities which are committed over our heads ; and, as I am informed, first occasioned the *Three Nuns & Hare*, which we see so frequently joined together. I would therefore establish certain rules for the determining how far one tradesman may give the sign of another, and in what case he may be allowed to quarter it with his own.

In the third place, I would enjoin every shop to make use of a sign which bears some affinity to the wares in which it deals. What can be more inconsistent than to see a bawd at the sign of the *Angel*, or a tailor at the *Lion* ? A cook should not live at the *Boot*, nor a shoemaker at the *Roasted Pig*, and yet, for want of this regulation, I have seen a *Goat* set up before the door of a perfumer, and the *French King's Head* at a sword-cutler's. . . .

As for the *Bell Savage*, which is the sign of a savage man standing by a bell, I was formerly very much puzzled upon the conceit of it, till I accidentally fell into the reading

* 2 April 1710 : No. 28.

of an old romance translated out of the French, which gives an account of a very beautiful woman, who was found in a wilderness and is called *La Belle Sauvage*, and is everywhere translated by our countrymen, the *Bell Savage*★. This piece of philology will I hope convince you that I have made signposts my study, and consequently qualified myself for the employment which I solicit at your hands. But before I conclude my letter, I must communicate to you another remark which I have made upon the subject with which I am now entertaining you—namely, that I can give a shrewd guess at the humour of the inhabitant, by the sign that hangs before his door. A surly, choleric fellow generally makes choice of a *Bear*, as men of milder dispositions frequently live at the *Lamb*. Seeing a *Punch-bowl* † painted upon a sign near Charing Cross, and very curiously garnished, with a couple of angels hovering over it, and squeezing a lemon into it, I had the curiosity to ask after the master of the house, and found upon inquiry, as I had guessed by the little *agremens* upon his sign, that he was a Frenchman.

Another reason for 'quartering' signs was on removing from one shop to another, when it was customary to add the sign of the old shop to that of the new one : ‡ The process continued after Queen Anne's time thus :—

Whereas Anthony Wilton, who lived at the *Green Cross* publick-house against the new Turnpike on New Cross Hill, has been removed for two years past to the new boarded house now the sign of the *Green Cross & Cross Keys* on the same Hill, etc. (1718)

Thomas Blackall and Francis Ives, Mercers, are removed from the *Seven Stars* on Ludgate Hill to the *Black Lion & Seven Stars* over the way. (1718)

Peter Duncombe and Saunders Dancer, who lived at the *Naked Boy* in Great Russell St., Covent Garden, removed to the *Naked Boy & Mitre* near Somerset House, Strand, etc. (1711)

The *Crown* and the *Angel* were two separate inns in Norwich in 1781, but they had disappeared when Borrow's father lodged in Norwich in 1814, and he stayed at the *Crown & Angel*. The *Dolphin & Anchor*, Chichester, is an amalgamation of the *Dolphin* and the *Anchor*.

To increase this complexity still more came the corruption of names arising from pronunciation. The *Castle & Ball*, Marlborough, may be a corruption of *Castle & Bull*, two charges in the arms of the borough. Thus Burn in his introduction to the *Beaufoy Tokens* mentions the sign of *Pique et Carreau*, on a gambling-house at Newport, I. of W., which was Englished into the *Pig & Carrot* ; again the same sign at Godmanchester was metamorphosed into the *Pig & Checkers*. The sign of the *Island Queen* Larwood had frequently heard either in jest or in ignorance called the *Iceland Queen*. Hotten in his *Slang Dictionary* says he has seen the name of the once popular premier *George Canning*, metamorphosed on an alehouse-sign into the *George & Cannon* ; so the *Golden Farmer* became the *Jolly Farmer* : while the *Four Alls*, Whitechapel, was altered into the *Four Awls*.

★ Addison is wrong in this derivation. (See under Miscellaneous Signs.)
† Actually the *Punch Bowl* was a famous Whig sign.
‡ *Post Boy*, 4 January 1711 ; *Weekly Journal*, 22 November 1711 ; *Daily Courant*, 17 November 1718.

Along with this practice, there is a tendency to translate a sign into a sort of jocular slang phrase : thus, in the 17th century the *Blackamoorshead & Woolpack* in Pimlico, was called the *Devil & Bag of Nails* by those that frequented it, and by the last part of that name the house is still called at the present day. So the *Elephant & Castle* is vulgarly rendered as the *Pig & Tinderbox* : the *Bear & Ragged Staff*, the *Angel & Flute* : the *Eagle & Child*, the *Bird & Bantling* : the *Hog in Armour*, the *Pig in Misery* : the *Pig in the Pound*, the *Gentleman in Trouble*.

The *Adventurer* in 1752 * has an essay on the subject of signs, plainly inspired by Addison's work :—

. . . Hence the *Hand & Shears* is justly appropriated to tailors, and the *Hand & Pen* to writing-masters, though the very reverend and right worthy order of my neighbours, the Fleet parsons, have assumed it to themselves as a mark of 'marriage performed without imposition'. The *Woolpack* plainly points out to us a woollen draper, the *Naked Boy* elegantly reminds us of the necessity of clothing, and the *Golden Fleece* figuratively denotes the riches of our staple commodity ; but are not the *Hen & Chickens* and the *Three Pigeons* the unquestionable right of the poulterer, and not to be usurped by the vendor of silk or linen ? . . .

The publicans' extravagance in this affair calls aloud for reprehension and restraint. Their modest ancestors were contented with a plain *Bough* stuck up before their doors but . . . they have ransacked earth, air and seas, called down sun, moon, and stars to their assistance, and exhibited all the monsters that ever teemed from fantastic imagination. Their *Hogs in Armour*, their *Blue Boars*, *Black Bears*, *Green Dragons* and *Golden Lions*, have already been sufficiently exposed. . . .

There can be no objection made to the *Bunch of Grapes*, the *Rummer*, or the *Tuns* ; but would not any one inquire for a hosier at the *Leg*, or for a locksmith at the *Cross Keys* ? And who would expect anything but water to be sold at the *Fountain* ? The *Turkshead* may fairly intimate that a seraglio is kept within, the *Rose* may be strained to some propriety of meaning, as the business transacted there may be said to be done 'under the rose', but why must the *Angel*, the *Lamb*, and the *Mitre* be the designations of the seats of drunkenness or prostitution ? Some regard should likewise be paid by tradesmen to the propriety of the place ; and in this, too, the publicans are notoriously faulty. The *King's Arms*, and the *Star & Garter*, are aptly enough placed at the court end of the town, and in the neighbourhood of the royal palace, *Shakespeare's Head* takes his station by one playhouse, and *Ben Jonson's* by the other. *Hell* is a public-house adjoining to Westminster Hall, as the *Devil* Tavern is to the lawyer's quarter in the Temple, but what has the *Crown* to do by the Change, or the *Gun*, the *Ship*, or the *Anchor* anywhere but at Tower Hill, at Wapping or Deptford ? . . .

I know not whence it happens that publicans have claimed a right to the physiognomies of kings and heroes, as I cannot find out, by the most painful researches, that there is any alliance between them. *Lebec* [Lebeck], as he was an excellent cook, is the fit representative of luxury, and *Broughton*, that renowned athletic champion, has an indisputable right to put up his own head if he pleases ; but what reason can there be why the glorious *Duke William* should draw porter, or the brave *Admiral Vernon* retail flip ? Why must *Queen Anne* keep a ginshop, and *King Charles* inform us of a skittle-ground ?

Propriety of character, I think, requires that these illustrious personages should be deposed from their lofty stations, and I would recommend hereafter that the alderman's

* No. 9.

effigy ★ should accompany his Intire Butt Beer, and that the comely face of that public-spirited patriot † who first reduced the price of punch and raised its reputation *Pro Bono Publico* should be set up wherever three penn'orth of warm rum is to be sold. . . .

By the middle of the 18th century, when the *Adventurer* appeared, the necessity for signs was not so great as formerly. Reading had become a very general acquirement, yet it would appear that the exhibitors of signboards wished them to make up in extravagance what they had lost in usefulness.

A contemporary writer says that long after signs became unnecessary it was not unusual for an opulent shopkeeper to lay out as much upon a sign and the curious ironwork with which it was fixed in his house as would furnish a less considerable dealer with a stock-in-trade. I have been credibly informed that there were many signs and sign-irons upon Ludgate Hill which cost several hundred pounds, and that as much was laid out by a mercer on the sign of the *Queen's Head*, as would have gone a good way towards decorating the original for a birthday. Misson, a French traveller who visited England *c.* 1698, thus speaks about the signs :—

> At London they are commonly very large, and jut out so far that in some narrow streets they touch one another ; nay, and run across almost quite to the other side. They are generally adorned with carving and gilding, and there are several that with the branches of iron which support them, cost above a hundred guineas. They seldom write upon the signs the name of the thing represented in it. This does not at all please the German and other travelling strangers ; because for want of the things being so named, they have not an opportunity of learning their names in England, as they stroll along the streets. Out of London, and particularly in villages the signs of inns are suspended in the middle of a great wooden portal, which may be looked upon as a kind of triumphal arch to the honour of Bacchus.

Grosley, another Frenchman who made a voyage through England in 1765, makes very similar remarks upon a fact which he notices as soon as he has landed at Dover.

But gaudy and richly ornamented as they were, it would seem that after all the pictures were bad. The absence of inscriptions was not to be lamented, for those that existed only made fritters of English. The *Tatler* No. 18 amused his readers at the expense of their spelling :—

> Many a man has lost his way and his dinner by this general want of skill in orthography ; for considering that the paintings are usually so very bad that you cannot know the animal under whose sign you are to live that day, how must the stranger be misled, if it is wrong spelled as well as ill painted ? I have a cousin now in town, who going to see a relation in Barbican, wandered a whole day by the mistake of one letter ; for it was written ' This is the Beer ', instead of ' This is the Bear '. He was set right at last by inquiring for the house of a fellow who could not read, and knew the place mechanically, only by having been often drunk there. . . . I propose that

★ Samuel Whitbread I, ? –1796. Actually Entire is said to have been invented by Ralph Harwood. (Bickerdyke, *op. cit.*, 366.)

† The Earl of Wilmington, who was responsible for the passing of the 1743 act (16 Geo. II, c. 8) which reduced the retail licence duty from £50 to £1, and abolished the prohibitive retail sales duty of 20s. per gallon, while only slightly increasing the duty on manufacture. (Webb, *op. cit.*, 27, 33.)

every tradesman in the city of London and Westminster shall give me a sixpence a quarter for keeping their signs in repair as to the grammatical part ; and I will take into my house a Swiss count * of my acquaintance, who can remember all their names without book, for despatch sake, setting up the head of the said foreigner for my sign, the features being strong and fit to hang high.

On occasion the signs murdered not only the King's English but also his subjects. Apart from their preventing the circulation of fresh air, a more serious charge was brought against them in 1718, when a sign in Bride's Lane, Fleet St., by its weight dragged down the front of the house, and in its fall killed two young ladies, the king's jeweller and a cobbler. A commission of inquiry into the nuisance was appointed, but while the commissioners were deliberating public interest and excitement abated, and matters remained as they were.

In the year 1762 considerable attention was directed to signboards by Bonnell Thornton, a wag who organized an Exhibition of Signboards in order to burlesque the exhibitions of the Society of Artists. In a preliminary advertisement and in his published catalogue, he described it as the ' EXHIBITION OF THE SOCIETY OF SIGN-PAINTERS of all the curious signs to be met with in town or country, together with such original designs as might be transmitted to them, as specimens of the native genius of the nation '. Hogarth, who understood a joke as well as any man in England, entered into the spirit of the humour, was on the ' hanging committee ', and added a few touches to heighten the absurdity. The whole affair proved a great success.

While discussing signboard exhibitions it may be noted that another more serious —but still very enjoyable—signboard exhibition was held in New Bond St. in 1936 under the auspices of the Brewers' Society, the Council for the Preservation of Rural England, the Building Centre, and the Victoria and Albert Museum and with a member of the Royal Academy as Chairman of its Committee. Another very interesting display of inn signs was at the Inn Crafts Exhibition at the Suffolk Galleries in 1948.

Thornton's exhibition was the greatest glory to which signboards were permitted to attain. Not more than four years after, they had a fall from which they never recovered. Education was now becoming more widely spread, and perhaps a majority of our people could read sufficiently well to decipher a name and a number. The continual exhibition of pictures in the streets and thoroughfares consequently became useless, the information they conveyed could be imparted in a more convenient and simple manner, while their evils could be avoided. The strong feeling of corporations too had set in steadily against signboards, and henceforth they were doomed.

In 1762 London followed the example which Paris had set a year before. ' The signs in Duke's Court, St Martin's Lane, were all taken down and affixed to the front of the houses.' Westminster procured an act with ample powers to improve the pavements, etc., of the streets. This act also sealed the doom of such of the signboards as obstructed the streets. These as in Paris were now ordered to be affixed

* Probably John James Heidegger, Director of the Opera.

Plate
I

BEXLEY PUBLIC LIBRARIES.

PLATE
2

to the houses. This was enforced by a statute of 1762, enlarged at various times. Other parishes were longer in making up their minds, but the great disparity in the appearance of the streets westward from Temple Bar and those eastward at last made the Corporation of London follow the example, and adopt similar improvements. Suitable powers to carry out the scheme were soon obtained. In 1766 the Court of Common Council appointed commissions, and in a few months all the parishes began to clear away the signboards, St Botolph's in 1767, St Leonard's Shoreditch in 1768, St Martin's-le-Grand in 1769, and Marylebone in 1770. The last streets that kept the signs were Wood St. and Whitecross St., where they remained till 1773 ; while in Holywell St., Strand, less than a century ago some were still dangling above the shop doors. In the suburbs many might be observed in Larwood's time. A few remain still. A legal decision ruled against a pawnbroker's sign being considered a nuisance, notwithstanding its projection over the footway, unless it also obstructed the circulation of light and air, or was inconvenient or incommodious. By the acts referred to :—

> The commissioners are empowered to take down and remove all signs or other emblems used to denote the trade, occupation, or calling of any person or persons, signposts, signirons, balconies, penthouses, showboards, spouts and gutters, projecting into any of the said streets, etc., and all other encroachments, projections, and annoyances whatsoever, within the said cities and liberties.

With the signboards, of course, went the signposts. The removing of the posts and the paving of the streets with Scotch granite gave rise to the epigram :

> The Scottish new pavement well deserves our praise ;
> To the Scotch we're obliged, too, for mending our ways :
> But this we can never forgive, for they say
> As that they have taken our posts all away.

Now numbers appeared everywhere. The numbering of houses in France was fairly general by 1787, and became compulsory in 1805. In London it appears to have been attempted in the beginning of the 18th century, but in all probability reading was not sufficiently widespread to bring the novelty into general practice. How much more simple is the method of numbering for giving a clear and unmistakable direction may be seen from the means resorted to in order to indicate a house under the signboard system : e.g.

> To be let, Newbury House, in St. James's Park, next door but one to Lady Oxford's, having two balls at the gate, and iron rails before the door . . . etc. . . .
> At her house, the *Red Ball & Acorn* over against the *Globe* Tavern, in Queen Street, Cheapside, near the *Three Crowns*, liveth a Gentlewoman . . . etc. . . .

At night the difficulty of finding a house was greatly increased, since the light of the lamps was generally but faint. Other means therefore were adopted, as we see from the advertisement of ' Doctor James Tilbrough, a German Doctor ' who resides ' over against the New Exchange in Bedford St., at the sign of the *Peacock*, where you shall see at night two candles burning within one of the chambers before the balcony,

c

and a lanthorn with a candle in it upon the balcony'. Others resorted to painting their house, doors, balconies, or door-posts, in some striking colour; hence those *Red, Blue* or *White Houses* still very common, and the *Blue Posts* still to be found in the centre of the West End. So we find a *Dark House* in Chequer Alley, Moorfields, a *Green Door* in Craven Building, and a *Blue Balcony* in Little Queen St., all of which figure on the 17th-century trades tokens. Those who did much trade by night, as coffee-houses, quacks, etc., adopted lamps with coloured glasses, by which they distinguished their houses. This custom has come down to us, and is still adhered to by doctors. In Larwood's time it survived also among chemists, public-houses and occasionally sweeps. In some parts of the Continent it still remains quite generally among ladies pursuing none of these professions.

Similar names to those mentioned above occur, of course, in the provinces. There was, for example, a *Wooden House* at Camberley, Surrey, at the end of the 18th century, and the *Thatched House* occurs at Walsall, while there are three *Red Houses* in various parts of Staffordshire.

After the numbers were established, many shopkeepers still clung to the old traditions, and for years continued to display their signs though affixed to the houses. As late as 1803 a traveller writes about London :—

> The whole front of a house is frequently employed for this purpose.* Thus, in the vicinity of Ludgate Hill, the house of S—— who has amassed a fortune of £40,000 by selling razors, is daubed with large capitals three feet high, acquainting the public that 'the most excellent and superb patent razors are sold here'. A grocer in the city, who had a large *Beehive* for his sign hanging out before his shop, had allured a great many customers. No sooner were the people seen swarming about this hive than the old signs suddenly disappeared, and Beehives, elegantly gilt, were substituted in their places. Hence the grocer was obliged to insert an advertisement in the newspapers, importing that he was the sole proprietor of 'the original and celebrated *Beehive*'. A similar accident befell the shop of one E . . . in Cheapside. . . . The sign of this gentleman consists in a prodigious *Grasshopper*, and as this insect had quickly propagated its species through every part of the city, Mr. E . . . has in his advertisements repeatedly requested the public to observe that 'the genuine *Grasshopper* is only to be found before his warehouse'. He issued to young beginners licences for hanging out the sign of a Grasshopper before their shops, expressly adding this clause in large capitals, that 'they are genuine descendants of the renowned and matchless *Grasshopper* of Mr. E . . . in Cheapside'.

Such practices as these however necessarily gave the deathblow to signboards. Gradually the signs began to dwindle away, first in the principal streets, then in the smaller thoroughfares and the suburbs, finally in the provincial towns also. Only the publicans retained them, and even they in the end were often satisfied with the name without the sign.

Signs which had been sung in sprightly ballads or often formed the groundwork for a biting satire continued to inspire the popular muse until the end, but her latter

* Of a sign.

productions had more of the dirge than the ballad about them.   There is certainly a
rollicking air of gladness about this song, but it was the last flicker of the lamp :—

The Mail Coach Guard

At each inn on the road I a welcome could find
  At the *Fleece* I'd my skin full of ale ;
The *Two Jolly Brewers* were just to my mind,
  At the *Dolphin* I drank like a whale.
Tom Tun at the *Hogshead* sold pretty good stuff ;
  They'd capital flip at the *Boar* ;
And when at the *Angel* I'd tippled enough,
  I went to the *Devil* for more.
Then I'd always a sweetheart so snug at the *Car* ;
  At the *Rose* I'd a lily so white ;
Few planets could equal sweet *Nan* at the *Star*.
  No eyes ever twinkled so bright.
I've had many a hug at the sign of the *Bear*,
  In the *Sun* courted morning and noon,
And when night put an end to my happiness there
  I'd a sweet little girl in the *Moon*.
To sweethearts and ale I at length bid adieu,
  Of wedlock to set up the sign :
Hand-in-Hand the *Good Woman* I look for in you
  And the *Horns* I hope ne'er will be mine ;
Once guard to the mail. I'm now guard to the fair ;
  But though my commission's laid down,
Yet while the *King's Arms* I'm permitted to bear,
  Like a *Lion* I'll fight for the *Crown*.

This was written in the beginning of the 19th century.   A considerable falling
off may be observed in the following, contributed by a correspondent of William
Hone :—

Signs of Love at Oxford

BY AN INN-CONSOLABLE LOVER

She's as light as the *Greyhound*, as fair as the *Angel*,
Her looks than the *Mitre* more sanctified are ;
But she flies like the *Roebuck* and leaves me to range ill,
Still looking to her as my true polar *Star*.
New Inn-ventions I try, with new art to adore,
But my fate is, alas, to be voted a *Boar* ;
My *Goats* I forsook to contemplate her charms,
And must own she is fit for our noble *King's Arms* . . . etc.

But tame as is this last performance, it is merry compared with a ballad sung in the streets some twenty years later, entitled *A Laughable and Interesting Picture of Drunkenness*. Speaking of the publicans, who call themselves ' Lords ', it says :—

> If these be the Lords, there are many kinds,
> For over their doors you will see many signs ;
> There is the *King*, and likewise the *Crown*,
> And beggars are made in every town.
>
> There is the *Queen* and likewise her *Head*,
> And many I fear to the gallows are led.
> There is the *Angel* and also the *Deer*.
> Destroying health in every sphere . . .
>
> and so on . . .

With the decline of the signboard came the rage for ' arms ' and the curious notion that every inn sign must be the ' arms ' of somebody or something ; whence we find such anomalies as the *Dunstan's Arms* (City Rd.), *Digger's Arms* (Petworth, Surrey), *Farmer's Arms* and *Gardener's Arms* (Lancs.), *Grand Junction Arms* (28 Praed St.), and the other horrors dealt with below.★

It is to be noted that some such signs which appear to be meaningless in fact are not so ; for example, the *Angel Arms*, Clapham Rd., noted by Larwood as an example of a foolish sign, is really the *Angell* (Family) *Arms*, and the *General's Arms*, Little Baddow, Essex, commemorates General Strutt, 1762–1848.

By Larwood's time many other types of new-fangled, high-sounding, but quite unmeaning names had been adopted for gin palaces and refreshment houses. Instances are *Perseverance*, *Enterprise*, *Paragon*, *Criterion*. Here again some names of this class are from those of coaches, but most are entirely meaningless.

However in recent years there has been among the leading brewery companies an admirable return to the old tradition. Many modern signs are well chosen and well designed by competent artists. The modern owners of a tied house often fully appreciate the historical value and human interest of the sign, and they would no more dream of renaming the house than of destroying a building of architectural interest in order to replace it by some modern spiritless abomination. Unfortunately much damage was done in the Victorian era but in general an old house and an old sign are both quite safe nowadays.

Notwithstanding all innovations, the majority of the signs still survive in name at least on the signboards of ale-houses and taverns somewhere or other. Their use may still be regarded as a rule with publicans and innkeepers, although they have become the exception in other trades. There are still many painted signboards : most new houses are given such, and in recent years many old signboards have been restored.

The head-quarters of the sign painters † were in Harp Alley, Shoe Lane, where,

★ P. 80.

† Signs are usually painted, more rarely of wrought metal or of earthenware. A very unusual one is the *Merry Maidens* at Shinfield, Berks., which consists of four half-length stone figures each fitting in its own niche.

until shortly before Larwood's time gilt grapes, sugar-loaves, lasts, teapots, etc., were displayed ready for the market.   Here Barlow, Craddock, and others, whose names are now as completely lost as their works, had their studios, and produced some very creditable signs, both carved and painted.   A few signs, however, were the productions of really front-rank artists.   The *Spectator*, in 1743,* says :

> The other day, going down Ludgate St., several people were gaping at a very splendid sign of Queen Elizabeth, which by far exceeded all the other signs in the street, the painter having shown a masterly judgment and the carver and gilder much pomp and splendour.   It looked rather like a capital picture in a gallery than a sign in the street.

Unfortunately the name of the artist who painted this has not come down to us.

Many of the best signs, however, were produced not by the Harp Alley sign-painters, but by the coach-painters who often united the two branches of art.   Two centuries ago both the coaches and sedans of the wealthy classes were moving picture galleries, the panels being painted with all sorts of subjects.   Two or three good examples of these are to be seen in the South Kensington Museum.   When the men that painted these turned their hands to sign-painting, they were sure to produce something good.   Such were Nathaniel Clarkson, to whom John Thomas Smith ascribed the beautiful sign of *Shakespeare*, that formerly hung in Little Russell St., Drury Lane—and Charles Catton (d. 1798), who painted several very good signs, particularly a *Lion* for his friend Wright, a famous coachmaker at that time living in Long Acre.   This picture, though it had weathered many a storm, was still to be seen in Smith's time at a coachmaker's on the west side of Well St., Oxford St.   A *Turk's Head* painted by him was long admired as the sign of a mercer in York St., Covent Garden.   Giovanni Cipriani (d. 1783), a Florentine carriage-painter living in London and a Royal Academician, painted several signs.   Samuel Wale, Academy Professor 1763 (d. 1786), painted a celebrated *Falstaff* and various other signs, the principal one was a whole length of *Shakespeare*, about five feet high, which was executed for and displayed at the door of a public-house at the north-west corner of Little Russell St., Drury Lane.   It was enclosed in a most sumptuous carved gilt frame, and was suspended by rich ironwork.   But this splendid object did not hang long before it was taken down, in consequence of the Act of Parliament for removing the signs and other obstructions in the streets of London.   Such was the change in the public appreciation consequent on the new regulations in signs that this was sold for a trifle.   This sign has also been ascribed to Edward Penny.   Catton, Clarkson, Cipriani, and Wale were all foundation or early members of the Academy, Penny was its first professor of painting, Wale its librarian and its professor of perspective. There is some substance in the argument of Hackwood † in which he derives the English school of painting from the more primitive craft of sign-painting.

The universal use of signboards furnished employment for the inferior rank of painters and sometimes even to artists of the first order.   Sir Godfrey Kneller painted

---

* No. 44, 8 January 1743.   † *Op. cit.*, n. 307–8.

the head of Lebeck, the famous 17th-century tavern-keeper, and this was used as the sign of another tavern long after the man was dead. Isaac Fuller, who painted altarpieces for Magdalen and Wadham Colleges, also excelled in tavern sign-painting. Among the most celebrated practitioners in this branch of art was a certain Lamb, who possessed considerable ability. 'His pencil was bold and masterly and well adapted to the subjects on which it was generally employed.' Gwynne, another coach-painter, acquired some reputation as a marine painter, produced a few good signs. Robert Dalton, Antiquary and Keeper of the Pictures to King George III, had been apprenticed to a sign- and coach-painter, so were Ralph Kirby, engraver and portrait-painter, drawing master to George IV, when Prince of Wales, Thomas Wright of Liverpool, the marine painter, Robert Smirke, R.A., and many other artists who acquired considerable reputation in later years.

Peter Monamy, the marine painter (d. 1749), was apprenticed to a sign- and house-painter on London Bridge. He decorated the carriage of Admiral Byng with ships and naval trophies, and painted a portrait of Admiral Vernon's ship for a famous public-house of the day, well known by the sign of the *Portobello*, a few doors north of the church in St Martin's Lane. John Bowen the celebrated heraldic painter and genealogist painted the sign of the *Hen & Chickens*, Shrewsbury. It was based on one of Bewick's woodcuts, with bacchanalian symbols and other embellishments.

Many of the 'great professors' occasionally painted signs for a freak. At the head of these stands William Hogarth, whose *Man loaded with Mischief* was formerly to be seen at 414 Oxford St., where it was a fixture in the alehouse of that name. It is now in private hands at St Albans. David Cox painted a *Royal Oak* for the alehouse at Bettws-y-Coed, Denbighshire; fortunately this has been taken down and is now preserved behind glass inside the inn. He is said also to have painted a *Blue Bowl* in Bristol. Old Crome, who was actually apprenticed as a sign-painter, also painted a *Jolly Sailor*, at Yarmouth, which was sold in Norwich for twelve guineas in 1906. He produced a sign of the *Top Sawyers* at St Martin's, Norwich. It was afterwards taken down by the owner, framed and hung up as a picture. It is now in the Pockthorpe Brewery. He also painted signs of these Norwich houses, the *Three Cranes*, the *Lame Dog*, the *Lamb* and the *Maid's Head*. For painting the *Lame Dog* he received a guinea, for writing and gilding the *Lamb* 18s., for writing and gilding the *Maid's Head* five shillings! The *Three Cranes* sign was bought by the late Sir Samuel Hoare.

In more recent years Walter Crane, R.A., painted the *Fox & Pelican* at Grayshott, Hants. J. E. Hodgson with — Leslie painted the sign of the *George & Dragon* at Wargrave, Berks. This also is said to have been painted in order to settle a score— in 1876. Tradition says that one side of the sign, depicting the Saint in combat with the dragon was painted by Leslie; the other, showing the dragon lying dead, and the Saint refreshing himself from a tankard by Hodgson. The original sign is now inside the house and outside hangs a good modern sign by H. Whiteside. Similarly a sign at Singleton, Lancashire, was the work of an 'R.A.', and an 'R.S.', each painting one side of it. On the front was represented a wearied pilgrim, at the back the same traveller duly refreshed. Leslie painted the *Row Barge* at Wallingford, and the *King John's Head*, Southwark St., Abbey St., S.E., Miss Leighton the *Smoker* at Plumbley, and no less a person than H.R.H. Princess Louise, the *Ferry* at Roseneath, Dumbartonshire.

At New Inn Lane, Epsom, Harlow painted a front and George Henry a back view of *Queen Charlotte*, to settle a bill they had run up. Harlow imitated Sir Thomas Lawrence's style, and signed the work 'T. L. Greek St. Soho'. When Lawrence heard this he said in a rage that if Harlow were not a scoundrel he would kick him from one street's end to the other ; upon which Harlow very coolly remarked that when Sir Thomas should make up his mind to it he hoped he would choose a short street. Herring is said to have painted some signs. Amongst them are the *Flying Dutchman*, Cottage Green, Camberwell, and the *Stag, Coach & Horses*, and the *White Lion*, Doncaster.

J. C. Ibbetson, the friend of Morland, to settle a bill run up in a sketching and fishing holiday, painted a sign still to be seen over the village alehouse at Troutbeck, near Ambleside. This represented two faces, the one thin and pale, the other jolly and rubicund ; under it was the following rhyme :

> Thou mortal man that liv'st by bread,
> What made thy face to look so red ?
>
> Thou silly fop that looks so pale,
> 'Tis red with Tommy Burkett's ale.

Tommy Burkett was of course the name of the host. The painting is now gone, but the verses remain.

George Morland painted several signs—in one instance charging a fee of ' unlimited gin '. The *Goat in Boots*, a sign in Fulham Rd., has been attributed to him, but it was painted over several times, and finally replaced by a carved sign. He also painted a *White Lion* for an inn at Paddington, where he used to carouse with his boon companions, Ibbetson and John Rathbone ; and in a small public-house near Chelsea Bridge, there was as late as 1824 a sign of the *Cricketers* painted by him. This painting by Morland at the date mentioned had been removed inside the house, and a copy of it was hung up for the sign. Unfortunately, however, the landlord used to travel about with the original, and put it up before his booth at Staines and Egham races, cricket matches, and on similar occasions, so the painting suffered.

In his younger days Sir Charles Ross painted a sign of the *Magpie* at Sudbury, and the landlady of the house with no small pride gave an inquirer to understand that more than thirty years after, the aristocratic portrait-painter came in a carriage to her house, and asked to be shown the old sign once more. Richard Wilson, R.A. (d. 1782), or according to another account David Cox, painted the *Three Loggerheads* for an alehouse in North Wales, which gave its name to the village of Loggerheads, near the town of Mold. The painting was still exhibited as a signboard in 1824, though little of Wilson's work remained, as the sign had been repeatedly touched up. Sir

John Millais painted a *George & Dragon*, with grapes round it, for the *Vidler's Inn*, Hayes, Kent.

Good pierced-metal signs have recently come into favour. Two fine examples of these are the *Lamb* at Burford and the *Plough* at Clanfield, both made by local crafts-men for Messrs. Garner to the design of Captain W. R. W. Kettlewell. In recent years Messrs. Youngers have had many excellent signs painted by Mr. S. T. Weeks, President of the London Sketch Club, and a well-known provincial house, Messrs. Parkers of Burslem, have had the whole of their signs re-designed by Mr. G. Forsyth.

It is curious how different parts of the country seem to have marked predilections for different signs. According to Mr. Bloch,★ the *White Lion* and the *Black Swan* are more common in the south of England than are their black and white counter-parts. The *Dolphin* also he says is specially common in the same area. The *Wheel* and the *Seven Stars* he notes as specially common in Cornwall. I find myself unable to subscribe to his theories, and so far have not been able to check the data upon which he bases them. Certainly it is a fact that the *Blue Posts* is a favourite in the *West* End of London. The *Staffordshire Knot* is common of course in the county concerned, the *One & All* (the fifteen roundels of the Cornish badge) in Cornwall, for example at Penrhyn. Some of these are understandable enough, and there is no puzzle in the popularity of the *Vulcan's Arms* and the *Miner's Arms* in the Black Country and in the neighbourhood of Sheffield, in that of the *Jolly Potters* in Staffordshire, and in that of ' ship ' signs of various kinds along the whole of the coast. Similarly it is clear why the *Cornish Chough* occurs rarely except in the Duchy. Along the main roads, particularly the old coaching roads, one finds the *Coach & Horses*, the *Flying Horse*, and such names as the *Express*, the *Tallyho*, etc., names of former coaches. Similarly along the lines of canal there occur such signs as the *Navigation*, the *Steam Packet*, the *Packet*, the *Duke of Bridgwater*, etc. It does not appear on the surface however why ' blue ' signs, the *Blue Man*, the *Blue Boar*, the *Blue Dog*, etc., should be specially favoured in Lincolnshire,† why the *George* should be specially common in Gloucester-shire, and the *Marquis of Granby* in Surrey,‡ far from the main Manners estates. The *Board* or *Table* occurs rarely except in or near Durham,§ the *Cat & Fiddle* is commoner in Hampshire than elsewhere. The *Case is Altered* and the *Rose & Crown* are to be found often in Hertfordshire, and in some parts of Middlesex—there were at one time four inns of these signs within six miles of Harrow, and formerly the *Thorn* or *Thorntree* was almost peculiar to Derbyshire. Four signs are commoner in Yorkshire than else-where. It is easy to understand why the *Bay Horse* is one of them, since this repre-sents the Cleveland Bay, the old coach-horse breed which developed locally. It does not appear, however, why Yorkshire should also have a taste for the *Heifer* signs rarely found elsewhere, and for the *Blacksmith's Arms*. Nor is it plain why the

---

★ *Op. cit.*, 216, etc.

† At Grantham the blue signs are certainly political—the Whig colours of the Earls of Dysart.

‡ There may be a political reason for this. The Duke of Rutland was patron of two or three pocket boroughs in Surrey.

§ The Board seems to be originally a blank signboard, the mark of a house having no formal sign.

Brunswick should be a favourite in the same county. Similarly the *Davy Lamp* in one form or another is universally used throughout the coalfields, but the sign rarely occurs except in Northumberland. The *Anvil*, the *Smith*, and the *Smithy* are quite rare except near Sheffield, the *Forge*, the *Three Forges*, etc., except in the Midland iron districts. Again it is perhaps understandable how the *Cricketers' Arms* should be common in Surrey and Hampshire (though of course many odd instances of it occur elsewhere). So far as is known, however, no one has yet produced a satisfactory explanation why the *Crooked Billet* should be greatly favoured in London and in Essex, especially in those parts of the county neighbouring the Thames Estuary. No less than sixteen London taverns bear this sign. The *Rose & Crown* is also said to be particularly common in Essex, where the *Running Mare* is also commoner than elsewhere.

Armorial signs tend of course to cluster in the districts where the families concerned had great estates. No doubt many of the *Talbots* and *Shrewsbury Arms* signs in the Cotswolds are connected with the fact that the Earl of Shrewsbury had estates centring round his manor house at Heythrop, twelve miles from Banbury. Similarly the *Green Man* is commonest in the Midlands. Cheshire has a taste for vivid picturesque signs, some of which have disappeared in recent years. Instances are the *Naked Child* at Timperley, Cheshire, the *Romping Kitling* at Styal, and the *Comfortable Gill* at Stockport. Lancashire also has still its *Doff Cockers*, but it has lost the *Dog i' th' Thatch*, formerly at Wigan. There are few *Hop Poles* in London and (surprisingly) in Kent, but many in the Midlands and the West. The *White Horse* is common in Kent. Here of course it is the badge of the county.

In connexion with this general survey of signboard history it is worth noting how many village names and street names are originally those of local inns. A glance at the Underground or 'Bus map of London will supply many instances. Other provincial illustrations are *Loggerheads*, *Black Bull*, and *Red Bull*, all in Staffordshire, *Black Bull*, Yorkshire, *White Post*, Nottinghamshire and Somerset, *Cross Keys*, Norfolk, *Cross in Hand*, Leicestershire and Sussex, *Halfway House*, Shropshire and Kent, *World's End*, at least five examples in England, *Five Crosses*, Lancashire, *Craven Arms*, Shropshire, etc. As to street names, any old town will supply numerous examples. A walk down Fleet St. now as in Larwood's time, brings out the point well, since such courts as still remain are nearly all christened after signs formerly displayed in them or at their entrances.

It is doubtful how far there is substance in the old idea that not only streets but families also have to thank signs for their names. According to Camden :—

> Many names that seem unfitting for men, as of brutish beasts, etc., come from the very signs of the houses where they inhabited ; for I have heard of them which sayd they spake of knowledge, that some in late time dwelling at the signe of the *Dolphin, Bull, White Horse, Racket, Peacocke*, etc., were commonly called Thomas at the Dolphin, Will at the Bull, George at the White Horse, Robin at the Racket, which names, as many other of like sort, with omitting *at the*, became afterwards hereditary to their children.

Perhaps some of the following surnames *may* have developed in this way :—
Arrow, Axe, Barrell, Bullhead, Bell, Block, Banner, Bowles, Baskett, Cann, Coulter,
Chisell, Clogg, Crosskeys, Crosier, Funnell, Forge, Firebrand, Grapes, Griffin, Horns,
Hammer, Hamper, Hodd, Image (the sign originally in honour of some saint perhaps),
Jugg, Kettle, Knife, Lance, Maul, Mattock, Needle, Pail, Pott, Potts, Plowe, Plane,
Pipes, Pottle, Patten, Posnet (a purse or money-bag), Pitcher, Rule, Rainbow, Sack,
Saw, Shovel, Shears, Scales, Silverspoon, Swords, Tabor (drum), Tubb, Wedge, etc.

Larwood concludes his first chapter with an enumeration of the inn, tavern, and
public-house signs which occurred most frequently in London in 1864 :

Adam & Eve 12, Albion 13, Alfred's Head 5, Anchor & Hope 13, Angel 18, Angel &
Crown 8, Antigalliean 3, Artichoke 5, Barley Mow 13, Beehive 9, Bell 31, Ben Jonson 7,
Bird in Hand 5, Black Boy 6, Black Bull 16, Black Dog 5, Black Horse 29, Black Lion 10,
Black Swan 6, Blue Anchor 19, Blue Coat Boy 5, Blue Last 6, Blue Peter 14, Bricklayers'
Arms 27, Bridge House 5, Britannia 22, Brown Bear 15, Builders' Arms 8, Bull 17 (some
combined with Bells, Butchers, etc.), Bull's Head 22, Camden Head 4, Cape of Good Hope 6,
Carpenters' Arms 14, Castle 19, Catherine Wheel 6, Champion 7, Chequer 5, Cherry-tree 5,
Cheshire Cheese 8, City Arms 11, City of London and other cities (as Canton, Paris, Quebec,
etc.) 18, Coach & Horses 52, Cock 12, Cock in combination with Bottle, Hoops, Lion,
Magpie, etc., 16, Constitution 6, Coopers' Arms 17, Crooked Billet 7, Cross Keys 5, Crown 61,
Crown & Anchor 18, Crown & Cushion 5, Crown & Sceptre 11, Crown combined with
other objects as Anvil, Barley Mow, Thistle, Dolphin, etc., 17 (in all Crown 112) ; Devon-
shire Arms 12, Devonshire Castle 2, Dolphin 10, Dover Castle 6, Duke of Wellington 34,
Duke of York 32, Duke of Sussex 6, Duke of Clarence 16, Duke of Cambridge 7, other Dukes
(including Albemarle, Argyle, Bedford, Bridgewater, Gloucester, etc.) 26, various Duchesses
(as Kent, York, Oldenburgh, etc.) 7, Duke's Head 14, Earls (Aberdeen, Cathcart, Chatham,
Durham, Essex, etc.) 18, Edinburgh Castle 6, Elephant & Castle 5, Falcon 9, Feathers 21,
Fishmongers' Arms 4, Five Bells 4, Fleece 5, Flying Horse 6, Fortune of War 4, Fountain 24,
Fox 8, Fox (combined with Grapes, Hounds, Geese, etc.) 12, Freemasons' Arms 8, various
Generals (Elliott, Hill, Abercrombie, Picton, Wolfe, etc.) 8, George 52, George & Dragon 14,
George the Fourth 19, Globe 31, Gloster Arms 6, Goat 7, Golden Anchor 5, Golden Fleese 5,
Golden Lion 15, Goldsmiths' Arms 6, Grapes 56, Green Dragon 15, Green Gates 4, Green
Man 24, Greyhound 9, Griffin 7, Grosvenor Arms 5, Gun 8, Guy of Warwick 4, Half-moon 6,
Hercules 4, Hercules Pillars 2, Hole in the Wall 5, Hoop & Grapes 5, Hop-pole 4, Hope 12,
Horns 11, Horse & Groom 21, Horseshoes 7, Horseshoe & Magpie 5, Jacob's Well 6, John
Bull 5, various 'Jolly' people, as Jolly Anglers, Caulkers, Gardeners, etc., 16, King of
Prussia 12, Kings & Queens 10, King's Arms 89, King's Head 63, Lamb 8, Lamb & Flag 3,
Lion & Lamb 4, different Lords 55, among whom were Lord Nelsons 23, Magpie & Stump 4,
Mail-coach 3, Man in the Moon 3, Marlborough Arms 2, Marlborough Head 6, Marquis of
Granby 18, Marquis of Cornwallis 6, various Marquisses 14, Masons' Arms 9, Mitre 17,
Mulberry-tree 4, Nag's Head 15, Nell Gwynne 3, Noah's Ark 7, Norfolk Arms 7, North
Pole 4, Northumberland Arms 9, Old Parr's Head 3, Olive Branch 6, Oxford Arms 6, Pea-
cock 10 (Peahen 1), Perseverance 5, Pewter Platter 5, Phoenix 10, Pied Bull 3, Pine Apple 5,
Pitt's Head 9, Plough 15, Portland Arms 6, Portman Arms 5, Prince Albert 19, Prince Alfred 5,
Prince Arthur 3, other Princes (mostly of the Royal family)15, Prince of Wales 43, Prince
Regent 12, Princess Royal 6, Princess Victoria 3, and a few of the younger Princesses,
Punch-bowl 2, Queen 3, Queen & Prince Albert 3, Queen Victoria 17, Queen's Arms 22,
Queen's Head 49, Railway Tavern 8, Red Cow 8, Red Cross 4, Red Lion 73, Rising Sun 26,

Robin Hood 9, Rodney Head 5, Roebuck 10, Rose 14, Rose & Crown 48, Royal Albert 4, various *Royal* personages and objects as *Champions, Cricketers, Crowns, Dukes, Forts,* etc., 28, *Royal George* 8, *Royal Oak* 26, *Royal Standard* 13, *Running Horse* 8, *Saints* (*St Andrew* 3, *St Martin* 2, *St Paul* 2, etc.) 23, *Salisbury Arms* 5, *Salmon* 2, *Salutation* 4, *Scotch Store* 6, *Seven Star* 4, *Shakespeare Head* 8, *Shepherd & Flock* 2, *Shepherd & Shepherdess* 2, *Ship* 53 (in combination, on launch, aground, etc.) 23, *Ship & Star* 3, *Ship & Whale* 2, knights and baronets (including *Sir John Falstaff* 4, *Sir John Barleycorn, Sir Hugh Myddleton, Sir Isaac Newton, Sir Christopher Wren, Sir Ralph Abercrombie, Sir Paul Pindar, Sir Robert Peel, Sir Walter Raleigh, Sir William Walsworth,* etc.) 19, *Skinners' Arms* 5, *Southampton Arms* 5, *Sportsman* 4, *Spotted Dog* 3, *Spread Eagle* 14, *Stag* 3, *Staghound* 3, *Star* 11, *Star & Garter* 17, *Sugar-loaf* 8, *Sun* 19, *Swan* 19, *Talbot* 9, *Telegraph* 4, *Thatched House* 3, *Thistle & Crown* 5, *Three Compasses* 21, *Three Crowns* 8, *Three Cranes* 3, *Three Cups* 3, *Three Kings* 3, *Three Tuns* 19, *Tigers* 8, (*Tiger Cat* 1), *Turk's Head* 10, *Two Brewers* 28, *Two Chairmen* 5, *Unicorn* 4, *Union* 10, *Union Flag* 2, *Victoria* 11, *Vine* 5, *Waggon & Horses* 3, *Watermen's Arms* 9, *Weavers' Arms* 9, *Westminster Arms* 3, *Wheatsheaf* 20, *White Bear* 15, *White Hart* 63, *White Horse* 44, *White Lion* 25, *White Swan* 35, *Whittington & Cat* 3, (*Whittington & Stone* 1), *William the Fourth* 16, *Windmill* 11, *Windsor Castle* 12, *Woodman* 4, *Woolpack* 8, *York Arms & York Minster* 10, *Yorkshire Greys* 12.

Verses on signs would fill a book by themselves. Many of them will be found in the text below. They have been an unfailing source of interest to passers-by for centuries. It does not appear, however, that the major poets have contributed as generously to signboard versification as their brothers the artists have to signboard pictorial art. Such cases as are quoted in the text will be found duly recorded in the index under Verses.

Chapter II

NICKNAMED, PERVERTED, CORRUPTED AND 'REFINED' SIGNS AND JOCULAR VARIATIONS UPON SIGNS

SIGNBOARD Corruptions are referred to by Ben Jonson—

> . . . It even puts Apollo
> To all his strength of art to follow
> The flights, and to divine
> What is meant by every sign.

For two and a half centuries at least signboard etymology has been the happy hunting-ground of theorists. A great many of their suggested derivations are ingenious, but far-fetched in the extreme. Many of them, probably by their very ingenuity, have passed into common currency, though frequently there is not a jot of evidence in their favour. A recent writer instanced among these the derivation of *Barley Mow* (the origin of which is clear enough, in all conscience), from *Bel Amour* ! Other choice specimens of these pseudo-derivations are *Goat & Compasses* from *God Encompasseth Us*, *Leg & Seven Stars* from *League & Seven Stars* (The Seven United Provinces), *Axe & Bottle* from *Battleaxe*, *Bag o' Nails* from *Bacchanals*, *Bull & Mouth* from *Boulogne Mouth*, and so on. The author has noted many such on the pages below. Perhaps he may have perpetuated (or perpetrated) a few.

But even discounting to the full the efforts of antiquarian ingenuity, there is abundant evidence that some very queer transformations have taken place. Many of them have arisen from the use of classical names which conveyed nothing or little to the habitués of the taverns which adopted them. *The Andrew Mac*, for example (shown as a kilted Highlander), was originally the frigate *Andromache*, the *Billy Ruffian* the *Bellerophon*. Other signs originate from the mispronunciation of words—sometimes quite everyday words, in other cases words in a foreign tongue, and those which once were in everyday use but which now are somewhat archaic.

The *Crown & Woodpecker* thus developed from the *Crown & Woolpack*, the *Iron Devils* from the (Arundel) *Hirondelles*, the *Ranged Deer* from the *Reindeer*, the *Hope & Anchor* from the *Hope Anchor*. It is said locally that the *Diglis Hotel*, Worcester, which certainly once belonged to the Dean and Chapter commemorates in its name its former ownership, the title being—originally ' d'Eglise '. The derivation seems however somewhat fanciful. One hopes that the *Rose of the Quarter Sessions* really does represent *La Rose des Quatre Saisons*, *St Peter's Finger*, Lytchett Minster, Dorset (p. 178), *St Peter* ad *Vincula*, the *Pig & Carrot*, *La Pique* (spade) *et le Carreau* (diamond), and the *Queer Door*, the *Cœur Dorée* (the Golden Heart of Our Lady).

28

In a few—probably a very few—instances, corruptions have been due to popular ignorance of the terms of heraldry. The *Bird in Hand* was probably as often as not originally a *Falcon* on a *Gauntlet*, the *Bleeding Horse* a *Horse's Head* (erminois), the *Spangled Bull* the *Pied Bull*, and the *Cats* the *Leopards*. Certainly it seems likely that the *Loggerheads* was once the *Libber* (i.e. Leopards') *Heads*. It is not so certain that the *Bonny Cravat* is the *Bonny Carvette* (i.e. hedge). A likelier suggestion would be that it repre-sented the *Bonny* (*Corvette*). Probably many curious double signs may be explained in this way, for example, the *Sheep & Anchor* is pretty certainly the *Ship & Anchor*. In several English counties ship is correct dialect for sheep. It may be that the *Buck & Bell*, Banbury, is derived from the mediæval curse by *book*, *bell* and *candle*, though on the face of it this seems hardly likely.

Sometimes changes owe their origin to fresh notions of verbal propriety. Thus the *Ass in a Bandbox* is a refined version of *My Arse in a Bandbox*, a satirical reference to Napoleon's proposed invasion of England. The *Devils House*, Hornsey, was refined by the landlord in 1767 to the *Summer House*. *Hell Cellar*, Norwich, was similarly renamed by the landlord, who advertised that it was ' laid into one large handsome public house, which will be inhabited by civil honest people '. He hoped that ' no person will reflect on the same for the scandalous name of the other ' and offered ' civil usage, good beer and a hearty welcome ', with the additional inducement that ' any gentleman may sit and see the Judge go to the Assizes '. The new name of this House was the *Globe & Seven Stars*.

Sometimes a sign has been deliberately altered in order to destroy its religious or political significance. Thus the early Protestants converted the *Catherine Wheel* into the *Cat & Wheel*, or the *Clockwheel*, the *Salutation* into the *Flower Pot*, the *Three Nuns* into the *Three Widows*, and Puritans changed the *Salutation* into the *Soldier & Citizen*. Some signs are clearly parodies of others, for example, the *Coach & Dogs* of the *Coach & Horses*, the *Goose & Gridiron* of the *Swan & Harp*. Probably many such signs developed first as nicknames. In the North Country today the *Eagle & Child* is almost invariably known as the *Bird & Babby*, the *Swan & Sugarloaf* appears elsewhere as the *Duck & Acid-drop*, the *Swan* as *Paddy's Goose*, or if it is a *Black Swan*, the *Mucky Duck*, the *Legs of Man* as the *Kettle with Three Spouts*, and so on. Since the *Red Lion* at Paddlesworth, Kent, is known—as it invariably is—as the *Cat & Custard Pot* it is easy to see how a cat and a custard-pot eventually appeared on its sign. This, of course, is in some ways an improvement upon the original sign. A very vulgar and unnecessary nickname, which seems unlikely to cause a change of sign is the *How de do & Spew*—an attempt equally feeble and coarse at humour upon the charming old sign of the *Salutation & Cat*. The figures of the *Salutation* sign have had many changes. Elsewhere (p. 165) it is explained how the Angel Gabriel in the *Salutation* of Our Lady became converted to a *Soldier & Citizen* (or later two citizens) politely bowing to one another, and still later to a pair of hands conjoined in a friendly clasp. The *Case is Altered* often originated as a nickname. A house of this title at Banbury is properly styled the *Weavers Arms*. The explanation given locally for the change is that the Bloxham Weavers occasionally paid a visit to their confrères at Banbury and that these visits usually wound up in a mass fight in or near the house on the Bloxham Rd. Usually the Bloxham weavers had the best of it, but on one occasion they were completely vanquished by the Banbury men, who changed the name of the house to commemorate their victory. Elsewhere the name is explained as commemorating the advent of a new landlord who began his régime by abolishing the 'slate', and there are half a dozen other explanations all equally plausible.

This list of nicknamed houses (all in Bristol) I owe to the kindness of Mr. H. Ll. George of the Bristol Brewery :—

Cauliflower :	*Rose* (from a badly painted sign).
Dollar, Market Place :	*Crown* (originally *Guilder*).
Dotty House :	*Steam Packet.*
Gluepot, Gloucester Rd. :	*Golden Lion* (? from the old custom of testing the purity of ale with a pair of leathern breeches).
Goose & Gridiron :	*Swan & Lyre.*
Hole in the Wall :	*Coach & Horses* (said to have kept a look-out posted for the press-gang).
Monkey shaves the Cat :	*Exeter Railway Tavern* (the incident is represented by stuffed animals).
Mouse, Westbury-on-Trym :	*Royal Oak* (the original house was 'down a hole').
Mucky Duck :	*Black Swan.*
Penniless Corner, Staple Hill :	*Portcullis.*
Quiet House, Old Market :	*Mason's Arms.*
Shant or Shanty, Cockshott Hill :	*Crown.*

The reader may find it interesting to work out a similar list of nicknamed houses in his own area, and to try to discover the reasons for them.

In the short table below I give notes of the major houses mentioned in the text or falling within the author's personal knowledge in which changes of the types indicated above seem to have taken place. The reader will probably be able to find many other instances for himself, and may care to take my list as the basis of his own. It should be used, of course, in conjunction with the list of heraldic and symbolic signs on pp. 88–97, that of changed signs on pp. 279–86, and the general index :

All Macks in the East :	A double pun on *Almacks* (in the West), and on the fact that Max = gin.
Andrew Mac :	(Sign displaying a kilted Highlander—the frigate (?)) (?) *Andromache.*
Angel :	Protestantization of *Nun.*
Angel & Crown :	A misinterpretation of a *Crown* sign, in which in Renaissance style the crown was supported by a cherub.
Angel & Flute :	Jocular variation upon *Bear & Ragged Staff* (see p.14).
Angel & Woolpack :	*Naked Boy & Woolpack.*
Ass in a Bandbox :	'Refinement' of *My Arse in a Bandbox.*
Axe & Bottle :	*Battle Axe* (see p. 12).
Babes in the Wood :	Appears on the signboard as two men in the stocks.

Bag o' Nails :	Possibly from *Woodnymph*, via *Bacchanals*. In other cases perhaps a perversion of *Blackamoor's Head* and *Wool-pack* (see pp. 14, 32).
Barley Mow :	Emphatically *not*, of course, ' *Bel Amour* '.
Barrel, Tunstall, Stoke-on-Trent :	Nickname for *Crown & Anchor* (from a ' barrel ' sign).
Bear & Bacchus :	Perhaps a corruption of *Bear & Baculus*, or *Bear & Ragged Staff*, *q.v.*
Bear & Billet :	*Bear & Ragged Staff*.
Beggars Bush :	(?) *Badger's Bush*, that is, a house furnishing the entertainment of badger baiting.
Bell & Dragon :⎫ *Bell & Griffin* :⎭	*Bel and the Dragon*.
Belle Sauvage, La :	An incorrect ' correction ' of *Bell Savage*.
Bible & Key :	Possibly a misreading of *Half Eagle & Key*.
Billy Ruffian :	Alleged to be a corruption of *Bellerophon*.
Bird & Babby :⎫ *Bird & Bantling*:⎭	*Eagle & Child*, *q.v.*
Bird in Hand :	(?) *Falcon* (on gauntlet).
Bleeding Horse :	*Horse's Head* (erminois).
Block & Cleaver, Burslem, Stoke-on-Trent :	Nickname for *Cresswell Arms*.
Blue Ball :	(?) *Globe*, *q.v.*
Blue-eyed Maid :	*Minerva* (see p. 51).
Bonny Cravat :	(?) *Bonny Carvette*—yew hedge, or more probably *Bonny—Corvette*.
Borough Arms, Hanley, Stoke-on-Trent :	Generally known as *Travellers' Rest*, a former sign.
Bosom's Inn :	*Blossoms* Inn—a nickname of *St Laurent's* Inn (see p. 180).
Boy & Barrel, York :	Nickname for *Jolly Bacchus*.
Broad Face :	Baldface (? d. Stag) (see p. 160).
Bull & Butcher :	Very improbably *Bullen Butchered* (see p. 37).
Bull & Mouth :	Alleged to be *Boulogne Mouth* (?).
Bull & Stirrup :	*Bull & Fetterlock*—a combination of two Yorkist badges, *q.v.*
Castle & Ball, Marlborough :	*Castle & Bull*.
Cat & Bagpipes, East Harlsey, N.R., Yorks. :	Supposed to be a skit upon the Highland drovers using the Great North Rd.
Cat & Custard Pot, Paddlesworth, Kent :	*Red Lion*.
Cat & Fiddle :	Alleged to be *Le chat fidèle*, or *Caton le fidèle* (the governor of Calais), and also referred to *Catherine la Fidèle* (Catherine of Aragon), and Catherine (Queen of Peter the Great, although it existed two centuries before her time, and in any case she was not particularly ' fidèle '. Probably merely from the nursery rhyme.
Cat & Kittens :	*Perhaps* quart pots and pint pots.
Cat & Lion :	*Tiger & Lion* (see p. 129).
Cat & Wheel :	Protestantization of *Catherine Wheel*.

Cats (Lewes) :	(*Leopard*) supporters of (*Sackville*) Dorsets.
Charlie Brown's :	Nickname of *Railway Tavern*, West India Dock Rd., the most famous 'museum' inn now remaining, so well known as to need no further description.
Clock Wheel :	Protestantization of *Catherine Wheel* (see p. 181).
Cock & Pie : *Cock & Magpie* : *Cock & Pynot* :	Very improbably *Peacock Pie*, or *Peacock & (Mag)pie*, often alleged to refer to the oath by *Cock & Pie*, that is, by God and the Mass (?).
Coach & Dogs :	Parody of *Coach & Horses*.
Cock & Bottle :	Alleged to refer to *Cocks in Battle* (i.e. *Fighting Cocks*). Probably, more prosaically, *Cork & Bottle*, or *Cock & Bottle*, that is, signifying liquors in bottle or on draught.
Cock & House, Norwich :	(?) *Cock* (fighting) *House*.
Colt & Cradle :	Translation from the Dutch *het Pardje in de Wieg*, for *het Partje in de Wieg*, that is, *The Couple in Bed*.
Corner Pin, York :	Nickname for *Unicorn*.
Cross in Hand :	Probably *Crossed* (clasped) *Hands* (as a symbol of unity and amity).
Crown & Woodpecker :	*Crown & Woolpack* (see pp. 28, 65).
Devil & Bag o' Nails :	*Blackamoor's Head & Woolpack* (see p. 209).
Devil in a Tub :	Possibly a corruption of *Labour in Vain*, *q.v.*
Dog & Crook :	Usually perhaps, a corruption of *Dog & Crock*, *q.v.*
Duck & Acid-drop :	*Swan & Sugarloaf.*
Duke's Motto, Bethnal Green Rd. :	The motto was 'I am here' (see p. 84).
Dusty Miller :	*Collier* (see p. 210).
Ere you are, Ipswich :	Jocular variation of *E(astern) U(nion) R(ailway)*.
Elephant & Castle :	Alleged to be *Infanta of Castle* (?).
Engine House, Tunstall, Stoke-on-Trent :	Nickname for *Oddfellows' Arms*.
Finish (Covent Garden) :	Nickname for *Queen's Head* (see p. 307).
First & Last :	Sometimes geographical, on other occasions, First (in), Last (out), the publicans' ideal customer, on still others a jocular variation of *Cradle & Coffin*, *q.v.*
Flower Pot :	Perhaps the *Vase of Lilies* symbolical of Our Lady.
Flying Horse :	*Pegasus.*
Foresters Inn, Liphook, Hants :	*Concert Inn.*
Flying Bull, Burslem, Stoke-on-Trent :	*Fly & Bull* (see p. 52).
Four Awls :	Nickname for *Four Alls* (see pp. 13, 266).
Fox & Owl :	*Owl & (Ivy) Tod*, hence *Tod & Owl*, *Fox & Owl* (see p. 109).
French Horn & Three Tuns :	The Company of *Bottlemakers' Arms—arg.* on a chevron *sa.*, three bugle horns of the first, between three leather bottles of the second.
Frighted Horse :	*Freighted Horse*, i.e. Packhorse.
Gentleman in Trouble :	*Hog in the Pound* (see p. 125).
George & Cannon :	Corruption of *George Canning* (see p. 49).
Globe & Seven Stars, Norwich :	See p. 282.

PLATE
3

PLATE
4

THE

BLACK   BEAR,

HUNGERFORD.

Dan.ᵉ Pashford.
Winchester.

Goat & Boot :	Corruption of *Goat in Boots*, *q.v.*
Goat & Compasses :	Said to be *God encompasseth us* (?) or a corruption of the Company of *Cordwainers' Arms*, the chevron being transmuted into a pair of compasses.
Good Woman : *Quiet Woman* : *Silent Woman* :	(Shown on sign as decapitated)—some female saint who suffered execution, or *Heedless Virgin* (in the parable), corrupted to *Headless Virgin*, so depicted on the sign, and then ironically renamed.
Goose & Gridiron :	*Swan & Harp*, *q.v.*
Green Lettuce :	Probably originally *Green Lattice* (?) (see p. 225).
Green Man : *Wild Man* :	Perhaps originally *Jack in the Green* ; in other instances *Archer* or *Robin Hood*.
Green Man & Still :	The Green Man was probably one of the Red Indian supporters of the arms of the Distillers' Company—the Company of *Distillers Arms*.
Hare & Billet (Blackheath) :	Combination of *Harrow* and *Crooked Billet*, with corruption of the latter.
Hawk & Buck :	(?) Corruption of *Hawk & Buckle*, *q.v.*
Hawk & Buckle :	(?) *Falcon & Fetterlock*, *q.v.*
Hole in the Wall (Shrewsbury) :	Nickname for *Star Vaults*. The original *Hole in the Wall* is said to have been at Grantham.
Hope & Anchor :	*Hope* (i.e. Spare) *Anchor* (see p. 52).
Horse & Dorsers :	*Horse & Dorsiters* (i.e. Pack Horse).
Horse & Magnet :	*Horse-shoe & Magnet*, *q.v.*
Horseshoe & Magnet :	Corruption of *Horse-shoe & Magpie*.
Horseshoe & Magpie :	Corruption of *Horseshoe & Falcon*.
How de do & Spew :	Vulgar would-be-jocular variation upon *Salutation & Cat*.
Iceland Queen :	*Island Queen* (see p. 40).
Iron Devils :	Said to be Hirondelles—swallows—the arms of the Arundels, now quartered by the (Howard) Dukes of Norfolk—*Arundel Arms*.
Jack of Both Sides, Reading :	A house situated at a V-shaped cross-roads—what is vulgarly called a flat-iron building. The phrase is also used as a term in rustic cricket.
Jigpost, Burslem, Stoke-on-Trent :	*Royal Express*—a colliers' house of call. A jigpost is the wooden post carrying a wheel and a drum placed at the top of an incline in the pit, so that the heavy descending tubs may draw up the light ascending ones.
Jolly Farmer (Bagshot) :	Corruption of *Golden Farmer*, *q.v.*
Kettle with Three Spouts :	(Nickname for) *Legs of Man*.
Kings & Keys :	*Three Kings & Cross Keys*.
Leg & Star :	*Star & Garter* or (?) originally *League* (the Seven United Provinces) *& Seven Stars*.
Leg of Mutton & Cauliflower :	(?) *Star & Garter*.
Lion & Pheasant :	*Lion & Cock* or *Dog & Pheasant* (see p. 98).
London Apprentice (Shrewsbury) :	Refinement of *George Barnwell* (c. 1780).
Maggoty Pie :	*Magpie*.
Magpie & Horseshoe :	See *Horseshoe & Magpie*.

D

Mr. Bunches (Tavistock Rd.) :	Nickname for *Salutation*.
Mucky Duck : } *Muddy Duck* : }	*Black Swan*.
Naked Man :	*Adam*.
Ostrich :	(At any rate that at Colnbrook, Bucks), *Ostry—Hospitalaria*—Monastic Guest House.
Paddy's Crut (Mostyn Arms, Hanley, Stoke-on-Trent) :	An Irish mining contractor or 'cruttler' paid out his men here.
Paddy's Goose :	*Swan*.
Pig & Carrot (?) : } *Pig & Checkers* : }	(?) *Pique et Carreau*—spade and diamond (see pp. 13, 28).
Pig & Tinderbox :	*Elephant & Castle*.
Pig & Whistle :	Probably the English inn sign about which most theorizing has taken place. Suggested explanations include *Pige Washael* (the *Salutation* of Our Lady (?), *Piggin of Wassail* (?) Pyx and Housel, (?) the Scottish '*pig*' for a pot and 'whistle' for small change, (?) and the idea that the name is a facetious rendering of *Bear & Ragged Staff* (?). The reader may choose according to his taste from these and a dozen or so other explanations. Probably the obvious derivation is the correct one, and the name is as meaningless (and as charming) as *Goat in Boots, Cat & Fiddle*, etc.
Pig in Misery :	*Hog in Armour* (see p. 258).
Plum & Feather (formerly near Oxford) :	*Plume & Feathers, q.v.*
Pyewipe (in Lincolnshire) :	*Peewit*.
Queer Door :	Alleged to be a corruption of *La Cœur Dorée*—the *Golden Heart* of Our Lady (?) (see p. 28).
Quiet Woman :	See *Good Woman*.
Ramping Horse :	*Horse Rampant*.
Ranged Deer :	*Reindeer*.
Rat Pie (York) :	Nickname for *Garden Gate*.
Rope & Anchor :	(?) *Hope & Anchor, q.v.*
Rose of Quarter Sessions :	Alleged corruption of *La Rose des Quatre Saisons* (?).
Shanghai, Hanley, Stoke-on-Trent :	Nickname for *Golden Lion*.
Same Yet, Prestwich, Lancs. :	*Seven Stars* (see p. 285).
Sheep & Anchor :	*Ship & Anchor* (see p. 200).
Shovel & Boot :	*Shovel & Boat* for *Ship & Shovel* (see p. 11).
Silent Woman :	See *Good Woman*.
Simpson's (Cheapside) :	Invariably so called, but properly the *Queen's Arms*.
Soldier & Citizen :	*Salutation, q.v.*
Spangled Bull :	*Pied Bull, q.v.*
Spotted Dog :	*Talbot, q.v.*
Stag & Thorn :	Q.v. Corruption of *Buck & Thorn* itself a corruption of *Buckthorn* (?).
Straw Hat Hotel, Newton, Mon. :	The *Chequers* (? the only thatched house in the town).
Summer House, Hornsey :	'Refinement' of *Devil's House* (see p. 180).

Swan with Two Necks : Often alleged to be *Swan with Two Nicks* (i.e. swan marks) on his bill (see p. 138).

Thomases (Lombard St.) : Invariably so called, but properly the *George & Vulture*.

Three Frogs : Travesty of *Three Flowers de Luce*.

Three Goats (Lincolnshire) : Possibly *Three Gowts*, i.e. drains or sluices.

Three Leopards' Heads :
Three Libbards' Heads :
Three Logger Heads :
Three Lubber Heads : } Probably originally the *Three Leopards*. Arms of the Goldsmiths (and of the town of Shrewsbury, etc.). Now a well-known jocular sign, for which see pp. 86, 268.

Three Pheasants & Sceptre : *Three Pigeons & Sceptre* (see p. 98).

Three Widows : Puritanization of *Three Nuns*.

Two Kings & Still : Probably originally *Indians & Still* (of Distillers' Arms).

Under World, Hanley, Stoke-on-Trent : Nickname for *Sea Lion*.

Weighing Chains, Norwich : Nickname for *Magpie* (from weighing machine on front house).

William's (22 Artillery Lane) : Invariably so called. Properly the *Ship*.

Whip & Egg (Norwich) : Often alleged as a corruption of *Whip & Nag*. On this see p. 216.

Woman : *Sparerib*. From Genesis ii. 21–2.

Chapter III

HISTORIC AND COMMEMORATIVE SIGNS

THE Greeks honoured their great men and successful commanders by erecting statues to them. The Romans rewarded their popular favourites with triumphal entries and ovations. Modern nations make the portraits of their celebrities serve as signs for public-houses :—

> Vernon, the Butcher Cumberland, Wolfe, Hawke,
>   Prince Ferdinand, Granby, Burgoyne, Keppel, Howe,
> Evil and good have had their tithe of talk
> And fill'd their sign-post then like Wellesley now.*

As Byron hints, popular admiration is generally very short-lived ; when a fresh hero is gazetted, the next new alehouse may possibly adopt him for a sign in preference to the last great man. In Larwood's time the *Duke of Wellington* was already neglected and in his place was seen *General Havelock* (which still survives as a sign in Birmingham, as do *Sir Colin Campbell* at Kilburn, *Lord Palmerston*, *Mr. Gladstone* and *Lord Beaconsfield* in many places). Other instances are the *Earl of Cardigan* at Norwich, *Lord Raglan*, a house much older than its sign, at St Martin's-le-Grand, and the *Princess of Denmark* which later became *Queen Alexandra*. Not only on these modern celebrities but also upon many of the illustrious dead have signboard honours been bestowed in bygone ages. In more recent years the custom has rather fallen into disuse, though there is a *General Gordon* at Stamford, a *General Garibaldi* at Staines, and a *Lord Roberts* at Scunthorpe, Lincs. In the 1914–18 War one or two houses were named after *Earl Haig* and *Lord Kitchener*. It does not appear that so far either *Generals Alexander* or *Montgomery* or *Lord Wavell* have been elevated to the signboard, although a house at Paddock Wood has been named *John Brunt, V.C.*, after a local hero, and a house at Hastings renamed *G.I.* as a tribute to our wartime ally.

Many signboards have an historic connexion of some sort with the place where they are exhibited. Thus the *Alfred's Head* at Wantage in Berkshire was in all probability chosen as a sign because Wantage was the birthplace of King Alfred. The *Canute Castle* at Southampton owes its existence to a local tradition, while admiration for the Scottish patriot made an innkeeper in Stowell Street, Newcastle, adopt *Sir William Wallace's Arms*. The *Caesar's Head* was in 1761 to be seen near the New Church in the Strand, and in the beginning of the 19th century was the sign of a tavern in Soho, which afterwards removed to Great Palace Yard, Westminster. Even at the present day his head may be seen outside certain village alehouses. Heroines and beauties are less common on signboards than are heroes, though there was formerly

* Byron, REF.

36

a *Cleopatra* in Savoy Street. *Cromwell* is still honoured with signboards in places where his memory lingers as, until a few years ago, at Kate's Hill, Dudley.

In most cases, however, signboard popularity is rather short-lived. Horace Walpole noticed this fickleness of signboard fame in one of his letters :

> I was yesterday out of town, and the very signs, as I passed through the village, made me make very quaint reflections on the mortality of fame and popularity. I observed how the *Duke's Head* had succeeded almost universally to *Admiral Vernon's*, as his had left but few traces of the *Duke of Ormond's*. I pondered these things in my breast, and said to myself ' Surely all glory is but as a sign ! '

Some favourites of the signboard have, however, been more fortunate than others. Former kings occasionally occur, but their memories seem to have been revived rather than handed down by successive innkeepers. If we are to believe a Chester legend, however, the *Old King Edgar* which still stands in Bridge St. has existed by the same name since the time of the Saxon king ! The sign represents King Edgar rowed down the river Dee by the eight tributary kings. The present house has the appearance of being built before the reign of Elizabeth, and the sign appears almost as old, but certainly it would be unwise to credit the legend. *King John* was the sign under whose auspices Jem Mace the pugilist kept a public-house, now extinct, in Holywell Lane, Shoreditch. The same sign also figures in Albemarle St. and in Bermondsey. *John of Gaunt* may be seen in many places, perhaps as a feudal lord, or possibly as a reformer and supporter of Wycliffe. The sign occurs at Leeds, Preston, Sandy, New-castle-under-Lyme, etc., though by no means as often as the *Red Rose*, his cognizance. The *Black Prince* may not unlikely have come down to us in an uninterrupted line of signboards ; so little has his identity sometimes been understood that in bills and on inn signs, he is occasionally represented as a negro ! The sign occurs among many other places in the Walworth Rd., and at Farnham, Surrey.

There is a *Queen Eleanor* in London Fields, Hackney, probably the beautiful and affectionate queen of Edward I, buried in Westminster Abbey in 1290. In honour of her Charing Cross, Cheapcross and seven other crosses were erected on the places where her body rested on its way to the great Abbey. What prompted the choice of this sign it is hard to say. *King Henry II* is a sign at Newcastle-under-Lyme. He gave a charter to the town and probably this is why he is so honoured here. Henry VIII is a great favourite for a *King's Head* sign.

At Hever, Kent, a rude portrait of him might formerly be seen. Near this village the Boleyn family formerly held large possessions, and old people in the district yet show the spot where the story goes, King Henry often used to meet Sir Thomas Boleyn's daughter Anne. It is alleged that for years after the unhappy death of Anne, the village alehouse had for its sign, *Bullen Butchered*, but the place falling into new hands, the name of the house was altered to the *Bull & Butcher*. The legend seems very unconvincing. This last sign is said to have existed till about a century ago, and might have swung at this moment but for the desire of the resident clergyman to see something different. He suggested the *King's Head* ; and the village painter was forthwith commissioned to make the alteration. He accepted the task, drew the bluff features of the monarch, and represented it as other *King's Heads*, but in his hands placed a large axe. This signboard—if indeed it ever did exist—is certainly not there today.

As for *Queen Elizabeth*, she was the constant type of the *Queen's Head*, as her father was of the *King's Head*, and like him, she may still be seen in many places. It is somewhat more difficult to ascertain who is meant by the *Queen Catherine* in Brook St., Ratcliffe Highway, whether it be Queen Catherine of Aragon or Queen Catherine of Braganza. *Queen Anne*, South St., Walworth, came down to Larwood's time as the token of that house since the day of its opening, just as the *Queen of Bohemia*, who until a century and a quarter ago continued as a sign in Drury Lane. The first-named has now, however, been replaced by an excellent modern sign. The beautiful and unfortunate lady was Elizabeth, daughter of James I, married to Frederick V, Elector-Palatine. After her husband's death she lived at Craven House, Drury Lane, and died there on 13 February, 1661. There is a *King of Bohemia* at Hampstead.

Of *King's Heads*, Henry VIII's is the oldest on authentic record. But this does not prove that he was the first. Among Henry's successors, we find the head of Edward VI on a trades token, while *Charles the First's Head* was the portrait hanging from the house of the scoundrel Jonathan Wild in the Old Bailey. Today there is a sign of *Charles the First* at Goring Heath, Reading. The *Martyr's Head* in Smithfield, 1710, seems also to have been a portrait of Charles I ; so at least, this allusion ★ suggests :—

> May Hyde, near Smithfield, at the *Martyr's Head*,
> Who charms the nicest judge with noble red.
> Thrive on, by drawing wines, which none can blame,
> But those who in his sign behold their shame ;

No doubt this is an allusion to puritanical water-drinkers. To this king belongs also the sign of the *Mourning Bush* set up by Taylor the Water Poet over his tavern in Phoenix Alley, Long Acre, to express his grief at the beheading of Charles I. He was soon compelled to take it down, when he put up the *Poet's Head*, his own portrait, with this inscription :

> There is many a head hangs for a sign ;
> Then, gentle reader, why not mine ?

At the same time that he put up his new sign, he issued a rhyming pamphlet, in which occur the following lines :

> My sign was once a *Crowne*, but now it is
> Changed by a sudden metamorphosis.
> The crowne was taken downe, and in the stead
> Is placed John Taylor's, or the *Poet's Head*.
> A painter did my picture gratis make,
> And (for a signe) I hang'd it for his sake.

★ In the *Quack Vintners*, 1710.

Now if my picture's drawing can prevayle,
'Twill draw my friends to me, and I'll draw ale.
Two strings are better to a bow than one ;
And poeting does me small good alone.
So ale alone yields but small good to me,
Except it have some spice of poesie.
The fruits of ale are unto drunkards such,
To make 'em sweare and lye that drinke too much.
But my ale, being drunk with moderation
Will quench thirst, and make merry recreation.
My book and signs were published for two ends.
T'invite my honest, civil, sober friends.
From such as are not such, I kindly pray,
Till I send for 'em, let 'em keep away.
From *Phoenix Alley*, the *Globe Taverne* neare
The *middle of Long Acre*, I *dwell* there.

JOHN TAYLOR. *Poeta Aquaticus.*

The *Mourning Crown* was afterwards revived, and in the 18th century it was the sign of a tavern in Aldersgate, where on Saturdays when Parliament was not sitting, the Duke of Devonshire with other aristocrats, Bagford the antiquary, and Britton the musical small-coalman, used to refresh themselves, after having passed the fore-part of the day in hunting for antiquities and curiosities in Little Britain and its neighbourhood. According to Hearne and Rawlinson the *Mitre* also was put in mourning at the death of Charles I. ' Of Daniel Rawlinson, who kept the *Mitre* Tavern in Fenchurch St., and of whose being sequestered in the Rump time, I have heard that upon the king's murder he hung his sign in mourning. He certainly judged right ; the honour of the mitre was much eclipsed through the loss of so good a parent of the Church of England. Those rogues (the Whigs) say this endeared him so much to the Churchmen that he soon throve amain, and got a good estate.'

The *Rose Revived* found at New Bridge, Oxon, is sometimes said to commemorate the Restoration. It seems, however, to have been so called quite recently when the *Rose* was first closed, then reopened again, the new sign being of a rose flourishing in a glass of ale. *Charles the Second's Head* swung at the door of a music-house for seafaring men and others in Stepney at the end of the 17th century. There is a *Charles the Second* in Northdown St., and the King's memory is still kept alive on a signboard in Herbert St., Hoxton, under the name of the *Merry Monarch*.

To his miraculous escape at Boscobel we owe the *Royal Oak*, which notwithstanding a lapse of nearly three centuries and a change of dynasty, still continues a favourite sign. In London alone Larwood reckons twenty-six occurrences of it in public-houses, exclusive of beer-houses, coffee-houses, etc. One instance of many is at Epping. Sometimes it is called *King Charles in the Oak*, as at Ely and at Willenhall, Warws. The *Royal Oak* soon after the Restoration became a favourite with the shops of London ; and tokens of some half a dozen houses bearing that sign are extant.

It is a curious fact (if it is true as Larwood asserts) that a century or so ago one of the descendants of Richard Pendrell kept an inn called the *Royal Oak* at Lewes.

There is a trades token of ' William Hagley, at the *Restoration* in St. George's Fields '; but how this event was represented does not appear. At Charing Cross it was commemorated by the sign of the *Pageant*, which represented the triumphal arch erected at that place on occasion of the entry of Charles II, and which remained standing for a year after. This was evidently the same house which Pepys called the *Triumph*. It seems to have been a fashionable place, for he went there on 25 May 1662 to see the Portuguese ladies of Queen Catherine. He did not care for their appearance or their dress, but was pleased to note that they have ' learned to kiss '. The *Triumph* is or was the sign of a public-house in Skinner St., Somers Town.

Queen Mary was in her day a very popular sign, as may be gathered from many of the shop-bills in the Banks Collection, whilst *William & Mary* are still to be seen in Maiden Causeway, Cambridge. The accession of the house of Brunswick produced the *Brunswick*, still very common, particularly in the West Riding of Yorkshire. Sometimes as with the *Brunswick* at Worthing the sign is a form of the *Black Brunswick*, i.e., a Brunswick Hussar. The regiment adopted a black uniform in memory of the defeat and death of Charles William Ferdinand in action at Auerstadt in 1806, when Davout's victories at Jena and Auerstadt brought Prussia completely under Napoleon's power. Then come the Georges, of whom *George III* and *George IV* still survive in nearly as many instances as their successor, *William IV*. With them are a few of the royal *Dukes of Clarence* and of *Suffolk*, and, above all, the Butcher *Cumberland*. *Princess Victoria* occurs occasionally, and there are many instances of *Queen Victoria*, the *British Queen*, *Island Queen*, *Albert*, *Jubilee*, etc. Under one of the Queen's signs at Coopersale, in Essex, is or was the following inscription :—

> The Queen some day
> May pass this way
> And see our Tom and Jerry.
> Perhaps she'll stop
> And stand a drop
> To make her subjects merry.

There are few *Edward VII's* or *VIII's*, or *George V's* or *VI's*, though there is a well-known house near Chatham which commemorates his late Majesty under the title he was proud to claim, the *Ordinary Fellow*.

Among the foreign kings and potentates who have figured upon signboards, the Turkish sultans seem to have stood foremost. *Morat* (Amurath) and *Soliman* (Suleiman) were constant coffee-house signs in the 17th century. Trades tokens are extant in the Beaufoy and other collections of a coffee-house in Exchange Alley under the sign of *Morat*. The same house figures in advertisements of the time in *Mercurius Publicus*.* There is still a *Sultan* at Camberwell and a *Grand Sultan* at Dover. The

---

* 12–19 March 1662.

Great Mogul also had his share of signboards of which a few still survive; one at Maghull, Lancs., may be intended as a pun on the place-name. There was an *Old Mogul* in Drury Lane, now extinct. *Kouli Khan* we find only in one instance (though there were probably many more), namely, on the sign of a tavern by the Quayside, Newcastle, in 1746.★ This house had formerly been called the *Crown*, but changed its sign in honour of Thomas Nadir Shah, or Kuli Khan, who, from having been chief of a band of robbers, at last seated himself on the throne of Persia. He reigned 1736–48. One of the reasons of his popularity in this country was the permission he granted to the English nation to trade with Persia, the most extravagant ideas being entertained of the advantages to be derived from this commerce. There is another *Shah of Persia* at Poole, Dorset, with a fine ornamental sign, displaying four Persian celebrities, Bahram the Hunter, Rustum the Warrior, glorious Jamshyd, and Omar Khayam, who of course mentions the other three.

The *Indian King* which is met with frequently, is an extremely vague personage, and may refer to any of various Indian potentates. The sign was generally set up when some king from the Far East or some Red Indian chief visited the metropolis, and for a short time created a sensation. Thus, in 1710, there were four Indian 'Kings' from 'states between New England, New York and Canada' who had audiences with Queen Anne, and who seem to have been a good deal talked about. The visit is referred to in the *Spectator*, No. 50. Again, in 1762, London was honoured with the visit of a Cherokee king. *Indian Chiefs*, *Kings* and *Queens* are dealt with below (p. 252).

Visits of European monarchs were also commemorated by complimentary signs. One of the oldest was the *King of Denmark* at the Old Bailey, which now appears under its earlier sign of the *Magpie & Stump*. Few kings deserved better an exalted place at the alehouse door. The sign originated in the reign of James I, who married a daughter of Frederick II of Denmark. In July 1606 the royal brother-in-law Christian IV came over on a visit, when the two kings began 'bousing' and carousing royally, the court, of course, duly following example. According to Sir John Harrington, the English nobles were so wrought upon by his example that they 'wallowed in beastly delights'. The Old Bailey house was very notorious. It used to be open all night for the benefit of the drunkard, the thief, the night-walker, and other profligates of every description. On execution nights the landlord used to reap a golden harvest. The visit of another crowned monarch is commemorated by the sign of the *Czar's Head* still existing in Great Tower St. This is the house where Peter the Great and his companions, having finished their day's work, used to resort to smoke their pipes and drink beer and brandy. The sign is now removed, but the public-house still bears the same name.

Prince Eugene also was at one time a popular tavern portrait in this country, more particularly after the Prince's visit to England in January 1712. It is named as one of the signs in Norwich in 1750, but is now apparently completely extinct in England. The *Grave Maurice* is of very old standing in London, being named by Taylor the

★ *Newcastle Journal*, 28 June 1746.

Water Poet as an inn at Knightsbridge in 1636 ; there are still two such signs left, one in Whitechapel Rd., the other in St. Leonard's Rd. Count Maurice of Nassau, afterwards Maurice Prince of Orange, was very popular in this country on account of his successful opposition to the Spanish domination in the Netherlands. When he was installed as a Knight of the Garter in 1612 the Garter conferred was that which had been previously worn by another Protestant hero Henry IV, King of France and Navarre. Another Maurice, about this period, was very popular in England—viz. Maurice Landgrave of Hesse-Cassel, who 'carried away the palm of excellency in whatever is to be wished in a brave prince'. He was a good musician, spoke ten or twelve languages, was a universal scholar, could dispute 'even in boots and spurs', for an hour with the best professors on any subject, and was the best bone-setter in the country. He gained, too, much of his popularity by his adherence to the Protestant cause during the Thirty Years War.

Probably however the first-named Maurice is the one commemorated. Signs referring to his father the Pfaltzgraaf are noted below, and one relating to his mother, the Queen of Bohemia, has been referred to above (p. 38).

The *Paltsgrave* became a popular sign at the marriage of Frederick Casimir, Elector and Count Palatine of the Rhine, King of Bohemia, with Elizabeth daughter of James I. Trades tokens are extant of a famous tavern, the *Paltsgrave Head* without Temple Bar, which gave its name to Palsgrave Head Court in the Strand, while the *Palatine Head* was an inn near the French Change, Soho. *Prince Rupert*, the Palgrave's son, who behaved gallantly in many of the fights during the Civil War, was no doubt a favourite sign after the Restoration. We have an instance of one on the trades token of Jacob Robins in the Strand.

One of the last foreign princes to whom signboard honours were accorded was the *King of Prussia*. This was quite common until the 1914–18 War. After the battle of Rosbach, Frederick the Great our ally became a popular hero in England. Ballads were made in which he was called 'Frederick of Prussia, or the Hero'. According to Macaulay 'portraits of the hero of Rosbach with his cocked hat and long pigtail were in every house. An attentive observer will, even to this day, find in the parlours of old-fashioned inns and in the portfolios of print-sellers twenty portraits of Frederick for one of George II. The sign-painters were everywhere employed in touching up *Admiral Vernon* into the *King of Prussia*.' The sign still occurs at Ringland, Norfolk, though at Abergavenny it has evolved into the *King of Russia*. In the same way the *Prince of Saxe-Coburg* in the Old Kent Rd., is now the *Prince of Windsor*, the *Prince of Prussia*, Windsor, is now the *Kitchener's Arms*. There are still, however, a *Crown Prince of Prussia* at Acton, a *Prince Teck* at Bermondsey and a *Prince of Teck* at Earl's Court, a *Prince of Brunswick* at Barnsbury, and a *Prince of Hesse* in Feldgate Street.

If one may credit the *Mirror* * in 1739 after the capture of Portobello, Admiral Vernon's 'portrait dangles from every signpost' and he may be figuratively said to have sold the ale, beer, porter, and purl of England for six years. Towards the close

* 19 February 1780.

of that period the admiral's favour began to fade apace with the colours of his uniform, and the battle of Culloden was total annihilation for him . . . The *Duke of Cumberland* kept possession of the signboard a long time. In the beginning of the last war (i.e. the Seven Years War), our admirals in the Mediterranean and our generals in North America did nothing that could tend in the least degree to move his Royal Highness from his place, but the doubtful battle of Hamellan, followed by the unfortunate convention of Stade, and the rising fame of the King of Prussia obliterated the glories of the Duke of Cumberland as effectually as he had effaced Admiral Vernon. The Duke was completely displaced by his Prussian majesty. 'One circumstance, indeed, was much against him; his figure being marked by a hat with the Kevenhuller cock, a military uniform and a very fierce look, a slight touch of the painter converted him into the *King of Prussia*. But what crowned the success of his Prussian majesty was the title bestowed upon him by the brothers of the brush, "The Glorious Protestant Hero", words which added splendour to every signpost, and which no Briton could read without a peculiar sensation of veneration and of thirst.

'For two years the glorious Protestant hero was unrivalled; but the French being defeated at Minden upon the 1st of August 1759 by the army under Prince Frederick of Brunswick, the *King of Prussia* began to give place a little to two popular favourites who started at the same time; I mean *Prince Ferdinand* and the *Marquis of Granby*. Prince Ferdinand was supported altogether by his good conduct at Minden, and by his high reputation over Europe as a general. The Marquis of Granby behaved with spirit and personal courage everywhere, but his success on the sign-posts of England was very much owing to a comparison generally made between him and his commander Lord George Sackville, who was supposed not to have behaved so well. Perhaps too he was a good deal indebted to another circumstance, the baldness of his head', and the fact that he wore a short coiffure in the days when other people were much bewigged. According to another account, at the Battle of Minden he 'won the battle but lost his wig'.

Though more than a century and a half has elapsed since the Marquis's death in 1770, his portrait is still one of the most common signs. In London alone in Larwood's time he presided over eighteen fully licensed public-houses besides numerous beer-houses. The first *Marquis of Granby* sign is said to have been hung out at Hounslow by one Sumpter, a discharged trooper of the regiment of Horse Guards, which the Marquis of Granby had commanded as colonel.

Crowned heads as well as other human beings were subject to the law of change on the signboard, according to an anecdote told by Goldsmith * :

> An alehouse keeper near Islington who had long lived at the sign of the *French King*, upon the commencement of the last war pulled down his old sign, and put up that of the *Queen of Hungary*. Under the influence of her red nose and golden sceptre he continued to sell ale, till she was no longer the favourite of his customers; he changed

---

* In the Essay on the Versatility of Popular Favour.

her therefore some time ago for the *King of Prussia*, who may probably be changed in turn for the next great man that shall be set up for vulgar admiration.

Of all great men, successful soldiers appear at all times to have captivated popular signboard favour much more than those men who promoted the welfare of the country in other ways. We find hundreds of admirals and generals on the signboard, but there seems to be but one *Watt*, and we have noted only one *Sir Walter Scott*, while there are relatively few *Shakespeares* and only one *Newton* is recorded. Booksellers formerly honoured the heads and names of great authors with a signboard as do publishers still, but that custom fell into disuse when signs became unnecessary. Few tradespeople but the publicans have signs nowadays and ' perhaps ', says Larwood, ' they and their customers can much better appreciate the pomp and pageantry of war than the subtlety of parliamentary debate '.

Sometimes such military signs are described in phrases which, common no doubt at the time, may well puzzle the inquirer nowadays. The *Hero* at Sheerness is apparently no hero in particular, the *Norfolk Hero* at Swaffham is presumably Lord Nelson, the *Hero of Switzerland* is dealt with elsewhere (p. 63). The *Hero of Alma*, Alma Square, is presumably Lord Raglan, the *Hero of Inkerman*, Bagshot, the same, the *Hero of Maida* in the Edgware Rd. is Sir John Stuart, the *Hero of Waterloo*, Lambeth, the Duke of Wellington, and the *Hero of Moultan*, Shrewsbury, which has a fine pictorial sign, is Lieutenant, later Sir H. B. Edwardes, who distinguished himself in the second Sikh War in 1848.

The high seas being considered almost a national possession, admirals have always had the lion's share of popular admiration, and their fame appears more firmly rooted than that of generals. Signs of *Admiral Drake*, *Sir Francis Drake*, or the *Drake Arms*, common at the water-side in our seaports, show that the nation has not yet forgotten one naval hero. *Sir Walter Raleigh* has not been quite so fortunate. Though he also came in for a great share of signboard honour perhaps this was less owing to his qualities as a commander than to his reputation of having introduced tobacco into England. Hence he became a favourite tobacconist's sign, and in that quality we find him on several of the shop-bills in the Banks Collection.

Admiral Blake is found at Ladbroke Grove. *Admiral Benbow* was far from uncommon in Larwood's time and still survives at Ludlow, Salop. *Admiral Duncan*, *Admiral Howe* and *Admiral Jervis* are found occasionally, while *Admiral Vernon* seems to have secured himself an everlasting place on the front of the alehouse by reason of his dashing capture of *Portobello*. The name of that town or sometimes the *Portobello Arms* is also frequently adopted instead of the admiral's name. There is an *Admiral Vernon* at Burwash (Sussex) and another at Over (? Cambs.) and a *Portobello* is sometimes found.

Possibly Vernon's signboard popularity is due as well to the part he played in the celebrated James Annesley Case in 1743, a good account of which is to be found in *Guy Mannering*, as to his naval victories, especially the capture of Portobello.

Admiral Keppel is another great favourite. There is a public-house with that sign in Hoxton St., and another in Fulham St., where, many years ago, the portrait of the admiral used to court the custom of the passing traveller by a poetical appeal to both man and beast :

> Stop, brave boys, and quench your thirst ;
> If you won't drink, your horses murst.

Above all *Admiral Rodney* seems to have obtained a larger share of popularity than even *Nelson* himself. In Boston there is still the *Rodney & Hood* and in Westminster the *Rodney*. According to Larwood the last addition to this portrait gallery before *Sir Charles Napier* was the head of *Lord Exmouth* who bombarded Algiers in 1816. In 1825 there was a house of this sign at Barnstaple, Devon, with a poetical address to the wayfarer. The sign formerly occurred at Stepney. There seems to be now no sign left in honour of *Captain Cook*. His name was formerly the sign of an alehouse in Mariner St., and was also to be seen in Cumberland St.

Jack Straw's Castle, Hampstead, and a former house of this name at Highgate seem to have a very dubious connexion with Jack Straw, Wat Tyler's lieutenant in the Peasants' Revolt of 1381. It is alleged that the house commemorates an incident when Straw took charge of a section of the mob that marched from Clerkenwell to Highbury and thence to Hampstead, after burning the mansion of Sir Robert Hales. This apparently is folk-lore rather than history. The house was damaged in air-raids during World War No. 2 but has been repaired.

Though the fame of generals seems to be more short-lived than that of admirals, yet a few ancient heroes still remain. There is, for example, a *Marquis Cornwallis* at Ipswich. *General Elliott* or *Lord Heathfield*, the defender of Gibraltar, seems to be one of the greatest favourites. Perhaps his popularity in London was not a little increased by the present which he made to Astley of his charger named Gibraltar, ' who performing every evening in the ring and shining forth in the circus bills would certainly act as an excellent puff for the general's glory'. This hero's popularity is only surpassed by that of the *Marquis of Granby* referred to above.

Among the generals of a later period are *General Tarleton* (or, as he is called on a sign in Clarence St., Newcastle, *Colonel Tarlton*), *General Wolfe*, *General Moore*, and *Sir Ralph Abercrombie*. There is a *General Wolfe* at Laxfield, Suff., a *General Picton* in Wharfdale Rd., and a *General Abercrombie* at Blackfriars. All these occur also in the provinces. At a tavern of this sign in Lombard St., about a century ago, used to meet the 'House of Lords' Club, composed not of members of the peerage, but simply of the good citizens of the neighbourhood each dubbed with a title. The president was styled Lord Chancellor, he wore a legal wig and robes, and a mace was laid on the table before him. The title bestowed upon the members depended on the fee—one shilling for a baron, two shillings a viscount, three shillings an earl, four shillings a marquis, and five shillings a duke. This club originated early in the 19th century at the *Fleece* in Cornhill, but removed to the *Three Tuns* in Southwark, that the members might be more retired from the bows and compliments of the London apprentices who used to salute the noble lords by their titles as they passed to and fro in the streets about their business. One of their last houses was the *Yorkshire Grey*, near Roll's Buildings. They are now long extinct.

The *Duke's Head* and the *Old Duke* are signs that for the last two or three centuries have always been applied to some ducal hero or other, for the time being basking in the sun of fame. There is a simple *Duke* at Deptford. One of the first Duke signs to be commonly used referred to Monk, *Duke of Albemarle*. Soon after the Restoration then came the *Duke of Ormond*, the *Duke of Marlborough*, the *Duke of Cumberland*, the *Duke of York*, the *Duke of Wellington* and the *Duke of Cambridge*. There is a *Duke of Marlborough* at Norwich, a *Duke of Wellington* at Ely and one in Wardour St., W., and an *Iron Duke* at High Wycombe. A much earlier duke appears to be commemorated in the *Duke William* at Burslem, Stoke-on-Trent, but actually it is likelier that the sign is political in origin and this Duke is the Duke of Cumberland, ' Sweet William ', or Billy the Butcher. The *Duke's Head* in Upper St., corner of Gad's Row, Islington, was the sign of a public-house kept by Thomas Topham, the strong man, who in 1741 in Coldbath Fields in honour of Admiral Vernon's birthday, lifted three hogsheads of water weighing 1,859 lb. There are one or two *Dukes of Ormond* and *Ormond's Heads*. The *Ormond's Head* in Long St., Tetbury, Glos., has had on it since 1656 an annual rent charge of 10s. to pay the vicar for preaching a sermon on Ascension Day. This is earlier than the famous rent-charge of 40s. on the *Angel* at Grantham, to pay for an annual sermon on the evils of drunkenness. The *Duke of Albemarle* figured on numberless signboards after the Restoration. At the same period there existed still older signs, on which his grace was simply called Mon(c)k ; as, for instance, that hung out by ' Well, Kidd, suttler to the Guard at St. James's ', which was the *Monck's Head*. A very few *Dukes of Marlborough* are also left. In the beginning of the 18th century the *Duke of Marlborough's Head* in Fleet St. was a tavern used for entertainments. Among the Bagford Bills and in the newspapers of the time it is constantly mentioned as the place where something wonderful or amusing was to be seen—panoramas, dioramas, moving pictures, marionettes, curious pieces of mechanism, etc. At Oxford there is a *Duke of Monmouth*.

The *Lord Craven* was once a very popular sign in London. It occurs amongst the trades tokens of Bishopsgate St. The *Craven Head* in Drury Lane has disappeared, but there is still a *Craven Arms* in Shropshire—perhaps from the family rather than the individual. Some of these signs were in honour of William Earl of Craven 1606–97. He had a brilliant military and public career, but probably owes his popularity rather to his civic virtues shown during the plague period, when he and General Monk were almost the only men of rank that remained in town to keep order. He even erected a pesthouse at his own expense in Pesthouse Field, Carnaby Market, and he was a great favourite with the Londoners because of his assistance during the frequent London fires.

The *Earl of Essex*, Elizabeth's *quondam* favourite, might have been met with on many signs long after the Restoration. There are trades tokens of a shop or tavern with such a sign in Banksides, Southwark, and tokens are extant of two other shops that had the *Essex Arms*. There is still an *Essex Head* in Essex St., and an *Earl of Essex* at Manor Park. In this former tavern the Robin Hood Society, 'a club of free and candid inquiry', used to meet. It was originally established in 1613, at the house of Sir Hugh Myddleton, the projector of the New River for supplying London with water, who himself is commemorated in the *Myddleton Arms*, Canonbury. Its first meetings were held at the houses of members, but afterwards, the numbers increasing, the meetings were removed to the tavern, and the club's name was altered into the 'Essex Head Society'. In 1747 it removed to the *Robin Hood* in Butcher Row, near Temple Bar. This was perhaps the leading private debating society of the mid-18th century. In the same house in 1794, Johnson established a club of twenty-four members, in order to insure himself society for at least three days in the week. The house at that time was kept by Samuel Greaves, an old servant of Mrs. Thrale. For each night of non-attendance was imposed a fine of threepence, and at each meeting members were to spend at least sixpence, besides a penny for the waiter. Each member had to preside one evening a month.

More difficult to explain than such signs as Nelson or Rodney is the presence on English signboards of the Dutch *Admiral Van Tromp*, yet we find him in Bethnal Green Rd. We have found, however, no Turennes, no Napoleons, Keys, or Soults, and certainly no von Brauelitz or Hitler.

Names of battles and glorious feats of arms have also been much used as signs— —thus *Gibraltar*, *Portobello*, the *Battle of the Nile*, and the *Mouth of the Nile* (so says Larwood but the house does not appear to be known nowadays). *Trafalgar*, the *Battle of Waterloo*, the *Battle of the Pyramids* and the *Alma* are all still more or less common. The *Bull & Mouth* surviving until 1888 and still found (in copies ?) in London and at Leeds and Sheffield is said to have had a similar origin, being a corruption of *Boulogne Mouth*, the entry in Boulogne Harbour, which grew into a popular sign after the capture of the place by Henry VIII. The first house with this sign was in Aldgate. However this may be, in less than a century after Henry VIII's time, the name was (? corrupted) into the *Bull & Mouth*, and the sign was represented by a black bull and a large (human) mouth. Thus it appears on the trades tokens, and also in a sculpture in the *façade* of the Queen's Hotel, St Martin's-le-Grand, formerly the *Bull & Mouth* inn. Of the same time also dates the *Bull & Gate*, a corruption of the Boulogne Gates, which Henry VIII ordered to be taken away and transported to Hardes in Kent, where they (?) still remain. The *Bull & Gate* in Holborn was a noted inn in the 17th century where Fielding's hero, Tom Jones, put up on his arrival in London. It is still in existence under the same name, though much reduced in size. There is another in Camden Town, and a few imitations of it were carried to distant provincial towns (? by the coaches of old times). Another sign of the same period, although not commemorative of a battle, was the *Golden Field Gate* mentioned by Taylor the Water-Poet in 1632, as the sign of an inn at the upper end of Holborn. It was put up in honour of the Field of the Cloth of Gold, where Henry VIII met Francis I in 1520.

The signs of great men who have distinguished themselves in the civil walks of life are much more scarce.   Brunel is found at Plymouth—a very appropriate spot—where presumably he is commemorated rather as designer of the *Great Eastern* or the *Great Britain* (both found as signs in Burslem, Stoke-on-Trent) than even as the builder of the Great Western Railway.   *Cardinal Wolsey* occurs in many places, particularly in London, Windsor, and the neighbourhood of Hampton Court.   *Sir Thomas Gresham*, the founder of the Royal Exchange, was a favourite in London after the opening of the first Exchange in 1566, and *Sir Hugh Myddleton*, the projector of the New River as mentioned above, was honoured with two or three signs in Islington.

Philanthropists are rarely commemorated.   There are instances, however, *General Gordon* and *Sir Paul Pindar* are dealt with elsewhere.   *George Peabody* is found at Shadwell.   *William Willett* of ' Summer Time ' is commemorated at Petts Wood, Kent, where he lived.   The sign is a good modern one by Ralph Ellis.   It shows a huge jovial sun face and two clock-dials, the one saying twelve o'clock, the other one o'clock.

Political signs occur here and there.   There exists a curious alehouse picture called the *Three Johns* in White Lion St., Pentonville.   The same sign many years ago, might have been seen in Bennett St., near Queen Square, Westminster.   It represented an oblong table with John Wilkes in the middle, the Rev. John Horne Tooke at one end, and John Glynn (Wilkes' counsel and his colleague as Knight of the Shire for Middlesex) at the other.   *John Wilkes*, once on many a signboard because of popular gratitude for his driving from power the Earl of Bute in 1763, still survives in a few spots.   In the small Staffordshire town of Leek there is a *Wilkes' Head*, while another one occurs at St. Ives.   *Sir Francis Burdett* is also not forgotten, and may still be seen in Nottingham and in a few other places.

Lord Grey appears in the Whig town of Wotton-under-Edge, Glos.   Sometimes signs have special reference to the locality of the inn.   A local dispute is commemorated by the *Parson & Clerk* at Streetley, Warws.   During a lawsuit between 'squire and rector the 'squire set up at the door of the inn a caricature of the rector.   The latter had his head bowed as in prayer, and the clerk stood behind him with an uplifted axe as though to cut off his head.   Hence the *Royal Oak* became known far and wide as the *Parson & Clerk*, and when the house was rebuilt the older sign was abandoned, and the popular name legitimatized by the erection of a suitable sign.   The *Child of Hale* at Liverpool is said to be named after a local ' giant ' who used the house in the 17th century.   The *Daniel Lambert* in Stationer's Hall Court, originally known as the *King's Head*, is named of course after the famous ' Fat Daniel ' who weighed 52 stone 11 lb. and who died in 1809.   The *Dick Whittington*, near Kinver, Staffs., a pleasant half-timbered inn, is presumably so named in honour of Whittington's birth at Pauntley, in the neighbouring county of Gloucester.   *Rattlebone* at Sherston, Wilts, commemorates the legendary hero of the parish who when mortally wounded in fighting against the Danes picked up a tile which he held to his stomach to prevent his bowels from gushing out, and so fought on.   This sign is based on an effigy in the church porch, but unkind antiquaries insist that it actually represents St Aldhelm, and that the ' tile ' is a book.

The *Marquis of Anglesey* is still to be seen at 39 Bow St. This is presumably one of the Paget Angleseys, raised to the Marquisate in 1815 for distinguished services in the Peninsular War. *Lord Anglesey*, in 1679, adopted by an inn in Drury Lane, is not the same man, but earned his popularity in that he, with Cavendish, Tillotson, Burnet, and a few others at the State Trial in 1683, appeared to vindicate Lord Russell in the face of the Court, and gave testimony to the good life and conversation of the prisoner. Other politicians are recorded in signs, though especially when they were also possessors of great landed estates it is not always clear whether they are commemorated as politicians or as landlords. There are, as one would expect, a great many such signs in London. Examples are the *George Canning*, Brixton (elsewhere this sign is sometimes corrupted to the *George & Cannon*), the *Duke of Grafton*, Euston Road, the *Duke of Bedford*, Seymour St., the *Duke of Devonshire*, Darnley Rd., the *Cobden Arms*, the *Earl of Aberdeen*, Mile End, the *Earl of Beaconsfield*, New Cross, the *Earl of Derby*, Cambridge, the *Earl Grey*, Ipswich, the *Earl Russell*, Bristol, the *Gladstone Arms*, Burslem, Staffs., the *Gladstone*, Brompton, the *Lord John Russell*, formerly in City Rd., the *Lord Holland*, Brixton, the *Lord Liverpool*, Clark St., the *Lord Palmerston*, Kilburn, the *Lord Rosebery*, Norwich, the *Marquis of Lothian*, Norwich, the *Marquis of Salisbury*, Balls Pond Rd., the *Sheridan*, Stafford, the *Pitt & Nelson*, Ashton-under-Lyne. Other ' political ' signs include the *Land of Liberty*, Herongate, Essex, the *Commonwealth*, Caterham, Surrey, the *Constitution*, Churton St., the *Magna Charta*, New Holland, Lancs., the *Daniel O'Connell*, Wolverhampton, and the *John Burns*, Chiswick. A rather puzzling political sign— the *Man with the White Hat*, was formerly to be seen in Manchester. The man was Henry (Orator) Hunt, whose taste in headgear made a white hat something of a (Radical) party badge in England in the early part of the 19th century.

Butler (*ob.* 1617), physician to James I, and according to Fuller the ' Aesculapius of that age ' invented a kind of medicated ale called Dr. Butler's ale, which says Hawkins, ' if not now (1784) was a few years ago, sold at certain houses that had the *Butler's Head* for a sign '. The sign is still to be seen at Mason's Avenue, E.C., and 11 Telegraph St., E.C.

Figures of a few of our poets are also common tavern pictures. As early as 1655 we find a (Ben) *Jonson's Head* tavern in the Strand, where Ben Jonson's chair was kept as a relic. Ten years later it occurs in a patent medicine advertisement.* There was formerly a *Ben Jonson's Head* with a painted portrait of the poet in Shoe Lane, Fleet St. There are still a *Ben Jonson* in the Harrow Rd., A *Ben Jonson's* inn at Pemberton, Lancs., and another at Weston-on-the-Green, Oxon.

Shakespeare's Head and variants of this sign are to be seen in almost every town where there is a theatre. There is a well-known example at Victoria. At a tavern with that sign in Great Russell St., Covent Garden, the Beefsteak Society (not to be confused with the Beefsteak Club) used to meet before it was removed to the Lyceum Theatre. George Lambert, scene-painter to Covent Garden Theatre, was its originator. This tavern was at one time famous for its beautifully painted sign. The well-known

---

* *The Newes*, 24 August 1665.

E

Lion's Head letter-box first set up by Addison at Button's was for a time placed at this house. There was at the beginning of the 19th century another *Shakespeare Head* in Wych St., Drury Lane. This was the last haunt of the Club of Owls, so called on account of the late hours kept by its members. After this it was for one year in the hands of Mr. Mark Lemon, sometime editor of *Punch*, then just newly married to Miss Romer, a singer of some renown who assisted him in the management of the place. The house was chiefly visited by actors from Covent Garden, Drury Lane, and the Olympic, and a club of writers, etc., used to meet on the first floor.

The *Andrew Marvell* is very appropriately at Hull. *Sir John Falstaff*, who dearly loved his sack, could not fail to become popular with the publicans, and may be seen on almost as many signboards as his parent Shakespeare. There is an example at Canterbury. At Windsor there is a *Merry Wives of Windsor* which shows them busy in packing Sir John into his basket. At present there are two *Milton's Head* public-houses in Nottingham and one at Chalfont St Giles, Bucks. *Comus* is found in Beverton St. At Kate's Cabin, on the Great North Rd., between Chesterton and Alwalton, there was a sign of Dryden's head painted by Sir William Beechey when engaged as a house-painter on the decoration of Alwalton Hall. The house is now de-licensed. Dryden was often in that neighbourhood when on a visit to his kinsman, John Dryden of Chesterton.

The *Man of Ross* is at the present day a signboard at Ross-on-Wye, Herfs., over the house in which dwelt John Kyrle, the ' Man of Ross '. After his death this was converted into an inn. A century or so ago a poetical effusion to his memory was to be read pasted up in the house. The pleasing sign to be seen there nowadays incorporates the arms of the Kyrle family, and was painted by the present tenant of the inn.

The *Camden Head* occurs as the sign of a London publican at 100 High St., N.W. *Addison's Head* was for above sixty years the sign of the then well-known firm of Corbett & Co.—first of C. Corbett, afterwards of his son Thomas, booksellers in Fleet St. from 1740 till the beginning of the 19th century. *Sir Richard Steele* still remains as an inn sign at Haverstock Hill. *Dr. Johnson's Head*, exhibiting a portrait of the great man, was in Larwood's time in Bolton Court, Fleet St., opposite where he lived. The sign is now extinct.

Of more recent poets *Lord Byron* is one of the few who has been exalted to the signboard. In the neighbourhood of Nottingham his portrait occurs in several places ; his *Mazeppa* also is a great favourite. It is found, for example, at Willenhall, Staffs. *Ghilde Harold* is in Railway St. *Don Juan* also occurs on a publican's signboard at Cawood, Selby, but is here merely the name of a Leger winner of 1838. *Robert Burns* is found at Darlington, and the *Burns* at Millwall.

Among the minor literary celebrities who attained sufficient popularity to entitle him to a signboard was *Sheridan Knowles*, dramatist and orator, who was chosen as the sign of a tavern in Bridge St., Covent Garden, facing the principal entrance to Drury Lane Theatre. There used to meet at one time the Club of Owls above mentioned.

Mythological divinities and heroes also have been very fairly represented on our

signboards.   At their head, of course, *Bacchus* (frequently with the epithet of *Jolly*)
well deserves to be placed.   In the time when the *Bush* was the usual alehouse sign,
or rather when it had swollen to a crown of evergreens, a chubby little Bacchus astride
on a tun was generally a pendant to the crown.   Such a sign survives in Bacchus
Walk, Hoxton.   Massinger's *Virgin Martyr* ★ illustrates how Bacchus includes both
wine and beer in his dominions.   Next to Bacchus, *Apollo* is most frequent, but whether
as god of the sun or leader of the Muses it is difficult to say.   Sometimes he is called
Glorious Apollo, which in heraldic language, means that he has a halo round his head.†
There is a house of this sign in Oxford.

Minerva also is not uncommon—probably not so much as the goddess of wisdom,
but because as Aubrey says, she was ' ye patroness of scholars, shoemakers, diers ', etc.
Juno had in Bristol a temple which has now disappeared.   This, like a similar sign in
Church Lane, Hull, may very probably refer to a ship.   *Neptune* of course is of
frequent occurrence in a maritime country.   There was an example of this sign at
Ipswich over an old tavern recently demolished.   Another *Minerva* in High St., E.C.,
was changed to the *Blue-eyed Maid* in honour of some verses by Peter Pindar (Dr.
John Wolcot).   Later the sign was repainted and the goddess converted into a buxom
dairymaid.   There was a *Blue-eyed Maid* coach, but it may have been named from the
house, not *vice versa*.

The smith being generally a thirsty soul, his patron *Vulcan* forms an appropriate
alehouse sign, and in that capacity he frequently figures particularly in the Black
Country.   There are a *Vulcan Arms* in Fenton, Stoke-on-Trent, a *Vulcan* at Huddersfield and many other examples elsewhere.   *Mercury* as god of commerce was of
frequent occurrence, as indeed might be expected.   Both *Cupid* and *Flora* were signs
at Norwich in 1750, and *Comus* is still found as a sign (though with reference to
Milton's poem rather than directly to the god).   There is still a *Cupid* at Cupid Green,
Hemel Hempstead, a *Cupid & Bow* at Norwich, and a *Flora* in the Harrow Rd.

Our admiration for athletic strength and sports suggested the sign of *Hercules* as
well as that of his biblical parallel *Samson*.   The *Hercules Pillars*, the Straits of Gibraltar
considered by the ancients the end of the world, was adopted on the outskirts of towns,
where it is more common now to see the *World's End*.   In 1667 it was the sign of
Richard Penck in Pall Mall and also of a public-house in Piccadilly on the site of the
present Hamilton Place, both at that period the ends of the inhabited world of London.
The sign still survives in Greek St. and in Great Queen St.   The signs generally
represented the demi-god standing between the pillars, or pulling the pillars down—a
strange cross between the biblical Samson and the pagan Hercules.   The *Pillars of
Hercules* in Piccadilly is mentioned in Wycherley's *Plain Dealer* in 1676, where ' betwixt
the *Hercules Pillars* and the *Boatswain* in Wapping ' is used as the London equivalent
of from Dan to Beersheba.   The Marquis of Granby often visited the former house,
and here Fielding in *Tom Jones* makes Squire Western put up.‡   In Pepys' time there

★ Act II, Sc. 1.   † ' Apollo in his glory ' is a charge in the apothecaries' arms.
‡ Bk. 16, ch. 2.

was a *Hercules Pillars* in Fleet St. Here the clerk of the Admiralty supped with his wife and some friends on 6 February 1668.

Atlas carrying the world was the very appropriate sign of the map- and chart-makers. There is still an *Atlas* licensed house in Seagrave Rd. The *Golden Fleece* often occurs as the sign of a woollen draper ; it is also found as an inn sign, especially of course in the woollen manufacturing towns where it is even commoner than the *Woolcomber's Arms* and the *Bishop Blaize*. In the 17th century there was a *Fleece* tavern in St James's, where one of the earliest public concerts on record in London was held in 1674.* Another example of this sign was the *Fleece* in York St., Covent Garden, which, says Aubrey, ' was very unfortunate for homicides ; there have been several killed—three in my time. It is now (1692) a private house. Clifton the master hanged himself, having perjured himself.' Pepys does not give him a better character when he refers to it under 1 December 1660.

Another sign of which the application is not very obvious is *Pegasus* or the *Flying Horse*, unless it refers to the rhyme—

> If with water you fill up your glasses,
> You'll never write anything wise ;
> For wine is the horse of Parnassus,
> Which hurries a bard to the skies.

Sometimes the *Flying Horse* sign is adopted as a compliment to the Templars, whose arms are a Pegasus on a field *arg*. Instead of the *Flying Horse*, a facetious inn-keeper at Rake, Petersfield, Hants, has put up a parody in the shape of the *Flying Bull*. The licensee of a *Flying Bull* at Liphook, Hants, explained the name by telling a story of a mad bull which charged into the inn and stampeded the customers. Actually the inn was formerly a posting-house, and it is much likelier that it takes its sign from two of the London Portsmouth coaches, the *Fly* and *Bull*. There is still a *Flying Horse* at Kegworth, Leics., a very fine one in Nottingham, and another in Wilson St. *Pegasus* still survives at Green Lanes, Stoke Newington.

The *Anchor & Hope* and the *Hope & Anchor* are constant signs with shop- and tavern-keepers. Probably the sign is really the *Hope Anchor*, i.e. spare anchor. It appears correctly in this form at Rye, Sussex. In other instances it may refer to St Paul's words.† Pepys spent his Sunday, 23 September 1660, at the *Hope* tavern in a not very godly manner, and his account shows the curious business management of the taverns of the time. The *Fortune* was adopted from considerations somewhat similar to those that prompted the choice of the *Hope*. It occurs as the sign of a tavern in Wapping in 1667. The trades tokens of this house represent the goddess by a naked figure standing on a globe, and holding a veil distended by the wind—' a sheet in the wind '. There is a *Fortune of War* in York Gateway, N. The *Fortune of War* and *Naked Boy* in Giltspur St. is an amalgamation of two separate signs. The second element is dealt with below (pp. 266–7). The *Fortune of War* was brought to the house in 1721 by a landlord who had previously had an inn of this name, so called

---

* *London Gazette*, 1–4 February 1674. † Acts x. 10.

because he acquired it on leaving the Navy after losing both legs and one arm in a sea-engagement.   Doubtless the name of the *Elysium*, a public-house in Drury Lane about a century ago, had also been adopted as suggestive of the happiness in store for the customers who honoured the place by their company.

Ballads, novels, chapbooks and songs have also contributed to signboard nomenclature.   Thus the *Blind Beggar of Bethnal Green*, still a public-house in the Whitechapel Rd., next to Messrs. Mann Crossman's brewery, has decorated the signpost for ages. Not only was the *Beggar* adopted as a sign by publicans, but he also figured on the staff of the parish beadle, and so convinced were the Bethnal Green folk of the truth of the story, that as late as Larwood's time a house called Kirby Castle was generally pointed out as the Blind Beggar's palace, and two turrets at the extremity of the court wall as the place where he deposited his guests.   Fairly general all over England is *Guy of Warwick*, who occurs amongst the signs on trades tokens of the 17th century.   That of Paul Rockford in Field Lane represents him as an armed man holding a boar's head erect on a spear.   His most popular feat is the slaying of the *Dun Cow* on Dunmore Heath, near Rugby, an act of valour commemorated on many signs.   There are at least five in Warwickshire, one each in Cheshire, and in Staffordshire, one at Shrewsbury, etc.   A public-house at Swainsthorpe, Norf., has the following inscription on the sign of the *Dun Cow* :

> Walk in gentlemen, I trust you'll find
> The Dun Cow's milk is to your mind.

Another formerly on the road between Durham and York, probably referred to the Dun Cow which led the monks bearing St Cuthberts body to the hill on which Durham Cathedral now stands.   It has a variant of the same doggerel :

> Oh come you from the east,
> Oh come you from the west,
> If ye will taste the Dun Cow's milk
> Ye'll say it is the best.

The *King & Miller* is another ballad-sign in many places.   It alludes to the adventure of Henry II with the Miller of Mansfield.   There is an old house (recently rebuilt) with this sign on the Great North Rd. near Retford, Notts., and a *Miller of Mansfield* at Goring-on-Thames.   Similar stories are told of many different kinds : of King John and the Miller of Charlton, of King Edward and the Tanner of Tamworth, and of King Henry VIII.   The sign of *King James & the Tinker* at Enfield Mx., is said to mark the *locus* of a story of the same kind concerning James I.

The most frequent of all ballad signs is unquestionably *Robin Hood*.   Often it appears as *Robin Hood & Little John*.   This sign is found in Kensal Rd.   It is frequently accompanied by the following inscription :

> You gentlemen, and yeomen good
> Come in and drink with Robin Hood.
> If Robin Hood be not at home
> Come in and drink with Little John.

The last line a country publican, not very expert either in ballad lore or in versification, thus corrected :—

Come in and drink with Jemmie Webster.

Variants of this are and were found all over the country, for example, at Bradford, Yorks., and at Overseal, Leics. At Turnham Green where the verse was

> Try Charrington's ale, you will find it good
> Step in and drink with Robin Hood.
> If Robin Hood . . . etc.

to show the perfect application of the rhyme the host informed the public that he was ' Little John from the old *Pack Horse* ', a public-house opposite. There is a fine modern *Robin Hood & Little John* sign (by Mr. H. G. Theaker) at Cherry Hinton, Cambs., in one of Messrs. Greene King's houses.

One of the ballads in *Robin Hood's Garland* has given to the signboard another hero, namely, the *Pinder of Wakefield*, George a Green. Drunken Barnaby mentions the sign in Wakefield before 1638, and it is still to be seen there and in the Gray's Inn Rd. There was formerly a public-house near St Chad's Well, Clerkenwell, bearing this sign, which in 1680, to judge from an inscription which Larwood prints, would seem to have been more famous than the celebrated Bagnigge Wells hard by.

Among the more uncommon ballad signs we find the *Babes in the Wood* at Hanging Heaton, Dewsbury, Batley and York. *Jane Shore* was commemorated in Shoreditch in the 17th century, as we see from the trades tokens. *Valentine & Orson* we find mentioned as early as 1711,* as the sign of a coffee-house in Long Lane, Bermondsey, and they remain there as the sign of an inn in Pepin Place to this present day. There is a *Flowers of the Forest* at Deptford and (a corrupted form) a *Flower of the Forest* at Blackfriars. A modern writer says that most of the ballad signs came into vogue about 1840, and that they rarely have any special connexion with the localities in which they are used. It is not clear on what evidence he bases his statement.

Other chapbook celebrities are *Mother Shipton*, Kentish Town and Knaresborough. The latter disputes with Shipton, near Londesborough, the honour of giving birth to this remarkable character in the month of July 1488. She is represented in literature of a kind, and should be depicted on signboards as of a most unprepossessing appearance. One might have expected this, since according to the chapbooks her father was a demon who had seduced her mother. ' Her body was long and very big-boned ; she had great goggling eyes, very sharp and fiery ; a nose of unproportionable length, having in it many crooks and turnings, adorned with great pimples and which, like vapours of brimstone, have such a lustre in the night, that the nurse needed no other light to dress her by in her childhood.'

Merlin, another necromancer, shares renown with *Mother Shipton* both in chapbooks and on signboards. *Merlin's Cave* was the sign of a public-house in Great Audley St., and is still to be seen in Upper Rosoman St., Clerkenwell. His cave

* Daily Courant, 19 February 1711.

was in Clerkenwell on the site where the alehouse now stands, and in the reign of James I was one of the London sights that strangers went to see.

A well-known chapbook hero appears in *Jack of Newbury*, who had already attained to signboard honours in the 17th century, when we find him on the token of John Wheeler in Soper Lane (now Queen St., Cheapside), while in Larwood's time he might be seen in a full-length portrait in Chiswell St., Finsbury Square. The sign was later preserved at Messrs. Whitbread's brewery. This Jack of Newbury *alias* John Winchcombe *alias* Smallwoode, was of course 'the most considerable clothier, i.e. cloth manufacturer, England ever had. He kept in his house a hundred looms each managed by a man and a boy. He feasted King Henry VIII and his first Queen Catherine at his own house in Newbury. He built the church of Newbury from the pulpit westward to the town. At the battle of Flodden in 1513 he joined the Earl of Surrey with a corps of one hundred men, well equipped at his sole expense, who distinguished themselves greatly in that fight . . .' An inn bearing his sign in Newbury is said to be built on the site of the house where he entertained Deloney, the ballad-writer, who wrote a tale about him which until quite recent years was reprinted in the chapbooks, and which lately appeared in Everyman's Library.

Whittington & His Cat is still very common, not only in London but in the country also. There is very properly an example at Highgate. Sometimes the cat is represented without her master, as on the token of a shop in Long Acre in 1657, and on the sign of a seal-engraver in New Court, Old Bailey, 1783. In Highgate Rd. there was in Larwood's time a skeleton of a cat in a public-house window, which was firmly believed to be the earthly remains of Whittington's cat. The house is not far distant from the Whittington Stone.

King Arthur's *Round Table* is to be seen on various houses. There is one in St Martin's Court, Leicester Square, where the American champion Heenan, the Benicia Boy, stayed when he came to contest the belt with Tom Sayers in 1860. The same sign is also often to be met with on the Continent. *John o' Groat's House* is also used for a sign; there was one many years ago in Windmill St., Haymarket. In Larwood's time there was a *John o' Groat's* in Gray St., Blackfriars Rd., and there is still one in Liverpool and one in Bradford. Both these and the *Round Table* may be intended to suggest that evenhanded justice is observed at the houses, where all comers are treated alike, and one man is as good as another. Perhaps the *Justice* at Birmingham may have a similar origin.

Darby & Joan, borrowed from an old nursery fable, is a sign at Crowle, Lincs., and in Cotton St., E.14, and *Hob in the Well*, with a similar origin, was formerly at King's St., Lynn. *Puss in Boots* is found at Macclesfield. *Sir John Barleycorn* at Newmarket is the hero of the ballad allegorical of the art of brewing, re-written by Burns. A favourite ballad of our ancestors originated the sign of the *London Apprentice*, of which there are still numerous examples as, for example, at Old St. and at Isleworth. The *Spectator* ★ says: the apprentice was represented 'with a lion's hetar

★ No. 428.

in each hand'. The ballad informs us that the apprentice came off with flying colours, after endless adventures in one of which like Richard Cœur-de-Lion he 'robbed the lion of his heart'. Naturally after 'his matchless manhood and brave adventure done by him in Turkey', he 'married the king's daughter of that same country'. The *Essex Serpent* is a sign in King St., Covent Garden, perhaps in allusion to a fabulous mediæval monster recorded in a catalogue of wonders and awful prognostications contained in a broadside of 1704. If Larwood had found any evidence that this was an old sign he 'would have been inclined to consider it as dating from the civil war, and hung up with reference to Essex, the Parliamentary general'.

Literature of a class rather loftier than the street ballads has likewise contributed material to the signboards. The *Complete Angler* was *the* usual sign of fishing-tackle sellers in the last century. This occurs often as an inn sign by the valleys of the Meece and the Dove which Walton loved well, and where he spent whole days tempting the trout. The essays of the *Spectator* made the character of Sir Roger de Coverley very popular with tobacconists. There are one or two instances of its use as an inn or tavern sign. There are numerous *Waverleys*, and *Ivanhoe* may be seen at Denmark Park, *The Lady of the Lake* at Oulton Broad, Norf., *Woodstock* in Woodstock St., Oxford St., W., and *Dandie Dinmont* at Westlinton, Carlisle. *Pickwick* appears in Manchester and elsewhere. *Oliver Twist* is at Leyton (though this is said by the proprietors to have no relation to Dickens' hero, but to be called from a 'twist' in Oliver Rd. !). A house of the same name at Camberwell displays the scene in the workhouse kitchen when Oliver asked for more. The *Mutual Friend* is at Stevenage, Herts. Some of the numerous inns mentioned by Dickens advertise themselves as the *Dickens* So-and-so. Examples are the *Dickens Maypole*, Chigwell, and the *Pickwick Leather Bottle*, Cobham. The *Red Rover* (? named after Fenimore Cooper's novel) is at Gloucester. *Tam o' Shanter* is to be seen in Laurence St., York, and in various other towns, for example, Longton, Stoke-on-Trent, and *Robin Adair*, at Benwell, Newcastle. Signs derived from popular songs also belong to this class, as the *Lass o' Gowrie*, Sunderland and Durham, *Auld Lang Syne*, Preston St., Liverpool, *Tulloch-Gorum* and *Loch-na-Gar*, both in Manchester, and *Rob Roy*, Tithebarn St., Liverpool. On the whole, however, this class of name is much more prevalent in the northerly than in the southerly districts of England. In the south, if we except the *Old English Gentleman*, who occurs everywhere, *Jim Crow* is almost the only instance of the hero of a song promoted to the signboard.

Uncle Tom, or *Uncle Tom's Cabin*, is to be found everywhere. Any little underground place of refreshment or beer-house difficult of access is considered as fittingly named after the novel. *Robinson Crusoe* is in Earl St., W., and in many seaports, and there is a *Vicar of Wakefield* in Shoreditch. *John Gilpin* is at Weybridge, the *Village Blacksmith* at Woolwich, and *Excelsior* in Charing Cross Rd.

A very appropriate and not uncommon public-house sign is the *Toby Philpot*. He well deserves this honour. According to his obituary notices in 1810 ★ :—

★ *Gentleman's Magazine*, December 1810.

Mr. Paul Parnell, farmer, grazier and maltster, during his lifetime, drank out of one silver pint cup, upwards of £9,000 sterling worth of Yorkshire Stingo, being remarkably attached to Stingo tipple of the home-brewed best quality. The calculation is taken at 2d. per cupful.

Between St Albans and Harpenden there was some years ago, and perhaps there is still, a public-house called the *Old Roson*. The name also appears to be borrowed from a formerly well-known song, ' Old Rosin the Beau ', which bears a suspiciously close resemblance to the one known nowadays as the *Tarpaulin Jacket*. The very common *Old House at Home* too, is borrowed from another once-popular ballad. The equally common *Hearty Good Fellow* is adopted from a Seven Dials ballad :—

> I am a hearty good fellow
>   I live at my ease ;
> I work when I am willing,
>   I play when I please . . . etc.

Of signboards portraying artists but few instances occur, and when they do they are almost exclusively the property of print-sellers. Larwood notes only three.

In old times even more than at present, music was deemed a necessary adjunct to tavern hospitality and public-house entertainment. The fiddlers and ballad singers of the taproom, however, gave way to the newer brass band at the doors. This in Larwood's time was gradually fading before the ' music hall ' and its concert arrangement. A survival of it was such a sign as *Paganini* at Liverpool, once of very common occurrence. Then musical arrangements in turn have given place in many taverns to a B.B.C. loud speaker, though still there are a great many houses in the industrial quarters of large towns which retain the traditional concert on Saturday or Sunday, and often on Friday as well. The *Insert* at Stoke-on-Trent has installed in its smoke-room a full-size church organ and an electric organ has been installed in a Leeds public-house.

The love for music is also expressed by the sign of the *Fiddler's Arms*, Gornal Wood, Staffs. *Jenny Lind* seems to be the only musician of modern times who has found her way to the signboard, for example, at Sutton, Surrey. In the 18th century *Handel's Head* was common, but no instance of its use remains. *The Maid & the Magpie*, which formerly existed in Oxford St., Stepney, is believed to be the only sign borrowed from an opera. In Queen Anne's time there was a *Purcell's Head* in Wych St., Drury Lane, the sign of a music house. It represented the musician in a brown, full-bottomed wig and green nightgown, and was very well painted.

Actors and favourite characters from plays have frequently been adopted as signs. The oldest instance we find is *Tarleton* or *Dick Tarleton* who, in the 16th century, seems to have been common enough to make Bishop Hall allude to him in his *Satyres*, as ' sitting on an alepost's sign '.★ *Tarleton* is seen on the trades token of a house in Wheeler St., Southwark, and it was but shortly before Larwood's time that this sign disappeared. He first kept in Paternoster Row an ordinary called the *Castle*,

★ Book VI.5.1.

much frequented by the booksellers and printers of St Paul's Churchyard ; afterwards he kept the *Tabor* in Gracechurch St. The *Garrick Head* was set up as a sign in Garrick's lifetime, and in 1768 it hung at the door of Griffiths, a bookseller of Catherine St., Strand. It is still common in the neighbourhood of theatres. There is one in Leman St., Whitechapel, not far from the place of his first successes. *Roxellana* was, in the 17th century, the sign of Thomas Lacy, of Cateaton St. (now Graham St.). It was the name of the principal female character in *The Siege of Rhodes*, and was originally the favourite part of the handsome Elizabeth Davenport, occasionally mentioned by Pepys (always under the name of Roxellana) with a few words of encomium on her good looks. Formerly there was a sign of *Joey Grimaldi* at a public-house nearly opposite Sadler's Wells Theatre ; not only had it the name, but also had a sign in the form of a clown with a goose under his arm and with a string of sausages issuing from his pocket. Joey's name had become less familiar to the public of a later day, and the house in Larwood's time was called the *Clown* and is now the *New Clown*. This is perhaps one of the last instances of an actor being elevated to signboard honours.

Paul Pry was very common in Larwood's time. The sign still remains at Prittlewell, Southend. Lower down the scale of celebrities and public characters, we find the court-jester of Henry VIII, *Old Will Somers* (Sommers), the former sign of a publichouse in Crispin St., Spitalfields. He also occurs on a token issued from Old Fish St., in which he is represented very much as in his portrait by Holbein, viz. wearing a long gown with hat on his head and blowing a horn. *Broughton*, the champion pugilist of England in the reign of George II, kept a public-house in the Haymarket, opposite the present theatre, his sign was a portrait of himself without a wig in the costume of a bruiser. Underneath was the following line from the Aeneid :

Hic victor caestus. Artemque repono.

Numerous public-houses in Larwood's time had adopted the sign of *Tom Sayers*, champion of England 1853–60. One in Pimlico, Brighton, deserves special mention, as it is said to be Sayer's birthplace. Another athletic Thomas, *Thomas Topham*, ' the strong man ', had also his share of signboards. He stabbed his wife and killed himself in 1749, but his more reputable feats were depicted on many signs remaining up to 1800. One in particular, over a public-house near the Maypole in East Smithfield, represented his first great feat of pulling against two dray horses. His name still appears as that of a street near Coldbath Fields.

Eugene Aram, the philologist, schoolmaster, and murderer of Knaresborough, is depicted on a sign in Knaresborough town. The house was formerly called the *White Horse*, and the cottage in which Aram kept his famous school was in White Horse Yard. Lord Lytton and Tom Hood both found inspiration for literary works in the life, character, and death of Aram. Over the entrance to Bullhead Court, Newgate St., there was formerly a stone bas-relief, according to Horace Walpole, once the sign of a house called the *King's Porter & the Dwarf*, with the date 1660. The sign occurs also in Houndsditch in 1725. The two persons represented are William Evans and Jefferey Hudson. Hudson the dwarf is a very interesting person. On one occasion at an entertainment given by Charles I to his queen he was served up in a cold pie; at another time at a court ball he was drawn out of the pocket of Will Evans, the huge door-porter or keeper at the palace. This is the incident to which the sign refers. Scott introduced Hudson in *Peveril of the Peak*. Thomas Fuller mentions Evans in the *Worthies* and Sir William Davenant wrote a comic poem upon one of Jefferey's misadventures. Jefferey is not the only dwarf who has figured on a signboard, for in the 18th century there was a *Dwarf* tavern in Chelsea Fields, kept by John Coan, a Norfolk dwarf. It seems to have been a place of some attraction, since in 1762, according to the *Daily Advertiser*,★ it was honoured by the repeated visits of an Indian king, that is, a Cherokee chief.

The name of *Dirty Dick's*, which graces a house in Bishopsgate St., E.C., otherwise known as the *Gates of Jerusalem*, and the *Old Port Wine House*, was transferred to it from the once famous *Dirty Warehouse* formerly in Leadenhall St. This was a hardware shop kept at the end of the 18th century by Richard Bentley *alias* Dirty Dick, in which premises until about a century ago the signboard of the original shop was still to be seen in the window. It is commonly supposed that Bentley was an eccentric character, the son of a wealthy merchant who had formerly kept his carriage and lived in great style, earned his nickname by his conduct after he had been 'crossed in love'. Actually his behaviour seems to have been an original (and very successful) advertisement. The outside of his house was as dirty as the inside, to the great annoyance of his neighbours, who repeatedly offered Bentley to have the place cleaned, painted and repaired at their expense. He would not hear of this, for his dirt had given him celebrity, and his house was known in the Levant and the East and West Indies, by no other denomination than the 'Dirty Warehouse in Leadenhall St.'

The house is so well known as to need no description. How exactly it comes to be in Bishopsgate St., not Leadenhall St., no one seems to know. Generally accepted explanations are :—

(1) that Bentley owned both this house and the Leadenhall St. Warehouse, and
(2) that the owner of the house bought the contents of Bentley's room at the warehouse, and removed them *en masse* to form a unique attraction in his own premises.

The real sign of the present *Dirty Dick's*—the *Gates of Jerusalem*—may be seen carved on the outside of the house. A provincial rival of *Dirty Dick* was the *Hermit of Redcoats* near Stevenage, Herts. On his mother's death he barricaded himself in the house and lived there in a condition of indescribable filth until his death in 1874. His title still appears over a local inn.

By a trades token we see that *Old Parr's Head* was already in the 17th century the sign of a house in Chancery Lane. A jingle as to the virtues of gin was displayed *c.* 1825 in Aldersgate over a house of this sign now extinct. Parr was of course the

★ 12 July 1762.

'old, old, very old man' who lived, according to tradition, 1483–1635.   He married his second wife at the age of 120 and had a child by her.   At the age of 105 he had been set in the stocks—for incontinence !   Signs of *Old Parr* still remain at Gravesend and at Rochester.   Thomas Hobson (of Hobson's Choice), the benevolent old carrier, is the sign of two public-houses in Cambridge—the one called *Old Hobson*, the other *Hobson's House*.   His own inn in London was the *Bull* in Bishopsgate St., where he was represented in fresco, having a £100 bag under his arm, with the words ' The fruitful mother of an hundred more '.   Milton who wrote two epitaphs upon him says ' he sickened in the time of his vacancy, being forbid to go to London by reason of the plague '.   Among this class of minor celebrities are also those who put up their own heads for signs.   Taylor, the Water Poet (see the *Mourning Crown*), was one of the first.   Next to him followed *Pasqua Rosee*, according to his handbill ' the first who made and publicly sold coffee-drink in England ' (in 1652).   His establish-ment was ' in St Michael's Alley, in Cornhill at the sign of his own head '.

Lebeck, who also used his own ' head ' as a sign, kept an ordinary about 1690 at the north-west corner of Half-Moon Passage, since called Bradford St.   The sign seems to have found imitators at the time, and there are one or two even yet.   There was a *Lebeck's Head* in Shadwell High St., there are still a *Lebeck's Inn* and *Lebeck's Tavern* in Bristol, and there was formerly a *Lebeck & Chaffcutter* at a village in Gloucester-shire.

A still more famous house was the *Pontack's Head*, formerly called the *White Bear*, in Abchurch Lane.   This tavern having been destroyed by fire, Pontack, the son of a president of the parliament of Bordeaux, opened a new establishment on its site. Assuming his father's portrait as its sign, he called it the *Pontack's Head*.   It was among the most fashionable eating-houses in London from soon after the Restoration until about the year 1780, when it was pulled down to make room for the building of the vestry hall of Christ Church.   Defoe mentions it in his *Tour*.   About the same time another tavern flourished, with its master's head for sign : this was *Caveac's*, celebrated for wine.   Though it cannot be said that *Don Saltero* put his portrait for a sign, yet his coffee-house was named after him, and is still extant under this denomina-tion in Cheyne Walk, Chelsea.   This house was opened in 1695 by a certain James Salter, who had been servant to Sir Hans Sloane, and had accompanied him on his travels.   Vice-Admiral Mundy on his return from the coast of Spain, amused with the pedantic dignity of Salter, christened him Don Saltero, and under that name the house has continued to this day.

From his connexion with the great Sir Hans Sloane, and perhaps because of the tradition of a descent from the Tradescants, Salter was of course in duty bound to have a museum of curiosities, which by gifts from Sir Hans and certain aristocratic customers in the army and navy soon became sufficiently interesting to constitute one of the London sights.   It existed until 1799, when it was dispersed by auction.   From his catalogue it is clear that the curiosities fully deserved that name, for amongst them were : ' a piece of St. Catherine's skin ', ' a painted ribbon from Jerusalem with which our Saviour was tied to the pillar when scourged, with a motto ', ' a very curious young mermaid-fish ', ' manna from Canaan, it drops from the clouds twice a year in May and June one day in each month ', ' a piece of nun's skin ', ' a necklace made of Job's tears ', ' the skeleton (*sic*) of a man's finger ', ' petrified rain', ' a petrified lamb, or a stone of that animal ', ' a starved cat in the act of catching two mice, found between the walls of Westminster Abbey when repairing ', ' Queen Elizabeth's chambermaid's hat ', etc.

A most amusing paper in the *Tatler*, No. 34, gives a full-length portrait of Salter. Richard Cromwell in his old age used to be a visitor to this house. Franklin when a printer's apprentice ' one day made a party to go by water to Chelsea in order to see the college and Don Saltero's curiosities '.

Innkeeper Adams ' at the *Royal Swan* in Kingsland Rd. leading from Shoreditch Church ' (1756) had also a *knackatory* which from his catalogue looks very like a parody on the Don's. He exhibited, for instance, ' Adam's eldest daughter's hat ', ' the heart of famous Bess Adams, that was hanged with Lawyer Carr, 18 January 1736–1737 ', ' the Vicar of Bray's clogs ', ' an engine to shell green pease with ', ' teeth that grew in a fish's belly ', ' Black Jack's ribs ', ' the very comb that Adam combed his son (*sic*) Isaac's and Jacob's head with ', ' rope that cured Captain Lowry of the headach, earach, toothach, and bellyach ', ' Adam's key to the fore and back door of the Garden of Eden ', and five hundred other curiosities.

The *Mother Redcap* is a sign that occurs in various places, as in the High St., Camden Town, etc. From the way in which Brathwaite mentions this sign in his *Whimsies or A New Cast of Characters*, 1631, it would seem to have been not uncommon at that time. Who the original Mother Redcap was is unknown, but not improbably she was Skelton's famous alewife ' Ellinor Rumming '. The *Mother Redcap* at Hollo-way is named also by Brathwaite's Drunken Barnaby in his travels. Formerly the following verses accompanied this sign :—

> Old Mother Redcap, according to her tale,
> Lived twenty and a hundred years by drinking this good ale !
> It was her meat, it was her drink, and medicine beside,
> And if she still had drank this ale, she never would have died.

Larwood says this was probably the same person we find elsewhere alluded to under the name of Mother Huff. Actually ' huffcap ' is an old name for beer froth, one of the few tests of quality in the days when beer was served in opaque vessels. There is a *Father Redcap* in Camberwell, evidently named in imitation of *Mother Redcap*.

There are a few other varied inn-sign celebrities so heterogeneous that they can scarcely be ranged under any of the former divisions : thus we meet with the stern reformer *Melancthon's Head* as the sign of an orthodox publican in Park St., Derby. *Nell Gwynn* occurs on several London public-houses, there is one in Chelsea, where she must have been well known since her mother resided in that neighbourhood, and popular tradition allows Nell to have been one of the principal promoters of the erection of the hospital there.   Another house named after her was to be observed in Drury Lane, in which street she lived, and where Pepys on May Day 1667 saw her standing at her lodgings door in her smock, sleeves and bodice and thought her a mighty pretty creature.   There is another in the Strand.

The *Sir John Oldcastle*, a tavern in Coldbath Fields at the beginning of the 17th century, was apparently the headquarters in 1707 of the Clerkenwell Archers.   Opposite this house stood the *Lord Cobham's Head*, celebrated in 1742 for its beer at threepence a tankard, and for its concerts and illuminations.   Both these houses were named after the *Good Lord Cobham*—Sir John Oldcastle—*c.* 1417—one of the first authors as well as one of the first martyrs of noble family in England.   Lord Cobham's estates were close to the site of these two public-houses, which were supposed to comprise a part of his ancient mansion.   The *Sir Paul Pindar* public-house, in Bishopsgate St. Without, was, when Larwood wrote, all that remained of the splendid mansion of the rich merchant of that name, who had here a beautiful park well stocked with game.   Sir Paul was a contemporary of Gresham, the founder of the Exchange.   James I sent him as ambassador to the Sultan, from whom he obtained valuable concessions for English trade throughout the Turkish dominions.   After his return he was appointed farmer of the customs, and frequently advanced money to King James I and afterwards to Charles I.   In 1639 he was esteemed worth more than a quarter of a million sterling. He spent vast sums in repairing St. Paul's Cathedral, and was in other ways a munificent benefactor to the City.

The *Welch Head* was the sign of a low public-house in Dyot St., St Giles.   In the 18th century there was a mendicants' club held here, the origin of which dated as far back as 1660, when it used to hold its meetings at the *Three Crowns* in the Poultry. Saunders Welch was one of the justices of the peace for Westminster, and succeeded Fielding as a metropolitan police magistrate.   He died 31 October 1784, and lies buried in the church of St George's, Bloomsbury.   He was a very popular magistrate.   It is said that in 1766 he went unattended into Cranbourne Alley to quell the riotous meetings of the journeymen shoemakers there, who had struck for an advance of wages.   One of the crowd soon recognized him, when they at once mounted him on a beer-barrel, and patiently listened to all that he had to say.   He quietened the rioters, and prevailed upon the master shoemakers to grant an additional allowance to the workmen.   Incidents of this kind, plus his well-known benevolence and his skill in capturing malefactors, gave him deserved signboard popularity.

The *Bedford Head*, Covent Garden, represented the head of one of the Russell Bedfords, ground landlords of that district, perhaps Francis, the fourth earl, who laid out Covent Garden in 1631.   Pope twice alludes to this tavern as a place to obtain a delicate dinner.   There was another *Bedford Head* in Southampton St., which was kept by Wildman, the brother-in-law of Horne Tooke.   There used to meet at this house for several years a Liberal club of which Wilkes was a member.   There is still a *Bedford Head* at 41 Maiden Lane, and another in Tottenham Court Rd.

Under the historical signs may be ranged a class of more modern signs, referring to local celebrities, many of them probably sportsmen, such as are dealt with elsewhere. *Captain Digby* (? the name of a wrecked vessel) is found at St Peter's, Margate. The *Don Cossack* frequently seen dates from the celebrity acquired by those troops in the harrying of Napoleon's half-starved and frozen soldiers on their retreat from Moscow, though later a more intimate acquaintance with the Cossacks in the Crimea considerably damaged their popularity as signboard figures. The signs of the *Druid*, for example, at Birchover, Derbys., the *Druid's Head* still found at Kingston-on-Thames, the *Druid & Oak*, and the *Royal Archdruid* are more to be attributed to the friendly society than as a mark of respect to the early clergy. The *Union* originated with the union of Ireland with this kingdom, as did the *Rose, Thistle & Shamrock*, found, for example, at Burslem, Stoke-on-Trent. The *Jubilee*, found, for example, at Hednesford, Staffs., usually dates either from Queen Victoria's Jubilee of 1887 or the Diamond Jubilee in 1897. That at Folkestone is named in honour of the Silver Jubilee of King George V in 1935. Occasionally it may commemorate the centenary of the revolution of 1688, celebrated with great pomp and national rejoicing in 1788. Most of such political signs are dealt with above (pp. 48–50). Here it will be sufficient to note that the *Reform* (as near Eccleshall, Staffs.), like the *Lord John Russell*, and the *Three Johns* mentioned elsewhere, refers to the agitation leading to the Act of 1832. The *Hero of Switzerland*, Loughborough Rd., Brixton, and in a few other places, refers to William Tell, and the *Spanish Patriot*, Lambeth, dates from the excitement of our proposed intervention in the Spanish Succession question in 1833. The *Spanish Galleon*, Church St., Greenwich, owes its origin simply to the pictures of our naval victories in the Greenwich Hospital.

These then are some of the principal and most curious historical signs. From the catalogue may be drawn one conclusion—that only a few of what may be termed 'historical signs' outlive the century which gave them birth. If the term extends over this period there is some chance that they will remain in popular favour for a long time. Thus considering most heroes of the 18th century, few publicans certainly will know anything about the *Marquis of Granby, Admiral Rodney*, or the *Duke of Cumberland*, yet their names are almost as familiar as the *Red Lion* or the *Green Dragon*, and have indeed become public-household words. Of the last century perhaps the same may be said of *Nelson* and *Wellington*, and certainly it would be true of *Lord Liverpool, Canning, Cobden* and *Peel*, and of such battle names as the *Alma* and the *Inkerman*. Once such names have persisted for two or three generations they have a chance of continuing for centuries. In due course, when these heroes are completely forgotten, the very mystery of their names becomes their recommendation. No doubt this is one of the reasons for the present-day survival of such signs as *Grave Maurice, Will Summers* and *Jack of Newbury*.

Chapter IV

HERALDIC AND EMBLEMATIC SIGNS

A MODERN writer says, 'Tenants of taverns in the old days were often the retired stewards from some ancient house either of the church, the state, or nobility and landed gentry, therefore it was only natural for them to desire to show their connexion with the powers of their day by painting on their signboards a crest or a coat of arms, or even using the predominant tincture of the heraldic shield to signify their close association with a prominent person. This is the cause of so many signs having a colour prefix such as the *Golden Lion*, the *Blue Lion*, the *Red Lion*, etc.' However this may be, there is no doubt that a great proportion of inn signs are heraldic. Emblems of royalty are at the head of the heraldic signs with the *Crown* (no coronets ever occur), the *King's Arms*, or *Queen's Arms*, and the various royal badges.

The *Crown* seems to be one of the oldest of English signs. It is recorded at least as early as 1467. It is certainly the commonest. According to Monson-Fitzjohn there are no less than 1,008 houses of this sign in England, fairly evenly distributed throughout the whole country. The sign certainly does *not* invariably signify, as some writers say, that the house has at some time or other been Crown property.

The *Crown Inn*, a famous house in the Cornmarket, Oxford, was kept by Davenant, Sir William Davenant's father. Shakespeare, on his frequent journeys between London and his native place, generally put up at this inn, and the malicious world said that young Davenant was somewhat nearer related to him than as a godson only. Some Tudor wall paintings were unearthed here in 1927 behind 17th-century panelling in what was probably the principal guest-chamber of the house, so may well have been Shakespeare's room if he travelled London, Oxford, Stratford. The *Crown* sign still exists, but the licensed house is now on the west of the Cornmarket. The wall paintings are in the old building on the east. The paintings have been properly preserved by the Oxford Preservation Trust with the aid of a liberal grant from the Oxford City Council. There are other interesting Elizabethan wall paintings in the *Crown*, Amersham, Bucks. On the site occupied by the present Bank of England there used to stand several taverns; one of them bore the sign of the *Crown*. About the same period there was another *Crown*, in Duck Lane, West Smithfield. One of the rooms in that house was decorated by Isaac Fuller (1606–72) and 'much employed in tavern painting', with pictures of Muses, Pallas, Mars, Ajax, Ulysses. According to Ned Ward 'The dead figures appeared with such lively majesty they begot reverence in the spectators towards the awful shadows.' Such painted rooms in taverns were not uncommon at that period.

The *Three Crowns*, found, for example, in Wells St., off Jermyn St., W., originated of course from the Three Kings—the Magi. It still appears as the arms of the city of

PLATE
5

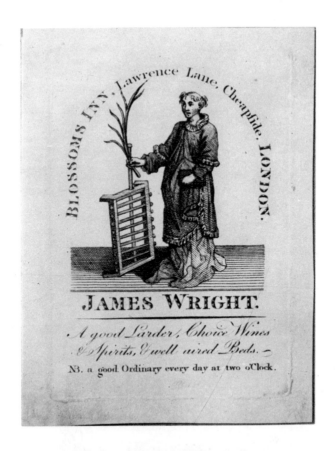

BLOSSOMS INN, Lawrence Lane, Cheapside, LONDON.

JAMES WRIGHT.

A good Larder, Choice Wines
& Spirits, & well aired Beds. —

N3. a good Ordinary every day at two o'Clock.

Neat Post Chaises
ION^N TOMKINS

NEWPORT Isle of Wight.

Haskoll
Sculp

PLATE
6

Cologne, and it is said that the sign in England was used by Cologne merchants. The point is dealt with on p. 183. Altogether there are at least ten houses of the name in Staffordshire alone. The Guildhall Museum has a *Three Kings* sign from Lambeth and a *Three Crowns* from the same borough, probably from the same house. Both are dated 1667. Afterwards, like all other signs, this was used promiscuously, and thus it gave a name to a good old-fashioned inn in Lichfield, later the property of Dr. Johnson, and the very next house to that in which the doctor was born. In a Buckinghamshire village an inn has the sign *15/-*, a play on the *Three Crowns*.

Frequently the royal Crown is combined with other objects to amplify the meaning, or to express some particular royal prerogative, such as the *Crown & Cushion*, found, for example, at Derby and at Chesterfield, which is the Crown as it is carried before the king in coronation and other ceremonies. The *Crown & Glove* refers to the well-known ceremony of the Royal Champion at the Coronation. It formerly occurred as a sign at Shrewsbury, and is still found at Chester, etc. The *Royal Champion* himself figures in George St., Oxford.

The *Crown & Sceptre* is another sign based upon the royal insignia; there is a house of this name at Brompton. The *Crown & Mitre*, indicative of royalty and the church is the sign of a High Church publican at Taunton, and another at King's Lynn, and the *Bible & Crown* is dealt with later as the sign of Messrs. Rivington the publishers. The King and Parliament are represented by the well-known *Crown & Woolpack*, at Stamford, which at Gedney near Holbeach, Lincs., has been corrupted into the *Crown & Woodpecker*. The *Crown & Woodpecker* in St John St. was frequented by Lenin when he was living in London. The *Crown & Tower*, at Taunton, may refer to the regalia kept in the Tower, or to the king being 'a tower of strength'. A similar symbol seems to be intended in the *Crown & Column*, Devonport, perhaps implying the strength of royalty when supported by a powerful and united nation. There is a *Crown & Harp* at Cambridge, a *Crown & Leek* at Mile End, a *Crown & Raven* at Bridgnorth, Salop, a *Crown & Stirrup* at Lyndhurst and a *Crown & Thistle* at Leicester. Probably the significance of most of these is fairly obvious. Such examples as the *Crown & Appletrees*, Berwick St., *Crown & Compasses*, Cambridge, *Crown & Dolphin*, Royston, *Crown & Seven Stars*, Royal Mint St., and *Crown & Sugarloaf*, Garlick Hill, are probably mere fortuitous amalgamations of two signs. It is suggested, however, that the frequent occurrence of the *Crown & Seven Stars* may indicate that here the stars are the Seven Sorrows of Our Lady. The *Crown & Horns*, East Ilsley, Berks., seems to have about it a flavour of high treason. The *Crown & Anchor*, with well-known naval associations, is a great favourite. One of the most famous taverns with this sign was in the Strand, where Dr. Johnson often used to make a night of it. There is another house of this name at Ipswich. The famous 'Crown and Anchor Association' against so-called *Republicans and Levellers*—as the reformers were styled by the ministerial party in 1792—owed its name to this tavern. It was because of the democratic speech at the *Crown & Anchor* in 1798 that the Duke of Norfolk was dismissed from the West Riding lieutenancy, an incident which is of some little importance

F

in constitutional history. When in 1800 the Farming Society had its famous experimental dinner in order to ascertain the relative qualities of the various breeds of cattle in the kingdom, the execution of it was entrusted to Mr. Simpkins, landlord of the *Crown & Anchor*. The *Anchor & Crown* was also the sign of the great booth at Greenwich fair. (The other booths also had signs : amongst them were the *Royal Standard*, which is found to be an inn sign at Derby, the *Lads of the Village* which occurs at St Mary Cray, Kent, the *Black Boy & Cat*, and the *Moonrakers*.) The *Crown & Dove*, Bristol, may refer to the order of the Holy Ghost, or may have been suggested by the *Three Pigeons & Sceptre*.

Objects of various trades with a crown above them were very common but generally refer to occupations other than innkeeping ; The *Crown & Fan* was an ordinary fan-maker's sign. The *Crown & Rasp*, belonging to snuff-makers, occurs as the sign of Fribourg and Treyer, tobacconists, at the upper end of Pall Mall near the Haymarket in 1781 ; it is still to be seen on the *façade* of the house, and is still the firm's trade mark. The *Crown & Last* originated with shoemakers, but the gentle craft having the reputation of being thirsty souls it was also adopted as an alehouse sign : we find it as such in 1718. The *Crown & Halbert* was in 1790 the sign of a cutler in St Martin's Churchyard, the *Crown & Can* formerly occurred in St John St., and there is a *Crown & Trumpet* at Broadway, Worcs. ; this last may either allude to the trumpet of the royal herald or simply signify a crowned trumpet. There is a *Crown & Liver* at Ewell, Ches., a *Crown & Greyhound* at Dulwich, a *Crown & Shears* in the Minories, a *Crown & Two Chairmen* at 32 Dean St., and a *Crown & Treaty House*, a beautiful old red-brick building, at Uxbridge. This is where in 1645 the sixteen plenipotentiaries of Cromwell and of Charles I met in the effort to agree upon conditions for an armistice. The house was not however actually an inn until the 18th century.

Of the *King's Arms* and the *Queen's Arms*, there are innumerable instances ; the signs are to be found in almost every town and village. Grinling Gibbons, the celebrated carver and sculptor, lived at the sign of the *King's Arms* in Bow St. from 1678 until his death in 1721. At the Haymarket corner of Pall Mall stood in the reign of Queen Anne the *Queen's Arms*. At the accession of George I it was called the *King's Arms*, and there in 1734 the Whig Party used to meet to plan opposition to Sir Robert Walpole. Their association went by the name of the Rump-steak Club. At the *King's Arms*, in Fulham High St., until at any rate 1813 the Great Fire of London was annually commemorated on 1 September. The custom is said to have taken its rise from a number of Londoners who had been burnt out and who, having no employment, strolled out to Fulham, on their way collecting from the hedges a quantity of hazel nuts, with which they resorted to the house. A good picture of the Fire used to be exhibited on the commemoration day.

In 1568 the prizes of the first lottery held in England were exhibited at the *Queen's Arms* in Cheapside, the house of Dericke goldsmith to Queen Elizabeth. The profits were to go towards repairing the havens of the kingdom. The drawing was also to have taken place at Dericke's house, but finally was done at the west door of St Paul's. 'On Friday, 6 April 1781,' says Boswell, 'Dr. Johnson carried me to dine at a club, which, at his desire, had been lately formed at the *Queen's Arms* in St Paul's Churchyard. . . . Garrick kept up an interest in the city by appearing about twice in a winter at Tom's coffee-house in Cornhill, the usual rendezvous of young merchants at Change times; and frequented a club established for the sake of his company at the *Queen's Arms* Tavern.'

Royal badges and the supporters of the arms of various kings were in former times largely used as signs. Notes on the various supporters and on the badges used by the Kings of England will be found in tabular form on pp. 88–90 and in the alphabetical table on pp. 90–7. The *Antelope* is not very common now, although in 1664 there was a tavern with this sign in West Smithfield, and there is an *Antelope* in Oxford. The antelope rarely appears as a charge in a coat of arms, but it is very common as a supporter. Macklin, the comedian who died in 1797, used for thirty years and upwards to visit a public-house called the *Antelope* in White Hart Yard, Covent Garden, where his usual beverage was a pint of stout made hot and sweetened almost to a syrup. This he said balmed his stomach, and kept him from having any inward pains.

The *Dragon* appears to have been one of the oldest heraldic charges of this kingdom. It was the standard of the west Saxons and continued so until the arrival of William the Conqueror. In the Bayeux Tapestry a winged dragon on a pole is constantly represented near the person of King Harold. It was likewise the supporter of the royal arms of Henry VII and all the Tudor sovereigns except Queen Mary. Before that time it had been borne by some of the early Princes of Wales and also by several of the English kings. Thus it is recorded that in 1243–4 the king ordered to be made 'a dragon in the manner of a banner, of a certain red silk embroidered with gold; its tongue like a flaming fire must always be seen moving; its eyes must be made of sapphire or of some other stone suitable for that purpose'.

At the battle of Lewes, 1264, the chronicler, Peter of Langtoffe,[*] says that :—

'The king schewed forth his schild his Dragon full austere.'

In that time, however, the Dragon appears not to have been the royal standard, but was borne along with it, for Matthew of Westminster says, 'The king's place was between the Dragon and the standard.' Edward III at the battle of Crécy also had a standard 'with a dragon of red silk adorned and beaten with very broad and fair lilies of gold'. Then again it occurs on a coin struck in the reign of Henry VI, and was also one of the badges of Edward IV. Probably all this is little to the point, however, since Dragon was a celebrated horse belonging to Tregonwell Frampton, 'Father of the Turf', 1641–1727.

The *Green Dragon* was of very frequent occurrence on the signboard. When Taylor the Water Poet wrote his *Travels through London* there were not less than seven

[*] Chronicle of Robert of Brunne, p. 217.

Green Dragons amongst the metropolitan taverns of that day. One of these has disappeared since Larwood's time, the well-known *Green Dragon* in Bishopsgate St., for nearly two centuries one of the most famous coach and carriers' inns. Probably most *Green Dragons* are named after this one. There are at least four of them in Staffordshire and three in Derbyshire. An odd *Green Dragon* at Hurst, Yorks., exhibits its sign indoors. The *Red Dragon* is much less common. It occurs at Kirkby Lonsdale, while the *White Dragon* occurs only on a trades token of Holborn representing a dragon pierced with an arrow. Evidently this was some family crest.

The *White Hart* was the favourite badge of Richard II. At a tournament held in Smithfield in 1390 in honour of some newly elected Knights of the Garter, ' all the kynges house were of one sute : theyr cotys, theyr armys, theyr sheldes, and theyr trappours, were browdrid all with whyte hertys, with crownes of gold about their neck, and cheynes of gold hanging thereon whiche hertys was the kinges leverye, that he gaf to lordes, ladyes, knyghtes and squyers, to knowe his household people from others '.* The origin of this White Hart with a collar of gold round its neck was in the most remote antiquity. Aristotle reports that Diomedes consecrated a white hart to Diana, which, a thousand years after, was killed by Agathocles, King of Sicily. Pliny states that it was Alexander the Great who caught a white stag and placed a collar of gold round its neck. This marvellous story highly pleased the fancy of mediæval writers. They substituted Julius Cæsar for Alexander the Great, and transplanted the fable to western regions, in consequence of which various countries now claim the honour of having produced the white hart collared with gold. One was said to have been caught in Windsor Forest, another on Rothwell Haigh Common, Yorks., a third at Senlis, in France, and a fourth at Magdeburg. This last was killed by Charlemagne. The same emperor is also reported to have caught a white stag in the woods of Holstein and to have attached the usual golden collar round its neck. More than three centuries after, in 1172, this animal was killed by Henry the Lion, and the whole story is to this day recorded in a Latin inscription on the walls of Lubeck Cathedral.

Amongst the oldest inns which bore this sign, that in the Borough High St. ranks foremost in historical interest. Here it was that Jack Cade established his headquarters, 1 July 1450. *King Henry VI* (Pt. II) † mentions this house by name. The original inn that had sheltered Cade and his followers remained standing till 1676, when it was burnt down in the great fire that devastated part of Southwark. It was rebuilt and the structure was in Larwood's time still in existence. It has since disappeared. In Hatton's time (1708) it could boast of the largest sign in London except one other which was that of the *Castle*, Fleet St. Dickens (in *Pickwick Papers*) gives a most graphic description of the place. The *White Hart* in Bishopsgate was also of very respectable antiquity. It had the date 1480 in the front. It is probable that this building standing on the boundary of the old hospital of Bethlehem formed part of

---

* Caxton's *Chronicle* at the end of Higden's *Polychronicon* edn. 1482, lib. ult. chap. vi.
† Act I, Sc. 8.

the religious house. Doubtless it was the hostelry for the entertainment of strangers, which was a usual outbuilding of the greater monastic houses and hospitals.

In the reign of Queen Elizabeth there was a *White Hart* in the Strand, mentioned in 1570. It is not improbable that this inn gave its name to Hart St. and White Hart Yard in that neighbourhood. There was another inn of this name in Whitechapel, connected with the name of that curious character Mrs. Mapp, the female bone-setter, who created a great sensation in the early part of the 18th century.

A fine modern *White Hart* sign at Charlbury, Oxon, over a house belonging to Messrs. Hitchman, was painted by Captain W. R. D. Kettlewell. A photograph of this has been reproduced in *The Studio*. The *White Hart* at Scole, Norf., had certainly the most expensive sign ever produced. It is mentioned by Sir Thomas Browne, 4 March 1663-4—' About three miles further, I came to Scole, where is a very hand-some inne, and the noblest sighnepost in England, about and upon which are carved a great many stories as of Charon and Cerberus, Actæon and Diana, and many others ; the signe itself is a *White Hart*, which hanges downe carved in a stately wreath.' A century later, Blomfield says—' The *White Hart* is much noted in these parts, being called by way of distinction *Scole Inn* ; the house is a large brick building adorned with imagery and carved work in several places, as big as the life ; it was built in 1655 by James Peck, whose arms impaling his wife's are over the porch door. The sign, which was made at a cost of over £1,000, is very large, beautified all over with a great number of images of large stature carved in wood, and was the work of Fair-child ; the arms about it are those of the chief towns and gentlemen in the country. . . . There was lately a very round large bed, big enough to hold 15 or 20 couples in imita-tion (I suppose) of the remarkable great bed at Ware.' The sign there survived until after 1795.

We obtain full details of this wonderful erection from an engraving of 1740. The sign passed over the road, resting on one side on a pier of brickwork, and joined to the house on the other ; its height was sufficient to allow carriages to pass beneath. Its ornamentation was divided into compartments, which contained the following subjects according to the numbers in the engraving. 1. Jonah coming out of the fish's mouth. 2. A lion supporting the arms of Great Yarmouth. 3. A Bacchus. 4. The arms of Lindley. 5. The arms of Hobart. 6. A Shepherd playing on his pipe. 7. An Angel supporting the arms of Mr. Peck's lady. 8. An Angel supporting the arms of Mr. Peck. 9. A White Hart (the sign itself) with this motto—' *Implentur veteris bacchi pinguisque ferinae. Anno Dom.* 1655.' 10. The arms of the Earl of Yar-mouth. 11. The arms of the Duke of Norfolk. 12. Neptune on a Dolphin. 13. A Lion supporting the arms of Norwich. 14. Charon carrying a reputed Witch to Hades. 15. Cerberus. 16. A Huntsman. 17. Actæon (addressing his dogs with the words ' *Actæon ego sum dominum cognoscite vestrum* '). 18. A White Hart, couchant (underneath, the name of the maker of the sign, *Johannes Fairchild*). 19. Prudence. 20. Fortitude. 21. Temperance. 22. Justice. 23. Diana. 24. Time devouring an infant (underneath, ' *Tempus edax rerum* '). 25. An Astronomer, who is seated on a

' circumferenter and by some chymical preparations is so affected that in fine weather he faces that quarter from which it is about to come '.   There is a ballad on this sign in Brome's *Songs and other Poems*, 1661.   The house is still there, though much reduced in size, and contains some fine 17th-century woodwork.   The sign, however, mysteriously disappeared at a sale in the early 19th century.

There are one or two other ' gallows ' signs still surviving in various parts of the country.   Notable among them are the *Crown*, Edenbridge, Kent, the *Four Swans*, Waltham Cross, Herts., the *Fox & Hounds*, Barley, Herts., the *George*, Stamford, the *George*, Crawley, Sussex, the *Green Man & Black's Head*, Ashbourne, Derbys., the *Magpie*, Stonham Parva, Suff., the *Old Star*, York, the *Red Lion*, Hampton, and the *Swan*, Fittleworth, Sussex, the *Swan*, Enford, Wilts.   There is a kind of gallows sign to the *Swan*, Swan Lane, Stroud, Glos., and there is a fine modern one by Professor Richardson at the *Rose & Crown*, Stanton, Suff.   The Scole sign was perhaps the most famous inn sign that ever existed and must surely have been the most expensive and elaborate one.

Of other royal badges one may note the *Hawk & Buckle* at Etwall, Derbys., and in various other places.   This is simply a popular rendering of the *Falcon & the Fetterlock*, one of the badges of the House of York.   The *Hawk & Buck* which appears to be only another version of this last corruption occurs at St Helens, Lancs.   The *Falcon & Horse-shoe*, a sign in Poplar in the 17th century (and found on trades tokens), may have had the same origin, while the *Bull & Stirrup* at Chester probably comes from the *Bull & Fetterlock*, another combination of badges of the House of York.

From this family are also derived the *Blue Boar* and the *White Boar*.   One of the badges of Richard Duke of York, father of Edward IV, was ' a blewe Bore with his tuskis and his cleis and his membres of gold '.   The heraldic origin of this sign, of which there are still innumerable instances all over England, is now so completely lost sight of that in many places, as at Bellerby, N.R. Yorks., and at Grantham, it passes as the *Blue Pig*.   The *White Boar* was the popular sign in Richard III's time, that king's cognizance being a boar passant *arg.*, whence the rhyme which cost William Collingbourne his life :—

> The Cat, the Rat, and Lovell our Dogge,
> Rules all England under *an Hogge*.

The cat was William Catesby, the rat Sir Richard Ratcliffe, our dog Lord Lovell. The fondness of Richard for this badge appears from his wardrobe accounts for the year 1483, one of which contains a charge ' for 8,000 bores made and wrought upon fustian ', and four thousand more are mentioned shortly afterwards.   He also established an officer of arms called *Blanc Sanglier*, and it was he who carried his master's mangled body from Bosworth battlefield to Leicester.

After Richard's defeat and death the *White Boars* were transformed into *Blue Boars*, this being the easiest and cheapest way of changing the sign.   So the boar of Richard passed for the boar of the Earl of Oxford, who had largely contributed to place Henry VII on the throne. Even the *White Boar* at Leicester, in which Richard passed the last night of his life, followed the general example, and became the *Blue Boar*, under which sign it continued until taken down about a century ago. Another *Blue Boar* still preserves the sign in Leicester. The bed in which the king slept was preserved and continued for many generations one of the curiosities shown to strangers at Leicester. The sign of the *White Boar* did not become quite extinct with the overthrow of the Yorkist faction, for it was used as a printer's sign in 1542.

The *Firebeacon*, a sign at Fulston, Lincs., was a badge of Edward IV, and also of the Admiralty. The *Hawthorn* or *Hawthornbush* which we meet in many places, for example, Walsall and West Bromwich, may be Henry VII's badge, but various other May Day customs may have contributed to the popularity of the sign. According to Reginald Scott's *Discovery of Witchcraft*, 1584, 'Hawthorne, otherwise whitethorne, gathered on Maiedaie' was a specific against witchcraft. A *Haw Bush* is noted elsewhere (p. 152).

The *Gun* or *Cannon* was the cognizance of King Edward VI, Queen Mary and Queen Elizabeth. In the beginning of the 18th century it was of such frequent occurrence that the *Craftsman* observed, 'Nothing is more common in England than the sign of a cannon.' Sarah Milwood, the wanton who led George Barnwell astray, lived according to the ballad, in Shoreditch 'next door unto the *Gun*'. The sign is still fairly common, especially in the neighbourhood of arsenals, where its adoption is easily explained.

About a century and a half ago there was a famous *Cannon* coffee-house at the corner of Trafalgar Square, at the end of Whitcombe St., or Hedgelane; its site is now occupied by the Union Club. From this coffee-house Hackman the murderer saw his victim drive past on her way to Covent Garden Theatre, when he followed and shot her as she was entering her coach after the performance. There is a *Gun* in Lupus St., a *Cannon* at Sunninghill, a *Morning Gun* at Bridgwater, an *Evening Gun* at Norwich, a *Gun & Tent* in Spitalfields and a *Battery* at Stonehouse, Devon. Presumably military in their origin are the *Rifle* at Hammersmith, the *Cross Rifles* at Bridgwater, with perhaps the *Halberd* at Ipswich and the *Battleaxes* at Wraxhall.

The *Swan* was a favourite badge of several of our kings; as Henry IV and Edward III. At a tournament in Smithfield the last king wore the somewhat profane motto :

> Hay, hay, the wyth Swan,
> By God's soule I am thy man.

Thomas of Woodstock used the same cognizance, whence Gower styles him 'cignus de corde benignus'; whilst Cicely Nevil, Duchess of York, mother of Edward IV and Richard III, likewise had a swan as supporter of her arms.

There are numerous provincial *Swans*. Perhaps the best known is that at Clare, Suff., which has possibly the oldest carved sign in the country.

The sign of the *Swan & Maidenhead* at Stratford-on-Avon may have originated in one of the royal badges, for in 1375 among the bequests of the Black Prince to his son Richard was hangings for a hall, embroidered with mermen, and a border of red and black empaled, embroidered with ' *swans having ladies' heads* '. The *Swan & Falcon* (compounded of two badges of Edward III) was a sign in Hereford in 1775, that of a well-known coaching inn. The *Swan & White Hart* may have been originally the *Swan & Antelope*, supporters of the arms of Henry IV, but as it at present stands two distinct royal badges are represented. This sign occurs on a trades token of St Giles-in-the-Fields in the second half of the 17th century.

The *Rising Sun* was the badge of Edward III, and forms part of the arms of Ireland : but the *Sun Shining* was a cognizance of several other kings. Various other causes may have led to the adoption of this sign, which is dealt with here under Miscellaneous Signs.

Lions have been at all times and still continue greater signboard favourites than any other heraldic animals. The lion rampant most frequently occurs, although in late years naturalism has crept in, and the animal is often represented standing or crouching, quite regardless of his heraldic origin. The lion of the signboard, especially the *Red Lion*, being seldom seen *passant*, it is probable that it was not derived from the national coat of arms (in any case the three English lions are properly leopards), but rather from some badge, often that of Edward III. The *White Lion* is probably often that of Edward IV, though silver in general was not used on English signboards, yet the *White Lion* was and is anything but uncommon. Several examples occur amongst early booksellers. Over inns, also, it was not uncommon. Thus the *White Lion* in St John's St., Clerkenwell, was originally an inn frequented by cattle-drovers and other wayfarers connected with Smithfield market. Formerly it was a very extensive building. Two of the adjoining houses and part of White Lion St. are all built on its site. The house occupied in Larwood's day by an oilshop was, in those days, the gateway to the inn-yard, and over it was the sign, in stone relief, a lion rampant painted white. It was inserted in the front wall where it still remained in its original position in 1861 with the date 1714, when probably it had been renewed. Pepys's cousin, Anthony Joyce, drowned himself in a pond behind this inn. He was a tavern-keeper himself, and kept the *Three Stags* at Holborn, a house of which tokens are extant. Sir Thomas Lawrence's father kept the *White Lion* at Bristol. He afterwards removed to the *Bear* at Devizes, where he failed in business. It seemed that it was this last speculation in hotel-keeping which ruined him, with reference to which local wits used to say, ' It was not the Lion but the Bear that eat him up.'

Since pictorial or carved signs have fallen into disuse, and only names given, the *Silver Lion* is not uncommon, though in all probability simply adopted as a change from the very frequent *Golden Lion*. Thus there is one at 65 Pennyfields, Poplar. The *Red Lion* is by far the most common. It is said to occur in 921 houses all over England, and is second in popularity only to the *Crown*. Doubtless in general it originated with the badge of John of Gaunt, Duke of Lancaster, married to Constance of Leon and Castile. The Duke bore the lion rampant *gules* of Leon as his cognizance, to represent his claim to the throne of Castile, when that was occupied by Henry of Trastamara. In after years the red lion may often have been used to represent the lion of Scotland.

The *Red Lion* at Sittingbourne is a very ancient establishment. According to an advertisement of *c.* 1820 Henry V rested here on his return from the Agincourt campaign (his bill being 9*s.* 9*d.* for wine at a penny a pint). The *Red Lion*, Drury Lane, is the inn where dwelt Goldsmith's indigent poet, Scroggen. Red Lion Square, Holborn, was called after another *Red Lion*. Aubrey says, ' Andrew Marvell lies interred under ye pews in the south side of St Gile's church in ye fields, under the window wherein is painted on glass, a red lyon (it was given by the Inneholder of the Red Lyon Inne, Holborn).' Another celebrated tavern was the *Red Lion* still to be seen in St John's St., Islington—which has been honoured by the presence of several literary personages. Thomson of the *Seasons* and Paine of the *Rights of Man* lived here, and Dr. Johnson with his friends used the house. Hogarth introduced its gable end in his picture of 'Evening'. At the *Red Lion* in Whitechapel (so the house asserts), in a struggle between Dick Turpin and the Bow Street Runners, Tom King was killed. A famous provincial *Red Lion* is that at Colchester. The history of the house is recorded from 1529, and is well documented from 1604, and the fabric dates back apparently to *c.* 1400 or some time earlier. Apparently it was built as a private mansion but converted into an inn by *c.* 1500. The sign is an interesting one. The lion is crowned and holds a fleur-de-lys tipped sceptre. This suggests that here at any rate this house takes its sign from John of Gaunt, pretender to the throne of Leon.

The *Black Lion* is somewhat uncommon ; it may have been derived from the coat of arms of Queen Philippa of Hainault, wife of Edward III. Owen Glendower also bore a lion rampant *sable,* ' the black lion of Powyse ' ; his arms were Paly of eight *arg.* and *gules,* over all a lion *sable.* The black lion was the royal ensign of his father, Madoc ap Meredith, last sovereign prince of Powys, who died at Winchester in 1160. The black lion consequently might sometimes be set up by Welshmen.

Among the badges of the Tudors, Henry VII and Henry VIII left the still common sign of the *Portcullis.* It is the principal charge in the arms of the city of Westminster and is to be seen everywhere within and without the beautiful chapel of Henry VII, whose favourite device it was, as importing his descent from the House of Lancaster. It was also one of the badges of Henry VIII, with the motto, *Securitas altera,* and occurs on some of his coins. There is an example at Hillesley, Glos., and another in Bristol, where it is taken from the arms of the Beauforts, Dukes of Somerset.

To this same Tudor family we also owe the *Rose & Crown,* which sign in Larwood's day might be observed on not less than forty-eight public-houses in London alone, exclusive of beer-houses. One of the oldest in the High St., Knightsbridge, has been licensed above three hundred years, though not under that name, for anciently it was called the *Oliver Cromwell.* We do not know what was its original sign. The Protector's bodyguard is said to have been quartered here, and an inscription to that effect was formerly painted in front of the house. It was accompanied by an emblazoned coat of arms of Cromwell on an ornamental piece of plaster work, which last is all that remained of it in 1861. It was the oldest house in Brompton, was formerly the largest inn, and not improbably the house at which Sir Thomas Wyatt put up while his Kentish followers rested on the adjacent green. Richard Corbould painted this inn under the title of ' The Old Hostelrie at Knightsbridge ' exhibited in 1849, but he transferred the date to 1497, altering the house according to his own fancy.

One princely badge remains to be mentioned—The *Feathers* or *Prince of Wales' Feathers*, occasionally found as the *Prince of Wales' Arms*. Ostrich feathers were from a very early period among the devices of our kings and princes. King Stephen, for instance, according to Guillim, bore a plume of ostrich feather with a motto signifying *No force alters their fashion*, meaning that no wind can ruffle a feather into lasting disorder. Not only the Black Prince, but also Edward III and his other sons bore ostrich feathers as their cognizances, each with some distinction in colour or metal. The badge originally took the form of a single feather. John Arderne, physician to the Black Prince, who is the first to mention the derivation of the feathers from the King of Bohemia, says, ' And observe that such a white feather was borne on his crest by Edward the eldest son of King Edward : and this feather he conquered from the King of Bohemia whom he killed at Cressy in France, and so he assumed the feather, called the ostrich feather, which that most noble king had formerly worn on his crest.'

The feather is drawn in the margin of the manuscript as single, and in that shape too it is represented on the Black Prince's tomb. This feather, however, appears only to have been an ornament on the helmet of King John of Bohemia. A contemporary Flemish poem describes his heraldic crest ' as were two vultures sprinkled all over with finely-gilt linden leaves '. In that shape it also occurs on the king's seal. Concerning the origin and meaning of the motto which in full is *Hou Moet Ich Dien*, the first two words of which are certainly not German, much ink has been shed and some acres of paper wasted. Larwood suggests very reasonably that since in Flemish the words mean ' Keep courage, I serve ', or ' Keep courage, I serve with you, I am your companion in arms ', though no parentage has as yet been found for this motto, it may not improbably have been derived from the Black Prince's maternal family, since his mother Queen Philippa of Hainault was a Flemish princess. The *Feathers* ' at the side of Leicester Fields ' was evidently named in compliment to its neighbour Frederick, Prince of Wales, son of George II, who lived at Leicester House, ' the pouting house of princes ' when on bad terms with his father, and died there in 1751. The back parlour of this tavern was for some years the meeting-place of a club of artists and well-known amateurs, among whom were James (Athenian) Stuart, the famous architect, Samuel Scott, the marine painter, Luke Sullivan, the miniaturist and engraver, Francis Grose, author of *Antiquities of England*, and the greatest wit of his day, Thomas Hearne, the antiquary, John Ireland, Hogarth's biographer, and several others. When this house was taken down to make way for Dibdin's theatre called the *Sans-souci*, the club adjourned to the *Coach & Horses* in Castle St., Leicester Fields. In consequence of the members not proving good enough customers the landlord one evening ventured to let them out with a farthing candle, so they betook themselves to Gerard St., and thence to the *Blue Posts* in Dean St., where the club dwindled to two or three members and at last died out.

A lodge of Oddfellows was held at the *Feathers*, Grosvenor St. West, into which George, Prince of Wales one night intruded very abruptly with a roystering friend. The Prince and his companion were at once initiated, and the Prince was chairman for the remainder of the evening. In 1851 the old public-house was pulled down and a new gin palace built on its site, in the parlour of which the chair used by the distinguished Oddfellow is still preserved, along with a portrait of his Royal Highness in the robes of the order.

A famous provincial *Feathers* is that at Ludlow, Salop, one of the loveliest half-timbered houses of the Welsh border.

Among the badges and arms of countries and towns, the national emblem the *Rose* is most frequent, and has been so for centuries. Bishop Earle seems to suggest that the *Rose* was a general sign, like the *Ivy Bush*. It was long held that upon the death of Richard III all the signboards with white roses were pulled down, ' and that none are to be found at the present day'. The *White Roses* were not however all immediately done away with. Larwood knew of none, but there are a few now, especially of course in Yorkshire. There is another in Norwich and another at Wolverhampton. There was in 1503 a *White Rose* tavern near the chapel of Our Lady behind the high altar of the abbey church of Westminster, later demolished to make room for the building of Henry VI's chapel. At present, however, as the rose on the signboard is in general simply the *Rose*—the Queen of Flowers—its heraldic history has been forgotten long ago, and it is painted any colour according to taste, or occasionally gilt. Long after disputes of the rival factions had ceased, the custom was continued of adding the colour to the name of the sign. Thus, in Stow, ' Then have ye one other lane called Rother Lane, or *Red Rose* Lane, of such a sign ', etc. In Lancashire we meet in one or two instances, with the old heraldic flower, as at Springwood, Chadderton, Manchester, where the red *Rose of Lancaster* is still in bloom on a signboard.

Machyn, in his *Diary*, mentions many instances of the *Rose* sign :—' The vij day of Aprill (1563) at Seint Katheryns beyond the Toure, the wyff of the syne of the Rose a taverne, was set on the pelere for ettyng of rowe flesse and rostyd boyth ', which in modern English means that she was put in the pillory for breaking fast in Lent. The *Rose*, now no more, in Russell St., Covent Garden, was a noted place for debauchery in the 17th century. Constant allusions are made to it in the old plays, for example, in Shadwell's *The Scowrers*,★ ' a man could not go from the Rose Tavern to the Piazzi once but he must venture his life twice '. In this house in 1712 was arranged the duel between the Duke of Hamilton and Lord Mohun, in which the latter was killed (the celebrated duel described in *Henry Esmond*). In the reign of Queen Anne the place was still a great resort for loose women, it is mentioned as such in the *Rake Reformed*, 1718. Hogarth represented one of the rooms of the house in his ' Rake's Progress '. In 1766

★ 1691, Act X, Sc. x.

this tavern was swallowed up in the enlargements of Drury Lane by Garrick, but the sign was preserved and hung up against the front wall. Two other *Roses*, not without thorns, are mentioned by Tom Brown ; the *Rose* by Temple Bar, and the *Rose* in Wood St. The *Rose* by Temple Bar stood at the corner of Thanet Place. Strype says it was ' a well customed house, with good conveniences of rooms and a good garden '. Horace Walpole mentions a painted room in this tavern in one of his letters in 1776. The *Rose* in Wood St. was a sponging-house.

Innumerable other *Rose* inns and taverns might be mentioned. One of the best known is the *Rose* at Wokingham, once famous as the resort of Pope and Gay. There was a room here called Pope's room. And a chair was shown in which the great little man had sat. It is also celebrated in the well-known song Molly Mog, attributed sometimes to Gay, sometimes to Swift. Molly was the daughter of John Mog, the landlord of that inn, and died a spinster at the age of 67. Mr. Standon of Arborfield, who died in 1730, is said to have been the lover to whom the song alludes. The current tradition of the place is that Gay and his poetic friends having met at the *Rose*, and being detained within doors by the weather, it was proposed that they should write a song, each person present contributing a verse ; the subject agreed on was the Fair Maid of the Inn. It is said that by mistake they wrote in praise of Molly, but that in fact the song was intended to apply to her sister Sally, who was the greater beauty. A portrait of Gay still remained at the inn in Larwood's time, though the house had been changed into a mercer's shop.

Sometimes the Rose is combined with other objects, as the *Rose & Ball*, which may have originated in the rose as the sign of a mercer, and the ball as the emblem or device which silk dealers formerly hung at their doors as the Berlin wool shops did in more recent years. The *Rose & Key* was a sign in Cheapside in 1682. This combination looks like a hieroglyphic rendering of the phrase ' under the rose ', but the key is of very common occurrence in other signs, so that the sign may have no particular meaning. There is a *Rose* in the Old Bailey, a *Blooming Rose* at Hunslet, Leeds, a *Little Rose* at Cambridge, a *Handford Rose* at Ipswich, a *Moss Rose* at Preston, a *Rosebud* at Accrington, a *Rose in June* at Margate, a *Rose of Denmark* at Roman Rd., E.7, a *Rose of England* at Ipswich, a *Rose of Kent* at Deptford, and one in Trundley Rd., a *Rose of Lee* at Catford, Kent, and at High Rd., Lee, a *Rose of Normandy* in Marylebone High St. (dealt with below, p. 153), a *Rose & Lily* at Bermondsey, a *Rose & Shamrock* at Chester-le-Street, a *Rose & Thistle* at Burnley, and a *Rose, Shamrock & Thistle* at Eton, with a *Rose, Thistle & Shamrock*, at Burslem, Stoke-on-Trent. These last signs are dealt with elsewhere (p. 63). The *Rose Revived* sounds as though it may have had in some instances a political significance, and is dealt with elsewhere (p. 39).

The Scottish *Thistle & Crown* is another common national badge, originally adopted no doubt mostly by publicans of Scottish origin. There is a *Scotch Thistle* at Birkenhead. The *Crown & Harp* is less frequent, but there is one at Bishop's Cleeve, Glos. Of the *Crown & Leek* we know only two examples, in Dean St., Mile End, and at Newton. The *Shamrock* also is of common occurrence, as, for example, at Bath, but is rarely or never combined with the Crown. No doubt those professing much reverence for the former symbol have rarely a great deal for the latter. The *Crown Posada*, Newcastle, was originally the *Crown*. The second part of the name, the Spanish word for a wineshop, was presumably added by some travelled landlord.

Among heraldic signs referring to towns are the *Bible & Three Crowns*, the coat of arms of Oxford, which was not uncommon with the booksellers in former times. To one of them probably belonged the carved stone specimen walled up in a house at the corner of Little Distaff Lane and St Paul's Churchyard. There was formerly an *Oxford Arms* in Warwick Lane, Newgate St., a fine old galleried inn, with exterior staircases leading to the bedrooms. This was already a carriers' inn before the Fire. The *Buck in the Park*, Curzon St. and Friargate, Derby, is the vernacular rendering of the arms of that town, which are—a hart *cumbant* on a mount *vert* in a park *paled*, all *proper*. The three legs are the Manx arms, and they still form a not uncommon ale-house sign, often as at Burslem, Stoke-on-Trent, appearing as the *Legs of Man*. There is one in Leeds, which is generally known under the jocular denomination of the *Kettle with Three Spouts*. County arms also are sometimes represented on the signboards ; as the *Fifteen Balls* (which refer to the Cornish arms, fifteen roundels arranged per pile 5, 4, 3, 2, 1) in Union St., Bodmin ; *One & All*, the motto of the county of Corn-wall, occurs in Market Jew St., Penzance. The *Staffordshire Knot* is common in the Potteries ; there are many instances of this sign in Stoke-on-Trent. Almost every county is represented on one or more houses within its territories by its own arms, such as the *Northumberland Arms*, etc., but about these little need be said.

The *Three Balls* of the pawnbroker are said to be taken from the lower part of the coat of arms of the Florentine Medici, from whose states and from Lombardy came nearly all the early bankers. These also advanced money on valuable goods, and hence gradually became pawnbrokers. The arms of the Medici family were five bezants *azure*, whence the balls formerly were blue, and only within the last century and a quarter have they assumed a golden colour. (Larwood suggests to gild the pill for those who have dealings with Uncle.)

The *Lion & Castle*, of which there were a few instances, for example, at Rotherhithe and at Norwich, both now gone, need not be derived from royal marriage alliances with Spain. Probably it was merely borrowed from the brand of the Spanish arms on the sherry casks, and had been put up by the landlord to indicate the sale of genuine Spanish wines, such as sack, canary and ' mountain '.

The *Flower de Luce* was a frequent English sign in old times, either taken from the quartering of the French arms with the English, or set up as a compliment to private families who bear this charge in their arms or as crest. There is a *Fleur de Lis* at Stoke under Ham, and a *Fleur de Lys* at Nuneaton and at Lawsonford, Warws., and one at St Albans. Tokens are extant of an inn at Dover in the 17th century with the sign of the *French Arms*, a tavern name sufficiently common also in London at that period to attract the travellers from across the Channel. Thus James Johnson was a goldsmith that kept running cash—i.e. a banker—in Cheapside in 1677 living at the sign of the

Three Flower de Luces. From the 15th century, strangers in London were allowed to keep hostels for their countrymen, and by way of advertisement they most probably put up the arms of those countries as their signs. No doubt the *Three Frogs*, still existing at London Rd., Wokingham, is a travesty of *Johnny Crapaud's Arms.* There is another house of this name still extant at Bracknell, Berks.

Another sign, apparently of Flemish origin, is the *Dolphin & Crown*, the armorial bearing of the French Dauphin, and the sign of C. Willington, a bookseller in St Paul's Churchyard, 1700.

In 1769 there was the *Geneva Arms* among the London signs, before the shop of Le Grand, a ' pastry-cook and cook ' as he styled himself, in Church St., Soho. Formerly most pastrycooks and confectioners were Swiss. This last sign has found imitators in Soho, and at the present day it figures at a public-house in Hayes Court, where it is put up, no doubt, in honour of the spirit which many call Geneva, but which is quite properly called Gin.

The *Cross Keys* are the arms of the Papal See, the emblem of St Peter and his successors, concerning which Milton gives an unkind interpretation. This sign was frequently adopted by innkeepers and other tenants of religious houses, even after the Reformation ; for the *Cross Keys* figure in the arms of the old dioceses of York, Exeter, Gloucester, and Peterborough, and the new ones of Blackburn, Bradford, Ripon, and Sheffield. At the *Cross Keys* in Gracechurch St., Banks in the days of Queen Elizabeth used to perform with his wonderful bay horse before a crowded house. Then the inn consisted of a large court with galleries all round, which like many other old London inns, was often used as an extempore theatre by our ancestors. It is named in 1681 amongst the carriers' inns and it remained until Larwood's time. The *Cross Keys* was also the sign of a tavern near Thavies Inn in 1712, and it still remains a very common one in some parts of the country.

Most numerous among heraldic signs were the crests, arms and badges of private families. Concerning the history of arms and crests the reader is referred to works on heraldry. Of the badges it will suffice to note that they consisted of the master's arms, crest or device, either on a small silver shield or embroidered on a piece of cloth and fastened on the left arm of domestics and retainers. The causes which dictated the choice of such subjects were various. According to Wright one of the earliest was that :—

> In towns it was a common custom even amongst the richer merchants to make a profit by receiving guests. These letters of lodgings were distinguished from the inn-keepers or *hostelers* by the name of *herbergeors*, and in large towns they were submitted to municipal regulations. The great barons and knights were in the custom of taking up their lodgings with those herbergeors rather than going to the public hostel, and thus a sort of relationship was formed between particular nobles or kings and particular burghers, on the strength of which *the latter adopted the arms of their habitual lodgers as their sign.*

This again led to the custom of prefixing to inns and arms of men of note who had sojourned in the house, as may be seen in Machyn's *Diary*, which says under 25 January 1560 that the Earl of Bedford on his embassy to France took with him 'iij dozen of logyng skochyons' (lodging escutcheons). Similarly, on the road from London to Westchester might formerly have been observed the coats of arms of several of the lords-lieutenant of Ireland, either as signs to inns or else framed and hung in the best rooms. Sir Dudley Digges' *Compleat Ambassador*, 1654, alluding in his preface to the reserve of English ambassadors observed : 'We have hardly any notion of them but their arms, which are hung up in inns where they passed.' Montaigne also mentions this practice as usual in France.

Possibly the feudal relations between the classes were the main reason for the adoption of this description of signs. It is reasonable to suppose that a vassal might have set up the arms or crest of his feudal lord.

Bagford, in his manuscript notes about the art of printing, has jotted down a list of signs originating in badges, which has been incorporated here in the alphabetical table on pp. 30-5. He says that :

> Then for ye original of signes used to be set over ye douers of tradesmen, as inkepers, Taverns etc., they having been domestic sarvants to some noblemen, they leaving ther Masters sarvis toke to themselves for ther signes ye crest, bag,[*] or ye arms of ther Ld., and thes was a destincsion or Mark of one Mannes house from another and (not) only by printers but all outher trades : and these servants of kinges, queenes, or noblemen, being ther domestic sarvants, and wor ther Leuire and Bages, as may be sene these day ye maner of the Levirs [†] and Bagges by ye wattermen.

The arms of the lord of the manor were often put up as a sign, a custom that has continued to our day, particularly in villages where the inn often displays the name or coat-armour of the ground landlord. Should the estate pass into other hands, the inn will most probably change its sign for the arms of the new purchaser. The house, as it were, wears the livery of the master. An explanation commonly given, though one for which there seems little evidence is this. In former times to some extent the great landowner himself performed the duties of innkeeper, and his arms were hung or carved at the entrance to his castle or manor house for the information of wayfarers. Probably many such houses were rarely without a stranger or two, either travelling mechanics, entertainers and chapmen of various kinds, or vagabond soldiers on the tramp for a new master to fight under. Greater people were admitted further into the castle, but the common sort fared with the servants. According to the good nature of the lord and his steward the fare was good or bad, plentiful or meagre. It was, however, generally the custom to be profuse in all matters of food bounty. The house-steward made charges for extras, and the comfort obtainable generally depended largely on his liberality or greediness. As population increased, travellers became too numerous for the accommodation provided. Stewards also became old and by way of pensioning them off detached premises were allotted to them to carry on business away from the castle or great house. The arms of the land-

---

[*] Badge.   [†] Liveries.

lord were of course put up outside the house, and on occasion of predatory excursions or family fights, when other nobles joined their troops with those of the landlord, the soldiers were usually quartered at the inn outside the castle. As with all places of public resort visitors began to have their special fancies, and this *Red Lion* and that *Greyhound* became famous through the country for the good entertainment to be had there. In this manner *Red Lions* and *Greyhounds* found their way on to the signboards of the inns within the walled cities. The men of the castle, too, used those houses bearing their master's arms when they visited the town. To a good business man the name of a favourite tavern would quickly suggest its adoption elsewhere, and in this way the heraldic emblem of a family might be carried where that family had never been known.

Latterly, however, as all traces of the origin and meaning of these ' Arms ' have died out, or become removed from the understanding of publicans and brewers, the uses to which the word has been applied are most absurd and ridiculous. Not only do we meet constantly with arms of families nobody ever heard of, nor cares to hear about, but all sorts of impossible ' Arms ' are invented as the *Junction Arms*, still existing in Southampton St., *Griffin's Arms*, *Chaffcutter's Arms*, *Union Arms* (Tom Cribbs' old house, still to be seen in Panton St.), *General's Arms*, *Antigallican Arms*, *Farmer's Arms*, *Drover's Arms*, *Boat-Builders' Arms*, Reading, *Boilermakers' Arms*, Norwich, *Brush-makers' Arms*, Oulton, Staffs., *Colliers' Arms* and *Miner's Arms*, to be seen all over the country, *Flagcutters' Arms*, *Footballers' Arms*, Burnley, *Fanciers' Arms*, Norwich, *Gold-diggers' Arms*, Peckham, *Graveldiggers' Arms*, Denham, Bucks., *Flintmillers' Arms*, *Hot-pressers' Arms*, Norwich, *Mechanics' Arms*, Glossop, *Minders' Arms*, Oldham, *Oilmillers' Arms*, Grimsby, *Platelayers' Arms*, Hatfield, *Thatchers' Arms*, Great Warley, Berks., *Welldiggers' Arms*, Petworth, Surrey, *Worsteddeallers' Arms*, Oldham, *Yachtsman's Arms*, Wivenhoe, Essex, etc. etc.

In tavern heraldry the *Adam's Arms* ought certainly to have the precedence. The publicans generally represent these by a pewter pot and a couple of crossed tobacco pipes. In this they differ from Sylvanus Morgan the writer on heraldry, who says that Adam's Arms were ' Paly Trenchy divided every way and tinctured of every colour '. The shield was naturally in the shape of such a spade as was used in the Golden Age, before escutcheons of war were needed (when Adam delved and Eve span). From the spindle of our first mother the female lozenge-shaped shield is said to be similarly derived.

In some instances armorial signs express the arms of the craft guilds or livery companies, as with the *Turners' Arms*, Crawford St., Baker St., W. In still others they refer to local celebrities, not necessarily manorial lords ; for example, in Shrewsbury there is only one house with the sign of some family arms, the *Hill Arms*. This recalls a bitterly contested election of 1796, fought between the Hills of Hawkstone and the Hills of Attingham. By way of exception to the general rule the *Butcher's Arms* at Sheepscombe, Glos., has a very pleasing sign. Its main part is the usual arms of the Butchers' Company, but this is surmounted by the carved figure of a butcher. In

PLATE
7

BEXLEY PUBLIC LIBRARIES.

PLATE
8

both hands he holds a huge pot containing, say, a gallon of ale ; round his wrist is the end of a rope tied to the legs of a young pig. The rope has, however, become tangled around the butcher's leg, and he is faced with the problem of missing his beer or losing his pig.

One of the most popular heraldic signs is the *Bear & Ragged Staff*, the crest of the Warwick family which is referred to in *King Henry VI (Pt. II)*.*

According to legend Arthgal, the first Earl of Warwick in the time of King Arthur, was called by the ancient British the Bear, for having strangled such an animal in his arms. Morvidius, another ancestor of the house, slew a giant with a club made out of a young tree : hence the family bore this cognizance. Robert Dudley when governor in the Low Countries, disusing his own coat of the Green Lion with two tails, signed all instruments with the crest of the Bear and Ragged Staff. He was then suspected by many of his jealous adversaries to hatch an ambitious design to make himself commander over the Low Countries, as the lion is king of beasts.

The *Bear & Ragged Staff* was lately the sign of an inn at Cumnor, Oxon, to which an historic interest is attached owing to its connexion with the dark tragedy of Amy Robsart, who it is said in this very house fell a victim to that stony-hearted adventurer, Robert Dudley, Earl of Leicester. Sir Walter Scott introduces the house in the first chapter of *Kenilworth*. There were formerly several houses of this name in East Anglia, far from the Warwick Estates. Other instances of this sign occur at Derby, Portsea, Romsey, and in London. Some of them may have dated from the suppression of Kett's Revolt by a royal Army under the Earl of Warwick. The heraldic designation of this sign has been better preserved than is the case of some others : only occasionally, as, for example, at Lower Bridge St., Chester, it has been altered into the *Bear & Billet*. Sometimes the sign of the *Bear & Ragged Staff* is jocularly spoken of as the *Angel & Flute*. The *Ragged Staff* figures also as a sign. A carriers' in West Smithfield possessed this sign in 1682. In the wall of a house at the corner of Little St Andrew St., and West St., St Giles, there is still a stone *bas-relief* sign of two ragged staves placed saltire-wise, with the initials S.F.G., and the date 1691. It was doubtless put there as a compliment to Robert Sidney, Earl of Leicester, who in the reign of Charles II built Leicester House, which gave a name to Leicester Fields, now the site of Leicester Square.

Equally well known with the last sign is that of the *Eagle & Child*, occasionally called the *Bird & Bantling*, or vulgarly the *Bird & Babby*, to obtain the favourite alliteration. This consists of an eagle hovering over a cradle which contains a tightly swathed baby. There are said to be eighteen houses of this name in Lancashire and there are others in London, at Conisborough, Yorks., Derby, Oxford, Sheffield, Stoke-on-Trent, etc. etc. Often they occur on Stanley estates. One at Norwich was established by the retired butler of Bishop Stanley of Norwich in 1849. The sign represents the crest of the Stanley family, which has an interesting legendary origin. In the reign of Edward III, Sir Thomas Lathom, ancestor of the house of Stanley and

* Act V, Sc. 1.

G

Derby, had only one legitimate child, a daughter named Isabel, but at the same time he had an illegitimate son by a certain Mary Oscatell. This child he ordered to be laid at the foot of a tree on which an eagle had built its nest. Taking a walk with his lady over the estate, he contrived to bring her past this place, pretended to find the boy, took him home, and finally prevailed upon her to adopt him as their son. This boy was afterwards called Sir Oscatell Latham, and considered the heir to the estates. Oscatell's daughter (or according to another account his half-sister) married Sir Thomas Stanley, and brought the Stanleys the Lathom estate, the legend and the crest.

The family of Culcheth also in Lancashire has arms of an infant in swaddling-clothes *proper* mantled *gules* swaddled in bands *or*, with an eagle standing upon it, with its wings expanded *sable* in a field *argent*. Taylor the Water Poet also names some instances of the sign among inns and taverns and particularly extols one at Manchester.

Another crest of the Derby family also occurs as a sign, namely, the *Eagle's Foot*, which was adopted in the 16th century by John Tysdall, a bookseller at the upper end of Lombard St., and which is found as an inn-sign in Lancashire. The frequency of eagles in heraldry made them very common on the signboard, although it is now impossible to say whose armorial bearings each particular eagle was intended to represent. It is fairly common on inn signs as an eagle displayed *sable*. There is an example at Epsom, and there was formerly one at Sutton Bonington, Notts., where it represented the armorial bearings of the Parkyns family, then lords of the manor.

Milton's father, a scrivener by trade, lived in Broad St., Cheapside, at the sign of the *Spread Eagle*, which was his own coat of arms, and in this house the author was born in 1608. The house was destroyed by the Fire of 1666. Perhaps its memory is preserved locally in Black Spread Eagle Court. Another *Spread Eagle* was a noted 'porter-house' in the Strand at the end of the 18th century—

> And to some noted porter-house repair :
> The several streets or one or more can claim
> Alike in goodness and alike in fame
> The Strand her Spreading Eagle justly boasts.
>
>   .   .   .   .   .
>
> Facing that street where Venus holds her reign,
> And Pleasure's daughters drag a life of pain,[*]

---

[*] Catherine St. in the Strand, full of bawdy houses in the 18th century.   Gay alludes to it in his *Trivia* :

> Oh, may thy virtue guard thee through the roads
> Of Drury's many courts and dark abodes.
> The harlot's guileful path, who nightly stand
> Where Catherine Street descends into the Strand.
> With empty bandbox she delights to range
> And feigns a distant errand from the 'Change
> Nay, she will oft the Quaker's hood profane
> And trudge demure the rounds of Drury Lane.

Tom Brown describes the wickedness of that part of the town. To this day Drury Lane cannot be called the most virtuous part of London.

There the Spread Eagle, with majestic grace
Shows his broad wings and notified the place.

. . . .

There let me dine in plenty and in quiet.*

The *Grasshoppers* on the London signboards were all descendants of Sir Thomas Gresham's sign and crest, which is still commemorated by the weather-vane on the Royal Exchange, of which he was the first founder. The original sign appears to have been preserved up to a very recent date.

† The shop of the great Sir Thomas Gresham, says Pennant, stood in this (Lombard) street : it is now occupied by Messrs Martin, bankers, who are still in possession of the original sign of that illustrious person—the Grasshopper. Were it mine that honourable memorial of so great a predecessor should certainly be placed in the most ostentatious situation I could find.

The ancients used the grasshopper as a talisman and grasshoppers in all sorts of human occupations were worn about the person to bring good luck. The grasshopper sign seems to have been a lucky one. According to the *Little London Directory* ‡ Charles Duncombe and Richard Kent, goldsmiths, lived at the *Grasshopper* in Lombard St. (no doubt Gresham's old house). They throve so well that Duncombe, later Sir Charles, and the richest commoner in England, gathered a fortune large enough to buy the Helmsley estate in Yorkshire from George Villiers, Duke of Buckingham. The land is now occupied by the Earl of Feversham under the name of Duncombe Park.

It is impossible to determine whether the *Maidenhead* was set up as a compliment to the Duke of Buckingham, to Catherine Parr, or to the Mercers' Company, for it is the crest of all three. The Mercers' crest is of course considerably the oldest. Amongst the badges of Henry VIII it is sometimes seen issuing out of the Tudor Rose :—

This combination does not appear to have been an entire new fancy, but to have been composed from the rose-badge of King Henry VIII, and from one previously used by the queen's family who had before this time assumed as one of their devises a maiden's head couped below the breast, vested in ermine and gold, the hair of the head and the temples encircled with a wreath of red and white roses : which badge they had derived from the family of Rose of Kendal.

This sign occurs occasionally as the *Maid's Head*, but since Queen Elizabeth's reign it has doubtless frequently referred to the virgin queen.

The *Cross Foxes*, that is, two foxes counter salient in saltire *gules*, is a common sign in some parts of England and Wales. It is the sign of the principal inn at Oswestry, Salop, of a house at Birkenhead, and of very many public-houses in North Wales, and has been adopted from the Williams element in the armorial bearings of the (Watkin) Williams-Wynns, a family holding extensive possessions in these parts.

* *Art of Living in London*, 1768.
† Pennant's *Account of London*, 1813, p. 618.　　　　　　　　　　　‡ 1677.

Guillim remarks upon this coat of arms, which he says belongs to the Kalrod Hard family of Wales :—

> These are somewhat unlike Samson's foxes that were tied together by the tails. They came into the field like to enemies, but they meant nothing less than fight, and therefore they pass by each other like two crafty lawyers, which come to the Bar as if they meant to fall out deadly about their clients' cause ; but when they have done, and their clients' purses are well spunged, they are better friends than ever they were, and laugh at those geese that find themselves foxbitten.

At Northwich, Altrincham, and Mobberly, Ches., there is a sign called the *Bleeding Wolf*, which is rarely found anywhere else. One explanation that can be offered for it is from the crest of Hugh of Avranches, surnamed Lupus, and of Richard, Earls of Chester. This was a wolf's head erased. The neck of the animal, being erased, may by primitive sign-painters have been represented less conventionally than is done now, and probably exhibited some of the torn parts, whence the name of the *Bleeding Wolf*. Another possible tradition is that it relates to the tradition that the last wolf in England was killed in Cheshire in 1746. A similar sign at Lawton, Cheshire, is taken from the crest of the Lawton's, a local family. There is another equally puzzling sign, peculiar to this county and to Lancashire—namely, the *Bear's Paw*. Of this sign, it must be confessed that we can offer no explanation ; it certainly looks heraldic, and lions' jambs erased are the crest of many families. A very old Latin sign is that of the *Cross Hands*, Little Sodbury, Glos., which bears the inscription 'Caivs Marius Imperator Concordia Militvm'. When the author last visited the house the licensee was unable to offer any suggestion as to the origin of the sign, but he readily agreed to the suggestion that probably it meant 'Free beer tomorrow'.

It is easy enough to explain the sign of *Parta Tueri*, 'To maintain acquired possessions', Cellarhead, Staffs., which is the motto of the (Powys) Barons Lilford. This is the only instance as yet met with of a family motto standing for a sign, though there is a *Duke's Motto* in Brick Lane, and in Essex a public-house sign representing a sort of Bacchic coat of arms with the motto *In Vino Veritas* may be seen. There is a similar sign at Abingdon, Berks. The *Oakley Arms* at Maidenhead, near Bray, deserves passing mention on account of some amusing verses connected with the place. These inform an inquirer who asks why the sign was not the *Vicar*, that the Vicar of Bray would undoubtedly prefer being inside the house to hanging near the door.

The *Wentworth Arms*, Kirby Mallory, Leics., may also be mentioned on account of its peculiar inscription, which has a strange moral air about it.

> May he who has little to spend, spend nothing in drink
> May he who has more than enough, keep it for better uses.
>
> May he who goes in to rest never remain to riot
> And he who fears God elsewhere never forget him here.

Other heraldic animals different from those just mentioned belong to so many various families, that it is utterly impossible to say in honour of whom they were first set up : such, for instance, is the *Griffin*, the armorial bearing of the Spencers (Marlborough), Spencer-Churchills, and innumerable other houses. Besides being an heraldic emblem the griffin was an animal in whose existence the early naturalists firmly believed. Its supposed eggs and claws were carefully preserved, and are frequently mentioned in ancient inventories and lists of curiosities.

In the original edition of the *Spectator*, No. 33, the *Griffin* is mentioned as the sign of a house in Sheer Lane, Temple Bar. It appears that John Crome was born at the *Griffin* in Norwich. There is a *Griffin* still at Danbury, Essex. The *Golden Griffin* was a famous tavern in Holborn issuing tokens in the 17th century. Tom Brown talks of a ' fat squab porter at the Griffin Tavern, in Fulwood's rents ', which is the same house as appears from Strype :—' At the upper end of this court is a passage into the Castle Tavern, a house of considerable trade, as is the Golden Griffin Tavern on the west side which has a passage into Fulwood's rents.'

The variously-coloured lions come under the same category of heraldic animals. Amongst them the *Golden Lion* stands foremost. A public-house with that sign in Fulham Rd. deserves notice. The old house was one of the most ancient in the district, having been built in the reign of Henry VII. The interior in Larwood's time was not much altered—the chimney-pieces in their original state, and in good preservation. Formerly there had been two staircases in the thick walls. Tradition says that the house once belonged to Bishop Bonner, and that it had subterranean passages communicating with the episcopal palace. When the old hostelry was pulled down in 1836, a tobacco-pipe of ancient and foreign fashion was found behind the wainscot. The stem was a crooked bamboo, and a brass ornament of an Elizabethan pattern formed the bowl of the pipe. This pipe an antiquary tried to identify as the property of Bishop Bonner, who on 15 June 1596 died suddenly at Fulham ' while sitting in his chair and smoking tobacco '. If the authority was right this inn should also have been honoured by the presence of Shakespeare, Fletcher, Henry Condell, Shakespeare's fellow actor, John Norden the topographer, Florio the translator of Montaigne, and divers other notabilities.

The *Blue Lion* is not common ; but there is a house of this sign in Gray's Inn Rd. It may possibly have been first put up at the marriage of James I with Anne of Denmark. The *Purple Lion* occurs but once—at Great Baddow, Essex. There is, or was, a sign of the *Green Lion* in Short St., Cambridge, which is almost or quite unique.

Signs borrowed from Corporation arms include the *Three Compasses,* a charge in the arms of both the carpenters and masons. This sign is a particular favourite in London, where in Larwood's time there were no less than twenty-one public-houses of this name. Perhaps this is partly owing to the compasses being a masonic emblem, and in the past a great many publicans worthy brethren. Frequently the sign of the compasses contains between the legs the good advice :—

Keep within compass
And then you'll be sure,
To avoid many troubles
That others endure.

The *Three Compasses*, in Pimlico, formerly a well-known starting-point for the Pimlico omnibuses, was once called the *Goat & Compasses*. The Wine-Coopers' Company of Cologne had a pair of compasses on their shield, and a couple of goats as supporters. So the sign may have been imported together with Rhenish wine.

Others have considered the sign a corruption of a puritanical phrase 'God encompasseth us'. But why may not the Goat have been the original sign to which the host added his masonic emblem in accordance with a practice still occasionally followed? The *Globe & Compasses* seems to have originated in the Joiner's arms, which are a chevron between two pairs of compasses and a globe. The *Three Goatsheads*, Wandsworth Rd., Lambeth, takes its sign from the Cordwainers' arms which are *azure* a chevron *or*, between three goats' heads, erased *argent*. Gradually the heraldic attributes have fallen away, the chevron has developed into a compass, and the goats' heads now alone remain. As there were rarely names under the London signs, the public unacquainted with heraldry gave a vernacular title to the objects represented. By way of exception it may be noted that the *Three Goats* found at Bury St Edmunds and in Lincolnshire is said to refer not to the animals but to gouts, that is, sluices.

The *Three Leopards' Heads* is given on a token as the name of a house in Bishopsgate, yet the tokens represent a chevron between three leopard's heads, the arms of the Weavers' Company. The sign of the *Leopard's Head* was anciently called the *Lubber's Head*. Similarly the *Three Lubberheads* is said to be the three leopard's heads which appear in the arms of the Goldsmiths. Thus in *King Henry IV* (Pt. II), the hostess says that Falstaff 'is invited to dinner at the Lubbar's Head in Lumbert Street, to Master Smooth's the silkman'. 'Libbard' *vulgo* 'lubber' is good Tudor English for 'leopard'. It is possible that the *Three Loggerheads* (p. 268), is in origin a corruption of this sign.

The *Green Man & Still* is a common sign. There is one in White Cross St. (the sign formerly represented a forester drinking 'drops of life' ★ from a glass barrel). The sign is still found also in Oxford St. This is a liberty taken with the Distillers' arms, which are 'a fess wavy in chief, the sun in splendour, in base a still, supporters two Indians with bows and arrows'. The Indians were transformed by the painters into wild men or green men, and the green men into foresters; and thus it was said that the sign originated from the partiality of foresters for the produce of the still. Monson Fitzjohn is probably quite wrong in thinking the sign is generally that of a herbalist.

The *Three Tuns* were derived from the Vintners', or the Brewers' Arms. On 9 May 1667 the *Three Tuns* in Seething Lane was the scene of a frightful tragedy

★ The 'drops of life' of course are *aqua vitæ*.

chronicled by Pepys. This seems to be a rather unlucky sign. In 1679 there was a murder * committed at the *Three Tuns* in Chandos St., and in this same house, Sally Pridden *alias* Sally Salisbury in a fit of jealousy stabbed the Hon. John Finch in 1723.

Sometimes the sign of the *One Tun* may also be seen. There is one at Saffron Hill. The sign also occurs in a newspaper advertisement of 1712, concerning four highwaymen drinking at the *One Tun* tavern near Hungerford Market in the Strand. Perhaps the sign may sometimes relate to the sale of ' entire ' since the usual *Three Tuns* covered houses selling ale, beer, and twopenny. The combined drink was invented by Harwood in 1722, so evidently this explanation will not cover at least one of the houses. Later ' entire ' was astutely re-christened ' porter ' to attract the custom of those thirsty souls, the London porters, and this name it retains to this day.

The *Golden Cup*, from the form in which it was generally represented, seems to have been derived from the Goldsmiths' arms, which are quarterly *azure* two leopards' heads *or* (whence the hall-mark), and two cups covered between two buckles *or*. It was a sign much fancied by booksellers from at any rate 1564 onwards, whilst the *Three Cups* was a famous carriers' inn in Aldersgate in the 17th century. There is a *Three Cups* still surviving at Colchester. The *Three Cups* appear also in the arms of the Salters. The *Ram's Head & Teazle*, Queensland St., Islington, is a part of the Clothworkers' arms, which are *sable* a chevron ermine between two habicks in chief *argent* and a teasel in base *or*. The crest is a ram *statant or* on a mount *vert*. The *Hammer & Crown* appears from a trades token to have been the sign of a shop in Gutter Lane in the 17th century. It was a charge from the Blacksmith's arms ; *sable* a chevron between three hammers crowned *or*. The *Lion in the Wood* was a tavern of some note about two centuries ago in Salisbury Court, Fleet St. It seems originally to have been the Woodmongers' arms, whose crest is a lion issuing from a wood. In Larwood's time it was the sign of a public-house, now no more, in the same Wilderness Lane, Dorset St. off Fleet St.

To these corporate arms we may add two belonging to a chartered trading company and to a friendly society. During the South Sea mania the *South Sea Arms* was a favourite sign. In 1718, the very year that Queen Anne had established the company and granted them arms, these appeared as the sign of a tavern near Austin Friars. They are a curious heraldic compound. *Azure* a globe representing the Straits of Magellan and Cape Horn, all *proper*. On a canton the arms of the United Kingdom of Great Britain, and in sinister chief two herrings saltirewise *argent* crowned *or*. The *Sol's Arms*, Sol's Row, Hampstead Rd., mentioned by Dickens in *Bleak House*, derives its name from the Sol's Society, who were a kind of convivial and friendly society imitating the freemasons. They used to hold their meetings at the *Queen of Bohemia's Head*, Drury Lane, but on the pulling down of that house the society was dissolved.

* *London Gazette*, 15–18 September 1679.

Chapter V

AN ALPHABETICAL TABLE OF SOME COMMON HERALDIC AND SYMBOLIC SIGNS

EVEN less than the other parts of our work does this section make any profession of completeness. Heraldic signs of one kind or another are perhaps the most numerous of all classes of inn sign. Probably even a bare hand-list of the heraldic signs in the country would fill a volume the size of this one. More than any other class of signs too these tend to be localized in particular areas, so that very few of the heraldic signs common, for example, in Northumberland will be found also in Dorset, or if they are they probably represent quite different families. This is of course because the signs are mainly found on or near the estates of the families commemorated. Below we give an alphabetical table of a few heraldic signs which are worth attention because they are very common, or because they are unique or almost so, because they are associated with particularly famous houses, or because they commemorate families now extinct in the places concerned. We have included among the heraldic signs a few of the commoner symbolic ones. The reader who is anxious to investigate signs of these two classes in his own area will find for the one class much help in any good dictionary of symbolism, or any of the standard books on emblems. Signs in the other group may usually be identified by reference to the county histories, and any available 'Visitations' of the county concerned, with such standard works of reference as Debrett, Fox Davies' *Armorial Families*, Burke's *General Armoury*, the *Book of Corporate Arms*, and a good *Ordinary*, say Papworth's. The arms of various city companies, the armorial and pseudo-armorial bearings of many English counties and boroughs, and the badges of many ships and regiments may supply the answers to some very puzzling signboard questions.

THE ROYAL ARMS OF ENGLAND

The history of the royal arms of England may be followed in any good book upon heraldry. The 'Supporters' varied from reign to reign until James I's time, and the royal badges also varied considerably :—

Supporters	*Badge*
H.M. the King : Lion and Unicorn.	Imperial Crown.
	Royal Cipher.
	Garter.
	Ostrich Feather *arg.* pen *or.*

Also of course, the Tudor Rose, the Thistle, the Harp, the Shamrock Leaf and the Red Dragon, and the badges of the Duchy of Lancaster (the Red Lion, the Red Rose, the Royal Arms with a label of three points, the Ostrich feather *arg.* penned *erm.*, the portcullis, etc.).

H.R.H. the Prince of Wales :—

Lion and Unicorn differenced with labels of three points, Ostrich Plume all *arg.*, Red Dragon with label.

Also, of course, the badges of the Duchy of Cornwall and the Earldom of Chester, etc. These have developed from the time of :—

Edward I :	Rose *or* stalk *vert.*
Edward II :	(?)
Edward III :	(Dragon *gu.* ?) Lion rampant *ppr.* armed *az.* langued *or*, Ostrich feather *or* pen *or*, Falcon *ppr.*, Swan *arg.* (p. 72), Sun rising.
(Queen Philippa of Hainault) :	Hind *arg.*, Lion *sa.*
(Black Prince) :	Swan and Maidenhead (p. 71).
(Edmund of Langley, Duke of York) :	Falcon *arg.* fetterlock *or.*
(John of Gaunt, Duke of Lancaster) :	Red Lion (from his wife Constance of Leon ? p. 95).
Richard I :	Two angels blowing trumpets, Hart *arg.* armed horned crowned *or.*
(Henry Duke of Lancaster) :	Rose *gu.* uncrowned, Ostrich feather and foxtail as below.
The House of Lancaster generally :	Portcullis. Rose *gu.* (from Duke Henry), Ostrich feather *arg.* pen *ermine*, Fox tail *ppr.*
The House of York generally :	Falcon and fetterlock, Bull and fetterlock, Rose *arg.* (from escheated earldom of Clifford, Dragon *sa.* (from Mortimer earldom of Ulster), Bull *sa.* horned and clayed *or* (from Duchy of Clarence), Hind *arg.* (from Joan Plantagenet the Fair Maid of Kent, Lion *arg.* (from Earldom of March).

Supporters	*Badge*
Henry IV : Swan *arg.*, Antelope *or.*	Swan *arg.*, Antelope *or.*
Henry V : Lion and antelope.	Antelope, armed crowned, spotted and horned *or*, Rose *gu.* uncrowned.
	Swan *arg.* crowned and collared *or* (from Earldom of Hertford).
Henry VI : Two antelopes.	As for Henry V.
(Cicely Neville : Duchess of York) :	Swan *arg.*
(Richard Duke of York) :	Boar *az.*
Edward IV : Lion and bull.	Lion *rampant arg.*
	Rose *arg.*
	Bull uncrowned *sa.*
Edward V :	Lion and Hind (Woodville badge).
Richard III : Two boars.	Boar *passant arg.*
(Queen Anne Neville) :	Rose *arg.* clayed *or*, Boar *arg.*
Henry VII : Dragon and greyhound.	Hawthorn tree *vert.*
	Portcullis.
	Tudor rose crowned.

Supporters	*Badge*
Henry VIII : Lion and dragon.	Antelope.
	Portcullis.
	Tudor rose crowned.
(In Catherine of Aragon's time) :	Rose dimidiated with pomegranate. Castle (of Castille) and Sheaf of arrows (of Granada).
and Anne Boleyn :	Falcon *arg.* crowned and sceptred *or.*
and Jane Seymour :	Demiphoenix ?
and Catherine Howard :	?
and Catherine Parr :	Castle and Falcon.
Edward VI : Lion and Dragon.	Phoenix in flames, later granted also Ostrich Feather *pen* and all *arg.* (to Seymour family). Cannon (p. 71) (and other Tudor badges ?).
Mary I : Eagle and Lion.	Marigold, Cannon (and other Tudor badges).
	Cannon.
Elizabeth : Lion and Dragon.	Falcon *arg.* as for Anne Boleyn. Welsh dragon (and other Tudor badges).
James I : Lion and Unicorn.	Scottish lion. Three Crowns ? Tudor rose or separate roses of Lancaster and York, often charged on Sunbeam. Other Tudor badges. Various royalist and Jacobite badges are dealt with separately in the text—the *Royal Oak, Raven, Black Boy, Oak and Crown,* etc.
From the time of James I the Supporters have been invariably the lion and Unicorn.	The only Georgian badge often found is the horse (courant *arg.*), the galloping *White Horse* of Hanover.

In the alphabetical table below the figures are sometimes the charges in armorial bearings, sometimes crests, sometimes supporters and occasionally badges which by long usage have been borne by the families concerned.

Adam and Eve :	Fruiterers' Company.
Anchor :	General nautical symbol. Lord High Admiral of England, hence Lords Commissioners of Admiralty. St Clement. General symbol of hope (see p. 52).
Angel :	Our Lady (from the Salutation). St Matthew.
(Red) *Antelope* :	(Russell) Earls and Dukes of Bedford.
(Gold) *Antelope* :	Henry IV and Henry VI.
Apollo in his Glory :	(Glorious Apollo) Company of Apothecaries.
Axe and Cleaver :	Butchers' Company.
Axe and Compass :	Carpenters' Company.
Bear (*sejeant* with ragged staff *arg.* muzzled *gu.*) :	(Neville) Earls of Warwick.
Bear and Ragged Staff :	(Neville) Earls of Warwick and (Dudley) Earls of Leicester.
Bell (Holborn) :	Crest of Sir Ralph Griggs, who formerly lived there.
Bird in Hand :	Sometimes falcon on gauntlet for ?
Bible and Three Crowns :	University of Oxford.
Black Bear :	(Dudley) Earls of Warwick.

Blackbird :	Perhaps properly *Raven*—Jacobite symbol.
Black Bull :	(armed *or*) House of Clarence.
Black Cross :	Teutonic Knights.
Black Dragon :	(Boleyn) Earls of Wiltshire.
Black Dragon :	(Clifford) Barons Clifford of Westmorland.
Black Eagle :	(Norris) Barons Norris of Ryecote or (Bertie) Barons Norreys.
Black Lion :	Queen Philippa—Consort of Edward III. Owen Glendower (Owain ab Gruffydd).
Black Raven :	King of Scots ; hence House of Stuart and Jacobites.
Black Staff :	(Grey) Earls and Dukes of Kent.
Bleeding Heart :	Five Mysteries of Rosary, (Douglas) Earls of Douglas.
Bleeding Wolf :	Hugh Lupus, Earl of Chester, hence several Cheshire families.
' *Blue* ' :	Signs in general. Whiggery as opposed to the scarlet of royalism. Truth and fidelity since blue is a ' permanent ' colour.
Blue Boar :	(With a mullet) (de Vere) Earls of Oxford (see p. 70).
Blue Lion :	Royal House of Denmark, especially Queen Anne, consort of James I.
Blue Plume :	(Scrope) Barons Scrope of Bolton.
Boar's Head :	Perhaps sometimes heraldic, as, for example, from the three Boars' Heads of the Gordons.
Broad Arrow :	H.M. Government—commonly explained as from the arms of Sidney, *or* a pheon *az.* the mark being generally adopted in the time of Henry Sidney, Earl of Romney, Master of Ordnance 1693–1702.
Buck in the Park :	County Borough of Derby.
Bull, and Bull's Head :	See *Dun Bull, White Bull, Red Bull,* etc.
Bull :	St Luke. (His symbol is properly an ox.) ? sometime monastic (from *bulla*)—the seal of the (abbot's) licence. Richard Duke of York and hence the House of York generally.
Bull and Stirrup :	i.e. Bull and Fetterlock, combination of two Yorkist signs.
Bull and Swan :	Possibly Yorkist, since both Bull and Swan are Yorkist badges.
Bull's Head :	Henry VIII.
	ppr. (Neville) Marquesses of Abergavenny (who had also bulls *ppr.* as supporters).
(White) *Butterfly* :	(Audley or Touchet ?) Barons Audley.
Cardinals Cap :	Thomas Wolsey, Cardinal and Archbishop of York.
Castle :	Castile—hence indicating sale of Spanish wines. Often it refers however only to a local manor house.
Castle and Falcon :	Queen Catherine Parr, Consort of Henry VIII.
Catamount :	(Penington) Barons Muncaster.

Catamount and Leopard :	(? Panther and Wyvern ?) (Beaufort) Dukes of Somerset and Marquesses of Worcester. (Sackville) Barons Sackville, Barons Buckhurst, and Earls and Dukes of Dorset.
Catherine Wheel :	(Lathe Wheel) Turners' Company.
Chequers :	Checky *or* and *az.*—Warrenne. One of quarterings of (Howard) Dukes of Norfolk and Earls of Surrey (see also p. 97).
Chough :	? Originally Raven. Royalist symbol.
Cock :	(Republican) France. Often used for a cock-fighting house.
Cock and Trumpet :	(Acheson) Earls of Gosford (p. 135).
(Wool) Comb :	Bishop Blaize, hence Woolcombers generally.
Crescent :	See *Half Moon.*
Cresset with Burning Fire :	Edward IV. The Admiralty.
Crooked Billet :	(See pp. 294–5.)
Cross :	The Christian faith and such ecclesiastics as Archbishops, Bishops and Abbots.
(Maltese) Cross :	Knights of St John (as at the *Cross House,* now the *White Horse,* Dorking).
(St Julian's) Cross :	Knights of St Julian. Innholders' Company. See also *White Cross, Red Cross, Green Cross,* etc.
Cross Daggers :	(Hallamshire) Cutlers' Company.
Cross Foxes :	(*Arg.* two foxes counter salient in saltire *gu.*) Williams quartering of Watkin-Williams-Wynn family of Wynnstay.
Cross Keys :	St Peter. The Papacy. Any abbey, diocese, or church with a Peter dedication, especially the dioceses of York, Exeter, Gloucester, and Peterborough.
Crossed Swords :	Corruption of *Cross Daggers, q.v.*
Cross in the Oak :	Combination of two Royalist or Jacobite Symbols.
Crown and Glove :	Dymoke Family of Scrivelsby, Lincs. (the Champions of England).
Crown and Harp :	(Formerly) Kingdom of Ireland.
Crown and Thistle :	Kingdom of Scotland.
Dolphin :	Watermen's Company. Also (French) Dauphin or Crown Prince.
Dove :	Stationers' Company.
Dun Bull :	(Neville) Barons Abergavenny. (Neville) Barons Latimer. (Neville) Barons Neville and Earls of Westmorland. (Wriothesley) Barons Wriothesley and Earls of Southampton.
Eagle :	St John the Evangelist. (Hamilton) Dukes of Hamilton and Earls of Cambridge.
Eagle and Child :	(Lancashire) Lathom Family and hence (Stanley) Earls of Derby, also certain other Lancashire families such as the Culcheths.

(Russet) *Eagle and* (Crowned) *Maidenhead* :	Honour of Conisborough.
Eagle :	See also *Spread Eagle*.
Eagle's Foot :	(Stanley) Earls of Derby.
Elephant :	Sir Francis Knollys.
Falcon :	Queen Elizabeth. Stationers' Company. (Paulet) Marquesses of Winchester. (Armed and collared) (St John) Barons St John of Bletso, (Zouche) Barons Zouche. See also *White Falcon*, etc.
Falcon and Fetterlock :	House of York, also Henry VIII as descendant of Edmund of Langley (pp. 70 and 90).
Feathers :	See *Plume*.
Fetterlock :	(De la Pole, Brandon, or Howard ?) Dukes and Earls of Suffolk.
Fifteen Balls :	See *Fifteen Roundels*.
Fifteen Roundels :	County of Cornwall.
Five Lions :	City of York.
Fire Beacon :	See *Cresset*.
Fleur de Lis : *Flower de Luce* :	(Properly Three Flowers.) Kings of France.
Flower Pot :	The Vase of Lilies—Our Lady.
Flying Horse :	See *Pegasus*.
Fool's Head :	(Grenville ?) Earls of Bath.
Fountain :	Stourton of Stourton, Wilts.
Four Crosses :	Diocese of Lichfield. (Note anciently including in addition to its present area, Derbyshire, Cheshire, southern Lancashire, north Warwickshire and part of Worcestershire.)
Four Lions :	University of Cambridge.
Fox and Goose :	Perhaps indicating the provision of facilities for gaming—Goldsmith's ' Royal Game of Goose '.
French Horn and Three Tuns :	(See p. 32.)
Globe :	Portugal—hence indicating sale of Portuguese wines. South Sea Company.
(White) *Goat* :	(Russell) Earls and Dukes of Bedford.
Goat and Compasses :	Wine-Coopers' Company of Cologne.
Goat's Head (and *Goat*) :	(Bagot) Barons Bagot.
Golden Anchor :	Lord High Admiral of England, and hence Lords Commissioners of Admiralty.
(Three) *Golden Balls* :	St Nicholas. (Florentine) Medici Family and (hence ?) pawnbrokers generally.
Golden Cup :	Goldsmiths' Company.
Golden He(a)rt :	Our Lady.
Grasshopper :	Sir Thomas Gresham.
Green Cross :	Knights of St Lazarus.
Green Dragon :	(Herbert) Earls of Pembroke.
Green Lion with Two Tails :	(Dudley) Earls of Leicester.
Green Man and Still :	Probably Indians and Still, for Distillers' Company.
Greyhound(s) :	(Clinton) Barons Clinton, and (Pelham Clinton) Dukes of Newcastle.

Greyhound's Head :	(Rich) Barons Rich and Earls of Warwick.
Griffin (passant) :	(Wentworth Fitzwilliam) Earls Fitzwilliam.
Griffin (rampant) :	(Collared *gu.* and *az.*) (Wentworth) Barons Wentworth.
Griffin's Head (gu.) :	(Spencer Churchill) Dukes of Marlborough.
Gripe's Foot :	Same as *Eagle's Foot* for (Stanley) Earls of Derby.
Half Eagle and Key :	City of Geneva.
Half Moon, i.e. Crescent :	(Percy) Earls of Northumberland. ' ye Temporalati ' (Templars ?).
Hammer and Crown :	Blacksmiths' Company.
Hand :	(Perhaps symbolical of papal hand raised in blessing.) See also *Red Hand*.
Hand in Hand :	(Dorset) Cheverell Family, and corruption of *Salutation*.
Harp and Crown :	(Properly *az.* a harp *or* stringed *arg.*) the (former) Kingdom of Ireland.
Hedgehog :	(Sidney, hence Barons de l'Isle and Dudley.)
(Two) Herrings :	Barons Scales.
Hind :	Sir Christopher Hatton.
Key and Castle :	12th Suffolk Regiment.
Lamb :	Symbol of innocence, said to be found often in old monastic inns. St Agnes.
Lamb and Anchor :	Mystical symbol of hope in Our Lord.
Lamb and Flag :	Agnus Dei—symbol of Our Lord. Merchant Taylor's Company. St John's College, Oxford.
Leather Bottle :	Bottlemakers' Company. Horners' Company.
Leek :	Principality of Wales.
Legs of Man :	See *Three Legs*.
(Winged) Lion :	Symbol of St Mark.
Lion :	See also *Red Lion, White Lion, Golden Lion,* etc.
Lion and Castle :	Leon and Castile, i.e. Spain.
Lion and Key :	? Symbolizing Ciudad Rodrigo ?
Magpie :	See *Pye*.
Maidenhead :	Queen Catherine Parr. (Villiers) Dukes of Buckingham. Mercers' Company.
Marigold :	Symbol of Queen Mary I.
Mill Sails :	See *Windmill*.
Mitre :	(Some) Abbots, (all) Archbishops and Bishops.
Moon :	Symbol of the Church (Our Lord being the Sun), also of eternity for ' when most declined she renews again ', and (because of her changes) of inconstancy and fickleness.
Oak :	Symbol of strength, constancy and long life.
Oak and Black Dog :	Anti-Royalist symbol (see p. 131).
Olive Leaf :} *Olive Tree* :}	Symbol of peace and concord.
Ostrich Feathers :	(As set forth above, p. 89.) H.M. the King, H.R.H. the Prince of Wales and the (Seymour) Dukes of Somerset.)

Owl :	Emblem of prudence, vigilance, watchfulness and wisdom.
Ox :	St Luke.
Peacock :	Symbol of the Resurrection. (Manners) Earls and Dukes of Rutland.
Pegasus :	(Cromwell) Barons Cromwell. Inner Temple.
Pelican :	Symbol of Our Lord. Emblem of parenthood.
Phoenix :	Symbol of Our Lord. Emblem of immortality. Chemical symbol of rebirth and renewal. (Seymour) Dukes of Somerset. Matthew Parker, Archbishop of Canterbury.
Pinetree :	Emblem of death (since once cut it never sprouts again.
Plough :	Emblem of abundance and fertility, and of agriculture generally.
(White) *Plume of Feathers :*	H.R.H. The Prince of Wales. (Clinton) Earls of Lincoln, and (Pelham Clinton) Dukes of Newcastle. See also *Blue Plume.*
(Crowned) *Pomegranate :*	Emblem of royalty.
Pomegranate :	Symbol of populousness and of friendship.
Portcullis :	Beaufort Family, hence House of Lancaster, and Kings of England as Dukes of Lancaster. Henry VII and Henry VIII (from Beauforts). (Somerset) Dukes of Beaufort and Earls and Marquesses of Worcester.
Pye :	(Savage) Earls Rivers.
(White) *Ragged Staff :*	(Neville, Dudley, and Greville) Earls of Warwick.
(Black) *Ragged Staff :*	(Neville) Earls of Kent.
Rainbow :	Emblem of Hope. Dyers' Company.
Ram :	(As first Sign of Zodiac) Emblem of fruitfulness.
Ram and Teasel :	Clothworkers' Company.
Raven :	(Shropshire) Corbet Family.
Raven :	See *Black Raven* and *White Raven.*
Red Bull's Head (erased) :	(Ogle) Barons Ogle.
Red Cross : (*arg.* a cross of St George *gu.*) :	Knights Templar. St George. Kingdom of England (from time of Edward I).
Red Dragon :	West Saxons. Cadwaladr, son of Gruffnd ap Cynan, hence Principality of Wales and House of Tudor. (Clifford) Barons Clifford and Westmorland and Earls of Cumberland.
Red Fox :	Richard Fox, Bishop of Winchester.
Red Hand :	Province of Ulster and Order of Baronets.
Red Horse :	See *Roan Horse.*
Red Lion :	(Rampant in a treasure) Kingdom of Scotland (as at Martlesham, Suff.). County of Holland? (Russell) Dukes of Bedford. John of Gaunt, Duke of Lancaster as pretender, through his wife Constance, to throne of Leon.
Red Rose :	House, County Palatine, and Duchy of Lancaster.

Rising Sun (Sun in Splendour) :	House of York. Spirituality generally. Distillers' Company.
Roan Horse :	Pedro of Castille, father-in-law of John of Gaunt.
Rose :	Emblem of Our Lady. Emblem of Silence—hence Jacobite symbol. Badge of Queen Catherine Parr (from Ros Family of Kendal). Alehouse symbol generally (see pp. 75–6).
Rose and Crown :	Henry VII and Henry VIII.
Rose and Maidenhead :	King Henry VIII and Queen Catherine Parr.
Rose and Sunbeam :	Lord Warden of Cinque Ports.
(Collar of) *Roses and Suns* :	Edward IV and House of York.
Salamander :	Symbol of constancy.
Salt Cellar :	Salters' Company.
Sceptre :	Symbol of kingship and of justice.
Serpent :	Symbol of cunning, of wisdom, of health and of good fortune.
Serpent and Cross :	Or Serpent and Christ (according to Randle Home, 'the cognizance of every true believer'.
Shamrock :	The Holy Trinity. St Patrick, hence Ireland.
Silver Lion, etc. :	See *White Lion*, etc.
Ship and Castle :	City of Bristol.
Snake :	See *Serpent*.
Spearhead :	(Herbert) Earls of Pembroke.
Spread Eagle :	Holy Roman Emperors (hence indicating sale of German wines), Kings of Poland, Margraves of Brandenburg (later Kings of Prussia), and Czars of Russia. Many English families, for example, (Brown) Viscounts Montague and (Nottinghamshire) Parkyns family.
Staff :	(See White) *Ragged Staff*, (Black) Ragged Staff.
Staffordshire Knot :	County of Stafford.
Star :	Emblem of Our Lady (Stella Maris). Symbol of prudence, also of welcome, hence often found on monastic inns. (Radcliffe) Earls of Essex, and Viscounts and Baron Fitzwalter.
Stork :	Emblem of sonship.
Sun and Roses :	See *Roses and Suns*.
Sun in Splendour :	See *Rising Sun*.
Swan :	Emblem of innocence.
(gorged) :	King Henry IV, Henry Duke of Gloucester, (Carey) Barons Hunsdon.
Three Maidenheads :	See of Oxford.
Three Pelicans :	(Chichester and elsewhere), (Pelham) Barons Pelham (Pelham) Earls of Chichester, and (Pelham Clinton) Dukes of Newcastle.
Three Suns :	Brewers' Company. Vintners' Company.
Tiger's Head :	Sir Francis Walsingham.
(White) *Unicorn* :	Symbol of Our Lord. Emblem of virginity. Company of Apothecaries (see p. 103).

Wheatsheaf :	(Cecil) Earls of Burleigh. Bakers' Company. Brewers' Company (? Barleysheaf). Innholders' Company (same !).
White Bear :	Queen Anne Neville, consort of Richard III (p. 89). (Grey) Earls of Kent.
White Boar :	Richard III. (Windsor) Barons Windsor.
White Bull's Head (erased) :	(Wharton) Barons Wharton.
White Butterfly :	See *Butterfly*.
White Cross :	Knights of St. John.
White Falcon :	(Strictly speaking a demi falcon *ppr.*) Queen Anne Boleyn, Consort of Henry VIII.
White Hart :	Richard II. Sir Walter Raleigh.
White Horse :	Saxons generally. Kings of Kent and Wessex. Electors (later Kings) of Hanover.
(passant or rampant) with an acorn slipped in his mouth :	Duke of Norfolk as Earl of Arundel.
White Lion : *rampant* or *passant* :	Edward IV.
(*rampant*) :	(Howard) Dukes of Norfolk and all other Howards.
(*rampant*) :	(ducally collared *or*) (Herbert) Earls of Pembroke.
(*statant*) :	(Percy) Earls and Dukes of Northumberland.
(*passant*) :	(Mortimer) Earls of March, hence House of York.
White Ragged Staff :	See *Ragged Staff*.
White Raven :	(Neville) Earls of Cumberland, and (Clifford) Earls of Cumberland and Westmorland.
White Rose :	County and Duchy of York.
White Swan :	Edward III and Edward IV.
White Unicorn :	See *Unicorn*.
Wild Cat :	See *Catamount*.
Windmill Sails (Verney) :	Barons Willoughby de Broke.
Wounded Heart :	See *Bleeding Heart*.

H

Chapter VI

SIGNS OF ANIMALS AND MONSTERS

ANIMAL signs form perhaps the largest class of inn signs. Perhaps the most comprehensive of them is the *Zoological Hall*. It is in many cases impossible to draw a line of demarcation between signs borrowed from the animal kingdom, and those taken from heraldry : we cannot now determine, for instance, whether by the *White Horse* is meant simply an ordinary hack, the White Horse of the Saxons, or that of the House of Hanover ; nor whether the *White Greyhound* represented originally the supporter of the arms of Henry VII, or simply the greyhound used in the favourite sport of coursing. For this reason this chapter has been placed as a sequel to that on heraldic signs.

As a rule, fantastically coloured animals are unquestionably of heraldic origin : they are generally limited to the Lion, the Boar, the Hart, the Dog, the Cat, the Bear, and in a few instances the Bull ; all other animals are generally represented in what is meant for their natural colours. The heraldic lions have already been treated of in the last chapter ; but sometimes we meet with the lion in a natural form, recognizable by such names as the *Brown Lion* as at Watergates, Salop, the *Yellow Lion*, or simply the *Lion*. There is a public-house in Philadelphia, Durham, with the sign of the *Lion* having underneath the following lines :

> The lion roars, but do not fear
> Cakes and beer sold here,

and a *British Lion* at Ipswich.

Lions occur in numerous combinations with other animals and objects, which in many cases seem simply the union of two signs as the *Lion & Dolphin* at Leicester, and the *Lion & Tun* at Congleton. The *Lion & Swan* in the same locality may owe its joint title to the name of the street in which the public-house is situated, namely, Swan Bank. The *Lion & Mouse* no doubt owes its sign to one of Æsop's Fables. The combination of the *Lion & Pheasant*, Wylecop, Shrewsbury, and formerly at Broseley not far away seems rather mysterious unless the Pheasant has been substituted for the Cock, just as in the *Three Pheasants & Sceptre* the pheasants were substituted for the pigeons in the *Three Pigeons & Sceptre*. It has been suggested that this might be a corruption of *Dog & Pheasant*, but this is hardly likely since changes on the sign-board are usually from the unfamiliar to the familiar and that is *vice versa*. The *Cock & Lion*, once a common sign, is often in respect of the old fable that

> The lyon dreadeth the white cocke, because he breedeth a precious stone called allec-tricium, like to the stone that hight Calcedonius,

(and, of course, particularly deadly to lions). The magic stone was never greater in size than a bean. When taken by gladiators it relieved their thirst, and rendered them invincible !

The *Lion & Ball* owes its origin to another mediæval notion—

> that those who robe the tiger of her young use a policy to detaine their damme from following them, by casting sundry looking-glasses in the way, whereat she useth to long to gaze, whether it be to beholde her owne beauty or because when she seeth her shape in the glasse she thinketh she seeth one of her young ones, and so they escape the swiftness of her pursuit.

The looking-glass thrown to the tiger was spherical, so that she could see her own image reduced as it rolled under her paw, and would therefore be more likely to mistake it for her cub. The words lion and tiger being almost synonymous in mediæval zoology the spherical glass was generally represented with either. In sculpture it could only be represented by a ball, which afterwards became a terrestrial globe, and the lion resting his paw upon it, passed into an emblem of royalty.

The origin of the *Lion & Unicorn* at Brighton is of course heraldic. In the 18th century an innkeeper at Goodwood put up as his sign the *Centurion's Lion*, the figurehead of the frigate *Centurion*, in which Admiral Anson made a voyage round the world. Under it was the following inscription :—

> Stay, Traveller, a while and view
> One that has travelled more than you,
> Quite round the Globe in each Degree,
> Anson and I have plowed the Sea ;
> Torrid and Frigid Zones have pass'd,
> And safe ashore arriv'd at last.
> In Ease and Dignity appear
> He—in the House of Lords, I—here.

When Anson was in general disfavour about the Minorca affair, a somewhat biting reply to this inscription went the round of the newspapers. The interested reader will find it in full in the original *Larwood*.

The *Tiger* is of rare occurrence on signboards ; there is a house, however, with a naturalistic tiger, not a heraldic one as its sign at Camberwell Green, S.E., and there is a *Golden Tiger* in Pilgrim St., Newcastle. In 1665 there was a *Leopard* in Chancery Lane ; the same animal is still occasionally seen on public-house signs ; there is one at Bristol, and one at Burslem, Stoke-on-Trent.

Generally speaking, the carnivorous animals are not great favourites, and those named above are almost the only examples that occur. As for the popularity of the *Bear*, it is largely to be attributed to the old vulgar pleasure of seeing him ill-treated in the once common amusements of bear-baiting and whipping. The colours in which he is represented are the *Black Bear*, the *Brown Bear*, the *White Bear*, and in a very few instances (as at Leeds) the *Red Bear*. Perhaps sometimes the sign may refer to the constellation rather than the animal. Besides bear-whipping and bear-baiting, another barbarous fancy led sometimes to the choice of this animal for a sign—the lamentable pun which the publican made upon the article he sold, and the name of the animal. Thomas Dawson of Leeds perpetrated this pun on his token dated 1670 ; it says—*Beware of ye Beare*, evidently alluding to the strength of his beer.

Bears used often to be represented with chains round their neck (as on the stone sign in Addle St., with the date 1610), and the story of the chained bull (below, p. 119) is sometimes ascribed to the bear.

Among the most famous *Bear* inns and taverns were—the *Bear* ' at Bridgefoot ', that is, at the foot of London Bridge, on the Southwark side, for many centuries one of the most popular London taverns. As early as the reign of Richard III we find it the resort of the aristocratic pleasure-seeker. Probably the first part of the sign has reference to the neighbouring bear gardens. Thus in March 1464 it was repeatedly visited by Jockey of Norfolk, the then Sir John Howard who went there to drink wine and shoot at the target, at which he lost twenty pence. It was also frequently named by the writers of the 17th century. Pepys mentions it 3 April 1667. A 17th-century joke about it was to the effect that it was ' the first house in Southwark built after the flood '. When this old tavern was pulled down in 1761, at the removal of the houses from London Bridge, the workmen found several pieces of gold and silver coin of Queen Elizabeth, and other money to a considerable value.

There was another famous *Bear* at the foot of Strandbridge : the vicinity of the Bear and Paris Gardens had evidently suggested the choice of those signs. At the *Bear* in the Strand, the earliest meetings of the Society of Antiquaries took place. Subsequently they met at the *Young Devil* in Fleet St. and then at the *Fountain*, opposite Chancery Lane.

There was a *White Bear* in Thames St. of which the sign is still extant, a stone bas-relief with the date 1670, and the initials M. E. In King Edward VI's time, the French ambassadors after they had supped with the Duke of Somerset went to the Thames, and saw the bear hunted in the river. Such an incident as this might easily lead to the adoption of this animal as a sign in that locality. It is possible also that the *White Bear* was set up in compliment to Richard III's queen, Anne, daughter of the Earl of Warwick, who as a difference from her father's bear and ragged staff, had adopted as a badge the *White Bear*. In 1656, John Wardell gave by will to the Grocers' Company a tenement called the *White Bear* in Walbrook, upon condition that they should yearly pay to the churchwardens of St Botolph's, Billingsgate, £4 to provide a lantern with a candle, so that passengers might go with more security to and from the waterside during the night. The annuity in Larwood's time was still applied to a lamp lighted with gas in the place prescribed by the will.

The *White Bear* at the east end of Piccadilly was for more than a century one of the busiest coaching-houses. In this house died Luke Sullivan, engraver of some of Hogarth's works, also Chatelain, another engraver. It was in this inn that West passed the first night in London on his arrival from America. The sign of this *White Bear* (?) may still be seen near Croydon in a cottage garden at Fickle's Vale. The sign of the *White Bear* is still common ; at Springbank, Hull, there is a house called with zoological precision, the *Polar Bear*. This may however refer to the constellation.

The *Bear's Head* occurs in Congleton, Ches. ; probably like the *Bear's Paw* it is a family crest. Both of these it is believed occur only in Cheshire and in Lancashire. There is another *Bear's Head* and a *Bear's Paw* at Liverpool. The Bear is also met in frequent combinations : the *Bear & Bells* is at Beccles, Suff. Presumably dancing bears were decorated with small bells in their collars. One of the most common, as, for example, at Warwick and Southwark, is the *Bear & Bacchus*, which looks like a hieroglyphic rendering of the words *Beer & Wine*, having the additional attraction of alliteration. Since mythology does not mention a Beer-God, the animal was probably chosen as a rebus for the drink. Or the Bacchus may be really *baculus*—a rough staff, so that the name is a variant of the *Bear & Ragged Staff*. It so appears at Warwick, where the sign is *Bear & Baculus*. The *Bear & Billet* in Chester also is presumably a variant of the *Bear & Ragged Staff*. Presumably the *Bear* at Wantage, Berks., has originally been a *Bear & Bacchus*. At any rate the bear in the sign still carries a bunch of grapes in his mouth. In the *Bear & Rummer*, Mortimer St., the *Rummer* implies the sale of liquors in the same manner as the *Punchbowl* is often used. The *Bear & Harrow* seems to be a union of two signs. In the 17th century it formed the house-decoration of an ordinary at the entrance of Butcher Row (now Picket St., Strand). One night in 1692 Nat Lee the mad poet, in going home drunk from this house, fell down in the snow and was stifled.

The *Elephant* in the Middle Ages was nearly always represented with the castle, that is, the houdah, on his back, and so appears thus in inn signs, though there is an *Elephant* without a castle at Doncaster. In this form too he is found in early chess-men.

Cutlers in the 18th century frequently used the *Elephant & Castle* as their sign, on account of it being the crest of the Cutlers' Company, who had adopted it in reference to the ivory used in the trade. Hence the stone bas-relief in Bell-Sauvage Yard, which was the sign of some now-forgotten shopkeeper, who had chosen it out of regard to his landlords. The houses in the yard were the property of the Cutlers' Company. The *Elephant & Castle* public-house, Newington Butts, was formerly a famous coaching inn, but on the introduction of railways it dwindled down to a starting-point for buses. Concerning this Larwood tells a not very convincing story :—About 1714, an apothecary in Fleet St., a great collector of antiquities, was digging in a gravel-pit in a field near the Fleet, when he discovered the skeleton of an elephant and near it a spear with a flint head, fixed to a shaft of goodly length, whence the antiquaries of the time conjectured it to have been killed by the British in a fight with the Romans. ' The incident gave a name to the house, though, regardless of the venerable antiquity of its origin, it is often nowadays jocularly degraded into the *Pig & Tinder-Box*.'

What is meant by the whimsical combination of the *Elephant & Fish*, at Sandhill, Newcastle, is hard to say, unless we assume the fish originally to have been a dragon. Between elephants and dragons there was supposed to be a deadly strife, and their battles are recorded by Strabo, Pliny, Aelian and their mediæval followers. The fight always ended in the death of both, the dragon strangling the elephant in the windings of his tail, when the elephant falling down dead crushed the dragon by his weight.

The *Elephant & Friar*, formerly to be seen at Bristol, may possibly have originated from the representation of an elephant accompanied by a man in Eastern costume, whose flowing garment might be mistaken for the gown of a friar. That sign would have admirably suited the fancy of the landlord of the *Elephant & Castle*, formerly in Leeds ; his name happening to be Priest, he had the following inscription above his door :

> He is a priest who lives within,
> Gives advice gratis, and administers gin.

In the 17th century, the *Reindeer* began to make its appearance on the signboard, where it has kept its place to the present day. At first it was called the ' *Rained Deer* ', as we see from the newspapers of that period.—' Mr. John Chapman, York carrier in Hull, at the sign of the *Rained Deer*.' The first instance we find of this animal on the signboards of London is in 1682, when there was ' Right Irish Usquebaugh to be sold at the *Raindeer* in Tuttle Street (Tothill St.), Westminster '.

Pepys mentions the *Reindeer* as early as 7 October 1667 as the sign of a tavern kept by a Mrs. Elizabeth Aynsworth, expelled as a procuress from Cambridge by the University authorities, and subsequently making a modest fortune at the *Reindeer* at Bishop's Stortford.

There is a *Giraffe* in Penton Place and a *Gnu* at Stedham, Suss. Dragons, when apothecaries' signs, were not derived from heraldry, but were used to typify certain chemical actions.

In mediæval alchemy, the dragon seems to have been the emblem of Mercury, since Mercury like a dragon could ' eat its own poisonous tail ' and extract therefrom a valuable medicine, that is, the useful drug calomel could be prepared (and is in fact prepared to this day) by subliming together a mixture of metallic mercury and the deadly poison corrosive sublimate, mercuric chloride. It had another draconic property in that its colours ' increase in death ', that is, the oxidation of the silvery metal yields mercuric oxide, which is a vivid red or yellow colour, changing markedly according to the temperature.

Hence the dragon became one of the ' properties ' of the chemist and apothecary, was painted on his drug-pots, hung up as his sign. Some dusty stuffed crocodile hanging from the ceiling in the laboratory had to do service for the monster, and inspire the vulgar with a profound awe for the mighty man who had conquered the vicious reptile. Such a stuffed crocodile is still to be seen in a pharmacy at Arundel, Suss. There is a *Dragon on the Wheel* at Dinder, Som., but the dragon as an inn sign occurs somewhat rarely. Other instances of it are dealt with on p. 67.

The *Salamander* was another animal, which represented certain chemical actions, owing to its fabled powers of resisting the fire. The notions of early naturalists concerning this creature were very extraordinary.

The bestiaries say that it lives on pure fire, and produces a substance which is neither silk nor linen, nor yet wool, of which garments are made and can only be cleaned by fire (? asbestos), and that if the animal itself falls into a burning fire, it will at once extinguish the flames. Bossewell, in his *Armourie* attributes to the salamander some other qualities :—

> Among all venomous beastes he is the mightiest of poyson and venyme. For he creepe upon a tree, he infecteth all the apples or other fruit that groweth thereon with his poyson, and killeth them which eats thereof. Which apples, also, if they happen to falle into any pitte of water, the strength of the poyson killeth them that drinke thereof.

This incombustibility made the *Salamander* a very proper sign for alchemists and apothecaries, and with the last it still continues on the Continent. It has not been noted as an inn sign.

The qualities attributed to the *Unicorn* caused this animal to be used as a sign both by chemists and goldsmiths. The only way to capture one was to leave a handsome young virgin in one of the places where it resorted. As soon as the animal had perceived her, he would come and lie quietly down beside her, resting his head in her lap, and fall asleep. In this state he might be surprised by the hunters who watched for him. This laying his head in the lap of a virgin made the first Christians choose the unicorn as the type of Our Lord, born from the Virgin Mary. The horn, as an antidote to all poison, was also believed to be emblematic of the conquering of sin by the Messiah. Allusions to the unicorn occur frequently in the Old Testament, and commentators say that these references symbolized the coming Saviour. Religious emblems being in great favour with early printers, some of them for this reason adopted the unicorn as their sign ; thus John Harrison in 1603 lived at the *Unicorn & Bible* in Paternoster Row. Again the reputed power of the horn caused the animal to be taken as a supporter for the apothecaries' arms, and as a constant signboard by chemists. According to Albertus Magnus, ' It is reported that the unicorn's horn sweats when it comes in the presence of poison, and that for this reason it is laid on the tables of the great, and made into knife-handles, which, when placed on the tables, show the presence of poison. But this is not sufficiently proved.' Whatever it was that passed for unicorn's horn (probably the horn of the narwal), it was sold at an immense price. ' The unicorn whose horn is worth a city,' says Dekker in the *Gull's Hornbook*.

The belief in the efficacy and value of this horn continued to the close of the 17th century ; for the Rev. John Ward in his diary refers to it as valuable in curing the ague.

> It approved itself as a true one, as he said by this : if one drew a circle with itt about a spider, she would not move out off itt.

The great value set upon unicorns' horn caused the goldsmiths to adopt this animal as their sign. There is one recorded in Machyn's *Diary* in 1561, ' the syne of the Unycorne in Chepesyd'. In 1711 the *Unicorn & Dial* was the sign of a watch-maker near the Strand Bridge. There is a famous *Unicorn* at Ripon.

The *Wyvern* is rarely found. There is an example however at Church Cookham, Som. Another fabulous animal that though rarely occurs on signboards is the *Cockatrice*, which was the sign of a place of amusement in Highbury *c.* 1611. There is a surviving *Cockatrice* at Norton Subcourse, Norf. The historians give most extra-ordinary particulars about the birth of this creature :—

> When the cock is past seven years old an egg grows in his belly, and when he feels this egg, he wonders very much, and sustains the greatest anxiety any animal can suffer. He seeks, privately, a warm place on a dunghill or in a stable, and scratches with his feet, until he has formed a hole to lay his egg in. And when the cock has dug his hole he goes ten times a day to it, for all day he thinks that he is going to be delivered. And the nature of the toad is such that he smells the venom which the cock carries in his belly, consequently it watches him, so that the cock cannot go to the hole without being seen by it. And as soon as the cock leaves the place where he has to lay his egg, the toad is immediately there to see if the egg has been laid ; for his nature is such, that he hatches the egg if he can obtain it. And when he has hatched it, until it is time to open, it produces an animal that has the head, and neck, and breast of a cock, and from thence downwards, the body of a serpent.

No doubt the story originated from the fact that sometime in the Middle Ages a cock so far forgot himself as to lay an egg, as at Basle in 1474, and when this happened could be convicted, condemned, and with the egg burned at the stake as a sorcerer with great pomp and ceremony.

The *Ape* was, in bygone times, the sign of an inn in Philip Lane, near London Wall ; all that now remains of this ancient hostelry is a stone carving of a monkey squatted on its haunches, and eating an apple ; under it the date 1670, and the initial B. Later the house was known as the *Ape & Apple*. It is said that there is a drawing of the original sign in the Bristol Museum. The courtyard, where the lumbering coaches used to arrive and depart, was in Larwood's time an open space, round which houses were built. It is suggested that the sign may have been adopted as a symbol of antiquity and human frailty.

The *Racoon* is a painted sign at Dalston, but a hyaena seems to have sat for the portrait ; the *Hippopotamus* occurs in New-England St., Brighton ; the *Ibex* at Chaddleworth, Berks. ; the *Crocodile* at Heigham St., Norwich. The *Camel* may be met with in a few instances, as in Globe Rd., and at Weston Peverell, Plymouth, there is the sign of the *Camel's Head*. Occasionally an example may be seen of the *Kangaroo*, set up probably by some landlord who had tried his luck in Australia. There is a *Panther* at Reigate, a *Polar Bear* at Hull, a *Polecat* at Prestwood, a *Porcupine* at Charing Cross Rd., a *Wolf* at Dedsworth, Berks., and a *Zebra* at Cambridge. The *Civet* is common all over Europe as a perfumer's sign, in reference to the production of musk. There was a *Civet Cat* in Kensington High St., whose sign is still exhibited over some bank premises.

The *Hedgehog* was never very common.   In the reign of Queen Elizabeth it was the sign of William Seeres, bookseller, in St Paul's Churchyard, who put it up, according to Bagford, on account of its being the badge of his former master Sir Henry Sydney.

The hedgehog is now very scarce on signboards ; at Dadlington, Leics., there is a *Dog & Hedgehog*, doubtless borrowed from the well-known engraving of ' A Rough Customer '.   There is a *Mole* at Arborfield, Berks.

Signs relating to sport or the chase are comparatively common ; thus we have the *Rat & Ferret* at Wilson, near Ashby-de-la-Zouch.   There was a *Coney* in Shrewsbury in 1657, the *Three Conies* figure on an old trades token of Blackman St.   There is still a house of this sign at Thorpe Mandeville, Northants., and a *Three Rabbits* at 833 Romford Rd., E.   The *Rabbits* is at Thurrock, Essex, and the *Black Rabbit* at Littlehampton.   There is a *Hare*, on the token of John Perris in the Strand, 1666 ; and that of Nicholas Warren, in Aldersgate.   Warren evidently made a cockney mistake, thinking that hares, instead of rabbits, lived in *warrens*.   Another *Hare* was the sign of Philip Hause in Walbrook in 1682.   There is a *Hare* inn still at Long Melford Suff., and one at Coventry.   The *Hare & Squirrel* occur together on a sign at Nuneaton. What the combination means it is difficult to surmise.

The *Hare & Hounds* is very common.   About a century and a half ago it was the sign of a notorious establishment in St Giles's :—

> The *Hare & Hounds* was to be reached by those going from the west end towards the city, by going up a turning to the left hand, nearly opposite St Giles's churchyard. The entrance to the turning or lane was obstructed or defended by posts with cross bars, which being passed, the lane itself was entered.   It extended some twenty or thirty yards towards the north, through two rows of the most filthy, dilapidated, and execrable buildings that could be imagined ; and at the top or end of it stood the citadel, of which ' Stunning Joe ' was the corpulent castellan ;—I need not say that it required some determination and some address to gain this strange place of rendezvous.   Those who had the honour of an introduction to the great man were considered safe, wherever his authority extended, and in this locality it was certainly very extensive.   He occasionally condescended to act as a pilot through the navigation of the alley to persons of aristocratic or wealthy pretensions, whom curiosity or some other motive best known to themselves, led to his abode.   Those who were not under his safe conduct frequently found it very unsafe to wander in the intricacies of this region.

Cages with climbing squirrels and bells to them were formerly the indispensable appendages of the outside of a tinman's shop.   One still hung out in Holborn in 1826.

From this perhaps originated the *Squirrel* found as an inn sign at Hurtmore, Surr. The *Three Squirrels* was the sign of an inn at Lambeth, mentioned by Taylor in 1636 ; and from a trades token it appears that in the 17th century there was a similar sign in Fleet St.   Probably it was the same house which, in 1677, was occupied by Gosling the banker ' over against St Dunstan's Church ', where a triad of squirrels may still as in Larwood's time be seen in the ironwork of the windows.

In 1750 there was a sign of the *Hare & Cats* at Norwich, which was clearly a travesty of the *Hare & Hounds*. A very odd combination is the *Hare & Billet* to be seen at Crote's Place, Blackheath.

The *Stag* may in early times have been put up as a religious symbol. As such it is of constant occurrence in the catacombs and in the early Christian sculptures, in allusion to Psalm xlii., ' Like as the hart desireth the water brook, so longeth my soul after thee, O God !' The *Stag* is still a very common sign. A publican on the Fulham Rd. put up the sign and added to this on the tympanum : ' Rex in regno suo non habet parem ', the application of which was best known to the host himself. There seems about it neither rhyme nor reason.

Baldfaced is a term still applied to horses who have a white strip down the forehead to the nose. The *Baldfaced Stag* is seen in many places, for example, in Southampton where a Stag of this description is said to have been killed in the neighbourhood. Because of the rarity of beasts of this kind the head was hung over the door of the inn to attract custom, so that the house became known as the *Baldfaced Stag*, and a sign was painted accordingly. A very well-known house of this sign is that at Finchley. At Chigwell, Essex, there is a *Bald Hind*, and in the High St., Reading, a *Bald Face*, both evidently derived from the last-named stag. The *Broad Face*, formerly at Reading, was no doubt a corruption of this sign.

Various combinations also occur, as the *Stag & Castle*, at Thornton, near Hinckley, and the *Stag & Pheasant*, formerly rather common and still surviving at Leicester. Both these doubtless allude to the game seen in parks, or in the neighbourhood of noblemen's seats. The *Stag & Oak*, the Cape, Warws., points towards a similar origin, but the *Stag & Thorn* at Traffic St., Derby, seems to be a union of two signs, for the *Thorn* appears in the same street on another public-house. There is however a tree called Buckthorn, the name of which possibly may have been corrupted into the *Buck & Thorn*, and hence the *Stag & Thorn*. Perhaps more probably the sign might be explained as from the Borough arms. The *Rising Deer*, Brampton-en-le-Morthen, Yorks., and the *Rising Buck* (Sheinton, Salop) have a decided deer-stalking smack about them, affording us a glimpse of the cautious stag rising from the heather, pricking his ears and sniffing the wind.

The *Ranged Deer* was the sign of the King's gunsmith in the Minories, 1673. At that period this street was full of smiths—a fact which is referred to by Congreve.

This was simply intended for the *Reindeer*, which animal had then just newly come under the notice of the public whose knowledge of it was still confused, who spelled its name in a variety of ways, such as rain deer, rained deer, range deer and ranged deer. There are one or two *Reindeer* inns. Perhaps the best known is a fine old house shockingly ill used of late, at Banbury. There is a *The Hind* at Oundle.

The *Roebuck* is equally common with the *Stag*. Among the taverns with the sign of the *Roebuck* that have become famous may be mentioned the house in Cheapside, notorious during the Whig Riots in 1715. There is a *Buck* at Rumburgh, Suff., and one at Eavsham, Norf., a *Running Buck* at Ipswich, and a *Buck in the Vine* at Ormskirk,

Lancs. The *Buck & Bell* is a sign at Banbury. The bell was frequently added to the signs of public-houses in honour of the bellringers, who were in the habit of refreshing themselves there. Hence we have the *Bull & Bell*, Briggate, Leeds, the *Raven & Bell* at Salop and Newport, and in Ropemaker St., though this may refer to the bell which was hung round the neck of the bull before he was baited ; the *Bell & Talbot* at Bridgnorth, originally known as the *Talbot*, the *Dolphin & Bell* on the token of John Warner, Aldersgate, 1668, the *Fish & Bell* (evidently the same sign), Charles St., Soho, the *Three Swans & Peal* at Walsall, the *Nelson & Peal* and many others.

Not only the deer themselves, but their horns also make a considerable figure on the signboard. It is probably to the sign of the *Horns* that allusion is made in the ' roll of the Pardoner ', *Cocke Lorell's Bote*, to one dwelling at the sign of Cokeldes Pate. The *Horns* was a tavern of note in Fleet St. from 1385. The original sign was *le Horn* or *le Hook*. *Anderton's Hotel* was its lineal successor. According to Machyn's *Diary*, members of a Spanish embassy to the Queen in 1557 on their way to Dover stopped to drink at this House and at the *Greyhound* in Cheapside. Sometimes the *Horns* are specified as the *Hart's Horns Inn*, the house in Smithfield, near Pie Corner, in the yard of which Joe Miller used to play during Bartholomew Fair time, when he was associated with Pinkethman at the head of a troop of actors.

What most contributed to the popularity of this sign in the environs of London was the ancient and well-known custom of Highgate. Highgate was the headquarters for swearing on the horn. Hone says that

> An old and respectable inhabitant of the village says, that 60 years ago, upwards of 80 stages stopped every day at the *Red Lion*, and that out of every 5 passengers 3 were sworn. The oath was delivered standing. He gives it in the following form : *Take notice* what I now say unto you, for *that* is the first word of your oath—mind *that* ! You must acknowledge me to be your adopted father, I must acknowledge you to be my adopted son (or daughter). If you do not call me father, you forfeit a bottle of wine. If I do not call you son, I forfeit the same. And now my good son, if you are travelling through this village of Highgate, and you have no money in your pocket, go call for a bottle of wine at any house you think proper to go into, and book it to your father's score. If you have any friends with you you may treat them as well, but if you have money of your own you must pay for it yourself. For you must not say you have no money when you have, neither must you convey the money out of your own pockets into your friends' pockets, for I shall search you as well as them ; and if it is found that you or they have money, you forfeit a bottle of wine for trying to cozen and cheat your poor old ancient father. You must not eat brown bread while you can get white, except you like the brown the best ; you must not drink small beer while you can get strong, except you like the small the best. You must not kiss the maid while you can kiss the mistress, except you like the maid the best, but sooner than lose a good chance you may kiss them both. And now, my good son, for a word or two of advice ; keep from all houses of ill repute, and every place of public resort for bad company. Beware of false friends, for they will turn to be your foes, and inveigle you into houses where you may lose your money and get no redress. Keep from thieves of every denomination. And now, my good son, I wish you a safe journey through Highgate and this life. I charge you, my good son, that if you know any in this company

who have not taken the oath you must cause them to take it, or make each of them forfeit a bottle of wine, for if you fail to do so you will forfeit a bottle of wine yourself. So now, my good son, God bless you. Kiss the horns or a pretty girl, if you see one here which you like best, and so be free of Highgate.

After that, the new-made member became fully acquainted with the privileges of a freeman, which included, for example, these (said by some to be a later addition, introduced by a blacksmith who kept the *Coach & Horses*) :—

> If at any time you are going through Highgate, and want to rest yourself, and you see a pig lying in the ditch, you have liberty to kick her out and take her place ; but if you see three lying together, you must only kick out the middle one and lie between the other two.

Nearly every inn in Highgate used to keep a pair of horns for this custom. In Hone's time the principal inn, the *Gatehouse*, had stag-horns : the *Mitre*, stags' horns, the *Green Dragon*, stags' horns, the *Red Lion & Sun*, bullocks' horns, the *Bell*, stags' horns, the *Coach & Horses*, rams' horns, the *Castle*, rams' horns, the *Red Lion*, rams' horns, the *Coopers' Arms*, rams' horns, the *Fox & Hounds*, rams' horns, the *Flask*, rams' horns, the *Rose & Crown*, stags' horns, the *Angel*, rams' horns, the *Bull*, stags' horns, the *Wrestlers*, stags' horns, the *Lord Nelson*, stags' horns, the *Duke of Wellington*, stags' horns, the *Crown*, stags' horns, the *Duke's Head*, stags' horns.

Hone supposes the custom to have originated in a sort of graziers' club. Highgate being the place nearest London where cattle rested on their way from the north, certain graziers were accustomed to put up at the *Gatehouse* for the night. But as they could not wholly exclude strangers, who like themselves, were travelling on business, they brought an ox to the door, and those who did not choose to kiss its horns, after going through the ceremony described, were not deemed fit members of their society. Similar customs prevailed in other places as at Ware, and at the *Griffin* in Hoddesden, etc. There is another well-known *Horns* inn at Kennington, S.E., and a *Harts' Horns* at Knaresborough.

The *Fox*, as might be expected, is to be seen in a great many places ; there is one at Thame, Oxon, another at Newbourne, Suff., and another at Frandley, Ches., with these rhymes :—

> Behold the Fox, near Frandley stocks,
> Pray catch him when you can,
> For they sell here, good ale and beer,
> To any honest man.

A still more absurd inscription accompanies the sign of the *Fox* at Folkesworth, Hunts. ; the alehouse where George Borrow was first induced to sample gypsy life :—

> I ham a cunen fox
> You see ther his
> No harm atched.
> To Me it is my Mrs
> Wish to place me
> Here to let you no
> He sells good beere.

There is a *Young Fox* at Bath and a *Fox & Cubs* at Herts. Probably in the countryside the reference is the obvious one, but many of the *Fox* signs in the towns (like the similar *Beavers*) are originally the trade signs of furriers—in the latter case, perhaps of hatters. It is not known what was the origin of the *Wheatland Fox* at Much Wenlock, Salop.

Formerly there used to be a sign of the *Three Foxes* in Clement's Lane, Lombard St., carved in stone, and representing three foxes sitting in a row. A few years before Larwood's time the house came into the possession of a legal firm, who, no doubt afraid of the jokes to which the sign might lead, thought it advisable to do away with the carving by covering it over with plaster. One of the most favourite combinations, at Fressingfield, Suss., is the *Fox & Goose*, represented by a fox *courant* with the neck of the goose in his mouth and the body cast over his back. It seems suggested by an incident in the old tale of 'Reynard the Fox', and was a subject which mediæval artists were never tired of representing ; it occurs in stall carvings, as in Gloucester Cathedral ; in the border of the Bayeux tapestry, and in endless manuscript illuminations. It is, or was, a coat of arms borne by the families of Foxwist and Foxfield. An example of this sign is to be seen at Ham, Surrey. Derived from this sign are the *Fox & Duck* (two in Sheffield and another at Ham, Surrey), and the *Fox & Hen*, of which there is an example at Long Itchington, Warws. Reynard's predatory habits are further illustrated by the *Fox & Lamb* formerly to be seen in Pilgrim St., Newcastle, and in Allendale, and still extant at Huddersfield ; the *Fox & Coney* at South Cave, E.R. Yorks., the *Fox & Rabbit*, Lockton, N.R. Yorks., and perhaps the *Fox & Goat*, Hersham, Corn. The *Fox & Grapes* is of course borrowed from Aesop's fable. The sign occurs at Brewer St., W., and at Sheffield. The London example appears to be a combination of a furrier's sign with that of an innkeeper. From the same well-known source also arose the sign of the *Fox & Crane*. We see the punishment of all Reynard's misdemeanours in the *Fox & Hounds*, a sign which seems of old standing, as there is one at Putney on a house which professes to have been 'established above three hundred years'. There are many others, one, for example, at Barley, Herts. This has a huge sign stretching right across the road. The *Fox & the Yorkshire Grey* is in Whitechapel. The *Fox & Owl* at Nottingham seems to have a curious origin. A bunch of ivy or ivy tod was generally considered the favourite haunt of an *owl*, but *tod* also signifies a fox, and so the owl's nest, owls-tod, may have led to the owl and tod, the fox and owl. The *Owl's Nest* is still a sign at St Helens, Lancs.

The *Fox & Ball* at Kentford, Suff., appears to be heraldic in origin. In the sign of the *Fox & Bull* at Knightsbridge, now extinct, the bull had been added about 1820.

About a century and a quarter ago a magistrate used to sit once a week at this house to settle the small disputes of the neighbouring inhabitants. The innkeeper was also, it appears, a furrier. The voyage to London in those days was performed in a sort of lumbering stage-coach over an ill-paved and dimly lighted road. To this *Fox* inn, by a very old wooden gate at the back, the bodies of the drowned in the Serpentine used to be conveyed to the care of the Royal Humane Society, who had a receiving-house there.   Among the many unhappy young and fair ones who were carried thither was Harriet Westbrook, Shelley's first wife, who had drowned herself in the Serpentine upon hearing that her husband had run off to Italy with Mary Godwin.   The ancient inn remained much in its Elizabethan condition till the year 1799, when certain alterations cleared away the old-fashioned fire-places, chimney-pieces and dog-irons.

Some other combinations are not so easily explained such as the *Fox & Cap*, Long Lane, Smithfield, and at Birmingham and Leeds.   The mystery is explained by the shop bill of the first named.   It was the sign of Tho. Tronsdale, a capmaker, and represented a fox running, with a cap painted above him, to intimate the man's business. The *Fox & Pelican* at Grayshott, Surrey, which has a fine modern sign by Walter Crane, is evidently a combination of two signs, so is the *Fox & Crown*, Nottingham and Newark.   On Highgate Hill there was once an old roadside inn, the *Fox & Crown*, now a private house, which displayed on its front a fine gilt coat of arms with the following inscription underneath :—

6th July 1837
This Coat of Arms is a Grant from
Queen Victoria, for services rendered
to Her Majesty when in danger travelling down this hill.

The story does not seem to be well vouched for, but the tablet is certainly to be seen in the local museum at Highgate.

The *Fox & Knot*, Snow Hill, now extinct, seems to have been of old standing as it gave its name to a court close by ; its origin, doubtless, is exactly similar to that of the *Fox & Cap* ; the knot or top-knot being a head-dress worn by ladies in the 18th century.   The *Flying Fox* at Colchester probably neither alludes to some kind of bat or flying squirrel nor is merely a landlord's *caprice*, as Larwood suggests.   *Flying Fox* was a celebrated racehorse and is dealt with elsewhere among the racehorse signs.   There are at least two *Fox under the Hills*.   One is at the bottom of Ivy Lane off the Embankment.   Dickens knew it well and described it as a ' dirty little tumbledown public-house'.   The other is at Camberwell St. and replaces an older house of the same sign at the foot of Denmark Hill, and is said to mark a spot where nightingales once sang. There is an *Intrepid Fox* (not the animal but the politician Charles James Fox) in Wardour St., Soho.

Larwood considered it strange that in this sporting country the sign of the *Brush* or the fox's tail should be so rare.   He found ' no instance of its use, although beside the interest attached to it in the hunting field, it had the honour of being one of the badges of the Lancaster family'.   There is an example of it, however, at Ropsley, Hants.

DOMESTIC ANIMALS

Notwithstanding the ballad of the *Vicar & Moses* which refers to ' the sign of the *Horse*', the horse rarely, or never, occurs without a distinctive adjective to determine its colour, action or other attributes.   All natural colours of the horse, and some others,

are found on the signboard—black, white, bay, sorrel (rare), pied, spotted, red, sometimes golden ; and in one instance, at Grantham, a *Blue Horse* is met with.   Frequently
the sign of the horse is accompanied by the advice :—

> Up hill hurry me not ;
> Down hill trot me not ;
> On level ground spare me not ;
> And in the stable I'm not forgot.

Many years ago at Greenwich there was a *Horse*—advertised under the sign ' Good
Grass for Horses.   Long Tails three shillings and six-pence per week '.   An inquisitive
person went in and questioned the landlord as to the reason for the differentiation,
which the host explained was quite justified, ' for ', said he, ' long-tailed horses can
whisk off the flies, and eat at their leisure, but bob-tailed horses have to shake their heads
and run about from morning till night, and so do eat much less '.

The *Red Horse* is now almost extinct ; it occurs in an advertisement of 1711 as the
sign of a house in Bond St.   Red at this time meant not vermilion but roan.   The
Bay Horse is a great favourite in Yorkshire ; in 1861 there were, in the West Riding
alone, not less than seventy-seven inns, taverns, and public-houses, with such a sign,
besides innumerable alehouses.   As the *Cleveland Bay* it is found at Eston, N.R. Yorks.,
and at Middlesbrough.   This is of course the famous breed which provided the best
coach and brougham horses.   The *Yorkshire Grey* occurs in Gray's Inn Rd.   The
Welsh Pony is at Oxford, the *Shetland Pony* was formerly at Clenchwharton, Norf.
The *Suffolk Punch* found in East Anglia, refers of course to the celebrated local breed,
cousin of the Flanders mare, the modern Belgian ' Percheron ' lately becoming very
popular in England.   The *Dapple Grey* is apparently a reference to the nursery rhyme.
A house of this sign formerly existed in Peckham.   Dappled grey was the fashionable
colour of horses in the 18th century.

Of the *White Horse* innumerable instances occur, and many are connected with
names known in history.   Often, though not always, this is the galloping *White
Horse* of Hanover and dates from the years after 1714.   There was until lately a very
good double sign of this name at Stoke Ash, Suff.   There is another *White Horse* at
Framlingham in the same county.   Elsewhere it may be sometimes the old West Saxon
White Horse which is found in reference to the animal, for example, at Ashdown,
Berks. cut out in the chalk.   At the *White Horse* near Bushey, Rutland, the noted
George Villiers, Duke of Buckingham, spent the last years of his life and died.   At the
White Horse in Fleet St. (*teste* Titus Oates) the Jesuits held their general council in April
1678, and concocted their nefarious scheme for murdering the King and setting on the
throne James, Duke of York.   The old *White Horse* in Kensington, where Addison
wrote several of his *Spectators*, remained in its original state till a little more than a
century ago, when it was pulled down and the name changed to the *Holland Arms*.
The old sign is still preserved in the parlour of its successor, though the Holland Arms
are displayed outside.

Edinburgh also has its famous *White Horse* in a close in the Canongate, an inn dating from the time of Queen Mary Stuart, which is referred to by Scott.   It was well known to runaway couples, and hundreds were married at a moment's notice in its large room, in which as well as in the *White Hart* in the Grassmarket these *impromptu* marriages were as regularly performed as at Gretna Green.   The *White Horse Cellar*, Piccadilly, later a mere omnibus office, was for more than a century a bustling coaching-inn for the West Country coaches, admired by Hazlitt.   Another *White Horse Inn* shows the dark side of the picture—the danger of the roads, for the *White Horse* at the corner of Welbeck St., Cavendish Square, was long a detached public-house, where travellers customarily stopped for refreshment and to examine their firearms before crossing the fields to Lissen Green.

It is said that a Warwickshire innkeeper started a public-house near four others, with signs respectively of the *Bear*, the *Angel*, the *Ship* and the *Three Cups*.   Yet quite undaunted at his neighbours, he put up the *White Horse* as his sign, and under it wrote the following spirited and prophetic rhymes :—

> My *White Horse* shall bite the *Bear*,
> And make the *Angel* fly ;
> Shall turn the *Ship* her bottom up,
> And drink the *Three Cups* dry.

And so it did: the lines pleased the people, the other houses lost their custom, and tradition says that the fellow made a considerable fortune.   There is a *Great White Horse* at Ipswich, the scene of some of Mr. Pickwick's adventures.   The *Sorrel Horse* at Barham and at Shottisham, Suff., and the *Chestnut Horse* at Great Finborough no doubt represent the county breed—the Suffolk Punch, concerning which George Borrow is very enthusiastic.   The *Blue Horse* is in that very blue town Grantham, whose predilection for the colour is explained elsewhere.

The *Black Horse* at Markham Moor, Notts., is said to be so called in honour of Turpin's mount, Black Bess, actually, of course, a mare.   It is now called the *Markham Moor Inn.*

Possibly in some places the *Black Horse* is so named merely as a rival to a neighbouring *White Horse.*   This seems so at Nibley, Glos., where the rival Horses face one another across the village green.

The *Running Horse* or the *Galloping Horse*—perhaps originally the Horse of Hanover—is also very common.   In the *London Gazette* of 1699 it is mentioned in connexion with a horse race at Lilly Hoo in Hertford, followed by a woman's footrace for a smock worth £3.   The *Running Horse* at Leatherhead has an interesting pictorial sign. There is another *Running Horse* (a gig horse ?) in Shepherd's Market.   The *Rampant Horse* has often been corrupted into the *Ramping Horse.*   There is an example of the latter sign at Hanley, Stoke-on-Trent, and one of the former at Needham Market. There is a *Sumpter Horse* at Penwortham, Lancs., and a *Trotting Horse* at Ludlow.

The combinations in which we meet with the Horse are all very plain and require no explanation.   The *Horse & Groom*, found, for example, at Nottingham, and the *Horse & Jockey* found, for example, at Mansfield and at Newark, Notts., and at Wessing-

PLATE
9

BEXLEY PUBLIC LIBRARIES.

PLATE
10

ton, Derbys., are the most prevalent.   Racing, since at any rate the days of Henry II, has been a favourite English sport.

The *Bell & Horse* is an old and still frequent sign ; it occurs on trades tokens, as on that of John Harcourt at the *Bell & Black Horse* in Finsbury, 1668, and on various others ; whilst at the present day it may be seen at many roadside alehouses.   Bells were a favourite addition to the trappings of horses in the Middle Ages.   Chaucer's abbot's bridle ' rang as loud as doth a chapel bell '.   Perhaps from this developed the custom of giving a golden bell as the reward of a race.   In Chester, such a bell was run for yearly on St George's Day, it was ' dedicated to the kinge, being double gilt with the Kynge's Armes upon it ', and was carried in the procession by a man on horseback ' upon a septer in pompe, and before him a noise of trumpets in pompe'.   This custom of racing for a bell led to the adoption of the still common phrase bearing the bell.

Names of famous racehorses are often to be found upon signboards.   Through the kindness of Mr. G. A. Tomlin I am able to add many instances to the half-dozen given by Larwood.   The date given in each case is that when the horse won the race referred to.

Derby winners include *Amato* (1838) at Epsom, the Aga Khan's *Blenheim* (1930) also at Epsom, the filly *Blink Bonny* (Oaks and Derby 1857) which is still fairly common in Northumberland, as, for example, at Chathill, and in Durham (there was formerly an example at Embleton), *Cadland* (1828—when he also won the Two Thousand Guineas), at Chilwell, Notts. (the horse was owned by the Duke of Rutland, but bred by Sir John Borlase Warren, ' squire of the neighbouring village of Stapleford), *Diamond Jubilee* (1900) at Gaywood, Norf., *Flying Fox* (1899) at Colchester, *Ladas* (1894) at Epsom, *Little Wonder* (1840) at Harrogate (here the house has a pictorial sign representing the horse and his rider), and *Voltigeur* (1850) which formerly existed at Hart, Durh., at Barton, N.R. Yorks., and in several other places.   A well-known house named after a St Leger winner is *Altisidora*, Bishop Burton, E.R. Yorks.   This was formerly named *Evander,* and so for a time the house became known as the *Horse & Jockey*.   A still later landlord gave it its present name when Altisidora won the leger in 1813.   Other Leger winners are *Charles XII* (1839) at Heslington, E.R. Yorks, *Filho da Puta* (1815) formerly at Manchester, and still at Nottingham (this latter house was occupied on his retirement by the stud groom of Sir William Maxwell, owner of the horse, Hambletonian (1795) at Stockton-on-Tees), and *Rockingham* (Doncaster Cup and Leger 1833), very appropriately situated at Doncaster.   *Barefoot* (1823) was formerly at York, *Octavian* (1810) is at Crakehall, N.R. Yorks., *Windsor Lad* (Derby, St Leger, and Eclipse Stakes, 1835) is at Windsor.

Of steeplechasers, perhaps the one most often chosen is *Master Robert* (Grand National 1924).   He has given his name to a fine new house on the Great West Rd., with a most attractive pictorial sign, painted from life by Lynwood Palmer.   The horse was kept for some time at the artist's stables adjoining the inn.   Other famous horses sometimes found are *Alice Hawthorn* (winner of more than fifty races) at Wheldrake, N.R. Yorks., *Bay Malton* (which had a most distinguished career, 1764–7) in

I

Great Portland St., *Bay Childers*, formerly at Dronfield, Derbys., and still to be found in Sheffield, *Beeswing* the wonderful mare which had an almost uninterrupted career of success 1835–42, at Wellingborough and at York (but there was another *Beeswing* which won the Liverpool Autumn Cup in 1866, and it has been alleged that the names of these houses are rather from the ' beeswing ' which one finds on port, since both houses in 1791 were celebrated for their port !).

Dr. Syntax, formerly existing at Gateshead, Newcastle, and Oldham and still to be seen at Preston, is likelier to be named after the sire of Beeswing than directly after Combe's hero. The horse won the Preston Gold Cup in 1815 and 1821. *Eclipse* is at Loscoe, Derbys. There was formerly a house of this sign at York. Later it was renamed the *Black Swan*. *Ely* (Ascot Gold Cup 1865) is at Hartford Bridge Flats, Hants. A fine sign representing the horse was stolen in 1926. *Flying Childers* (Derby), son of the Darley Arabian, was formerly to be seen at Melton Mowbray, and is still found at Kirby Bellars, Leics., and at Stanton-in-the-Peak, Derbys. *Flying Dutchman* (Champagne Stakes 1848, Emperor's Plate 1850, and both Derby and Ledger 1849) is at Norwich and at Wombwell, W.R. Yorks. The sign of the Norwich house has been removed and is in the possession of Messrs. Steward and Patterson. Perhaps the York house was named after the horse ran his celebrated match with Voltigeur at York in 1851. *Highflyer* was sold to Richard Tattersall who had a house near Ely, and the inn of this name is at Ely. *Smoker* is at Plumbley, Ches. This house was named after a very famous horse of Lord de Tabley's. It has a fine modern sign painted by Miss Leighton. *Wild Dayrell* (Darrell ?) was formerly at Oldham.

Possibly a great many houses may be named after horses of less fame. A few examples taken at random of names which occur as those of licensed houses, and which certainly are also the names of horses are :—*King Alfred* and *Red Ensign* (Prince of Wales' Stakes 1868 and 1893), *Life Boat* and *Drummer* (Great Metropolitan Stakes 1859 and 1893), *Vulcan* and *Indian Queen* (Cambridgeshire Stakes 1841 and 1894), *Julius Caesar* (Royal Hunt Cup 1878), *Manfred* and *Lord of the Isles* (Two Thousand Guineas 1817 and 1855), *Frigate*, *Gamecock*, and *Why Not* (Grand National 1889, 1887, and 1894), *Red Deer* and *Tam O'Shanter* (Chester Cup 1844 and 1876). Instances of houses having each of these names are given elsewhere in the text.

Probably some of the dignitaries noted elsewhere owe their signboard popularity rather to their fame as owners of celebrated horses, than to their military, naval, or political eminence. *Admiral Rous*, formerly on Galleywood Common, Essex, was the undisputed dictator of the English Turf in the 1870's. The *Duke of Cumberland*, whose figure often appears on inn signs, is perhaps often rather the breeder of *Eclipse*, than ' the *Butcher* of Culloden'. Named riders are more rarely found, but at Natland, Westmd., over a house which has now disappeared was a figure of *Captain Ross on Clinker*. Ross was a great racing character, and gave his name to the Ross Memorial Stakes at Windsor.

The *Saddle* occurs at Fulford, E.R. Yorks., the *Spur* at Mortlake, the *Whip* at Loosley Row, Bucks., the *Steeplechase* at St Albans, the *Stakes* at Stalybridge, the *Turf* at Richmond, Yorks., and at Shrewsbury, the *Grandstand* near Knavesmire, York. The *Racehorse* is a house with a fine pictorial sign at Leatherhead, the *Running Horses* at Merrow, Surrey, the *Running Mare* at Cobham, Surrey, and the *Horse & Jockey* in many places, for example, at Oxford and at Newark. The *Horse & Leaping Bar* was in Whitechapel High St.

There is a *Chester Cup* at Plymouth, a *Gold Cup at* Ascot, and a *St Leger* at Doncaster, with another at Warrington. Often signs of this type are explained locally by the assertion that each was established from the proceeds of a lucky bet on the horse or in the race commemorated, so that the new licensee chose the name as a graceful acknowledgement to the source of his good fortune.

The *Horse & Tiger*, at Rotherham, is said to refer to the accident in a travelling menagerie which took place many years ago, when a tiger broke loose and sprang upon the leaders of a passing mail-coach. Probably it refers rather to one of the spruce grooms or horse attendants known as Tiger's.

Even that poor hack the *Manage Horse* is not forgotten, as he may be seen going through his paces before a house in Cottle's Lane, Bath. In one of the turnings in Cannon St., City, there was formerly an old sign of the *Horse & Dorsers* or *Horse & Dorsiter*, which is simply an old rendering of the more common *Pack Horse*, formerly the usual sign of a posting inn. Possibly the *Frighted Horse* which occurs in many places, for example, at Handsworth, Birmingham, belongs to this class of horses, the expression 'fright' being a corruption of *freight*. Some publicans who, with their trade combine the calling of farrier, set up the sign of the *Horse & Farrier*, sometimes rendered as the *Bleeding Horse*. There are examples at Penrith, Cumb., at Ramsbury, Wilts., and elsewhere. The *Bleeding Horse* is said sometimes, however, to be of heraldic origin—the original sign being a horse's head couped erminois *gu*. The ermine were supposed by those ignorant of heraldry to represent drops of blood. The *Pack Horse* is found, for example, at Burslem, Stoke-on-Trent, at Newark-on-Trent and at Turnham Green. There is a fine *Pack Horse* sign at Gerrard's Cross, Bucks. The *Pack Horse & Talbot* is at Turnham Green, and the *Horse & Sacks* occurs in the Harrow Rd.

The *Horse & Stag* (Finningley, Notts.) and the *Horse & Gate* are both hunting signs ; but the last may have been suggested by the *Bull & Gate*. The *Horse & Trumpet*, formerly a very common sign illustrating the warhorse, was found at Leeds, and is still to be seen at Medbourne and Market Harborough, Leics., and at Uppingham, Rutland ; The *Horse & Chaise* (or shaze, as it is spelt) in the Broad Centry (sanctuary), Westminster, is named in an advertisement in the *Postboy* of 1711 ; whilst the *Chaise & Pair* is still to be seen at Northill, Colchester, and at Ipswich. There were formerly a *Chaise & Horses* at Wickham Market, Suff., and a *Postchaise* at Ipswich. The *Omnibus & Horses* is in the Harrow Rd., N.W. Various coaching signs are dealt with below (p. 214).

The *Nag's Head*—which only in one instance at Brampton, Cumb., is varied to the *Horse's Head*, is a sign that has become famous in history. It is represented on the print of the entry of Queen Marie de Medici on her visit to her daughter Henriette Marie, Queen of Charles I, being the sign of a notorious tavern opposite the Cheapside Cross.   The sign is suspended from a long square beam, at the end of which a large crown of evergreens is seen.   As none of the other houses are decked with greens, this apparently represents the *Bush*.   This house is associated with the validity of the orders of the Church of England, and the place of that Church's bishops, priests and deacons in the apostolic succession.   The reader is referred to works on church history for details of the ' Nag's Head Fable '—(or the Nag's Head Fact—according to his religious predilections).   There are a fair number of provincial *Nag's Heads*.   One, for example, at East Retford, Notts., formed part of the foundation endowment of the local (King Edward VI) Grammar School.   Another *Nag's Head* is to be seen at Amersham, Bucks., and there is another at Holloway.

A curious anecdote is told of the sign of a *Gelding*.   Golden Square, it appears, was originally called Gelding Square, from the sign of a neighbouring inn.   The inhabitants, indignant at the supposed vulgarity of the name, changed it to its present title. Some publicans appear to be of opinion that the *Grey Mare* is the best horse for their signboards ; in Lancashire, especially, this sign abounds.   Others put up the *Mare & Foal* —but they are evidently not very well acquainted with the old ballad of the *Mare and Foal that went to church*, for there the mare curses publicans who ' fill their pots full of nothing but froth '.

To match the *Mare & Foal*, there is the *Cow & Calf*, which is very common, as, for example, in Eastcheap.   A still more happy mother, the *Cow & Two Calves*, was in 1762 a sign near Chelsea Pond, whilst a touching picture of paternal bliss might have been seen on a sign in Islington in the 18th century, namely, the *Bull & Three Calves*. It may be that animal was placed there in the company of his offspring, to illustrate the homely old proverb, ' He that bulls the cow must keep the calf.'   The *Goat & Kid* was a sign at Norwich in 1711, the *Sow & Pigs* is common, as, for example, at Thundridge, Herts., and the *Ewe & Lamb* occurs on a trades token of Hatton Garden in 1668, and may still be seen in many places, as, for example, at Dunstable.   A practical traveller in the coaching days, staying at the *Ewe & Lamb* in Worcester, wrote on a pane of glass in that inn the following very true remark :—

> If the people suck your ale no more
> Than the poor Lamb, th' Ewe at the door,
> You in some other place may dwell,
> Or hang yourself for all you'll sell.

The *Cat & Kittens* was, about 1823, a sign near Eastcheap ; it may have come from the publican's slang expression, *cat and kittens*, as applied to the large and small pewter pots.

Happy families of birds are equally abundant.   (The *Sparrow* is rare as a sign, but it occurs at Letcombe Regis, Berks.)   There was the *Sparrow's Nest* in Drury Lane, of which trades tokens are extant ; there is a *Spink Nest* at Huddersfield.   The *Owl's Nest* is dealt with elsewhere. The *Throstle's Nest* (a not inappropriate name for a house with a free-and-easy singing club) is the sign of a public-house at Buglawton, Ches., there is the *Crows' Nest* at Newcastle-on-Tyne, the *Martin's Nest* at Thornhill Bridge, Normanton, the *Kite's Nest* (an unpromising name for an inn, if there be anything in a name) at Stretton, Herts., and finally the *Brood Hens*, and *Hen-and-Chickens*, which last two are more common than any of the former. Not improbably they originated with the sign of the *Pelican's Nest*, to which several of the above-named nests may be referred, or it may perhaps refer to Matthew xxiii, 37. Under the name of the *Brood Hen*, it occurs on a trades token of Battle Bridge, Southwark. As the *Hen & Chickens*, it was also known in the 17th century, for there are tokens of John Sell ' at ye *Hen & Chickens* on Hammond's Key ' ; and is likewise mentioned in a newspaper account in 1761 of how :

> Wednesday night last, Captain Lambert was stopt by three footpads near the *Hen and Chickens*, between Peckham and Camberwell, and robbed of a sum of money and his gold watch.

The sign still remains in St. Paul's Rd. and there is a famous coaching house of this sign in Birmingham. Larwood suggests rather long-windedly that ' The prevalence of this sign may be accounted for by the kindred love for the *barleycorn* in the human and gallinaceous tribes.'

The *Horseshoe* is a favourite in combination with other subjects. It is of course in very general use to this day in the English countryside as a bringer of good luck and a defence against witchcraft. The horseshoe nailed up over a threshold must be U, not ∩. The first way it would ' hold the luck in ', otherwise ' the luck would run out '. The horseshoe must be found or stolen—a given or bought one would be worthless.

The charm of the horseshoe lies in its being forked and presenting two points ; thus Herrick says in *Hesperides*

> Hang up *hooks* and *sheers*, to scare,
> Hence the hag that rides the mare ;

Any forked object, therefore, has the power to drive witches away. Even the two forefingers held out apart are thought sufficient to avert the evil eye, or prevent the designs of the devil and his crew. In this country, at the present day, scarcely a stable can be seen where there is not a horseshoe nailed on the door or lintel. There was in Larwood's time one very conspicuous at the gate of Meux's Brewery at the corner of Tottenham Court Rd., now removed to Wandsworth and its site occupied by a cinema. Conspicuous on the horse brasses of this concern and many others, the shoe might be seen ; in fact, it became the trade-mark of this firm like the red triangle which distinguishes the pale ale of Messrs. Allsop. Its origin is said to be in a horseshoe brought with him from Lincolnshire many years ago by a certain Kelsey from whose inn the great brewing concern developed. The iron heels of workmen's boots were also in Larwood's time frequently seen fixed against the doorpost or behind the door of working-class houses.

Block suggests that the single horseshoe is essentially symbolic—The Greek Omega—a sign of Unity. The present author rather doubts this, though it is certainly curious that a single horseshoe should be found sometimes, a set of three very often, and four perhaps only in one instance where a rival house to the *Three Horseshoes* has tried to ' go one better ' (although horses generally have four feet, not one or three).

The *Horseshoe* by itself is found fairly often. There is one close to the site of the brewery just referred to. There is a *Horseshoe* Tavern, mentioned by Aubrey in con-nexion with one of those reckless deeds of bloodshed common in the 16th and 17th centuries, when

> Captain Carlo Fantom outside the *Horseshoe* Tavern in Drury Lane slew a lieu-tenant of Colonel Rossiter because he disliked the jingling of his spurs.

This tavern was still in existence in 1692, as appears from the deposition of one of the witnesses in the murder of William Mountfort, the actor, by Captain Charles Hill, fifth Baron Hill, who, with his accomplice, Richard Mohun, whilst they were laying in wait for Mrs. Bracegirdle, drank a bottle of canary which had been bought at the *Horseshoe* tavern. There is a *Horseshoes* at Bulwell, Notts.

The *Three Horseshoes*, a purely heraldic sign, is not uncommon ; there was formerly a *Nine Horseshoes* near Bassingham, Lincs., and the single shoe may be met with in many combinations, arising perhaps from the old belief in its lucky influences. The *Horse & Horseshoe* was the sign of William Warden at Dover in the 17th century, as appears from his token. The *Sun & Horseshoe* is still a public-house sign in Mortimer St., and the *Magpie & Horseshoe* may be seen carved in wood in Fetter Lane. The magpie is perched within the horseshoe, a bunch of grapes being suspended from it. The *Horns & Horseshoe* is represented on the token of William Grainge in Gutter Lane, 1666—a horseshoe within a pair of antlers. The sign is still found at Cable St., E. The *Lion & Horseshoe* appears in 1703 in an advertisement of a shooting match. The *Hoop & Horseshoe*, at one time on Tower Hill, was formerly called the *Horseshoe*. Here in 1681 Colonel John Scott a great supporter of Titus Oates

> took occasion to kill one John Buttler, a hackney coachman, at the *Horse Shoe* Tavern on Tower Hill, without any other provocation 'tis said, but refusing to carry him and another gentleman pertaining to the law, from thence to Temple Bar for 1s. 6d.

The *Horseshoe & Crown*, in Castle St. near the Seven Dials in St Giles', is named in an early 18th-century handbill issued by the Daughter of a Seventh Daughter, offering divination and fortune-telling of every kind. The *Horseshoe & Magnet* is said by Monson Fitzjohn to have a curious history. The original sign was the *Horse & Falcon*, referring to the sport of hawking. This degenerated first into the *Horse & Magpie*, then to the *Horse & Magnet*, after that the *Horseshoe*, and then into its present form.

Probably the corruption was aided by the fact that a landlord took away the sign which appeared long afterwards over a house in King St., Covent Garden, named the *Magpie & Horseshoe*.

Horned cattle are just as common as horses on signboards ; the *Bull* in particular, is a favourite, whether as a namesake, as the source of roast beef, or from the ancient sport of bull-baiting it is difficult to say. From Ben Jonson we gather that there was another reason which sometimes dictated the choice of this animal on the signboard. In the *Alchymist*, Act I, Sc. 1, there is reference to such a sign chosen on astrological grounds. Possibly in some cases the origin of the sign may be remoter still. The Bull for obvious reasons is a recognized phallic symbol. It occurs frequently in various fertility myths, and is to this day the totem of the White Gipsies.

There was formerly a *Bull* sign at Woodbridge, Suff. Another at Yaxley, Suff., took its origin from the name, not the arms, of the lord of the manor. Newton dates a letter from the *Bull* at Shoreditch, September 1693 ; it is addressed to Locke and a curious letter it is, containing an apology for having wished Locke dead.

The *Bull* is generally represented in his natural colour, black, white, grey, pied, ' spangled ' (in Yorkshire), and only rarely *red* and *blue*, yet these two last colours may simply imply the natural red, brown, and other common hues, for newspapers of the 16th and 17th centuries often contain advertisements about *blue* dogs. Whatever shade that was intended for, it may certainly with as much justice be applied to a bull as to a dog. The *Chained Bull* at Chapel Allerton, Leeds, and the *Bull & Chain*, Lincoln, doubtless refer to the old cruel pastime of bull-baitings. Occasionally we meet also with a Wild *Bull*, as at Gisburn, near Skipton. There is a *Little Bull* at Spalding, and a *Winged Bull* at Rake, Suss.

The old story of the *Chained Bear* is sometimes told of a *Bull & Chain*. According to one version of it Thomas Gainsborough's brother John (Scheming Jack) is said to have agreed to paint for a pound the sign of the *Bull*, Glensford, Suff. He was refused payment of an extra ten shillings for a chain, though he warned the landlord that without it the bull might run away. It did—since he painted the sign in water colour.

Leigh Hunt has a good deal to say of the old galleried inns of London. An excellent example of them was that famous house the *Bull* in Bishopsgate St., where formerly plays were acted by Tarlton and by Burbage, Shakespeare's fellow-comedian. This inn is also celebrated as the London house of the famous Hobson, of Hobson's choice, the rich Cambridge carrier. Here a painted figure of him was to be seen in the 18th century, with a hundred-pound bag under his arm, on which was the following inscription :—' The fruitful Mother of a Hundred More '. At the *Bull* public-house on Tower Hill, Thomas Otway, it is said, died of want at the age of 33, on 14 April 1685, having retired to this house to escape his creditors. Johnson gives a different account of his death, and the matter is still controverted.

The *Bull* at Ware, obtained a celebrity by its enormous bed. Taylor the Water Poet in 1636 remarked, ' Ware is a great thorowfare, and hath many fair innes, with very large bedding, and one high and mighty Bed called the Great Bed of Ware : a man may seeke all England over and not find a married couple that can fill it.' In Chauncy's *Hertfordshire* is a story of twelve married couples who lay together in the bed, each pair being so placed at the top and bottom of the bed, that the head of one pair was at the feet of another. Shakespeare alludes to the Bed in *Twelfth Night*, Act III, Sc. 2. Where the ' high and mighty Bed ' was located seems a moot point ; some say at the *Bull*, others at the *Crown*, and Clutterbuck places it at the *Saracen's Head*, where there is or was an oak bed of some twelve feet square, in an Elizabethan style but with the date 1463 painted on the back. Tradition says that it was the bed of Warwick the King-maker, and was bought at a sale of furniture at Ware Park. It was sold in Larwood's time and is said to have been bought by Dickens.

The *Bull* Inn at Buckland, Kent, deserves to be mentioned for its comical caution to customers :

> The Bull is tame so fear him not,
> All the while you pay your shot.
> When money's gone, and credit's bad,
> It's that which makes the Bull run mad.

The *Bull* at Long Melford is a magnificent building, dating back to *c.* 1450, and built probably by one of the wealthy wool-staplers of the district as a private house. The wings of the building were probably his warehouses and workshops, the front his residence. The house became an inn before 1580. It recently passed into the hands of Messrs. Trust Houses, who have restored it with much loving care. The sign of the *Bull*, Shrewsbury, is a painting of a (once-famous) bull named *Commandant*, transferred to this old house when the licence of another local *Bull* was transferred to a new house of a different name.

There is a *Bullocks* at Cold Norton, Essex, and there are still three *Pied Bulls* at Islington. The famous *Old Pied Bull Inn*, Islington, was pulled down *c.* 1827, the house having existed from the time of Queen Elizabeth. The parlour retained its original character to the last. There was a chimneypiece depicting Hope, Faith, and Charity, with a border of cherubims, fruit and foliage, whilst the ceiling in stucco represented the five senses. Sir Walter Raleigh is said to have been an inhabitant of this house. At what time the house was converted into an inn does not appear. The sign of the *Pied Bull* in stone relief, on the front towards the south, bore the date 1730, which was probably the year this addition was made to the building. That it was an inn in 1665 appears from an episode of the Plague-time related by Defoe in his *Journal of the Plague Year*. The *Pied Bull* accepted a plague-stricken Londoner refused accommodation at the *Angel* and the *White Horse*, and by so doing, introduced a very severe attack of the Plague into Islington.

Perhaps that very odd beast the *Spangled Bull*, in existence as late as 1927 at Kirkheaton, Yorks., may be a variant of the *Pied Bull* sign, possibly due to an unskilful repainting. There are numerous other Black, White and Red Bulls, and a *Grey Bull* at Penrith. The *Dun Bull* is at Mardale, Westmd. There is a *Black Bull* at Alsagey, Ches., and another, Bramwell Brontës haunt, near Patrick Brontë's church at Haworth, Yorks. The *Black Bull* was a famous carriers' inn in Bishopsgate St. and remained until Larwood's time. There is still a *Black Bull* in Whitechapel Rd., E.

The *Red Bull* was the sign of another of the inn-playhouses in Shakespeare's time. Like the *Fortune*, it was mostly frequented by the meaner sorts of people. It was situated in Woodbridge St., Clerkenwell (its site is still called Red Bull Yard), and is supposed to have been erected in the early part of Queen Elizabeth's reign. At all events, it was one of the seventeen playhouses that arose in London between that period and the reign of Charles I. Killigrew's troop of the king's players performed in it until the theatre in Lincoln's Inn Fields opened. The place was then abandoned to exhibitions of gladiators and feats of strength. There was still in Larwood's time a *Bull's Head* in this same street. It was built on the site of the house (now extinct) of Thomas Britton, the Musical Small Coal Man, where he gave his celebrated concerts for a period of thirty-six years, powdered duchesses and fastidious ladies of the Court tripping through his coal repository and climbing up a ladder to assist at these famous meetings.

The *Bull's Head* is often seen instead of the *Bull*; its origin may be from the butcher's arms, which are *az.* two axes saltire-wise *arg.* between two roses *arg.* as many *bulls heads* couped of the second attired *or* etc. At the *Bull's Head* in Clare Market used to meet the artists' club of which Hogarth was a member. The Clerkenwell *Bull's Head* still stands, and there are many other recurrences of the sign, for example in Holbeach, London, Loughborough, Manchester and Salford. A house of this name in Durham may have been called after a former licensee named Turnbull. Often the origin may be that the *Bull's Head* was a badge of Henry VIII. It is curious that in the pictured (?) sign the head is often surmounted by a coronet, perhaps once a crown. Certainly the *Bull's Head* was already used in signs three hundred years ago, since according to Machyn's *Diary* in 1560 the hostess of the *Bull* in Gracechurch St., and the *Bull's Head* beside London Stone were publicly punished as whores and bawds.

As a variation on the *Bull's Head* there is the *Cow's Face*. This is mentioned in an interesting advertisement of 1695 concerning a rascally servant at the *Cow's Face* in Miles Lane, Canon St.

The *Buffalo Head* is common in many places. The latter was the sign in one of the coffee-houses near the Exchange during the South Sea Bubble, and was hung up over the headquarters of a company for a grand dispensary, capital £3,000,000. At the *Buffalo Head* tavern, Charing Cross, Duncan Campbell, the deaf and dumb charlatan whose life was written by Defoe, used at one time to deliver his oracles. There is still an *Old Buffalo Head* at Charing Cross. Elsewhere, probably, as, for example at Ware, Herts., *Buffaloes* like *Druids*, *Foresters*, *Gardeners* and *Oddfellows* (and the ' Arms ' of these) record the meeting-places of the friendly societies which sprang up in the latter part of the 18th century.

Masons' signs are not very common. There is, however, a *Caveac* in Finch Lane,

E.C., which is called after a French refugee who gave his name to the *Caveac* Lodge of Freemasons meeting there.

Among the combinations in which the *Bull* is met with on signboards, the *Bull & Dog*, as for example at Stokesley, N.R. Yorks., and Tixall or Whixall, Salop, is one of the most common. It is derived, like the *Bull & Chain*, from the favourite sport of bull-baiting. A variation of this is the *Bull & Bitch* at Husborn Crawley, Beds. In the sign of the *Bull & Butcher* at Norwich, the Bull is placed in still worse company. The *Bull & Bush* at Hampstead, was made famous in the Victorian era by a comic song introducing its name.

The *Bull & Magpie*, which occurs at Boston, has been explained as meaning the Pie and the Bull of the Roman Church, but as Larwood says, this seems very like a cock-and-bull story. It may be asked whether this might not have arisen out of the sign of the *Pied Bull* thus leading to the *Pie & Bull* or the *Bull & Magpie*. The transition seems simple and easy enough, but should this not be considered satisfactory, since we have the *Cock & Bull* and the *Cock & Pie* we may by a sort of rule of three manœuvre obtain the *Bull & Pie* or *Magpie*. The *Bull & Ram* is in Old St. The *Black Bull & Looking-Glass* is named in an advertisement in the original edition of the *Spectator* as a house in Cornhill. It was evidently a combination of two signs. Still more puzzling is the *Bull & Bedpost*; but as the actual use of this sign as a house decoration remains to be corroborated, we may dismiss it with the remark that the Bedpost, in all probability, was a jocular name for the stake to which the bull was tied when being baited, in allusion to the stout stick formerly used in bed-making to smooth the clothes in their place. The *Bull & Swan*, Stamford, may be heraldic, both these animals being badges of the York family; in all probability, however, the *Swan* was the first sign, the *Bull* being added on account of the singular custom of Bull Running, which yearly took place at both Tamworth and Stamford on St John's Eve. The *Bull in the Pound* is the Bull punished for trespass, and put in the pound or pinfold—whilst the *Bull & Oak* at Sheffield (at Market Bosworth there is a house with the sign of the *Bull in the Oak*) may have originated from the sign of the *Bull* being suspended from an oak tree, or referring to an oak tree standing near the house. Bulls are often tied to trees or posts in pastures, and this also may have given rise to the sign.

Other odd combinations are the *Bull & Horseshoes*, Latton (? Ex), and the *Bull & Pump*, High St., Shoreditch, and formerly at Shrewsbury. At Shrewsbury was also the *Bull in the Barn*, notorious in the 18th century for the number of clandestine marriages celebrated there. It was said to stand on the site of an old chapel. The *Bull & Stars* was at Putney. The *Bull & Last*, Highgate, is said to have no connexion with cobblers, but to mark the last stage (at the *Bull*) of the coach journey from Scotland and the North Country to London.

Visitors to the Isle of Wight will have noticed the word *Bugle* frequently inscribed under the picture of a *Bull* on the inn signboards there. Bugle is a provincial name for a wild bull. It is an old English word, used by Sir John Mandeville, and it was still current in the 17th century. Randle Holme in 1688 classes the Bugle, or *Babalus*, amongst ' the savage beasts of the greater sort '. The horns of this animal used as a musical instrument gave a name to the Buglehorn. It may be remarked that the term *bugle* doubtless came, in old times, with other Gallicisms common to Sussex and Hampshire, from across the Channel, where the word *bugle* is still preserved in the verb *beugler*, the common French word for the lowing of cattle.

The *Ox* is rather uncommon. Perhaps when it occurs it may sometimes be as the symbol of St Luke. Both notable breeds and famous individual beasts are commemorated. There is a *Durham Ox* at Burslem, Staffs., and one at Lincoln, a *Castle Howard Ox* at Yorks, and a *Fat Ox* at Whitley Bay, Northumb., there is a *Craven Ox Head* in George St., York, and a *Grey Ox* at Hartshead, W.R. Yorks. The *Ox & Compasses* at Poulton Swindon, Cumb., is evidently a jocular imitation of the London sign of the *Goat & Compasses*.

The *Cow* is more common ; its favourite colours being Red, Brown, White, Spotted and Spangled. The *Spotted Cow* at Littlehampton, Sussex, one of Messrs. Henty & Constable's houses, has a fine modern sign by Ralph Ellis. The *Red Cow* appears as a sign near Holborn Conduit on the 17th-century trades tokens, and there is an old house of this name in Hammersmith Rd. It also gave a name to the alehouse in Anchor and Hope Lane, Wapping, in which Lord Chancellor Jeffreys was taken prisoner disguised as a sailor and trying to escape to the Continent after the abdication of James II. There is a *Cow* at Ilchester and one at Southampton, a *Cow & Pail* at Ipswich, a *Heifer* at Newbiggin, and there was a *Wensleydale Heifer* at West Witton, N.R. Yorks. The house is now known as the *Town of Ramsgate*, a sign adopted to attract the Ramsgate fishermen who came to sell their catches at Wapping Old Stairs.

A heraldic origin is not necessary for this colour of the cow. According to Misson, a French traveller in England in 1719 :—

> Cows (I mean that whole species of horned beasts) are more commonly black than *red* in England. 'Tis for this reason that they have a greater value for Red Cow's Milk than for Black Cow's Milk. Whereas in France we esteem the Black Cow's Milk, because Red Cows are more common with us.

In 1700 Tom Brown speaking of the Green Walks in St James's Park says : The senators talking of state affairs and the price of corn and cattle were disturbed with the noisy Milk folk crying : A can of Milk, Ladies ; a can of *Red* Cow's Milk, sirs ? The preference for the *Red* Cow's milk may, however, have a more remote origin, namely, from the ordinance of the law contained in Num. xix, 2, where a *red* heifer is enjoined to be sacrificed as a purification for sin. Hence, *Red* Cow's milk is particularly recommended in old prescriptions and panaceas.

The *Red Cow* in Bow St. was the sign of a noted tavern, afterwards called the *Red Rose*, which stood at the corner of Rose Alley. It was when going home from this tavern that Dryden was cudgelled by bravoes, hired by Lord Rochester. In Dryden's old age, Pope, then a boy, came here to look at the great man whose fame in after years he was to equal, if not eclipse.   The tavern was the famous mart for libels and lampoons.

Near Marlborough, Wilts., there is an alehouse having the sign of the *Red Cow* with the rhyme :—

> The Red Cow
> Gives good Milk now.

That under a *Brown Cow* at Oldham is even clumsier :—

> This Cow gives such liquor,
> 'Twould puzzle a Viccar [*sic*].

The *Heifer* is to be met with sometimes in Yorkshire, but almost always with some local adjective, as the *Craven Heifer* at Stainforth and at Skipton, the *Airedale Heifer* at Mirfield and at Keighley, the *Wensleydale Heifer* at West Witton, the *Wellington Heifer* at Ainderby Steeple.   There is a *Scotch Heifer* at Manchester, and one of the few occurrences of the *Heifer* is at New Biggin ;   The *Durham Heifer* is also found.   Probably in many such cases the original sign has been the *Red Cow* or the *Dun Cow*, but with the development of scientific cattle breeding and the growth of local specialized breeds in the late 18th and early 19th centuries, the landlord with the aid of a pot of paint, has transmogrified a nondescript beast into a member of the breed locally most in favour.   The *Pied Calf* at Spalding seems to present an almost solitary instance of a calf on the signboard.

Neither are sheep very common ;   the *Ram* was a noted carriers' inn in the 17th century in West Smithfield, and indeed continued as such until the destruction of this old cattle market.   The crest of the cloth-workers was a mount *vert*, thereon a ram *statant* ;   so that this sign in that locality was very well chosen, being in honour of the cattle-dealers on ordinary occasions, and serving for the cloth-workers in the time of Bartholomew Fair, for whose benefit the fair was founded.   There is a *Ram* at Tidworth, Hants., and another, a pleasant half-timbered building at Wotton-under-Edge, Glos., and a *Ram & Hogget* at Bradfield, Essex.   In 1668 there were two *Ram's Head* inns in Fenchurch St., one of them being a carriers' inn for the Essex people. The *Ram's Skin* which occurs at Spalding, Lincs., is another name for the *Fleece*.   The *Black Tup* figures on a sign near Rochdale.   Larwood suggests that this may be an allusion to the well-known custom associated with the claiming of free bench in copy-hold lands by a widow who has been guilty of incontinency.   All the instances cited in the standard authorities relate however to manors in Devonshire, Berkshire and Somerset, with one odd example from Salop, so this attractive theory, like many others concerning inn signs, rests upon a very insecure foundation.

Though the *Ram* is rarely, and the sheep never seen on the signboard, the *Lamb* is not uncommon.   There is a *Lamb* at Higham, Suff., and one at Ely.   In 1761 the *Lamb* in Abchurch Lane is mentioned in an Admiralty announcement as the house where the officers and company of H.M.S. *Boreas* might receive their prize money.

The *Wiltshire Lamb* is at Southsea, Portsmouth. There are two examples of the *Loving Lamb* in and near Dudley, Worcs. Doubtless, many *Lamb* signs favoured by booksellers had originally represented the *Lamb* with the flag of the Apocalypse. The sign was used by other trades also : in 1673 and according to the *London Gazette*, it was the distinctive sign of a confectioner at the lower end of Gracechurch St. There was a *Distressed Lamb* at Poole, Dorset, in 1666.

A few combinations also occur, but most of these are not inn signs as the *Lamb & Breeches*, the sign of Churches & Christie, leather-sellers and breeches-makers, on London Bridge in the 18th century. This was a sign like that of the *Hat & Beaver*, in which the animal and the article manufactured from its skin were displayed together. The *Lamb & Crown* was, to judge from the *Public Advertiser*, a sort of colonial or emigration office in Threadneedle St., near the South Sea House in 1759.

At the present day there is a *Lamb & Lark* inn at Keynsham, and one in Printing House Lane, Blackfriars. It is a representation of the proverb, 'Go to bed with the *Lamb* and rise with the *Lark*'. The *Lamb & Hare* figure together in Portsmouth Place, Lower Kennington Lane. The *Lamb & Still* is a combination intimating the sale of distilled waters. It was in 1711 the sign of a house in Compton St.

If we except the heraldic *Blue Boar* and the *Sow & Pigs*, we shall find few *Pigs* on inn signs except as, for example, the *Pig & Whistle*, the *Pig & Tinderbox*, the *Pig in Misery*, etc., *q.v.* There are a few *Hampshire Hogs* (Hampshire hogs have been celebrated since Michael Drayton's time), for example at Norwich and at Hampstead. The last house belongs to Messrs. Watney. It has a fine modern sign by Ralph Ellis. It is believed that the *Pretty Pigs* sign, Tamworth, Warws., is unique. There is a *Little Pig* at Amblecote, Worcs., and a *Black Pig* at Barnsole, Kent. The *Pig in the Pound*, Romford, and the *Hog in the Pound* at Oxford St., W., jocularly called the *Gentleman in Trouble*.

This sign was said to have been originally that of a butcher and depicted a well-fed pig in a stye. When the house became an inn the rails of the stye were mistaken for those of a pinfold. This latter was formerly a starting-point for coaches, and became notorious through the crime committed by its landlady, Catherine Hayes. She was induced by her lover to murder her husband, after which she cut off his head, put it in a bag, and threw it in the Thames. It floated ashore and was put on a pole in St Margaret's Churchyard, Westminster, in order that it might be recognized ; and by this primitive means the murderess was detected. The man was hanged, and Catherine burned alive at Tyburn in 1726.

The *Goat* is not very common ; there was a *Goat* Inn at Hammersmith, taken down in 1826, and rebuilt under the name of the *Suspension Bridge Inn* ; up to that time, the sign and the woodwork from which it was suspended used to extend across the street. The *Goat in Boots*, on the Fulham Rd., was in old times called simply the *Goat*. It has a sign in relief in terra-cotta. Besides these there is a *Black Goat* in Lincoln, and a *Grey Goat* in Penrith and Carlisle, and there are a few others without addition of colour.

It is no wonder that the *Dog* should be of frequent occurrence on the signboard. Pepys mentions a tavern of that name in Westminster which he used occasionally to visit. Taylor mentions a *Dog* at ' Riple ', i.e. Ripley, Surrey, in 1636. The house is still extant, but is known as the *Talbot*. It is mentioned below (p. 285). In 1768, the author of the *Art of Living in London* recommended the *Dog* in Holywell St. for a quiet good dinner :—

> Where disencumbered of all form or show
> We to a moment might or sit or go ;
> Eat what the palate recommends us hot,
> Yet not considered as a useless guest.

The *Dog* in Newgate St. was a house of resort of William Davis the Golden Farmer. There is a *Dog* extant at Bedfield, Suff., and one at Hempstead Rd., Catford.

For some unknown reason the *Black Dog* seems the greatest favourite ; perhaps it refers to the English terrier formerly very popular. In the 17th century there was a *Black Dog* Tavern near Newgate, a house of old standing, of which trades tokens are extant. Akerman in his *Trades Tokens* makes a mistake in surmising that Luke Hutton's *Black Dogge of Newgate* had anything to do with this tavern. That poem is simply against ' coney-catchers ', that is roguish detectives or informers of the Jonathan Wild stamp. Such a one is personified under the name because the coneycatchers used to hunt people down by threatening them with Newgate. This *Black Dog* may have derived its name originally from the canine spectre that until late years frightened the timorous in rural districts, just as the terrible *Dun Cow* and the *Lambton Worm* were the terror of rustics in former times. Near Lyme Regis there is an alehouse which has this black fiend in all his ancient ugliness painted over the door. Its adoption arose from a legend that the spectral black dog used to haunt at nights the kitchen fire of a neighbouring farm-house. The dog would sit opposite the farmer ; but one night a little extra liquor gave the man additional courage and he struck at the dog, intending to rid himself of the horrid thing. Away flew the dog and the farmer after it from one room to another, until it sprang through the roof, and was seen no more that night. In mending the hole a hoard of money was discovered, which of course was connected in some way or other with the dog's strange visit. Near the house is a lane still called Dog Lane, which is now the favourite walk of the black dog, and to this *genius loci* the sign is dedicated.

There was another notorious *Black Dog* next door to the *Devil* Tavern, the shop of Abel Roper who was the original printer of *Lillibulero*. There is also a *Black Dog* still at Emsworth, Hants., and one at Sunbury, Mx., and there is or was a *White Dog* at York. There is still a *Red Dog* at High Halston, Kent. Tokens are extant of the *Pied Dog* in Seething Lane, 1667, and the sign is still to be seen occasionally. We very rarely meet with the *Blue Dog* ; but there is an example in Grantham, and the sign occurs in a few other places.

Sometimes a peculiar breed is chosen, as the *Setter Dog* formerly at Retford, Notts., and still at Rainow, Ches. ; many such signs are dealt with below (p. 259), the *Pointer* at Peckfield, N.R. Yorks, and Alresford, Hants., and the *Beagle* at Shute, near Axminster. The *Merry Harriers* are common in hunting counties. There is a *Harrier* at Link Hill, Kent, and a *Merry Harriers* at Cullompton. Equally common is the *Greyhound*, particularly in the North Country, where coursing has long been a favourite sport. In the 17th century the *Greyhound* was the sign of a fashionable tavern in London, for in a ballad in the Roxburgh collection a young gallant is introduced who is about to forsake his evil courses and turn over a new leaf. He gives a last farewell to all his doxies and remembers all those delightfully wicked places he used to haunt formerly, and amongst them :

> Farewell unto the *Greyhound*
> And farewell to the *Bell*
> And farewell to my landlady,
> Whom I do love so well.

This was probably the same *Greyhound* mentioned by Machyn, apparently situated in Fleet St., where the gaudily dressed Spanish ambassador took his stirrup-cup before leaving London. The same author mentions the sign elsewhere, apparently in Westminster in 1557.

There are many provincial *Greyhounds*. One at Carshalton has a fine modern painted sign by A. Houghton, a local schoolmaster.

The *White Greyhound* seems to occur only as a bookseller's sign.

The sign of the *Black Greyhound* is also of frequent occurrence, and at Grantham there is a *Blue Greyhound*. It may be noted that in Colsterworth, Lincs., are the *Blue Bull*, the *Blue Cow*, the *Blue Dog*, and the *Blue Fox* ; there is a *Blue Dog* also at Stainby, Lincs., besides the *Blue Pig*, the *Blue Ram*, etc., in Grantham,* which town can also boast of the unique sign of the *Blue Man*.

Elsewhere a contrast in signs is probably merely an indication of trade rivalry between the landlords as the *Young Devil* in Fleet St. was merely a short-lived rival to the famous (old) *Devil*, so the names of the two inns at Putney in Taylor's time—1636 —the *Red Lion* and the *White Lion* suggest that one was adopted in opposition to the other.

The *Talbot*, an old and now almost obsolete term for a large kind of hunting dog, has acquired a literary celebrity from having been substituted for the old sign of the *Tabard* Inn in Southwark, whence the pilgrims started on their merry journey to Canterbury. A *Talbot* Inn in the Strand is mentioned in a quaint advertisement which

---

* Grantham is the best historical example of Party colours in inns. Lord Dysart was a Whig and owned most of the inns in Grantham, so had them all called Blues—*Blue Lion, Blue Boar*, and so on. Probably this explanation applies only occasionally to blue signs elsewhere.

The party colours varied in different constituencies. In Newark, for example, Tory was red and Whig blue. This was from the old Royalist (King's) scarlet, contrasting with ' Presbyterian True Blue '. Then after the Home Rule split, the Conservative Liberal Unionist married the Tory-Whig colours and had the joint colours—red and blue—while the Radical-Liberals had yellow. Gladstone as a Tory, fought his 1832 election as a red, and his banner and red-election cards, etc., are in the Newark Museum.

Larwood quotes from the *Public Advertiser* of 1759. The *Talbot*, Ripley, Surrey, is a well-known house of call on the London-Portsmouth road. There was a *Gilded Talbot* at Shrewsbury up to *c.* 1820.

At the foot of Birdlip Hill, Gloucs., there is a *Talbot* which has a sign painted with two inscriptions. At the side where the road is level it says :—

> Before you do this hill go up,
> Stop and drink a cheerful cup.

On the side of the hill there is :—

> You're down the hill, all danger's past,
> Stop and drink a cheerful glass.

Probably in general both the *Talbot* and the *Spotted Dog* are adopted in honour of the House of Talbot, earls of Shrewsbury.

A publican at Odell, Beds., has chosen the *Mad Dog*, possibly as having a great horror of water (another at Pidley, Hunts., not to be behind the *Mad Dog*, has put up the *Mad Cat*). There was once an odd and apparently unmeaning sign in Tabernacle Walk, now Tabernacle St., namely, the *Barking Dog*.

Almost all the combinations of the sign of the dog point towards sports, as the *Dog & Bear*, which was very common in the 17th century, when bear-baiting was the fashion and kings and queens countenanced it by their presence. The sign is still found at Nottingham, at Leek, Staffs., at Stamford, etc. The *Dog & Duck*, though it sometimes relates to fowling, in general refers to another barbarous pastime, styled in 1665 the 'Royal Diversion of Duck Hunting', in which ducks were hunted in a pond by spaniels. The pleasure consisted in seeing the duck make her escape from the dog's mouth by diving. It was much practised in the neighbourhood of London till the beginning of the 19th century, when it went out of fashion and most of the ponds were gradually built over. One of the most notorious *Dog & Duck* taverns stood in St George's Fields, where Bethlehem Hospital was built later. It had a long room with tables and benches, and an organ at the upper end. In its last days it was frequented only by thieves and prostitutes, and similar characters. After a long and wicked existence it was at length put down by the magistrates. In the 17th century it was famous for springs, but already in Garrick's time its reputation was very equivocal. He referred to it in the *Maid of the Oaks*, 1774.

> St George's Fields, with taste and fashion struck,
> Display Arcadia at the *Dog & Duck*
> And Drury Misses, here in tawdry pride,
> Are there 'Pastoras' by the fountain side ;
> To frowsy bowers they reel through midnight damps,
> With Fauns half drunk and Dryads breaking lamps.

The old stone sign was in Larwood's time still preserved, embedded in the brick wall of the garden of Bethlehem Hospital. It represented a dog squatted on his haunches with a duck in his mouth, and the date 1617. It is now in the Cuming Museum.

PLATE
II

BEXLEY PUBLIC LIBRARIES.

PLATE
12

Another famous *Dog & Duck* Inn formerly stood on the site of Hertford St., Mayfair. It was an old-fashioned wooden public-house extensively patronized by the butchers and other rough characters during May Fair time. The pond in which the sport took place was situated behind the house, and was surrounded by a gravel walk shaded with willow trees. It was boarded round to the height of the knee, to preserve the over-excited spectators from being crowded into the water during the performances. Pepys refers, 26 March 1664, to the ducking-pond near the *King's Head* at Islington. There are numerous provincial *Dog-&-Ducks*, for example, at Sutton-in-Ashfield, and there is one at Rotherhithe.

There is a *Dog & Otter* at Great Harwood, Lancs. The *Dog & Badger*, Kingswood, Glos., and Medmenham, Bucks., refers to the now obsolete sport of badger-baiting. More genial sports, however, are called to mind by the *Dog & Gun*, *Dog & Partridge*, both of which are found, for example, at Nottingham, the second also at Dovedale Thorpe, Derbys., and the *Dog & Pheasant*, which is quite common. Monson Fitzjohn suggests that the two last-named signs may indicate houses having game retailers' licences, either before or after they were licensed to retail beer. The matter seems rather dubious. There are said to be thirty-five *Dog-&-Pheasants* in Lancashire alone. The *Dog & Rabbit* is at Warsop, Notts. Probably this refers to rabbit coursing with whippets. There is a *Dog & Fox* (or dog fox?) at Wimbledon. The *Rat & Ferret* was at Breedon-on-the-Hill, Leics.

The incident of the cat-hater, told in the *Spectator*, is a proof of the presence of cats on the signboard, where indeed they are still to be met with, but very rarely. There is a *Cat* sign at Egremont and one at Whitehaven, both in Cumberland, a *Black Cat* at St Leonard's Gate, Lancaster, and a *Red Cat* at Birkenhead. These are undoubtedly heraldic, the (wild) cat being the crest of the (Pennington) Barons Muncaster. Probably the *Cat* in Whitecross St. is a more domestic creature. This is a rather rare sign.

The *Cat & Lion*, which we meet with sometimes, as at Stockport and Stretton, was probably at one time the *Tiger & Lion*. It is occasionally accompanied by the distich :—

> The Lion is strong, the cat is vicious,
> My ale is strong, and so is my liquors.

The *Cat & Tiger* is at Sevenoaks.

The sign of the *Cat in the Basket* or *Cat in the Cage* doubtless originated from the cruel game once practised by our ancestors of shooting at a cat in a basket. The *Cat i' th' Wall* and *Cat i' th' Window*, both at Halifax, are supposed to be named after stuffed pet cats which gave first nicknames, then names to the houses. The next sign may be a corruption of that first named. There is a *Cat in the Well* at Halifax, a *Squinting Cat* at Pannel near Harrogate, and a *Tabby Cat* at West Grinstead, Sussex. The *Civet Cat* is dealt with elsewhere (p. 104).

Serpents and snakes are very uncommon. There is a *Snake*, however, outside Sheffield on a well-known pass over the Pennines.

K

Chapter VII

BIRDS AND FOWLS

BIRD signs were never very general in England, though certainly the *Cock* and the *Swan* appear to have found more votaries than many other signboard animals. The *Eagle* is not nearly so common : some instances of it already mentioned are undoubtedly of *heraldic* origin. There is an *Eagle* at Snaresbrook, Essex, and another at Chesham, Bucks., an *American Eagle* at Bristol, a *Black Eagle* in Brick Lane, a *White Eagle* at Brighton, and an *Eaglet* in the Seven Sisters Rd. From heraldry also the *Golden Eagle* may be derived ; it was the emblem of the Eastern Empire, and occurs in various family arms (though there actually do exist golden eagles). The *Eagle & Ball*, of which there are three in Birmingham, was suggested by the imperial eagle standing on the globe, or the spread eagle with the globe in his talons. The *Eagle & Serpent* found at Kinlet, Salop, or the *Eagle & Snake* to be seen at Burslem, Stoke-on-Trent, is a mediaeval emblem of courage united to prudence. Other signs occurring less often are the *Bustard*, South Rauceby, Lincs., the *Condor*, Wye St., the *Hawk*, Halesworth, Suff., and the *Kite*, Osney, Oxon.

Mythical birds also have been in great favour. The burning and reviving of the *Phoenix* for instance, like the curious habits of the salamander and the dragon, typified certain transformations obtained by chemistry, whence he was a very general sign with chemists, and may still be sometimes seen on their drug-pots and transparent lamps. The firm of Godfrey and Cooke, for instance, have adhered to it ever since the opening of their business, A.D. 1680.

Not only apothecaries used this emblem, but all kinds of shops adopted it. In the time of James I it was the sign of one of the places where plays were acted in Drury Lane—sometimes also called the Cockpit Theatre.

The character ascribed to the Pelican was fully as fabulous as that of the Phoenix. From a clumsy, gluttonous, piscivorous water-bird, she was transformed into a mystic emblem of Christ. Jerome gives the story of the pelican restoring her young ones destroyed by serpents, as an illustration of the destruction of man by the old serpent, and his salvation by the blood of Christ. Heraldically a pelican in her piety is one feeding her young from the flesh upon her own bleeding breast. In this form she often appears upon church lecterns, etc., and in many mediaeval choir stalls.

The *Pelican* at Speenhamland, Berks., is famous in economic and social history as the birthplace in 1795 of the notorious Speenhamland System, by which farm labourers' wages were subsidized from the poor rates. It has another claim to fame as the target of a wit who wrote :

The Pelican at Speenhamland,
That stands below the hill,
May well be called the Pelican,
From his enormous *bill*.

It is amusing to see how public-house wit runs in the same channel. In 1792 an anecdote is fathered upon Foote. 'Pray what is your name?' said he to the Master of the *Castle* Inn at Salthill, near Windsor. 'Partridge, sir!'—'Partridge! it should be Woodcock by the length of your *bill*!'

Similarly Longfellow's celebrated verses on the *Raven* at Zurich have a suspicious family resemblance to a well-known epigram on the *Golden Lion* at Brecon, which we refrain from quoting here since we are restricting ourselves to the English inn. The stanzas may be turned up in Larwood and Hotten.

The *Pyewipe*, Lincoln, takes its name from a provincial term Peewit. The *Raven*, or the *Black Raven*, was never a common inn sign. On the Great West Rd. between Murrell Green and Basingstoke, the *Raven* Inn is still to be seen (or was a century or so ago), in which the incendiary John the painter, *alias* James Aitken, the man who set fire to Portsmouth Dockyard in 1776, was taken prisoner. This house was built in 1653 and preserved much of its original appearance.

Where the sign occurs it may sometimes be as a Jacobite emblem, since the bird is the badge of the old Scottish kings as well as of the St Aubins and Macdonalds. There is a *Black Raven* in Bishopsgate, E.C., of which trades tokens of the 17th century are extant, and a *Raven* at Norwich, and one at Cobridge, Stoke-on-Trent. The *Raven*, Shrewsbury, is no doubt from the arms of the Corbets, a local family. It is known that Sir Vincent Corbet in 1668 paid the Corporation a quit rent for the premises. The *Three Ravens* is found at Tilmanstone, Kent.

The common occurrence of the *Blackbird* and the *Cock & Blackbird* seems puzzling. Larwood and Hotten think, on the strength of one of Allan Ramsay's collected ballads, that it is due to the use also of the Blackbird as a Jacobite symbol. There is a passage in a letter of Sir John Hinton, physician to Charles II, which seems to imply that the black boy was a nickname for Charles II. What lends strength to the supposition is the occurrence of such a sign as the *Crow in the Oak*, at Foleshill, Coventry, which seems to have been a covert way of representing the royal oak during the times of the Commonwealth. The disguise continued after there was no more need of it, similarly to the *Cat & Wheel* and other signs dating from the same period, for no other reason than that the house had then become known by the sign. In the same manner the *Oak & Black Dog* (at Stretton on Dunsmore, Worcs.), if not a combination of two signs, may have been put up in derision of the Prince in the *Royal Oak*.

The *Crow* or the *Black Crow*, is also a common sign; so are the *Three Blackbirds*, then there is the *Chough*, at Chard in Somerset, the *Three Choughs* at Yeovil, and the *Three Crows*, all of which belong to the same family, and seem to have the same origin. The *Three Blackbirds, Choughs, Crows, Ravens*, etc., may allude to Charles, *de jure* King of England, James Duke of York and Prince Rupert of the Rhine.

The *Crow* rarely occurs as a sign by itself. There was however a *Split Crow* (a variant of the *Spread Eagle*) in the Broad at Oxford which retained the patronage of Balliol men long after the members of other colleges were generally patronizing the coffee-houses.

The *Stork* now occurs sometimes, although not among the older English signs. Traditionally the bird is an emblem of filial piety, just as the pelican is that of parental affection. When the old bird was too feeble to seek meat for himself, he was said to be fed by the young ones, and even carried about on their backs. If the young bird could find no other food for its parent, it would regurgitate its own previous day's dinner. Probably from this the stork became a harbinger of good luck for the house on which he alighted. To this day it is the stork that brings the babies. Its reputation for benevolence and affection and as an omen of good fortune has been continuous from classical times to those of Walt Disney. There are three *Storks* in and near Birmingham.

The *Three Cranes* was formerly a favourite London sign. Three birds were represented instead of three cranes, which in the Vintry used to lift the barrels of wine. The *Three Cranes* was a famous tavern as early as the reign of James I. It was one of the taverns frequented by the wits of Ben Jonson's time. In *Bartholomew Fair* he speaks of the 'pretenders to wit—Three Cranes, Mitre and Mermaid men'.

On 23 January 1661 Pepys dined at this tavern with some poor relations at the wedding of 'Uncle Fenner'. His sufferings were intense, the lady was pitifully ugly and illbred, her relatives sorry mean people, the room was a narrow, crammed dog-hole, and the dinner was a poor one. Opposite this tavern people generally left their boats to shoot the bridge, walking round to Billingsgate, where they would re-enter them. The Three Cranes Wharf still exists, but the house is gone. The *Three Cranes* sign occurs also at York.

The Cornish *Chough* is often found in south-west England, for example, at Yeovil and at Chard. This is a local bird and occurs in the bearings of many West Country families, for example, the Williams of Brideswell.

The *Cock* occurs frequently on the signboard. It is one of the oldest signs, already in use at the time of the Romans, who record that one Eros, a freedman of Licius Africanus Cerealis, kept an inn at Narbonne at the sign of the *Cock*—'a gallo gallinaceo'. In Christian times the sign acquired a new prestige. Skelton considered the bird to 'preche like a Postle' since he told man the night was past. This bird in the legends of the Middle Ages, was surrounded with a mystical, religious halo. Our Lord was born at the time of cock-crow. Cock-crowing symbolizes the morning of the Resurrection. Devils and ghosts disappear at the time of cock-crow. And, of course, there is in cock-crow the reminder of St Peter's denial of his Master.

There are well-known *Cock* signs at Camberwell Green, S.E., and Great Portland St., W. One of the oldest *Cock* taverns in London was that in Tothill St., Westminster, re-christened as the *Cock & Tabard* a century or so ago, and now no more. In the back parlour was the portrait of a jolly, bluff-looking man in a red coat, said to represent the driver of the first mail to Oxford, which started from this tavern. Tradition says that the men employed in building work at Westminster Abbey in the reign of Henry VII, used to receive their wages at this house. It was formerly entered by steps, the building which existed in Larwood's time exhibiting traces of great antiquity, and appearing at one time to have been a house of considerable pretensions. The rafters and timbers were principally of cedar wood. There was a curious hiding-place on the staircase, and a massive carving of Abraham about to offer his son Isaac with another in wood representing the Adoration of the Magi, said to have been left in pledge at some remote period, for an unpaid score. The cock may have been adopted as a sign here on account of the vicinity of the Abbey, of which St Peter was the patron, for in the Middle Ages a cock crowing on the top of a pillar was often one of the accessories in a picture of the apostle, a very unkind allusion to the saint's delinquencies.

The *Cock* in Bow St., witnessed a disgraceful scene in the reign of Charles II when

> Lord Buckhurst, with Sir Charles Sedley and Sir Thomas Ogle, got drunk, and going into the balcony, exposed themselves to the public, in very indecent postures. At last, as they grew warmer, Sedley stood forth naked, and harangued the populace in such profane language, that the public indignation was awakened. The crowd attempted to force the door, and being repulsed, drove in the performers with stones, and broke the windows of the house.

It was on his way home from supper at this house, 21 December 1670, that Sir John Coventry, who gives his name to the ' Coventry Act ' against mutilation, was attacked by several men, and had his nose cut to the bone. When Sir John proposed in the Commons to lay a tax on the theatres, this was opposed by the Court, the players being ' the King's servants and a part of his pleasure ' ; upon which Sir John asked whether the king's pleasure lay among the men or among the women that acted ? The assault was committed by four ruffians instigated by the Duke of Monmouth.

Pepys praises the *Cock* in Suffolk St. where he enjoyed the ordinary on 15 March 1669, and where three weeks later he took Mistress Pepys and a party of friends. At the same period there was another celebrated *Cock* still existing in Fleet St. near Temple Bar, properly called the *Cock & Bottle*, a sign still occurring, for example, in Cannon St., E.C., Preston, and at Hemel Hempstead, Herts. Nicholas Hart the famous five-day sleeping-boy mentioned in the *Spectator* had his visions of the other world at the *Cock & Bottle* in Little Britain in 1711.

The *Cock & Bottle* sign seems to be a figurative rendering of liquor *on draught and in bottle*, cock being good old English, and still a good provincial word for the spigot or tap in a barrel. The sign is, however, generally represented by a cock standing on a bottle. The present sign of the Fleet St. House, still conspicuous in gilt over the door, is said to have been carved by no less a hand than that of Grinling Gibbons. During the plague time of 1665 the landlord intending to close his house very honestly advertised for all holding his tokens to repair to it and receive their sterling equivalent. After the Plague Pepys on 23 April 1668 went by water to the Temple and then to the

Cock alehouse with Knipp and Mrs. Pierce to drink and eat lobster and sing in honour of the King's coronation day.

Exactly one hundred years later, the *Cock* is named with encomia on its porter, in the *Art of Living in London*, but Larwood thinks it is to be hoped that the porter was better than the poetry :—

> Nor think the Cock with these not on a par,
> The celebrated Cock of Temple Bar,
> Whose Porter best of all bespeaks its praise,
> Porter that's worthy of the Poet's lays.

In *Will Waterproof's Monologue*, the fame of the waiter of the tavern is handed down to posterity in Tennyson's verses.

Jackson the pugilist, who has a pompous epitaph on his grave in the Brompton burial-ground, kept for some time the *Cock*, Sutton, still standing on the Epsom Rd. Finally, some century ago, there was a *Cock & Bottle* in Bristol kept by a man named John England, who added to his sign the well-known words :—

> England expects every man to do his duty.

The sign of the *Three Cocks* in St John's Lane occurs in an advertisement of 1711 issued by a pawnbroker *cum* goldsmith. Then pawnbrokers did not always rigorously adhere to the *Three Balls*, they were occasionally goldsmiths, and in that capacity used any sign.

It is rarely that the sign of the *Cock* designates any particular colour. There is, however, a *Black Cock* in Owen St., Tipton, and one at Broughton-in-Furness, Lancs. A cock of this colour was always considered something more than an ordinary bird ; with the Greeks it was a grateful sacrifice to Esculapius and Pluto, and in the Middle Ages it played a prominent part in matters of witchcraft. There are one or two *White Cocks* in north Staffordshire, for example, at Blythe Bridge. The *Blue Cock* is a sign at Leicester ; but none of the colours is common. At Hargrave, Suffolk, there is a *Cock's Head*, put up either in imitation of a nag's, bull's, bear's, or boar's head, or as the crest of a fool's cap, which, in old times, usually terminated with a cock's head.

Though some sort of religious prestige may at first have prompted the choice of the cock, more profane ideas latterly contributed to make it popular. Such were those associated with the pastimes of ' cock-shying ' and cock-fighting. To this first practice alludes the sign of William Brandon, on Dowgate Hill, which was called *Have at it*, his token representing a man about to throw a stick at a cock. This cruel game was very common in alehouses in former times, the whole sport consisting in throwing a stick at an unfortunate cock who was tied to a stake. If the animal was killed it was the thrower's property, if not, he forfeited the small sum paid for each ' shy '. A variant of the ' sport ' was frequently practised in the old Grammar Schools on Shrove Tuesdays, the boys providing the cocks, and the bruised carcases of the unfortunate birds being the perquisite of the schoolmaster and usher. Medals are extant of the reign of William III, on which John Bull is represented throwing sticks at the French cock, not a very lofty allegory.

Cock-fighting was a favourite diversion with the Romans, and we find continual traces of it during their occupation here. Fitz-Stephen says it was the sport of school-boys in his time. According to Larwood and Hotten (who gives no reference for the statement) King Henry VIII, though not specially notable for kind-heartedness, ' felt his heart melt at the miseries of the cocks, and made edicts against cock-fights ', yet with Tudor inconsistency built a cock-pit for himself at Whitehall. James I also was a great follower of the sport. Though often suppressed by various sovereigns, the evil would always break out again, till it was finally abolished by Act of Parliament in 1849. In Staffordshire, Westmorland and other counties where the sport is still occasionally practised on the sly, the *Fighting Cocks* is a favourite sign. It occurs, for example, at Wolverhampton. The *Fighting Cocks*, Dartmouth St., S.W., had a fine sign, now preserved in a private house in Suffolk. The *Fighting Cocks* at St Albans is one of the numerous claimants to the honour of being the oldest inn in England—built A.D. 795 ! Actually the recorded history of the place goes back well into the 16th century, and the building is certainly much older than this. There is a *Gamecock* at Kingsdown. On the topic of cock-fighting it may be noted that a few old inns have still their cock-pits. The *Bear*, Woodstock, has a fine collection of cock-fighting equipment, hoods, spurs, etc.

The *Cock* occurs in innumerable combination with all kinds of heterogeneous objects, many of which seem merely selected for their oddity. The *Cock & Trumpet* is a common sign found, for example, at Garston, typifying those ideas about the cock expressed above. This simile is constantly used by the poets,[*] and most beauti-fully enlarged upon by Shakespeare in *Hamlet*, Act I, Sc. 1. Sometimes the sign is heraldic. The Cock *gu.* and Trumpet *Or* are the crest of the (Acheson) Earls of Gosford.

The *Cock & Bell* if not a simple combination of two signs may be derived from another Shrove Tuesday cock-fighting custom. The party whose cock won the most battles was held victorious in the cock-pit, and gained the prize—a small silver *bell* suspended to a button of the victor's hat, and worn for three successive Sundays. This is an old sign, and occurs on a Birchin Lane trades token between 1648 and 1672. It is still found in the provinces at High Easter, Essex.

The *Cock & Breeches* originated in a favourite form of gilt gingerbread at Bartholo-mew Fair. There is a very coarse anecdote in Joe Miller concerning such a sign. The *Cock & Bull* is still frequently seen, but though the meaning of the phrase is well under-stood, neither its origin, nor the meaning of the two animals on the signboard, have as yet been properly explained. Larwood suggests very reasonably that many of the explanations advanced of this (and several other) signs are truly cock-and-bull stories. The sign occurs amongst the 17th-century trades tokens.

The *Cock & Dolphin* was the sign of one of the London carriers' inns whence ran

[*] For example, Michael Drayton.

the Hampstead coach in 1681. Hatton in 1708 placed this inn 'on the east side of Gray's Inn Lane, near the middle'. At the present day there is an inn of this sign in Kendal, Westmorland. It is more likely to be a combination of two signs than to refer to the French Cock and the Dolphin in the arms of the Dauphin. Other similar 'impaled' signs are the *Cock & Anchor* at Gateshead and in Dublin, the *Cock & Swan*, and the *Cock & Crown*, both in Wakefield, the *Cock & Bear* at Nuneaton, and the *Cock & Ostrich* at Norwich. The *Cock & Serpents* in Church Lane, Chelsea, had a sign dated 1652. The *Cock & House* in Norwich may originally have been the cocking-house of the district, that is, the house where the cock-fights were held.

The *Hen & Chickens* sign is referred to elsewhere (p. 22). We have not found a *Hen*, but there lately was a *Wyandotte* at Kenilworth, Warws.

Fully as general as the sign of the *Cock* is that of the *Swan*; the reason is probably that this bird is so fond of liquid. Not only is there a conformity of aesthetic symbolism in various parts of Europe, observable in the constant recurrence of the same objects on signboards, but even the same jokes are found. On a couple of Irish houses of this sign are :—

> This is the Swan
> That left her pond
> To dip her bill in porter,
> Why not we,
>   As well as she
> Become regular Topers.

and this, which seems to be a trifle nearer the original verse :—

> This is the Swan that dips her neck in water,
> Why not we as well as she, drink plenty of (Beamish and Crawford's) Porter.

Often as noted the *Swan* sign is plainly heraldic, being taken from one of the supporters of the arms of Henry IV. The sign has always been a favourite. In 1829 there was along the river between Battersea Bridge and London Bridge the *Old Swan* at London Bridge, the *Swan* in Arundel St., the *Swan* at Hungerford Stairs, the *Swan* at Lambeth, lately destroyed, the *Old Swan* at Chelsea, long turned into a Brewhouse, the *New Swan* 'beyond the Physick Garden', and the two *Swan* signs at Battersea.

The *Swan* by London Bridge was a very ancient house and gave a name to the Swan Stairs. Trades tokens of this house are extant, representing a Swan walking on Old London Bridge, with the date 1657. This feat was performed by the *Swan* on the token, to intimate that it was the *Swan above* the Bridge in contradistinction to another tavern known as the *Swan below* the Bridge—the *Swan* at Dowgate. Pepys dined at this house on 27 June 1660, and he has not much good to say about it. The landlady of this tavern is mentioned in a curious manner in the *Quack Vintners* tract of 1712 :—

> May the chaste widow prosper at the *Swan*
> Near London Bridge, where richest wines are drawn,
> And win by her good humour and her trade
> Some jolly son of Bacchus to her bed.

Previous to 1598 there was a Swan *Theatre* on the Bankside, near the Globe ; so named from a house and tenement called the *Swan*, mentioned in a charter of Edward VI, granting the manor of Southwark to the City of London. It fell into decay in the reign of James I, was closed in 1613, and subsequently only used for prize-fighting exhibitions.

From an anecdote preserved by Aubrey, it appears that Ben Jonson did not always go to the *Devil*, but was also in the habit of having his cup of sack at the *Swan* near Charing Cross. In his famous *Extempore Grace before King James* :—

> Our king and queen, the Lord God blesse,
> The Palsgrave and the Lady Besse,
> And God bless every living thing
> That lives and breathes and loves the King.
> God blesse the Council of Estate,
> And Buckingham the fortunate.
> God blesse them all and keep them safe,
> And God blesse me, and God blesse Ralph,

he aroused the King's curiosity as to the identity of Ralph. Ben told him he was the ' drawer at the Swanne Taverne by Charing-crosse who drew him good canarie '. For his drollery his Majesty gave Ben £100. Tokens of this house of the plague year are extant, representing a Swan with a sprig in its mouth, and the inscription ' Marke Rider at the *Swan* against the Mewes, 1665 '.

The *Swan* at Knightsbridge had a somewhat lurid reputation. It was well known to young gallants, and was the terror of all such jealous husbands and fathers as the Sir David Dunce who figures in Otway's *Soldier of Fortune*, 1681. Dunce says ' 'tis a damned house that Swan ; that Swan at Knightsbridge is a confounded house ! ' Tom Brown also alludes to it, and Peter Pindar (Dr. Woolcot) commemorates a vestry dinner there. The old house was pulled down in 1788, and its name transferred to a public house in Sloane St., which, with three other houses, occupies the site of the old *Swan*.

The *Swan* in Exchange Alley, Cornhill, was well known among the musical world in the 18th century. In this house some celebrated concerts were given, at a time when there were no proper concert rooms ; they commenced in 1728, under the manage-ment of one Barton, formerly a dancing master, and continued for twelve years, when the place was burnt down. At the rebuilding, it was christened the *King's Head*.

In 1825 the landlord of the *Swan* at West Ham, a house still extant, recommended the charms of his place in poetical strains :—

> At the *Swan* Tavern kept by Lound
> The best accommodation's found,—
> Wine, Spirits, Porter, Bottled Beer,
> You'll find in high perfection here.
> If in the garden with your lass
> You feel inclined to take a glass,
> There tea and coffee of the best,
> Provided is for every guest,

And females not to drive from hence,
The charge is only fifteen pence,
Or if disposed a pipe to smoke,
To sing a song or crack a joke,
You may repair across the Green,
Where nought is heard, though much is seen,
There laugh, and drink, and smoke away,
And but a mod'rate reckoning pay.
Which is the most important object
To every loyal British subject.
              In short,
The best accommodation's found
By those who deign to visit Lound.

There is a *Swan* at Clare, Suff., notable since the actual sign is one of the oldest in England, and one at Burslem, Stoke-on-Trent, which appears in Arnold Bennett's books as the *Duck*. A *Cygnet* may be seen at York, a *Swan & Falcon* at Gloucester, a *Black Swan* at York, and a *White Swan* in New St. At Monmouth is a *White Swan* with outstretched neck and open bill hissing fiercely at the beholder, while a very callow-faced cupid endeavours to restrain the bird's indignation.

Another celebrated *White Swan* is to be seen at Stratford-on-Avon, a magnificent building dating back to *c.* 1450 with some very good recently discovered Tudor wall paintings of the story of Tobit. In Shakespeare's time the house was a tavern with the sign of the *King's Head*. It had formerly belonged to the Perrots, a local family much at feud with William Shakespeare. It is likely enough that he may have seen the paintings often when he called in the House. The Birthplace is only two minutes' walk away, and New Place is within a few yards. Shakespeare twice refers to such scriptural scenes, painted on the walls of inns and other houses of the time in the *Merry Wives of Windsor*, and in *King Henry IV*, in both cases the story chosen being that of the *Prodigal Son*. At Stratford also there is a house with the very appropriate sign of the *Swan's Nest*.

The *Black Swan* though formerly considered very much of a rare bird and indeed so learnedly described in Latin on the sign of a house of this name at Winchester, may now be seen in many places swinging at inn doors, the pictures painted just as fancy may have suggested, long before the actual bird was brought over from Australia. At the *Black Swan* in Tower St. the Earl of Rochester, when banished from the Court, took lodgings under the name of Alexander Bendo, his profession that of an Italian quack, and there he had comical adventures with the waiting-maids of the Court. Another *Black Swan* is named in a broadside of 1704 as the place of exhibition of a ' large sea monster found in the common-shore ' in New Fleet St., Spitalfields.

The *Swan with Two Necks* is another curious creature observable on the signboard, and said to owe its origin to the corruption of the word *nick* into *neck*. This explanation, however ingenious, is probably to be taken with a grain of salt. These *nicks* were little horizontal, vertical or diagonal notches cut in the swan's bill, in order that each owner might know his own swans. Those of the company of the Vintners had two nicks or marks on their bills, it is said, and hence the popular explanation of the sign. This nicking of swans on the river was formerly a matter of great state. The members of the Corporation of London used annually to go up the Thames in the month of August in gaily decorated barges, and after the swans were nicked and counted, to land off Barn Elms, and there partake of a dinner in the open air, and wind up the festivities with a dance. There is something entertaining in the thought of aldermen dancing after a Corporation dinner—if only one served upon picnic lines.

It is, however, a well known and established fact that the London signs of old had no inscriptions under them. Now, considering the small size of the nicks in question, they would scarcely have been perceptible at the height at which the sign was generally suspended, and even if visible, would never have been sufficiently noticed or understood to give a name to the sign. Moreover there are swan marks with three or four nicks. There was once a *Swan with Three Necks* in Lad Lane, but no-one ever saw a four-necked swan even on a signboard. Conventionally too, the swan has or should have its neck 'gorged' with a coronet. All this seems to suggest a heraldic origin for the sign.

Larwood suggests the alternative explanation that two swans represented swimming side by side may have given rise to the *Swan with Two Necks*. It is much likelier the origin may have been that the symbol of two birds' necks encircled by a coronet which was used by a foreign publisher,—taken, it has been conjectured, by him from the arms of some trade company.

Machyn in his *Diary* mentions the sign in 1556 in Milk St. In 1636, the *Two-Necked Swan* was already to be seen in Berkshire, at the town of Lambourne, where Taylor the Water Poet names it as the sign of a tavern. In later years it was the sign of a famous carriers' inn in Lad Lane, Cheapside, whence for more than a century and a half passengers and goods were despatched to the North. To this inn the following couplet alludes :—

> True sportsmen know nor dread nor fear,
> Each rides, when once the saddle in,
> As if he had a neck to spare,
> Just like the Swan in Ladlane.

Notwithstanding the ' double bill ' which Larwood thinks is suggested by the two heads, the sign still continues a favourite one.

Four is an uncommon number on the signboard, but it survived in Larwood's time in one instance, the *Four Swans*, Bishopsgate, which was internally one of the best remaining examples of the famous galleried inns of old London. There is another *Four Swans* at Waltham Cross.

The *Swan & Bottle*, Uxbridge, is perhaps a variant of the *Cock & Bottle* ; the *Swan & Rummer* was a coffee-house near the Exchange during the South Sea Bubble —the *Rummer* a common addition, being simply joined to the *Swan* to intimate that wine was sold. The *Swan & Salmon* are combined on many signs, doubtless in honour of the two ornaments of our English rivers.   The *Swan & Hoop*, Moorfields, now called the *Moorgate*, bears a commemoration plaque to say it was the birthplace of John Keats. The *Swan on the Hoop* ' on the way called old Fysshe Strete ', is mentioned as early as 1413.   The same combination may still be seen on London signboards.   There is a *Swan & Horseshoe* at 33 Little Britain, E.C.

The *Swan & Sugarloaf* occurs amongst the trades tokens, and is still seen (as in Fetter Lane, for instance).   The sugarloaf was at first added by a grocer, whose sign having gained popularity as a noted landmark, or from other causes, was imitated by rivals or juniors, particularly on account of it presenting the favourite alliteration. Combinations with the sugarloaf are very common, all arising from its being *the* grocer's sign : thus the *Three Crowns & Sugarloaf*, Kidderminster ; *Wheatsheaf & Sugarloaf*, Ratcliff Highway (17th-century trades token), the *Tobacco Roll and Sugarloaf*, Gray's Inn Gate, Holborn, the *Three Coffins & Sugarloaf*, Fleet St., 1720.   As the *Black Swan* is usually popularly styled the *Mucky Duck*, the *Swan & Sugarloaf* is very generally known as the *Duck & Acid-drop*.   In the sign of the *Swan & Rushes* at Leicester, the rushes were merely a pictorial accessory, placed in the background to bring out the white plumage of the *Swan*, while the *Swan & Helmet* at Northampton, no doubt originated from a helmet with a Swan for crest.

In one instance, a *Drake* occurs as a sign, namely on the token of Will Jonson at the *Drake* in Bell Yard, near Temple Bar, 1667.   The *Duck* is generally to be seen only in company with the *Dog* or the *Drake*, though in one instance it accompanies a *Mallard*.   The *Duck & Drake* is at Yaxley, Hunts.   The *Duck & Mallard* was apparently not an inn sign but appears as the sign of a lock- (and probably gun-) smith in East Smithfield in 1673.   There is a house with *Duck in the Pond* sign at Stanmore, Mx.

The *Pigeon* was a tavern at Charing Cross in 1675.   The *Three Pigeons* were very common : there still exists an inn of this name at 12 Romford Rd., Brentford.   It is a house of interest as being in all likelihood one of the few haunts of Shakespeare now remaining, as being indeed one of the few Elizabethan taverns existing in England, which in the absence of direct evidence one may fairly presume to have been visited by him.

It was kept at one time by Lowin, one of the original actors in Shakespeare's plays, and is often named by the old dramatists, for example, in Ben Jonson's *Alchymist*. There also George Peele played some of his merry pranks.   In the parlour is or was an old painting dated 1704, representing a landlord attending to some customers seated at a table in the open air, with these lines :—

> Wee are new beginners
> And thrive wee would fain,
> I am honest Ralph of Reading,
> My wife Susana to name.

There is another well-known *Three Pigeons* at Richmond, Surrey.
Most *Three Pigeons* in London were the signs of establishments other than inns,

for example, Bat Pidgeon, the famous hairdresser, immortalized by the *Spectator*, lived at the sign of the *Three Pigeons* ' in the corner house of St Clement's Churchyard '.

A famous fictional *Three Pigeons* is that favoured by Tony Lumpkin in *She Stoops to Conquer*.

There is a *Dove* at Ipswich and a *Doves* at Hammersmith. This last house has a very attractive painted sign and is known to public-house connoisseurs for a variety of literary associations with writers ranging from Thomson of the *Seasons* to Sir A. P. Herbert. The *Stockdove* is a sign at Romiley, Ches., the *Dovecote* one at Laxton, Notts., the famous village where open fields still remain. Perhaps it refers to the manorial dovecote ; certainly until very recent years the manor court was held here. There is a *Pigeon Box* at Prior's Lee, Salop. Pigeon-shooting matches may have something to do with the selection of this sign.

The *Falcon* was a favourite printers sign. These booksellers, perhaps, borrowed their device from the stationers' arms, which are, *arg.* on a chevron between three bibles, *or a falcon* volant between two roses, the Holy Ghost in chief. The Falcon was also a badge of some of the kings. At the *Falcon*, Stratford-on-Avon, there is or was a shovelboard on which Shakespeare is said often to have played. Another *Falcon* connected with Shakespeare's name used to stand on the Bankside, where he and his companions occasionally refreshed themselves after the fatigues of the performance at the *Globe*. It long continued celebrated as a coaching inn for all parts of Kent, Surrey, and Sussex till it was taken down in 1808. The name is still preserved in the *Falcon Glasshouse* which stands opposite its site, and in the *Falcon Stairs*. There was another *Falcon* in Fleet St., bequeathed to the Company of Cordwainers by a gentleman named Fisher, under the obligation that they were yearly to have a sermon preached in the church of St Dunstan in the West on 10 July. Formerly on that day sack posset used to be drunk in the vestry of the church if not to the health, at least to the pious memory of this Fisher ; but that good custom has long since been abandoned.

The *Falcon on the Hoop* is named in 1443. ' In the xxj yer of Kyng Harry the vj^{te} ' the brotherhood of the Holy Trinity received ' for the rent of ij yere of Wyllym Wylkyns for the Sarrecyn Head v li. vj s. viij d., paynge by the yer liij s. iiij d. and of the *Faucon on the Hope* for the same ij yer vi li., that is to say paynge by the yer iij li.' Six days before that period, there is an entry in the churchwardens accounts for ' kervyng and peinting of the seigne of the Faucon vj sh.' The mention of the sign clearly shows that it was not a picture but a carved and coloured falcon, suspended in a hoop, whence the name of the sign.

The Magpie being a bird of good omen was on that account very often chosen as a sign. With this another reason concurred namely the sign of the eatable pie falling into disuse, it was transformed into the *Magpie* (see *Cock & Pie*), and this transition was so much the easier as the original name of the magpie was *pie*, and only subsequently because of its knowing antics, did it receive the nickname of *maggoty* pie, which gradually was abbreviated into *Magpie*. The full form of the epithet is preserved in the nursery rhyme :—

Round about, round about,
Maggoty Pie,
My father loves good ale
And so do I.

The *Maggoty Pie* was an inn in the Strand during the reign of James I. It is alluded to in Shirley's Comedy *The Ball*, Act I, Sc. 1, as ' the Maggety Pie in the Strand, sir '. As late as 1654, we find the name *maggoty pie* used in *Mercurius Fumigosus*, 26 July to 3 August, where the Welshman's arms are described as including a fly, a *magotty pie*, etc. The coat is extremely libellous. It consists of ' A fly, a maggoty pie, a gammon of bacon and a ——— : the fly drinks before his master, a magpie doth prate and chatter, a gammon of bacon is never good till it be hanged, and a ——— when it is out never returns to its country, no more will a Welshman ; otherwise, his arms are two trees *verdant*, a beam *tressant*, a ladder *rampant*, and Taffe *pendant* '.

There is a *Magpie* at Carlisle. The *Magpie* at Stonham, Staffs., has a gallows sign with a cage on top, presumably formerly containing a live magpie. At Fairford, Glos., is the *Three Magpies* with an interesting sign.

The *Magpie & Stump* represents the magpie sitting on the stump of a tree ; it was the sign of one of the Whig pothouses in the Old Bailey during the riots of 1715, and still appears there. There was in Larwood's time an old house with such a sign in Cheyne Walk, Chelsea. It is now extinct. The *Magpie & Pewter Platter* formerly in Wood St. is said to have originated from a magpie standing by a dish and picking out of it. The *Magpie & Crown*, says the author of *Tavern Anecdotes* (1825) is a ridiculous association, but when once joined is not to be separated without injury to the concern, as it happened in the case of a certain Renton. He was originally waiter at a house of this name in Aldgate, famous for its ale, which was sent out in great quantities. The landlord becoming rich, pride followed, and he thought of giving wing to the *Magpie*, retaining only the royal attribute of the crown. The ale went out for a short time, as usual, but it was not from the *Magpie & Crown*, and the customers fancied it was not so good as usual. The business fell off. The landlord died, and Renton purchased the concern, caught the Magpie, and restored it to its ancient situation. The ale improved in the opinion of the public, and its consumption increased so much that Renton at his death left behind him property amounting to £600,000 (!) chiefly the profits of the *Magpie & Crown* ale.

The *Parrot* or *Popinjay* is an old sign now almost out of fashion, the *Green Parrot*, Leeds, being one of the few instances of it remaining. The *Popinjay* sign still remains at 105 Fleet St., but the house is no longer an inn. There is a *Parrot* still, however, at Aldringham, Suff. It is suggested that perhaps the sign may often refer to the popinjay target for archers rather than to the bird. A former *Popinjay* at Norwich was so called by the person who bought the house for conversion into an inn. It had been the residence of Richard Popinjay. Taylor the Water Poet mentions the Popinjay at Ewell in 1636.

The *Peacock*, in ancient times, was possessed of a mystic character. The fabled incorruptibility of the flesh led to its typifying the Resurrection; and from this incorruptibility doubtless originated the first idea of swearing ' by the Peacock ', an oath that was to be inviolably kept. It appears very early on the signboard—the oath was a common military one in early times. Near the *Angel* in Clerkenwell there still stands the *Peacock* which bears the date 1564. This was formerly a great house of call for the mail and other coaches travelling on the Great North Rd., in much the same way as was the *Elephant and Castle* for the southern counties. The *Peacock & Feathers* was a sign in Cornhill in 1711. There is another *Peacock* at Erith, and a *Peahen* at St Albans. There are still five *Peacocks* in various parts of Warwickshire.

The *Ostrich* seems more common at present than it was in ancient times. Generally the ostrich is represented with a horseshoe in his mouth, in allusion to his supposed digestive powers, referred to in *King Henry VI*, Act IV, Sc. 1. There is an *Ostrich* at Wherstead, Suff., and another at Colnbrook, Bucks., a house with a very old licence.

The landlord of an alehouse at Calverley near Leeds has put his premises under the protection of Minerva's bird, the *Owl*. There was another house of this sign at Over Whitacre, Worcs., and there is one in Silver St., Edmonton, and there is a *Blinking Owl* near Shaftesbury. At St Helens, Lancs., there is a still more curious sign, namely, the *Owl's Nest*, or the *Owl in the Ivy Bush*. A bush or tod * of ivy was formerly supposed to be a favourite place in which the owl made its nest. The old dramatists abound in allusions to this. Drayton has :—

> And, like an owl, by night to go abroad,
> Rooster all day within an Ivy Tod,

and Beaumont and Fletcher :—

> Michael von Owle, how doth thou?
> In what dark barn or tod of aged ivy
> Hast thou been hid.

In a masque of Shirley entitled *The Triumph of Peace* 1633, one of the scenes represented a wild, woody landscape ' a fit place for purse taking ' where, ' in the further part was scene an ivy-bush, out of which came an owle '. *Opinion*, one of the *dramatis personæ*, informed the public that this scene was intended for ' a wood, a broad-faced owl, an ivy-bush and other birds beside her '.

There is a *Pheasant* at Retford, Notts., and another at Carlisle, and a *Pheasant Cock* at Norwich. The *Swallow* is at Cley next the Sea, Norf. In districts where Grouse and Moorcock are found, these birds frequently court the patronage of the thirsty sportsman at the village alehouse door. One publican at Upper Haslam, Sheffield, invites at once the follower of two sports : his sign is the *Grouse & Trout*. There is a *Grouse* at Darley Dale, a *Moorcock* near Hawes, and a *Snipe* at Patcham, Brighton. The *Dotterel* is at Reighton, E.R. Yorks. Other bird signs occurring much less often are : the *Blackbird*, Salisbury, the *Crane*, Wandsworth Plain, the *Cuckoo*, Peterborough. There is a *Goose* at Burslem, Stoke-on-Trent, lately so called after the

* See p. 109.

goose of St Werburg, a patron of the parish in which the house stands. Probably the goose sign is sometimes a tailor's goose. Certainly it seems likely that the *Snob & Ghost* formerly at Middleton Cheyney, Northants., is really the *Snob* (i.e. tailor) *and (tailor's) Goose*.

The *Martlet*, presumably a heraldic martlet, that is, a swallow with no legs, is found at Langford Budville, Som., the *Nightingale* at Norwich, the *Redstart* at Barming, Kent, the *Robin* at Anerley, the *Rock Robin* at Wadhurst, Surrey, the *Rook* at Halifax, the *Quail* in Charlwood Rd., S.W.15, the *Stormy Petrel* at Landport, Portsmouth, the *Turkey Cock* at Hunsdon, Herts., the *Woodcock* at Hindhead, the *Woodpecker* at Leeds, and the *Wren* in Liverpool.

The last bird sign which remains to be noticed is unquestionably the most puzzling of all. It occurs on an old trades token of Cornhill and is there called *The Live Vulture*. That the proprietor should have kept a live vulture at his door seems very improbable. The only explanation which occurs to us, is the probability that, at some period or other, a live vulture had been exhibited at this house, and that from this event its name was derived. It will be seen from our notice of the *George & Vulture* under *Religious Signs*, that vultures were exhibited as great curiosities.

Chapter VIII

FISHES AND INSECTS

THE *Mermaid* as a sign had great attractions for our forefathers. Shakespeare, Ben Jonson and other dramatists notice their taste for strange fishes. The ancient chronicles teem with accounts of captures of mermen, mermaids, and similar creatures. Hollinshed gives a detailed account of a merman caught at Orford in Suffolk, in the reign of King John. He was kept alive on raw meal and fish for six months, but at last ' fledde secretelye to the sea, and was neuer after seen nor heard off'. Another chronicler says, ' About this time (1202) fishes of strange shapes were taken, armed with helmets and shields like armed men, only they were much bigger.' Gervase of Tilbury roundly asserts that mermen and mermaids live in the British Ocean. Even in more modern times, every now and then a mermaid (the mermen seem to have been more scarce) made her appearance. In an advertisement at the beginning of the 17th century we find :—

> In Bell Yard, on Ludgate Hill, is to be seen, at any hour of the day, a living Mermaid from the waist upwards of a party colour, from thence downwards is very strange and wonderful.

After which follows a most promising and tempting little bit of information in French :—' Son corps est de divers couleurs avec beaucoup d'autres curiosités qu'on ne pent exprimer.'

Again, according to the *General Magazine* of January 1747 :—

> We hear from the north of Scotland that some time this month a sea creature, known by the name of Mermaid, which has the shape of a human body from the trunk upwards, but below is wholly fish, was carried some miles up the water of Devron.

In 1824, a mermaid or merman made its appearance before ' an enlightened public', when, as the papers inform us, ' upwards of 150 distinguished fashionables' went to see it. At Bartholomew Fair, in 1830, a stuffed mermaid was exhibited. She was sketched by George Cruikshank ; and a wood-cut of her may be seen in Morley's *Memoirs of Bartholomew Fair*, p. 488. A very different specimen had been exhibited in Fleet St. in 1822, but she disappeared all at once most mysteriously, Larwood says not without a rumour of her being under the protection of the Lord Chancellor, which lies within the range of possibility, as she was a comely maiden with flaxen hair, ' mulier superne *et inferne* '. The sea-serpent has now almost done away with the mermaid ; yet Larwood saw in 1857 an article in the *Shipping Gazette*, under the intelligence of 4 June, signed by some Scottish sailors, and describing an object seen off the North British coast, ' in the shape of a woman, with full breast, dark complexion, comely face ', and the rest. The appearance of mermaids is still a ' silly season ' topic with some of the picture papers. The present author as a small boy, *c.* 1910, paid sixpence to see a mermaid in a tank of seawater, a ' wakes ' exhibit at Pontefract, Yorks. His principal recollection of the exhibit is a very definitely ancient and fish-like smell attached to it or to her.

At one time the *Mermaid* appears to have been a very common sign, if we may judge from the way in which it is mentioned by Brathwaite in his *New Cast of Characters,* 1631 :—The hostess having pulled down her birch pole ' A long consultation is had before they can agree what sign must be reared. " *A meere-mayde,*" says she, " for she will sing catches to the youths of the parish." " A lyon," says he, " for that is the onely sign he can make ; and this he formes so artlessly, as it requires his expression, *this is a lyon.*" '

Among the most celebrated of the *Mermaid* taverns in London that in Bread St. stands foremost. As early as the 15th century it was one of the haunts of the pleasure-seeking Sir John Howard, whose steward records in 1464 :—' Paid for wyn at the Mermayd in Bred Stret, for my mastyr and Syr Nicholas Latimer, x d. ob.' In 1603 Sir Walter Raleigh established a literary club in this house, doubtless the first in England. Amongst its members were Shakespeare, Ben Jonson, Beaumont and Fletcher, Selden, etc. It is frequently referred to by Beaumont and Fletcher in their comedies, but the best known allusion is in a quotation from a letter of Beaumont to Ben Jonson :—

> What things have we seen
> Done at the *Mermaid* ! heard words that have been
> So nimble and so full of subtle flame,
> As if that any one from whence they came
> Had meant to put his whole wit in a jest,
> And had resolved to live a fool the rest
> Of his dull life.

There was another *Mermaid* in Cheapside, frequented by Jasper Mayne, and in the next reign by the poet laureate, John Dryden. Mayne mentions it in the *City Match,* 1638. In 1681, there was a *Mermaid* in Carter Lane, which had a great deal of traffic as a carriers' inn.

The *Seahorse* may be seen at Birmingham, York, Chalford (Surrey), Ipswich and various other places. Bossewell in his *Armourie* of 1589 gave a quaint description of this animal :—

> This waterhorse of the sea is called an hyppotame, for that he is like a horse in back, mayne, and neying. He abideth in the waters on the day, and eateth corn by night *et hunc Nilus* gignit.

There is a *Sea Serpent* in High St., E.15, and a *Whale* at Swindon. Sometimes in the old seaports the sign has been adapted to attract the customers of sailors from whaling ships. In the *Blade Bone* at Reading and at Bracknell, Berks., and in the *Splaw Bone* at Hull, the sign—a whale or whaler, was painted on an actual whale's bone.

The *Dolphin* is another sign of very old standing. One of the first instances of its use was probably the inn referred to in Stow :—

> The other side of the High Street, from Bishopsgate and Houndsditch, the first building is a large inn for the receipt of travellers, and is called the *Dolphin*, of such a sign. In the year 1513, Margaret Ricroft, widow, gave this house, with the gardens and appurtenances, unto William Gam, R. Clye, their wives, her daughters, and to their heirs, with condition they yearly do give to the warders or governors of the Greyfriars' church, within Newgate, 40 shillings, to find a student of divinity in the university for ever.

Moser, in his *Vestiges Revived* mentions this same inn as the *Dolphin*, or rather *Dauphin* inn ; and says that it was adorned with fleurs-de-lis, cognizances, and dolphins and was reported to have been the residence of one of the dauphins of France, probably Louis the son of Philip Augustus who in 1216 came to England to contest the Crown with King John. Here he must be wrong as it seems that the French Crown Prince did not assume the title of Dauphin until 1349. The house was still in existence at the end of the 17th century, when it was a famous coaching inn. Perhaps it was to this tavern that Pepys and his company adjourned on 27 March 1661.

There is still a *Dolphin* in Ludgate Hill, E.C., and another (an old house transferred to a new site) at Bovey Tracey, Devon. The *Dolphin* at Southampton is associated with many literary personages, from Taylor the Water Poet to Gibbon, Jane Austen and Thackeray, who wrote part of *Pendennis* there. Its huge bay windows are said to be the largest in existence. In 1914 it was Haig's headquarters when the expeditionary force was embarking for France. There is an interesting *Dolphin* sign at Hastings and a house of this name at Sydenham with a pleasing modern sign.

Ancient naturalists made a wonderful animal of the dolphin. Bossewell, for instance, tells most extraordinary stories about him ; but they are unfortunately too long to quote. Londoners formerly might have seen the living fish from the riverbanks, for old chroniclers every now and then have entries to the effect that dolphins paid London a visit. Thus : ' 3 Hen. V. Seven dolphins came up the river Thames, whereof 4 were taken.' ' 14 Ric. II. On Christmas day a dolphin was taken at London Bridge, being 10 ft. long, and a monstrous grown fish.'

The *Dolphin & Anchor* is still a common sign ; and the *Fish & Anchor* at North Littleton, Warws., evidently implies the same emblem. This sign seems to have been taken by the publicans from the printers. Aldus Manutius, the celebrated Venetian printer, was the first to use the sign, adopting it from a silver medal of the Emperor Titus. Camerarius thus mentions this sign in his book on Symbols :—

> That the dolphin wound round the anchor was an emblem of the Emperors August and Titus, to represent that maturity in business which is the medium between too great haste and slowness ; and that it was also used in the last century by Aldus Manutius, that most famous printer, is known to everybody. Erasmus clearly and abundantly explains the import of that golden precept.

Our emblem is taken from Alciatus, and has a different meaning. He reports, namely, that 'when violent winds disturb the sea', as Lucretius says, and the anchor is cast by seamen, the dolphin winds herself round it, out of a particular love for mankind, and directs it, as with a human intellect, so that it may more safely take hold of the ground ; for dolphins have this peculiar property, that they can, as it were, foretell storms.   The anchor, then, signifies a stay and security, whilst the dolphin is a hieroglyphic for philanthropy and safety.

This sign was afterwards adopted by William Pickering, and another bibliophile Sir Samuel Egerton Brydges made some rather neat verses upon it :

> To the Dolphin as we're drinking,
>   Life and health and joy we send ;
> A poet once he saved from sinking,
>   And still he lives—the poet's friend.

The *Dolphin & Anchor* also occurs at Chichester.   Here, however, it is a combination of two separate and rival signs.   The *Dolphin* was the local Whig inn, the *Anchor* the headquarters of the Tories.   The *Dolphin* has a stone dated 1519 built into a chimney, so if the house was always an inn, it may challenge priority with the house mentioned by Stow.   Often the sign of the *Fish* is seen without any further specification ; in this case it is probably meant for the *Dolphin*, which is the sign-board fish *par excellence*.   The *Fish* sign is a very common public-house decoration at the present day, probably for the same reason as the *Swan*, that he is fond of liquor.   Does one not ' drink like a fish' ?   In Carlisle, however, there are two signs of the *Fish & Dolphin*, a rather puzzling combination, unless it has reference to the dolphin's chase after the shoals of small fishes.   The *Three Fishes* was a favourite device in the Middle Ages, the fishes crossing or interpenetrating each other in such a manner, that the head of one fish was at the tail of another.   It may have had no emblematic meaning, but very possibly it represents the Trinity, the fish being a common symbol for Our Lord derived from the Greek monogram ICTHYS.

The *Fish & Bell*, Soho, may either allude to a well-known anecdote of a numskull, who having caught a fish which he desired to keep for dinner on some future grand occasion, put it back into the river with a bell round its neck, so that he should be able to know its whereabouts the moment he wanted it ; or it may be the usual *Bell* added in honour of the bellringers.   A quaint variety of this sign is the *Bell & Mackerel* in the Mile End Rd.

The *Three Herrings*, the sign of James Moxton a bookseller in the Strand near York House in 1675, is evidently but another name for the *Three Fishes*.   In Larwood's time it was the sign of an alehouse now extinct in Bell Yard, Temple Bar.

The *Fish & Quart* at Leicester must be passed by in silence, as the combination cannot immediately be accounted for.   Were it in France a solution would be easier, for in French slang a ' poisson ' or fish means a small measure of wine.   The *Fish & Ring* at Stepney and near Keswick refers to a legendary incident in the life of St Kentigern, patron saint of Glasgow.   The saint dropped his ring in a stream and it was miraculously restored to him by a fish.   The *Fish & Eels* at Roydon, Essex, the *Fish & Kettle*,

Southampton, the *Whitebait* at Bristol and the *Eel's Foot* at Theberton, Suff., all tell their own tale, and need no comment. The *Salmon & Ball* is the well-known *Ball* of the silk-mercers in former times, added to the sign of the *Salmon* : there is an example of it in Bethnal Green Rd. The *Salmon & Compasses* which is found in Dorrington St. and Penton St., consists of the masonic emblem added to the sign. The *Fishbone* is rarely met with as a public-house sign, though there was an example of it at Netherton, Ches., now transformed into the *Whale Bone*, and also amongst the 17th-century tokens of New Cheapside, Moorfields. But generally it was the sign of a rag-and-bone shop or marine store. These shops as their name implies used to buy all the odds and ends of rubbish of which a ship is cleared after its return from a long voyage. Larwood suggests that no doubt bones of large fish would be often amongst the curiosities brought home by the sailors, and these being bought and hung up outside the doors of marine stores, in the end these bones became their distinctive sign. The *Sun & Whalebone*, still to be seen at Latton, Essex, may have originated either from a whalebone hanging outside the house, or because the landlord had laid the foundation of his fortune as a rag merchant. According to Mr. Lock ★ the sign occurs two or three times on the London–Norwich road as related to a masque at Norwich before Queen Elizabeth, at which on the last evening of her visit she was presented by 'Jupiter' with a whalebone riding-whip.

There is a *Lamprey* at Gloucester with a good painted sign, a *Pickerel* at Stowmarket, Suff., and a *Pike* at Stoke-on-Trent. The *Trout* and the *Perch* are neighbouring inns at Godstone and at Binsey, Oxon. The *Salmon* is seen occasionally near places where the fish is or was caught. There is an example at Bedford.

Insects are very rare occurrences. The industrious habits of the bees however made their habitation a favourite object to imply a similar industry in the Puritan shopkeepers. Many years ago there used to be at Grantham a signpost on which was placed a beehive with a full swarm and the lines under it :—

> Two wonders, Grantham, now are thine,
> A lofty steeple and a living sign.

The hive is still there and so is the inscription, but the bees are gone. The following is a common inscription under the sign of the *Beehive*, as, for example, at Abingdon, Berks. :—

> Within this hive we're all alive,
> Good liquor makes us funny ;
> If you are dry, step in and try
> The flavour of our honey.

There is a *Busy Bee* at Bradford, and one at Seacombe, Wallasey, a *Grasshopper* at Oxted, Surrey, and one at Westerham, Kent, and a *Midge* at Halton, Lincs. A very odd insect sign is the *Dumb Flea* at Meldreth, Cumb. The *Beetle & Pile* or the *Beetle and Wedge* do not refer to an insect, but to a pile driver or a mason's mallet.

★ *Op. cit.*, p. 289.

Although the frog cannot be considered either an insect or a fish, yet we may include it in this chapter. Of frogs there are some instances on the signboard; the *Three Frogs* (see under *Heraldic Signs*) and *Froghall*, formerly a public-house at the south end of Frog Lane, Islington. On the front of this house there was exhibited the ludicrous sign of a plough drawn by frogs. There is at the present day a *Froghall* Inn at Wolston, near Coventry, and one at Layerthorpe in the West Riding. Probably the sign as a rule developed from the place-name Frog Hall, which like Rats Castle, Bats Hall, Owl Castle, etc., is supposed to have been applied to a ruined building.

Chapter IX

FLOWERS, TREES, HERBS, ETC.

WHEN signboards flourished there would have been many reasons for choosing as house-decorations trees, plants and flowers. One was their symbolic meaning, for example, that of the olive-tree, the fig-tree and palm-tree. Another was to intimate what was sold within, as with the vine, the coffee-plant, etc. Some plants were used as badges. Often the reason was the vicinity of some well-known tree or road-mark near the place where the sign was displayed. Finally they seem often to have been chosen merely because of the desire of a landlord to have an unusual sign.

The oldest sign borrowed from the vegetable kingdom is the *Bush*. It was a bush or bunch of ivy, box or evergreen, tied to the end of a pole. The custom came evidently from the Romans, and with it the oft-repeated proverb ' Good wine needs no Bush '. *Vinum vendebile hedera non est opus.* Ivy was the plant commonly used : ' The Tavern Ivy clings about my money and kills it,' says the sottish slave in Massinger's *Virgin Martyr* (Act III, Sc. 3). Ivy may have been adopted as the plant sacred to Bacchus and the Bacchantes, or perhaps simply because it is a hardy plant, and long continues green. As late as the reign of King James I many inns used it as their only sign. Taylor the Water Poet in his perambulation of ten shires around London notes various places where there is ' a taverne with a bush only ' ; in other parts he mentions ' the signe of the *Bush* '. Even at the present day ' the Bush ' is a very general sign for inn and public-house, as, for example, at Farnham Cross and at Shrewsbury.

In Gloucestershire, Warwickshire, and other counties where at certain fairs the ordinary booth people and tradesmen enjoyed the privilege of selling liquors without a licence, they hung out bunches of ivy, flowers, or boughs of trees to indicate this sale. As far away as the western states of North America at the building of a new village or station it was in Larwood's time common to see a bunch of hay or a green bough hung from above the grocery or bar-room door until such time as a superior decoration could be provided. In England the bunch being fixed to a long staff was also called the *Alepole* ; thus among the procession of odd characters that came to purchase ale at the *Tunnying of Elinour Rummyng* :—

> Another brought her bedes
> Of jet and of coale,
> To offer to the *Alepole*.

How these *Alepoles* from the very earliest times continued to enlarge and encroach upon the public way has been shown already. The bunch gradually became a garland of flowers of considerable proportions, whence Chaucer says his Sompnour's garland was ' as gret as it were for an alestake '. Afterwards the garland became a still more elegant object, as exemplified by that of the *Nag's Head* in Cheapside in the print of the entry of Marie de Medici.   Finally it appeared as a crown of green leaves, with a little *Bacchus* bestriding a tun dangling from it.   Thus the sign was used simultaneously with the bush.   According to Lupton in 1632

> If these houses (alehouses) have a boxe-bush, or an old post, it is enough to show their profession.   But if they be graced with a signe compleat, it's a signe of a good custome.

In Shirley's *Masque of the Triumph of Peace* 1633, it is said that a tavern must necessarily have . . . 'but especially a conceited signe and an eminent bush' . . . 'Tavernes are quickly set up, it is but hanging out a bush at a nobleman's or an alderman's gate, and 'tis made instantly.'   An English host in *Good News and Bad News* says :—'I rather will take down my bush and sign than live by means of riotous expense.'   Gradually as signs became more costly the bush was entirely neglected, and the sign alone remained. Sometimes the *Bush* assumes the name of the *Ivy Bush*, or the *Ivy Green* (of which there are two in Birmingham).   There is an *Elder Bush* at Soham, Cambs., a *Furze Bush* at Aldermaston, Berks., a *Haw Bush* at Gidea Park, a *Holly Bush* at Bewdley, Worcs., and one at Loughton, and a *May Bush* formerly existed at Stowmarket, Suff.   The *Hand & Holly Bush* occurs among the London trades tokens and is mentioned in 1708. It was at Temple Bar 'about the middle of the backside of St Clement's'.   There is still a *Holly Bush* in Ladbroke Grove.   The *Beggars Bush* was a notorious house in Southwark in the 17th and 18th centuries.   Later it was rechristened the *Horse & Hounds*, after a hare had been hunted and killed on the premises, and afterwards cooked and eaten there.   There was another *Beggars Bush* in Lincoln's Inn Fields in 1660.   It is stated that such signs were really *Badgers' Brush*, signifying houses where there was badger baiting.

The *Hand & Flower* is a sign very frequently adopted by alehouses in the vicinity of nursery grounds, for example, Addison Rd., Kensington, King's Rd., Chelsea, a little past Cremorne, though there the nursery ground has been built over.   This seems a much likelier theory than that of Block, who gives the sign a very far-fetched mystical interpretation.*

The *Rose* besides being the queen of flowers and the national emblem, had yet another prestige which alone would have been sufficient to make it a favourite sign in the Middle Ages, this was its religious import.   On the monumental brass of Abbot Kirton, formerly in Westminster Abbey, there was a crowned rose with I.H.C. in its heart, and round it the words

SIS, ROSA, FLOS FLORUM. MORBIS MEDICINA MEORUM.

The rose was an emblem of the Virgin, and the fact may still survive in the terms the Rose of Jericho and the Christmas Rose.

Roses often appear as the rents payable under feudal tenures.   Very occasionally perhaps a *Rose* sign may have originated in the payment of a rose quit-rent.

* *Op. cit.*, p. 201.

At the present day some publicans take liberties with the old sign of the *Rose*, dealt with elsewhere (pp. 75–6). Here it will suffice to instance in Macclesfield and at Preston, the *Moss Rose*, at Silkstone Common, W.R. Yorks., the *Bunch of Roses*, in London Rd., Preston, the *Rosebud*, etc. The *Three Roses* was formerly a common sign; from the way they are represented, they appear to have been heraldic roses.

The colloquial phrase, *Under the Rose*, is sometimes used as a sign, or written under the pictorial representation of the rose; it occurs on a trade token of Cambridge, and may be seen on various public-houses of the present day. Numerous suppositions have been made concerning its origin, some holding that it arose from this flower being the emblem of Hippocrates; others from a rose painted on the ceiling, any conversations held under which were not to be divulged; whilst Gregory Nazianzen seems to imply that the rose, from its close bud, had been made the emblem of silence. 'Like the rose in spring hidden in its bud, so must the mouth be closed and restrained with strong reins, enforcing silence to the loquacious lips.' At Lullingstone Castle, Kent, there is said to be a representation of a rose nearly two feet in diameter, surrounded with the following inscription :—

> Kentish true blue,
>   Take this as a token,
> That what is said here
>   Under the Rose is spoken.

There is one *Rose* sign the origin of which it is difficult to ascertain, this is the *Rose of Normandy*, a public-house in High St., Marylebone. It was built in the 17th century, and in Larwood's time the original building remained and was the oldest house in the parish. The street having been raised, the entrance to the house was some steps beneath the roadway. The original form of the exterior had been preserved, and the staircases and balusters were coeval with the building; but the fine garden set with fruit trees and laid out with gravel walks and quickset hedges had disappeared, and the large bowling-green had dwindled into a miserable skittle-ground.

As a sign the *Marygold*, it is said, arose from a popular reading of the sign of the *Sun*. It may be mentioned that this flower (originally called *the Gold*) seems to have been considered as an emblem of Queen Mary I. So at least it would appear from a lengthy ballad of *The Marygolde* composed by one of her chaplains, William Forrest, in which amongst many other similar allusions, he says she may well be called Marygold as dear to Christ's Mother, and ' golde on earth to have no peere '.

> She (the Queen) may be called Marygolde well,
>   Of Marie (chiefe) Christes mother deere,
> That as in heaven she doth excell,
>   And golde on earth to have no peere,
> So certainly she shineth cleere,
>   In grace and honour double fold,
> The like was never erst seen heere,
>   Such as this flower the Marygolde.

The flower was a favourite one in the Middle Ages, deriving the first part of its name from the Virgin Mary. The first known mention of the sign, however, is in 1638, when it appears on the title pages of Eglisfield, a bookseller in St Paul's Churchyard. In 1673 when it was also the sign of a milliner in the Strand. This must have been the same house in which Blanchard and Child the goldsmiths kept the running cashes of the oldest banking firm in London. The old sign of the house is still preserved by its successors Messrs. Glyn, Mills & Co. (Fleet St., E.C.4), together with various relics of the *Devil* Tavern on the site of which part of the bank was built.

No doubt the *Lily* which is found for example at Hull and Norwich, often has a religious origin as the symbol of Our Lady, which may or may not be descended from the lotus flower of the east. According to Mr. Block * for obvious reasons the symbolic lily should possess no stamens. Sometimes perhaps the *Bell may* be a development of the stamened lily. The author very much doubts it !

Only a few other flowers occur, mostly modern introductions, for example, the *Daisy*, Bramley, Leeds, and in Brompton Rd., the *Tulip*, Springfield, Essex, and Richmond, Surrey, the *Lilies of the Valley*, Ible, Derbys., the *Snowdrop*, near Lewes, the *Woodbine*, South Shields, and Honey Lane, Essex, and the *Forest Blue Bell*, Mansfield. The *Blue Bell* is very common but apparently in general it signifies not a blue flower but a bell painted blue. There is a *Blooming Fuchsia* at Ipswich.

There were two *Myrtle Trees* in Bristol, and there is still one in Ipswich and one in Taunton, and the *Rosemary Branch* is found in Camberwell, Lewisham and in many other places. Rosemary was formerly an emblem of remembrance, in much the same way as the Forget-me-not is now : ' There's Rosemary, that's for *remembrance*,' says Ophelia, in *Hamlet*, Act IV, Sc. 5. In *The Winter's Tale*, Act IV, Sc. 5, Perdita refers to Rosemary and Rue for grace and remembrance (because both remained fresh and of sweet savour long after cutting). Hence Rosemary and gloves were of old presented to those who followed the funeral of a friend.

Fruit trees are much more common, particularly the *Apple-tree* and the *Pear-tree*, which (owing to the favourite drinks of cider and perry) are next to the *Rose* and the *Oak* the most frequent among vegetable signs. The *Apple-tree*, near Coldbath Fields prison, was one of the numerous public-houses kept at one time or another by Topham the strong man. He had this house in 1745. The sign is still to be seen, and there is a Topham St. near by. At the *Apple-tree* in Charles St., Covent Garden, four of the leading London Freemasons' lodges considering themselves neglected by Sir Christopher Wren met in 1716 and chose a Grand-master *pro tem.* until they should be able to place a noble brother at their head. The three lodges that joined with the *Apple-tree* Lodge used to meet respectively at the *Goose & Gridiron*, St Paul's Churchyard ; the *Crown*, Parker's Lane ; and at the *Rummer & Grapes*, Westminster. There are other *Apple-trees* at Carlisle and at Workington, Cumb. For obvious reasons this sign is common in the cider counties, especially Herefordshire, Gloucestershire and Somerset. The *Hand & Apple* was the sign in 1782, of a shop in Thames St., where ' syder, Barcelona,

* *Op. cit.*, p. 7.

cherry brandy, tobacco ', etc. were sold. It represented a hand holding an apple, and was chosen on account of the cider.

To this beverage other signs owe their origin ; for instance, the *Red-Streak Tree*, from the apple of which the best cider is made. Tickets used formerly to be placed in the windows of houses where cider was sold, with the words ' Bright Red-streak Cyder sold here ', illustrated with a cut of three merry companions in cocked hats, sitting under an apple-tree and drinking cider. On the other side was a pile of barrels, from which the landlord was drawing liquor. In Maylordsham, Herefs., this sign was rendered as the *Red-streaked Tree*. There was a *Red-streaked Tree* in that same town in 1775, and the town still has a *Red Stock Tree*. The *Apple-tree & Mitre* was when Larwood wrote an old painted sign, a great deal the worse for London smoke, in Cursitor St. It represented an apple-tree abundantly loaded with fruit, standing in a landscape with some figures and above it a gilt mitre. It was evidently a combination of two signs. The house still stands, but the sign is gone.

The *Pear-tree* is not as common as the *Apple-tree*. There is one at West Row, Ely, and another in the New Cut. The *Iron Pear-tree* at Appleshaw, and at Redenham and Andover, Hants., *may* have been derived from some noted pear-tree in that neighbourhood, whose hollow and broken stem was secured with plates or bands of iron. Very general, also, is the *Cherry-tree*. It was the sign of a once famous resort in Bowlinggreen Lane, Clerkenwell, and was adopted on account of the numbers of cherry-trees which grew upon its grounds until almost a century ago. There is a *Cherry-tree* at Bromeswell, Suff., and another at Welwyn Garden City, and a *Cherry Arbour* at Sparkhill, Birmingham. The *Cherry-tree* at East Dulwich has a pleasing painted sign. Down the river at Rotherhithe was the *Cherry-Garden*, a famous place of entertainment in Charles II's reign. Pepys went to it on 15 June 1664 and with his usual pleasant flow of animal spirits, ' came home by water singing merrily '.

According to Stow :—

> Over against the parish church (St Olave's Southwark) on the south side of the street, was some time one great house, builded of stone, with arched gates, which pertained to the Prior of Lewis, in Sussex, and was his lodging when he came to London ; it is now a common hostelry for travellers, and hath to sign the Walnut-tree.

The *Walnut-tree* was also the sign of a tavern at the south side of St Paul's Churchyard, over against the New Vault, in which place a concert is advertised in July 1718, which, from the high price of the admission tickets—5s. each—must have been something out of the common. The *Walnut-tree* was frequently adopted by cabinetmakers, and is at the present day a not uncommon alehouse sign, as for example, at Norwich. There is a *Cob-tree* at Ightham, Kent.

The *Mulberry Tree* was introduced at an early period, but does not seem to have been used as a sign until modern times. James I, in 1609, caused several shiploads of mulberry trees to be imported from abroad to encourage the home manufacture of silk. These were planted in St James's Park ; but the climate being too cold for the silk worms, it was changed into a pleasure garden, where even the serious Evelyn would occasionally relax, as he did on 10 May 1654. Here Dryden went to eat mulberry tarts, and Pepys occasionally dined. There is still a house of this sign at Ipswich.

Orange-trees were one of the ornaments of St James's Park in the reign of Charles II; and at that period and long after, were mostly used as signboards of the seed-shops, and by Italian merchants. The sign of the *Orange-tree* still occurs at Highgate, at Birmingham, and there is one in Euston Rd., which had once a good painted sign but is now disfigured by an advertisement. The *Lemon-tree* is at Beacon St., Lichfield, and at Bedfordbury, W.C.

The *Olive Tree* was a common Italian warehouse sign, but was occasionally used by other shops. Amongst the tokens in the Beaufoy Collection, there is the 'Olfa Tree, Singon Strete', the Olive Tree in St John's St., a sign now apparently extinct. The usefulness of the olive-tree made it in very early times a symbol of peace. An olive leaf occurs in this respect of course in Genesis viii, 2. The *Olive Leaf* is at Ipswich and there is an *Olive Branch* at Inkpen, Berks., and one in Homer St.

The *Vine*, or the *Bunch of Grapes*, is a very natural sign at a place where wine is sold. The last particularly was almost inseparable from every tavern, and was often combined with other objects. The *Compleat Vintner* has in 1720 :—

> Without there hangs a noble sign,
> Where golden grapes in image shine ;
> To crown the bush, a little Punch
> Gut Bacchus dangling of a bunch,
> Sits loftily enthron'd upon
> What's called (in miniature) a Tun.

There was an interesting old *Vine* in Mile End Rd., a house which has now disappeared. The *Grapes* in Seven Dials was a famous house drawn by Cruikshank for Dickens in 1836. Two other instances may be adduced from the hundreds which are available. There is a *Grapes* and a *Vineyard* at Rochester, and a *Bunch of Grapes* in the Brompton Rd. The *Vintage* is at Wellington, Salop.

The *Bunch of Carrots* at Hampton Bishop, Herefs., is probably meant as a joke upon the *Bunch of Grapes*. Vines were grown in England from Roman times. In London alone there were celebrated vineyards in East Smithfield, in Hatton Garden (giving its name to Vine St.), and in St Giles-in-the-Fields. Curiously enough, until about 1820, a public-house, the sign of the *Vine*, in Dobie St., St Giles, occupied the very site assigned to this last vineyard in Domesday Book, A.D. 1080.

In many alehouses a bunch of hops might formerly be seen suspended in some conspicuous place.

As the vine was set up as a sign in honour of wine, so the *Hop Pole*, or the *Hop & Barleycorn*, the *Barley Mow*, the *Barley Stack*, the *Malt & Hops*, and the *Hopbine*, are very general tributes of honour rendered to beer. There is a *Hopbine* at Cambridge, a *Hop Pole* at Tewkesbury, Worcs., and at Ollerton, Notts. *Hop Poles* at Tewkesbury, a *Malt & Hops* at Soham, Cambs., and a *Wurtemberger Hop* at Stepney. A fine brand of hops used formerly to be imported from Wurtemberg. There is a *John Barley-*

corn at Coton, Cambs., and a *Barley Mow* at Witnesham, Suff. John is of course a personification of malt liquor. Mow has nothing to do with mowing, but means a heap of barley. The *Barleycorn* is in Euston and the *Barley Sheaf* at Dogdyke, Lincs.

The *Pineapple*, in the end of the 18th and the beginning of the 19th century, was generally, though not exclusively, the emblem adopted by confectioners. It was the sign of an eating-house in New St., Strand, at which Dr. Johnson used to dine on his first coming to town. There is a *Pineapple* still in Lambeth. The sign is not in general use with public-houses. Probably its origin has been either to signify an eating-house, or possibly as a mere business-getting novelty. A house of this sign survived in Shrewsbury until *c.* 1906.

Of the *Fig Tree* there are several examples among the London trades tokens, some of them, no doubt, grocers' signs, but other trades may have adopted the sign, either in allusion to the text of every man sitting under his own fig-tree, or because the fig-tree was a symbol of quiet unassuming industry. As such, at least, a writer of 1697 represents it because in spring-time the fig-tree does not make any show of beautiful flowers or precocious fruit to deceive mankind with idle hope ; but in autumn it generally produces exceedingly sweet fruit with flowers as it were contained within them. The sign occurs to this day at Peterborough. The *Almond Tree* was the sign of John Webster in St Paul's Churchyard in 1663, and there is a house of this sign at Liverpool, and the *Peach Tree* occurs sometimes as a sign, as for example in Nottingham. Neither of these signs, however, is of frequent occurrence.

Not only fruit trees but various forest trees are constantly met with on the sign-board ; thus the *Green Tree* which is very common and found, for example, at Darlington, originally had allusion to the foresters of the merry greenwood, or was suggested by some large evergreen, or tree sheltering or standing near the inn ; of this green tree the *Green Seedling* in Chester is evidently a sprout. Again, in Sheffield there are two signs of the *Burnt Tree*, which name possibly originated from some tree having been damaged in a fire, and becoming a well-known landmark. The *Oak* is deservedly much used as a sign ; sometimes as at Berry Brow, Huddersfield, it is called the *British Oak*. The *Cuckoo Oak* and the *Friar's Oak* and the *Doodle Oak* are found ; there is the *Evergreen Oak* at Thelnetham, Suff., the *Holme Oak* (Horne Oak) at Winkfield, Berks., the *King's Oak* at High Beech, Essex, and the *Round Oak* at Padworth, Berks. The *Acorn* is in Nicholas Passage, the *Oak & Acorn* at Taunton. There is an *Oak Tree* at Richmond, Surrey, an *Oak* at Sudbury, Mx., an *Oak Shades* at Norwich, and a *Broad Oak* at Strelley, Notts. At Killpeck, Herefs., the rhyme accompanies it :—

> I am an oak and not a yew,
> So drink a cup with good John Pugh.

The *Oak & Ivy* at Bilston, Staffs., and at Walmer, Kent, has a Druidical flavour. *Hearts of Oak* is the material out of which according to the song our ships were constructed, and therefore well deserves its favourite place amongst the signboards of the present day, while the *Acorn* the fruit of the *British Oak* is nearly as common as the other oak signs. The *Old Oak* and the *Oak of Reformation* of which there were a few examples in Norfolk, for example at Wymondham, are of course in memory of Kett's Council oak of 1549. The *Royal Forest* at Chingford takes its name from its being built next to a fine Tudor building, which was Queen Elizabeth's hunting lodge in the heart of Epping Forest.

Next to the oak the *Elm* seems to have had most followers. From the trades tokens it appears that the *Three Elms* was the sign of Edward Boswell in Chandos St. in 1667; and also of Isaac Elliotson, St John St., Clerkenwell. Besides these there was about the same date the *One Elm*, and the *Elm*. At present we have the *Nine Elms*, and the *Queen's Elm*, Brompton, which is mentioned under the name of the *Queen's Tree* in the parish books of 1586. The tree is said to derive its name from the fact of Queen Elizabeth when on a visit to Lord Burghley, being caught in a shower of rain, and taking shelter under the branches of an elm-tree, then growing here. There was formerly an avenue of fine elms near the house. The *Seven Sisters*, the sign of two public-houses in Tottenham, were seven elm-trees, planted in a circular form, with a walnut-tree in the middle. They were said to be upwards of 500 years old and local tradition had it that a martyr had been burnt on that spot. They stood formerly at the entrance from the high road at Page Green, Tottenham. The *Chestnut*, the *Sycamore*, the *Beech Tree*, the *Fir Tree*, the *Birch Tree*, and the *Ash Tree*, all occur in various places where alehouses are built in the shadow of such trees. The *Thorn Tree* is almost peculiar to Derbyshire, though there is a *Thorn* at Bury, Lancs. The *Buckthorn Tree* was, in 1775, the sign of ' William Blackwell in Covent Garden, or at his garden in South Lambeth'. He had chosen this sign because he sold, amongst other herbs, ' buckthorn and elder-berries, besides leeches and vipers'. What the use of the first was is well known ; as for the vipers, they were eaten in broth and soups before the days of Coty and Max Factor by ladies who wished to continue young and beautiful for ever. The *Crab Tree*, the indigenous apple-tree, is also seen in a great many places. A house of this name in Fulham is well known to oarsmen on the Thames. It derives its denomination from a large crab-tree growing near the public-house, which gave its name to the whole village. The *Willow Tree* is very rare as an inn sign. In the 17th century it was the sign of a shop in the Old Exchange, as appears from a trades token, but what business was carried on under this gloomy sign does not appear. There is a house of this name at Eton. The frequency of the sign of the *Yew Tree* is said to be attributed not to the yew's association with the churchyard, but to its giving the wood from which English bows were made. The bows were however made, or supposed to be made, of *Spanish Yew*. A house of this name at Reigate has a fine painted sign.

The *Cotton Tree* is a sign generally put up in the neighbourhood of cotton factories, as at Manchester, Ancoats, Bury, Chorlton-on-Medlock, Colne and in some ten or a dozen other places in Lancashire. At Hull the same sign occurs near the mills where cotton seed is treated for the extraction of oil and the manufacture of cow-cake. The *Palm Tree* is one of the oldest symbols known : it was used as such by the Assyrians, the Greeks, and the Romans, and by them transmitted to the early Christians. St Ambrose in a very forcible image, compares the life of an early and faithful Christian to the palm-tree, rough and rugged below like its stem, but increasing in beauty upwards where it bears heavenly fruit. There is a house of this sign at Eythorne, Kent.

The *Cocoa-Tree* was frequently the sign of chocolate-houses when that beverage was newly imported and very fashionable. One of the most famous survived until recently in St James's St. ; it was, in the reign of Queen Anne, strictly a Tory house :— 'A Whig', says Defoe, 'will no more go to the *Cocoa Tree*, or Ozinda's (another chocolate house in the same neighbourhood) than a Tory will be seen at the coffee-house of St James.' It was notorious for high play, and is mentioned by Horace Walpole in this connexion. It afterwards became a club, of which Byron was a member. This gambling seems to have been inseparable from the chocolate-houses. Roger North said in 1657 :—

> The use of coffee-houses seems newly improved by a new invention called Chocolate-houses, for the benefit of rooks and cullies of all the quality, where gaming is added to all the rest, and the summons of whores seldom fails : as if the devil had erected a new university, and those were the colleges of its professors, as well as his school of discipline.

The *Coffee House* was in Larwood's time the inappropriate sign of a gin-palace in Chalton St., Somers Town. The house still survives. Early in the 18th century this neighbourhood was a delightful rural suburb, with fields and flower gardens. A short distance down the hill was the then famous Bagnigge Wells, and close by were the remains of Totten-Hall, with the *Adam & Eve* Tea-Gardens, and the so-called King John's Palace. Many foreign Protestant refugees had taken up their residence in this suburb on account of the retirement it afforded and the low rents asked for the small houses. The *Coffee-House* was then the popular tea- and coffee-gardens of the district, and was visited by the foreigners of the neighbourhood as well as by pleasure-seeking Cockneys from the distant city. The speciality of this establishment was its coffee. As the traffic increased it became a posting-house, uniting the business of an inn to the profits of a pleasure garden. Gradually the demand for coffee fell off and that for malt and spirituous liquors increased. Then the gardens were all built over and the old gateway formed part of the bar. Another old coffee-house, the *London Coffee-House* in Ludgate Hill, opened in 1731 is now known as the *Ye Old London*.

Flowers, fruit trees, and forest trees were represented on the signboard, and even the homely tenants of the kitchen garden found a place. The *Artichoke*, above all, used to be a favourite, and still gives a name to some houses. As a seedsman's sign it was common and rational ; not so for a milliner, yet among the shopbills there are several instances of its being the sign of such a business. Probably the novelty of the plant had more than anything else to do with this selection, for though it was introduced into this country in the reign of King Henry VIII, yet Evelyn observes that in his time artichokes were so rare as to be sold for a crown apiece. Houses of this sign still remain in Farringdon St. and at Bristol. The *Cabbage* is an alehouse sign at Hunslet, Leeds, and at Liverpool. *Cabbage Hall* however, once opposite Chaney Lane, Oxford, was formerly the name of a public-house kept by a tailor.   Cabbage is of course a recognized trade term for the tailor's perquisites in the matter of scraps of cloth, etc., and the name may well have originated in a nickname given by his customers.   There is a *Cauliflower* at Ilford.   The *Oxnoble*, a kind of potato, is the name of a house in Manchester, and there is a *Sacks of Potatoes* at Gorsty Green, Birmingham.   The homely mess of *Pease & Beans* was a sign in Norwich in 1750.

The *Wheatsheaf* is an extremely common inn, public-house and baker's sign ; it is a charge in the arms of the three livery companies catering for these trades, besides that of the brewers.   There is a *Wheatsheaf* in Rathbone Place off Oxford St., W., another with a good painted sign at Chichester, still another at Ide Hill, Kent, and there is a *Three Wheatsheaves* in Upper St., Islington.   In the middle of Farringdon St., opposite the Market, is Wheatsheaf Yard, called from the *Wheatsheaf* once a famous waggon inn, which also did a roaring trade in wine, spirits and Fleet St. marriages. Indeed, most of the large inns within the liberties of the Fleet served as ' marriage shops' between 1734 and 1749 ; amongst the most famous were the *Bull & Garter*, the *Hoop & Bunch of Grapes*, the *Bishop Blaize & Two Sawyers*, the *Fighting Cocks*, and numerous others.   The gateway entrance to the old coach-yard was adorned with very fine carvings of wheat ears and lions' heads intermixed, finished in a manner worthy of Grinling Gibbons himself.

The *Oatsheaf* is very rare as an inn sign ; it was the sign of a shop in Cree Church Lane, Leadenhall St., in the 17th century, as appears from a trades token.   It appears however over a house at Whittlesea, I. of E.

With the plants named we may also class Tobacco, the most abused of all weeds. Sometimes we see a picture of the *Tobacco Plant*, but most usually it occurs in the form of Tobacco Rolls, representing coils of the so-called spun or twist tobacco, otherwise pigtail, painted for the sake of ornament alternately brown and gold.   There is a *Virginia Plant* in Great Dover St., and a *Virginia Planter* in Virginia Rd., Bethnal Green.

PLATE
13

BEXLEY PUBLIC LIBRARIES.

PLATE
14

Chapter X

BIBLICAL AND RELIGIOUS SIGNS

THE earlier signs often depicted the most important article sold in the shops before which they hung. The *stocking* denoted the hosier, the *gridiron* the ironmonger, and so on. The early booksellers, whose trade lay chiefly in religious books, delighted in signs of saints, but after the Reformation they set up the *Bible* for their sign ; it became the popular symbol of the trade, and instances of its use still linger with us.

One of the last Bible signs was nearly a century ago at a public-house in Shire Lane, Temple Bar, E.C., over an old-established house of call for printers.

The Bible being such a common sign, booksellers had to adopt Bibles of different colours, amongst which the *Blue Bible* was one of the most common. Prynne's *Historio-Mastrix* was 'printed for Michael Sparke, and sold at the *Blue Bible*, in Green Arbour Court, Little Old Bailey, 1632'. This blue colour, common on the sign-board, was chosen not without meaning, but on account of its symbolic virtue. Blue, from its permanency, was an emblem of truth, hence it also signified piety and sincerity. It also had a party significance which is dealt with elsewhere in the text.

Other booksellers chose the *Three Bibles*, which was a very common sign of the trade on London Bridge in the 17th and 18th centuries : of one of them, Charles Tyne, trades tokens are extant,—great curiosities to the numismatist, as booksellers rarely issued them. The sign of the *Three Bibles* seems to have originated from the stationers' arms, which are *arg.* on a chevron between *three bibles or*, a falcon *volant* between two roses, the Holy Ghost in chief. One bookseller in 1711, better as a business man than as a herald, on account of his selling stationery, added *three inkbottles* to the favourite three Bibles and did a trade in ' Picket Cards ', ' Ombre Cards ', and ' Basset Cards ', from the *Three Bibles & Three Inkbottles* near St Magnus' Church on London Bridge.

Combinations of the Bible with other objects were very common, some of them symbolic, as the *Bible & Crown*, which originated from the conviction of the clergy and the court party as to the divine prerogative of the Crown. The *Bible & Crown* became the standing toast of the cavaliers and those opposed to the Parliamentary leaders. As a sign it has been used for well over two centuries by Messrs. Rivington the publishers. The old wood carving, painted and gilt in the style of the early signs, was taken down from over the shop in Paternoster Row in 1853, when this firm removed westward. It is still in their possession. Cobbett when setting up as a pub-lisher chose the sign of the *Bible, Crown & Constitution* ; but the general tenor of his life was such that his enemies said he put them up merely that he might afterwards be able to say he had pulled them down. A *Bible, Sceptre & Crown* carved in wood was in Larwood's time still to be seen on the top of an alehouse of that name in High Holborn. The crown and sceptre in this case were placed on two closed Bibles. The house is now extinct and the sign has gone.

The *Bible & Lamb*, i.e., the Holy Lamb, near Temple Bar, is mentioned in an advertisement of 1759. Books also were sold here, for booksellers and toyshops were then the usual repositories for quack medicines. There are many other *Bible* signs—almost all of booksellers rather than of innkeepers.

Of the Apocryphal books of the Bible there is only one doubtful example among the signboards, viz., *Bel & the Dragon*, which was at one time not uncommon, more particularly with apothecaries. It was represented by a Bell and a Dragon, as appears from the *Spectator* No. 28. Although at the first glance this sign seems taken from the doubtful books of the Old Testament, there seems nothing in the Apocryphal book which could in any way prompt the choice of it for a signboard. After all then it may possibly be only a combination or corruption of two other signs. There still remain a few houses which employ it, as at Cookham, Berks., and it was formerly to be seen also in Worship St., and at Norton-in-the-Moors, Staffs., etc., while in Boss St., Horselydown, there is a variation in the form of the *Bell & Griffin*. It was vulgarly called *King Astyages' Arms*. This was for no better reasons than that King Astyages is the first name in the story : the incident related in the *Book of Bel and the Dragon* having taken place after his death.

A very common sign of old as well as at present is the *Adam & Eve*. It occurs in London and at Windsor, Hitchin, Norwich, Ware, etc. According to Mr. Block ★ there were thirteen houses of this name in London in 1848. Our first parents were constant *dramatis personæ* in the mediaeval mysteries and pageants and this may account for some instances of the adoption of the sign. It was certainly used by various trades including the publishers of books. Often however the sign was from the arms of the Fruiterers' Company.

In Newgate St. there lately remained an old stone sign of the *Adam & Eve* with the date 1669. Eve was represented handing the apple to Adam, the fatal tree was in the centre, round its stem the serpent winding. There is another *Adam & Eve* in the High St., Kensington, where Sheridan, on his way to and from Holland House, used to refresh himself, and in this way managed to run up rather a long bill, which Lord Holland had to pay for him. Another London *Adam & Eve* is at the corner of Tottenham Court Rd. and Edgware Rd. It is on the site of the Adam and Eve Tea-Gardens in Tottenham Court Rd., part of which was the last remaining vestige ' of the once respectable, if not magnificent, manor-house appertaining to the Lords of Tottenhall '. In 1819, it was said that the place had long been celebrated as a tea-garden ; there was an organ in the long room, and the company was generally respect-able till the end of the 18th century. Then highwaymen, footpads, pickpockets and prostitutes beginning to take a fancy to it, the magistrates interfered. The organ was banished, and the gardens were dug up for the foundations of Eden St. Hogarth has

★ *Op. cit.*, p. 269.

represented the *Adam & Eve* in the *March of the Guards to Finchley*. One hopes it is true that a former licensee of the *Adam & Eve*, Norwich, was named Cain Abel!

The tree with the forbidden fruit always represented in the sign of *Adam & Eve* leads directly to the *Flaming Sword* ' which turned every way to keep the way of the tree of life '. As the first sword on record, it was not inappropriately a cutler's sign, and as such we find it in the Banks Collection, on the shop-bill of a sword cutler in Sweetings Alley, Royal Exchange, 1780. It is less appropriate at the door of a public-house in Nottingham, for the landlord evidently cannot desire to keep anybody out, whether saint or sinner. It is fitting that there should decorate the tavern the vessel by which the life of the first planter of the vine was preserved. Hence *Noah's Ark* is not an uncommon public-house sign. It appears, says Larwood, like a sarcastic reflection on the mixed crowd that resort to the house—not to escape the heavy wet, but in order to obtain some of it. Toy-shops also constantly used it, since Noah's Ark is generally a favourite toy of children. Often it appears the sign was used by a man who dealt in animals, birds, fishes, etc., as well as in beer and wine. In such cases it appears as, for example, the *Tun & Ark*. There is an *Ark* at 313 Oxford St., and another at Cattawade, Suff., near Manningtree, Essex. The *Noah's Ark* is the principal inn at Thetford, Norf.

The Deluge was one of the standard subjects of mediaeval dramatic plays. It was the mystery performed at Whitsuntide by the Company of Dyers in London, and from this the Dyers' sign of the *Dove & Rainbow* may have originated. There is evidently in its use a reference to the various colours of the rainbow. On the bill of John Edwards, a silk-dyer in Aldersgate St., the *Dove* with an olive branch in her mouth is represented flying underneath the *Rainbow* over a landscape with villages, fenced fields and a gentleman in the costume of the reign of Charles II. Besides this, there are among the Bagford and Banks Collections various other dyers' bills with the sign of the *Dove & Rainbow*. A few licensed houses at the present day still keep up the memory of the sign—there is one at Nottingham, and another at Leicester, and there is a *Rainbow & Dove* at Haslingwood Common, Essex.

Jacob's Well was once common in London as well as in the country. There is a house of this sign in New Inn Yard, S.E., and another in Leeds. The allusion here is to the well at which Our Lord met the woman of Samaria. The words ' Whosoever drinketh of this water shall thirst again ' * apply with special force to the tap, at which generation after generation drink, and after which they always thirst again. Possibly although the sign has a flavour of irreverence, the English use of it may date from the Puritan period. A *Jacob's Inn* in Redcross St. is recorded at least as early as 1708.

Not always, however, had the sign any direct relation to the trade of the inmate of the house which it adorned ; as, for example, *Moses & Aaron*, which occurs on a trades token of Whitechapel. In allusion to this or a similar sign, the ribald Tom Brown says, ' Other amusements presented themselves as thick as hops, as Moses pictured with horns, to keep Cheapside in countenance.' In London however the use of

* St John iv. 12.

this sign may at first have been suggested by the statues of Moses and Aaron that used to stand above the balcony of the Old Guildhall.   Connected with the history of Moses we find several other signs, one in particular is mentioned by Ned Ward in *A Step to Stirbitch Fair*, 1703, as the *Old Pharaoh*, Barley, Herts.   It was so named, says he, ' from a stout, elevating malt liquor of the same name, for which this house had long been famous '.   A story in the county is current that it was so named because the beer, like the Egyptian king of old, ' would not let the people go ! '   It is now no longer drunk in England, but a certain strong beer of the same name is or was lately a favourite beverage in Belgium.   Next in chronological order connected with the history of Moses, follows the *Brazen Serpent*, the sign of Reynold Wolfe, a bookseller and printer in St Paul's Churchyard in 1544, and also of both his apprentices, Henry Bynneman and John Shepperde.   It had probably been imported by the foreign printers, for it was a favourite amongst the early French and German booksellers.   In Larwood's time it was the sign of a licensed house in Richardson St., Bermondsey. What led to the adoption of this emblem was not the historical association, but the mystical meaning which it had in the Middle Ages.   According to Randle Holme the figure was :—

> A serpent torqued with a long cross ; others blazon Christ, supporting the brazen serpent, because it was an anti-type of the passion and death of our Saviour ; for as Moses lifted up the serpent in the wilderness, so must the Son of Man be lifted up (Num. xxi. 8, 9, John iii. 14), that all that behold him, by a lively faith, may not perish but have everlasting life.   This is the cognizance or crest of every true believer.

The *Two Spies* is the last sign belonging to the history of Moses ; it represents two of the spies that went into Canaan ' and cut down from thence a branch with one cluster of grapes, and they bear it between two upon a staff '.*   This bunch of grapes made it a favourite with publicans ; at many places it might formerly be seen, as in Catherine St., Strand (a house of old standing), in Long Acre, etc.   In Great Windmill St., Leicester Square, it was corrupted into the *Three Spies*.   All these houses are now extinct, and the sign is not recorded as existing nowadays.

After Moses there is a blank until we come to Samson, to whom our national admiration for athletic sports and muscular strength has given a prominent place on the signboard.   *Samson & the Lion* occurs on the sign of various houses in London in the 17th century, as appears from the trades tokens.   It is still of frequent occurrence in provincial towns, as at Birmingham, Coventry, etc.   *Samson* is found at Gilstead, W.R. Yorks, and the *Old English Samson* (? Topham, *q.v.*) at Sheffield.

This admiration of strong men which procured the signboard honours to Samson also made Goliah, or Golias, a great favourite.   The sign is found for example at Carlisle.   In the Horse Market, Castle Barnard, he is actually treated just like a duke, admiral, or any other public-house hero, for there the sign is entitled the *Goliah Head*. Some doubts, however, may be entertained whether by Golias or Goliah, the Philistine giant and champion Goliath was always intended.   Towards the end of the 12th cen-

* Numbers xiii. 23.

tury the Galiardic verses were composed probably by wandering scholars of whom Walter Mapes, quoted on our title page, was almost certainly one. Chaucer's *Miller* ★ was a 'junglere, and a goliardeys'. Such a Golias, whether or not he had ever a real existence, would certainly have been a very appropriate tutelary deity for an alehouse.

Goliah's conqueror King David shares the honours with his victim, and he still figures on various signboards. There is a *King David* in Bristol, and a *David & Harp* in Limehouse. *Absolom* was a peruke-maker's very expressive emblem both in France and in England, to show the utility of wigs. An old sign of *Absalom in the Oak* is now preserved in the Fonnerean Museum, Ipswich. It does not appear whether or not this belonged to a licensed house.

Psalm xlii. seems to have been very profanely hinted at in the sign of the *White Hart & Fountain*, Royal Mint St. (now extinct) which, if not a combination of two well-known signs, apparently alludes to the psalm. Solomon does not appear to have ever been honoured with a signboard portrait, but his enthusiastic admirer, the Queen of Saba, i.e. *Queen of Sheba*, figured before the tavern kept by Dick Tarlton the jester in Gracechurch St. This Queen of Saba was a usual figure in pageants. There is a letter of Secretary Barlow in *Nugæ Antique* telling how the Queen of Sheba fell down and upset her casket in the lap of the King of Denmark when on his drunken visit to James I, who 'got not a little defiled with the presents of the queen; such as wine, cream, jelly, beverages, cakes, spices, and other good matters'.

Balaam's Ass, again, was one of the *dramatis personæ* in the Whitsuntide mystery of the company of Cappers, and this is the only reason we can imagine for his having found his way to the signboard. The sign occurs in 1722 in a *Weekly Journal* paragraph.

Few signs have undergone so many changes as the well-known *Salutation*. Originally it represented the Angel saluting Our Lady, in which shape it was still occasionally seen in the 17th and 18th centuries, as appears from the tavern token of Daniel Grey of Holborn. In the time of the Commonwealth, however, the Puritans changed it into the *Soldier & Citizen*, and in such a garb it continued long after, with this modification, that it was represented by two citizens politely bowing to each other. The *Salutation* in Billingsgate shows it thus on its trades token, and so it was represented by the *Salutation* in Newgate St. (an engraving of which sign might in Larwood's time still be seen in the parlour of that old-established house). Formerly at Coventry a house of this sign showed a townsman holding out his hands towards a visitor, with the greeting 'Welcome to our Town'; the scene being laid on the outskirts of the town, with the spires of the Priory Church in the background. At present it is usually rendered by two hands conjoined. That *Salutation* in Billingsgate was a famous place in Ben Jonson's time; it is named in *Bartholomew Fayre* as one of the houses where there had been

> Great sale and utterance of wine,
> Besides beere and ale, and ipocras fine.

★ Prologue 560.

During the Civil War there was a *Salutation* in Holborn where if one may believe the Royalist paper : *The Man in the Moon discovering a world of wickedness under the Sun*— 4 July 1649 :—

> A hotte combat lately happened where some of the Commonwealth vermin, called soldiers, had seized on an Amazonian Virago, named Mrs. Strosse, upon suspicion of being a loyalist, and selling the Man in the Moon ; but shee, by applying beaten pepper to their eyes, disarmed them, and with their own swordes forced them to aske for forgiveness ; and down on their mary bones, and pledge a health to the king, and confusion to their masters, and so honourabile dismissed them. Oh ! for twenty thousand such gallant spirits ; when you see that one woman can beat two or three.

At the end of the 18th century there was a *Salutation* in Tavistock Row, called also *Mr. Bunches*, which was one of the haunts patronized by the Prince Regent. Lord Surrey and Sheridan were generally his associates in these escapades. The trio went under the pseudonyms of Blackstock, Greystock, and Thinstock, and were disguised in bob wigs and smockfrocks. The night's entertainment generally concluded with thrashing the Charlies, wrenching off knockers, breaking down signboards and not unfrequently in some of the choice spirits among their companions being taken to the roundhouse. The *Salutation* in Newgate St. some time called *Salutation & Cat* (a combination of two signs) was haunted by many of the great authors of the 18th century. A rhymed invitation to a social feast held at this tavern, 19 January 1736, issued by two stewards, Edward Cave (of the *Gentleman's Magazine*), and William Bowyer, the antiquary and printer, was replied to by Richardson the novelist in verse almost as bad as theirs.

In this tavern Coleridge in one of his melancholy moods, lived for some time in seclusion until found out by Southey, and persuaded by him to return to his usual mode of life. Here Coleridge had been in the habit of meeting Lamb when in town on a visit from the University. Christ's Hospital, their old school, was within a few paces of the place.

Shortly after they had terminated, with Coleridge's departure from London, he thus recalled them in a letter :—

> When I read in your little volume your nineteenth effusion, or what you call ' The Sigh ', I think I hear *you* again. I imagine to myself the little smoky room at the *Salutation & Cat*, where we have sat together through the winter nights, beguiling the cares of life with poesy.

This was early in 1769, and in 1818, when dedicating his works—then first collected—to his earliest friend, he spoke of the same meetings.

The vulgarization of the sign by a milkman, perhaps the best (or worst) example of corruption of this kind, is dealt with elsewhere (p. 29).

The *Angel* was derived from the *Salutation*. It is evident that it originally represented the angel appearing to Our Lady at the Salutation or Annunciation. Even as late as the 17th century on nearly all the trades tokens of houses of this sign the angel is represented with a scroll in his hands. This scroll we know, from the evidence of paintings and prints, to contain the words addressed by the angel to the Blessed Virgin : *Ave Maria, gratia plena, Dominus tecum.* Probably at the Reformation it was considered too Popish a sign, and so Our Lady was left out, and the angel was retained. Among the famous houses with this sign stood foremost the *Angel* at Islington, now Messrs. Lyons' Angel Café, but still known as a London Transport omnibus stage. A neighbouring house however still has the sign of the *Angel & Crown.* The old house was pulled down in 1819, until which time it had preserved all the features of a large country inn. It had a long front, an overhanging tiled roof with a square inn-yard, having double galleries supported by columns and carved pilasters, with caryatids and other ornaments. It is probably that it had often been used as a place for dramatic entertainments at the period when inn-yards were customarily employed for such purposes. A century and a half ago it was usual for travellers approaching London to remain all night at the *Angel* rather than venture after dark to prosecute their journey along ways which were almost equally dangerous from their bad state, and their being so greatly infested with thieves. On the other hand, persons walking from the city to Islington in the evening waited near the end of John St., in what is now termed Northampton St. (but was then a rural avenue planted with trees). When a sufficient party had collected they were then escorted by an armed patrol appointed for that purpose.

Another old tavern with this sign existed formerly behind St Clement Dane's Church. To this house Bishop Hooper was taken by the guards on his way to Gloucester, where he went to be burnt in January 1555. The house, until shortly before Larwood's time, preserved much of its ancient aspect ; it had a pointed gable, galleries, and a lattice in the passage. This inn is named in a curious advertisement in the *Publick Advertiser* of 1769 as to the sale of a Black Girl.

There was an *Angel* in Smithfield, where the famous Joe Miller used to play during Bartholomew Fair time. A play-bill of 1722 informs the public in large letters that :—

> Miller is not with Pinkethman, but by himself, at the *Angel* Tavern next door to the King's Bench, who acts a new Droll, called the *Faithful Couple* or the *Royal Shepherdess*, with a very pleasant entertainment between Old Hob and his Wife, and the comical humours of Mopsy and Colin, with a variety of singing and dancing.

> The only Comedian now that dare,
> Vie with the world and challenge the Fair.

Older than any of these is the *Angel*, now the *Angel & Royal* at Grantham. This building was formerly in the possession of the Knights Templar, and still keeps many remains of its former beauty, particularly the gateway, with the heads of Edward III and his queen Philippa of Hainault on either side of the arch ; the soffits of the windows are elegantly groined, and the parapet of the front is very beautiful. Kings have been entertained in this house ; but it seemed to bring ill-luck to them, for the reigns of those that are recorded as having been guests in it stand forth in history as disturbed by violent storms—King John held his court in it on 23 February 1213 ; King Richard III on 19 October 1483, and King Charles I visited it 17 May 1633. King Edward VII as Prince of Wales visited the house, and since then it has taken the name of the *Angel & Royal*.

Ben Jonson used to visit the *Angel* at Basingstoke, kept by a Mrs. Hope, whose daughter's name was Prudence. On one of his journeys, finding that the house had changed both sign and mistresses, Jonson wrote the not very elegant epigram :—

> When *Hope* and *Prudence* kept this house,
> the *Angel* kept the door,
> Now *Hope* is dead, the *Angel* fled,
> and *Prudence* turned a whore.

The *Angel* was the sign of one of the first coffee-houses in England, for Anthony Wood tells us that ' In 1650 Jacob, a Jew, opened a coffee-house at the Angel in the Parish of St Peter, Oxon, and there it (coffee) was by some who delight in noveltie drank '. This is apparently the *Angel* in the High St. Part of its site is now occupied by the Examination Schools, and the remaining scrap of the building, which had associations with Johnson and Boswell and with Nelson, is now occupied as a café by the local Co-operative Society. There was a famous half-timbered *Angel* at Bury St Edmunds.

There being such a profusion of *Angels* everywhere it became necessary to make some distinctions, and the usual means were adopted ; the *Angel* was gilded, and called the *Golden Angel* ; this, for instance, was the sign of Ellis Gamble, a goldsmith in Cranbourn Alley, Hogarth's master in the art of engraving on silver. Another variety was the *Guardian Angel*, which is still the sign of a house at Yarmouth.

Very common, also, were the *Three Angels*, which may have been intended for the three angels that appeared to Abraham,* or simply the favourite combination of three frequent on the signboard and in heraldry. Three angels were thought to possess mysterious power. The *Three Angels* was a very general linen-draper's sign. There seems no special reason for this unless the long flowing garments in which angels are generally represented suggest their having been good customers to the drapery business.

Angels appear in combination with various heterogeneous objects, in many of which, however, the so-called angel is simply a Cupid. The *Angel & Bible* was a sign in the Poultry in 1680. The *Angel & Crown* was a not uncommon tavern decoration. This stanza from the *Quack Vintners*, 1712, shows the way in which this sign was represented :—

> May Harry's Angel be a sign he draws
> Angelick nectar, that deserves applause,
> Such that may make the city love the Throne,
> And, like his *Angel*, still *support the Crown*.

---

* Genesis xviii. 1–22.

Doubtless the sign of the house had originally been the *Crown*, and the Renaissance Cupid had been added by way of ornament, but was mistaken by the public as a constituent of the sign. The verses probably applied to the *Angel & Crown*, a famous tavern in Broad St., behind the Royal Exchange. There was another *Angel & Crown* in Islington, where convivial dinners were held. It was a common practice in the 18th and preceding centuries for the natives of a county or parish to meet once a year and dine together. The ceremony often commenced by a sermon, preached by a native, after which the day was spent in pleasant conviviality, after-dinner speeches and mutual congratulations. The custom in Larwood's time had almost died out, but lately has been happily revived by the Society of Yorkshiremen in London, and the similar county societies. In 1737–8 another *Angel & Crown* in Shire Lane obtained an unenviable notoriety, for it was there that a Mr. Quarrington was murdered and robbed by Thomas Carr, an Attorney from the Temple, and Elizabeth Adams. They were hanged at Tyburn, 18 January 1738.

In 1718 we find the *Angel & Still* at Deptford noticed, as in an advertisement in the *Weekly Journal* of 1718 concerning a runaway negro. In this case the still was simply added to intimate the sale of spirituous liquors. The *Angel & Sun*, apparently a combination of two signs, is named as a shop or tavern near Strand Bridge, in 1663, and in Larwood's time the name of a house—now no more—in the Strand. The *Angel & Woolpack*, Bolton, is the same sign which formerly existed near London Bridge, called the *Naked Boy & Woolpack*. A woolpack with a negro seated on it was at one time very common : for a change or distinction, this negro underwent the reputedly impossible process of being washed white, and thus became a naked boy, who, in signboard phraseology, is equivalent to an angel. There is an *Angel & Elephant* at Widnes, and an *Angel & Trumpet* in Stepney.

The *Virgin* was unquestionably a very common sign before the Reformation, and may be met with even at the present day, as for instance at Worcester, and in various other places. An odd mixture is the *Virgins & Castle*, still seen at Kenilworth, Warws. The sign of the *Virgin* also appears as Our Lady, as indicated by Stow : ' Newe Inne was a guest Inne, the sign whereof was the picture of our Lady, and thereupon it was also called *Our Lady's Inne*.'

The prevalence of the *Baptist's Head* probably dates from the time when pilgrimages across the sea were considered good works, and the head of St John the Baptist at Amiens Cathedral came in for a large share of visits from English worshippers. The old monkish writers say that in A.D. 448 the head was found in Jerusalem, in 1206 it was transferred to Amiens, where it was kept in a salver of gold, surrounded with a rim of pearls and precious stones. Various other reasons may be adduced for the prevalence of this sign, as the conspicuous place occupied by St John in the Roman hagiology and hence in mediaeval plays and mysteries ; the festivities of Midsummer (a day of great moment in London for setting the watch) and finally his being the patron saint of the Knights of Jerusalem. Possibly in compliment to those knights was named the *Baptist's Head* still found in St John's Lane, Clerkenwell. This is often however said to commemorate Sir Baptist Hicks, first Lord Cambden, who built Hicks Hall also in Clerkenwell as a gift to the county of Middlesex. The present building is of no great interest, though its taproom contains a fine mantelpiece taken from the old tavern, formerly the mansion of Sir John Forster the judge, who died here in 1612. When the late house was adapted to its purpose it was distinguished by the Head of St John the Baptist in a charger, now gone. Johnson is said to have been an occasional visitor here when returning from the office of Cave the editor of the *Gentleman's Magazine*, which was close by at St John's Gate. Goldsmith, Garrick and Savage are also reported to have made frequent calls here, when business of a similar nature led them to the same spot. In later years it became the house of call of prisoners on their way from Clerkenwell detention prison to Newgate, the new prison in the parish—a circumstance commemorated by Dodd in the *Old Bailey Registers*. Another *St John's Head* 'within Ludgate' is mentioned by Stow in an account how the Drawer of the House for seditious speeches at the proclamation of ' Queen ' Jane Grey in 1553, was set in the pillory in Cheape ' with both his ears nailed and cleane cut off '. To this same St John also referred the *John of Jerusalem*, an extinct sign formerly in Rosoman St., Clerkenwell.

The *Good Samaritan*, which may be seen in Turner St., Whitechapel, Grimshaw Park, Blackburn, Ashton-under-Lyne, etc. was borrowed from the parable. When barbers combined with their trade the practice of letting blood, of drawing teeth, and setting bones they frequently adopted this sign. No doubt also taken from the parables are the signs of the *Prodigal's Return*, Battersea, and the *Fatted Calf*, Manchester.

Crosses of various colours were probably amongst the first signs put up by the newly-converted Christians on account of the recommendation of the early fathers, and for their beneficial influence. Lactantius, St Ephrem, St Chrysostom, and St Cyril of Alexandria all refer to the marvellous power of the sign of the Cross. Even in Protestant England the present author as a small boy engaged in games of Tig, when he was tired cried ' Kings ', and crossed his fingers, knowing that by so doing he was safe from his pursuers. At the Crusades the popularity of this emblem increased : a red cross was the badge of the Crusader, and perhaps would be put up as a sign by the men who had been to the Holy Land, or wished to court the patronage of those on their way thither. The different orders of knighthood settled each upon a particular colour as its distinctive mark. Thus the Knights of St John wore *white crosses*, the Templars *red crosses*, the Knights of St Lazarus *green crosses*, the Teutonic Knights *black crosses* embroidered with gold. By far the most common in England was the *red cross*, that of St George and of the Templars.

A more prosaic origin for some of the cross signs is from the position of their houses at cross-roads. An inn of the *Cross* sign which it seems to have acquired in this fashion is to be seen at Woodhide, Suff. Very few signs of the cross now remain. The *Golden Cross* in the Strand is one of these, and has been in that locality for centuries. It was one of the first upon which the Puritans vented their hatred of popery ; for in 1643 it was taken down by order of a committee from the House of Commons, as ' superstitious and idolatrous '. This was the precursor of the fall of Old Charing Cross itself. The sign, however, was put up again at the Restoration, and figures prominently in Canaletto's well-known view of Charing Cross in the Northumberland Collection. Probably the tavern was pulled down at the formation of Trafalgar Square.

The *Golden Cross* is the oldest inn in Shrewsbury, with a well-documented history from 1480. Up to some years before 1780 it was known as the *Sextry*, since it was originally the Sacristy of St Chad's Church. Up till 1794 a covered passage ran from the inn to the church (for the convenience of the vicar's *Choral*) singing the night offices in the collegiate church. There is another famous *Golden Cross* in the Cornmarket, Oxford, a fine old place with part of its gallery still remaining. A pleasant wayside *Cross* is just outside Stroud, Glos.

At a point on the road between Dunchurch and Daventry, where three roads meet, there was formerly an inn with the sign of the *Three Crosses*, in allusion to the three roads. Swift in one of his pedestrian excursions happened to stop at that inn. He was not very elegantly dressed and rather importunate to be served so the landlady told him that she could not leave her customers for ' such as he ', upon which the Dean, who was neither the most modest nor the most patient of men, wrote the epigram on one of the windows :—

> *To the Landlord.*
> Thou fool, to hang three crosses at thy door !
> Hurry up thy wife—she's cross enough for four.

The *Four Crosses* is common in Staffordshire and the other counties in the old diocese of Lichfield. This is no doubt from the arms of the see, described as party per pale *gu* and *arg*. A cross potent and quadrate in the centre between four crosses patée and countercharged. There is a good example of it at Shelfield, Walsall.

Although the English alehouses long continued to select fresh signs from the notabilities of the hour, they rarely chose anything of a religious or devotional cast. One instance occurs however, and that in the neighbourhood of London. In Kentish Town an inn which in Larwood's time was ' the noisiest and most objectionable public-house in the district ' bears the significant sign of the *Gospel Oak*. It was the favourite resort of navvies and quarrelsome shoemakers, and took its name not from any inclination to piety on the part of the landlord but from an old oak tree in the neighbourhood, near the boundary line of Hampstead and St Pancras parishes. This was a relic of the once general custom of reading a portion of the Gospel under certain trees during the parish perambulations on the gang-days in Rogation Week—' beating the bounds '. ' The boundaries and township of the parish of Wolverhampton are,' says Shaw, in his *History of Staffordshire*, ' in many points marked out by what are called 'Gospel Trees', and Herrick, in his *Hesperides*, says :—

> Dearest, bury me
> Under that holy oak, or gospel tree ;
> Where, though thou see'st not, thou may'st think upon
> Me, when thou yearly go'st procession.

The old Kentish Town *Gospel Oak* has long been removed, but not until it had given a name to the surrounding fields, to a village and to a chapel, as well as to the public-house.   The whole locality is still known as Gospel Oak.

Chapter XI

SAINTS, MARTYRS, ETC.

THE *All Saints* at Chorlton-on-Medlock is called after the neighbouring church of All Saints. Many of the saints were patrons of particular trades or crafts, and were constantly adopted as the signs of those that followed them. Thus *St Crispin* was generally a shoemaker's sign ; many publicans still have the sign of *Crispin, Saint Crispin, Jolly Crispin,* or *Crispin* and *Crispian,* and occasionally *King Crispin,* as at Morpeth and at Stroud, or *Bold Crispin* as at Ipswich, perhaps because as the old proverb has it ' Cobblers and tinkers are the best ale drinkers '. No doubt what mainly contributed to St Crispin's popularity in this country is the fact of the Battle of Agincourt having been fought on his day, 25 October 1415. There is a well-known purple patch on the subject in *King Henry V.*★

St Hugh's bones (i.e. the tools of the shoemakers' trade) was another sign of the gentle craft ; it seems to be extinct now, but a trades token shows that in 1657 it was the sign of a house in Stanhope St., Clare Market.

Bishop Blaze or Blaize, otherwise St Blasius of Sebaste in Cappadocia, is considered the patron of woolcombers, whence the sign is very common in the clothing districts. It is found in London and at Derby, Richmond, Yorks, Leicester, Wakefield, Rochdale, Burnley, etc. Blaize is represented with in his hands the instrument of his martyrdom in A.D. 289 an iron comb with which the flesh was torn from his body. From this instrument has been attributed to him the invention of wool-combing. His feast on 3 February was formerly celebrated every seventh year by a procession and feast of the masters and workmen of the woollen manufactures in Yorkshire and in Bedfordshire. In sheep-shearing festivals also a representation of him used to be introduced. There are still a few places where observance of his feast (3 February) survives in a vestigial form.

St Julian, the patron of travellers, wandering minstrels, boatmen, etc., made a very common inn sign, because he was supposed to provide good lodgings for such persons. There is still a house of this sign at Newport, Mon. Two St Julian's crosses, in saltire are in chief of the innholders arms and the old motto was :—' When I was harbourless ye lodged me.' This benevolent attention to travellers procured him the epithet of the good herbergeor.

Mediaevally *St Julian's Inn* is as a synonym for good cheer as appears in *Cocke Lorell's Bote,* where the crew, after the entertainment with the ' relygyous women ', from the Stews Bank, at Colman's Hatch,

> Blessyd theyr shyppe when they had done
> And dranke about a *Saint Julyan's torne.*

★ Pt. II, Act IV, Sc. 3.

St Martin's character as a saint was not unlike St Julian's ; hence we find him frequently on the signboard. The most favourite representation of him showed the saint on horseback, cutting off with his sword a piece of his cloak in order to clothe a naked beggar.

These two saints, it is believed, are no longer to be found on the signboard, though *St Martin's Raven* still exists in Pratt St., near to the old almshouses of the parish of St Martin's-in-the-Fields. Another powerful patron of travellers, St Christopher, may still occasionally be met with as in Bath, where in the 17th century he was still very common, and at Hengrave, Suff. Taylor the Water Poet mentions this as the sign of an inn at Eton, presumably the *Christopher Tap* which was the only licensed house the Eton boys were allowed to frequent. It occurs on various trades tokens of London shops, inns and taverns. The saint's intercession was thought efficacious against all danger from fire, flood and earthquake.

Travellers even carried his figure about with them either on their hats or on their breasts, as we gather from Chaucer's *Yeoman* :—

A Christofre on his breast of silver shene.

The practice has been revived in our own days by the general adoption of St Christopher as the patron saint of motorists, some of whom carry Christopher medalets attached to their cars.

St Luke still figures as the sign of two or three public-houses in London, for example in Old St. near St Jude's Church there is *St Luke's Head*. Since he was the patron of painters, it certainly was the least the sign-painters could do to honour his portrait with an occasional appearance on the signboard. But Luke possessed other attributes. Aubrey tells us : ' At Stoke Verdon, in the Parish of Broad Chalk, Wilts., was a chapell (in the chapel close by the farm-house) dedicated to St Luke, who is the Patron or Tutelar Saint of the Horne Beasts, and those that have to do with them ', etc. This arose evidently from the *Ox* being his emblem, as the *Lion* was of St Mark, the *Eagle* of St John and the *Angel* of St Matthew. For this reason St Luke was often chosen as the sign of inns frequented by farmers and graziers.

There is a *St Anne's* at St. Annes-on-Sea, a *St Anne's* at Buxton and a *St Bartholomew's* at Norwich. *St Etherington* (sic) is a house at Portsmouth, and there is a *St James* at New Cross, *St John of Jerusalem* in Clerkenwell, *St Olave* at Folkestone, *St Paul* in Chiswell St., and *St Petrock* at Bodmin.

Simon the Tanner of Joppa is an old established house in Long Lane, Bermondsey, and as a sign is supposed to be unique. It seems to have been adopted with reference to the tanners who frequented the house, or it may have been taken from the former occupation of the landlord. Simon is named in Acts x. 32 as the host of St Peter.

Of all the signs coming under this class, *St George & the Dragon* is undoubtedly the greatest favourite in England. In London alone there were in Larwood's time not less than sixty-six public-houses and taverns with this name, not counting the beer-houses, coffee-houses, etc. Sceptics doubt whether St George ever existed, and say he is only a popular corruption of St Michael conquering Satan, or Perseus' romantic delivery of Andromeda. Hence the little rhyme recorded by Aubrey:

To save a mayd St George the Dragon slew—
A pretty tale if all is told be true.
Most say there are no dragons, and 'tis sayd
There was no George; pray God there was a mayd.

It may be possible to distinguish in very old signs between St Michael and St George, since St George *should* use a lance and slay a dragon, while St Michael should use a sword and attack a basilisk, a dragon-like creature which unlike the ordinary dragon has a snake-like head at the end of its tail. Often the saint has been superseded by the King, one of the four who successively ornamented the English throne from 1714 to 1830. The *George* at Hampstead is known to have been established between 1750 and 1760, so the owners have had on their present sign the head of George III. By way of exception to the general rule there is a *George* at Hull, said to have been originally a merchants' hostelry under the local guild of St George, and reputed to have existed since 1449. It developed a dragon in the mid-19th century, and is now the *George & Dragon*. The original sign was a St George's Cross. As in the fine Tudor *George* at Winchcombe, Glos., and the famous *George* at Norton St Philip, Som., this sign seems to be much favoured by inns which have originated in the old monastic guest-houses.

St George is mentioned by Bede, who calls 23 April 'Natale S. Georgii Martyris'. He was, however, at that time a very recent importation. In the reign of Canute, there was already a house of regular canons dedicated to St George, at Thetford in Norfolk. The church of St George, Southwark, is also thought to have existed before the Conquest. After the Conquest chapels were frequently erected to the saint, and on the seals of this period he is often represented without the Dragon. Edward III had a particular veneration for him. Many of his statutes begin: *Ad honorem omnipotentis Dei Sanctæ Mariæ Virginis gloriosæ, et Sancti Georgii Martyris*. It was after the foundation of the Order of the Garter that the *George* became a favourite sign. The fact that St George was the patron of soldiers also assisted his popularity on the signboard.

There still exists an old and much dilapidated stone sign of *St George & the Dragon* in the front of a house on Snow Hill. There was an inn of this name, mentioned in 1554 as being situate on the north side of the *Tabard*. This inn was very much damaged by the great fire of Southwark in 1670, and completely burned down in 1676. It was rebuilt however and has come down to our time.

Machyn in his *Diary* mentions several *Georges*, one of them the *George* in Bread St., where there was a scandalous case of robbery during a fire in 1559. The *George* in Lombard St. was a very old house, once the town mansion of the Earl Ferrers, in which one of the Ferrers family was murdered as early as 1175. At this house died in 1524 Richard Earl of Kent, who had wasted his property in gaming and extravagance. It was then an inn, where the nobility used to put up. George Dowdall, Archbishop of Armagh, was buried from here in 1558. A *George Inn* at Derby occurs in connexion with a very interesting advertisement in the *Daily Advertiser* of 1758, for which the reader may be referred to Larwood. There is a fine *George & Dragon* at Codicote, Herts., recently carefully restored by Messrs. Trust Houses, who have published an admirable little pamphlet on the house.

As well as in association with the Dragon, St George is or was found in various other combinations, as the *George & Blue Boar*, High Holborn, an old inn which came to its end a century or so ago. In the 17th century this house was called the *Blue Boar*, and is said by the Earl of Orrery to have been the house in which Cromwell and Ireton disguised as troopers intercepted a letter of King Charles to his queen. Cromwell, the story goes on to say, finding by this letter that his party were not likely to obtain good terms from the king ' from that day forward resolved his ruin '. Unfortunately for lovers of the romantic there is no foundation for this dramatic incident.

The *George & Thirteen Cantons* once kept by the great Bob Travers is another odd combination, formerly occurring in Church St., Soho ; it is, however, easily explained when we learn that there is another public-house called the *Sun & Thirteen Cantons* in Great Pulteney St., also in Soho. The sign is of great interest and it is deplorable that the owners should have debased it into the ' *Scots Hoose* '. This sign was put up in reference to the thirteen Protestant cantons of Switzerland—a compliment to the numerous Swiss who inhabited the neighbourhood. The *George in a Tree* near Kenilworth was apparently once a *Royal Oak* until a mid-18th century landlord, without much historical knowledge, and desiring to move with the times, substituted George III for Charles II.

The strangest combination of all is that of the *George & Vulture*, familiar to all readers of Dickens. In Larwood's time there were three houses in London with this sign : one in St George-in-the-East, one in Wapping, and one in Pitfield St., Hoxton. The last named still survives, and there is another house of this sign, a chop-house, near Cornhill. As in the *Live Vulture* the only obvious explanation for part of this strange combination seems to be the possibility of a vulture having been exhibited at this house. Alternatively the sign is a combination of two quite separate ones, as in the *Salutation & Cat*, and the other instances on p. 165. Vultures were still considered great curiosities as late as the 18th century. In 1726 one of the attractions at Peckham Fair was a menagerie, and amongst the animals exhibited the *Vulture* was described in the following terms :—

> The noble Vulture Cock, brought from Archangall, having the finest talons of any bird that seeks her prey ; the forepart of his head is covered with hair ; the second part resembles the wool of a black ; below that is a white ring, having a ruff that he cloaks his head with at night.

According to Strype, the sign is of some standing. ' Near Ball Alley was the *George Inn*, since the Fire rebuilt with very good houses, well inhabited, and ware-

PLATE
15

PLATE
16

houses, being a large open yard, and called George Yard, at the farther end of which is the *George & Vulture* Tavern, which is a large house and of a great trade, having a passage into St Michael's Alley' (Cornhill). There was another tavern of this name on the east side of the high road, nearly opposite Bruce Green, Tottenham, in early times much frequented by the citizens of London taking their recreation. It is mentioned in the *Search after Claret* as early as 1691. Several coins of the reign of Queen Elizabeth and Charles I were discovered on pulling down the old house. A coat of arms of Queen Elizabeth was fixed over the front door, and at the demolition of the building it was put up at the back of a house in Hale Lane. After the fashion of the time the house was duly puffed up in newspaper poems. One of 1761–2 enumerates the attractions of a suburban tea-garden of the period and is perhaps worth quoting at full length :—

If lur'd to roam in Summer Hours,
Your Thoughts incline tow'rd Tott'nham Bow'rs,
Here end your airing Tour and rest
Where *Cole* invites each friendly Guest :
Intent on signs, the prying Eye,
The *George & Vulture* will descry ;
Here the kind Landlord glad attends
To wellcome all his cheerfull Friends
Who, leaving City smoke, delight
To range where various scenes invite.
The spacious garden, verdant field,
Pleasures beyond Expression yield,
The Angler here to sport inclined,
In his Canal may passtime find.
Neat racy Wine and Home-brew'd Ale
The nicest Palates may regale,
Nectarious Punch—and (cleanly grac'd)
A Larder stor'd for ev'ry Taste,
The cautious Fair may sip with Glee
The fresh'st Coffee, finest Tea.
Let none the outward *Vulture* fear,
No *Vulture* host inhabits here,
If too well us'd you deem ye—then
Take your Revenge and come again.

St Paul the patron saint of London was formerly a common sign in the metropolis, and still survives in Chiswell St. One of the trades tokens of a house or tavern in Petty France, Westminster, represents the saint before his conversion, lying on the ground with his horse standing by him. This house was called ' the *Saul* '. Larwood suggests that perhaps this originated in a monkish pleasantry of an earlier period (as Westminster was under the patronage of St Peter) representing an unpleasant event in the history of the great patron, and showing by comparison the vast superiority of the converted St Peter. The usual way, however, of commemorating the saint on the

N

signboard was the *St Paul's Head*. This was the sign of a very old inn in Great Carter Lane in Doctors' Commons in 1712. As an inn it is mentioned by Machyn in his *Diary* in 1562. Trades tokens of this house are extant in the Beaufoy Collection. In the 18th century, most of the celebrated libraries were sold at this inn : amongst others that of the bibliomaniac Rawlinson—the Tom Folio of the *Tatler*. To this tavern formerly the new sheriffs after having been sworn in used to resort to receive the keys of the different jails. That ceremony terminated, they were regaled with sack and walnuts by the keeper of Newgate. The *St Paul's* Coffee-house is built on the site of this old inn. About 1820 there was in Cateaton St. another *Paul's Head* where a literary club used to be held ' for the cultivation of forensic eloquence '. It was under the patronage of several distinguished characters, and had for a motto the modest words, ' Sic itur ad artra.' The vicinity of the cathedral evidently had suggested both these signs. On another sign in the same locality the two saints were united, viz. the *Saint Peter & Saint Paul*, St Paul's Churchyard. Of this house also trades tokens are extant. The sign *Paul's Head* still remains in Crispin St.

Although St Peter was it appears as common on the signboard before the Reformation as were the other great saints of religious history, yet no instances of his survival have come down to us. His keys, however—the famous *Cross Keys*—are very common. At Dawley, Salop, there was one, and another at Salisbury, Wilts. At Lychet Minster between Wareham and Bournemouth, there still is a very curious sign called *St Peter's Finger*. The sign is said to have originated here because a manor court was held in the inn on Lammas Day, the feast of St Peter ad Vincula. In all probability however this sign refers to the benediction of the Pope, the finger of His Holiness being raised whilst bestowing a blessing. St Peter being the first of the Papal line was doubtless often represented in old pictures and carvings with his finger raised in benediction. A passage by Bishop Hall [*] alludes to the finger :—

> But walk on cheerly 'till thou have espied
> *St Peter's finger*, at the churchyard side.

The famous tavern of the *Devil & St Dunstan* within Temple Bar took its name of course from the well-known legend. The identical pincers (with which this feat was performed) are still preserved (for the confutation of sceptics) at Mayfield Palace, Sussex. They are of a considerable size, and formidable enough to frighten the arch-fiend himself. This episode in the saint's life was represented on the signboard of the tavern. By way of abbreviation this house was called the *Devil*, though the landlord's token reads ' *The Devil and Dunstan* '. Child's Bank was built in 1788 on part of the site.

There are innumerable allusions to this tavern in the dramatists ; one of the earliest is in 1563, in the play of *Jack Jugeler*. William Rowley mentions it in his comedy of *A Match by Midnight*. So fond was Ben Jonson of this tavern that he lived ' without Temple Bar at a combmaker's shop ' according to Aubrey, in order to

[*] *Satires*, Bk. V, Set 2.

be near his favourite haunt. It must have been therefore in a moment of ill-humour when he found fault with the wine that he made the statement that his play of the *Devil is an Ass* was written ' when I and my boys drank bad wine at the *Devil* '. It sounds hardly likely that he should have established his favourite Apollo Club at a place where bad wine was sold. He himself composed for this club the famous *Leges Conviviales*, which are still preserved, with the respect due to so sacred a relic, by the Bank. They are twenty-four in number, some of them highly characteristic :—

4. And the more to exact our delight while we stay,
   Let none be debarr'd from his choice female mate.
5. Let no scent offensive the chamber infest.
10. Let our wines without mixture or scum be all fine,
    Or call up the master and break his dull noddle.
16. With mirth, wit, and dancing, and singing conclude,
    To regale every sense with delight in excess.
21. For generous lovers let a corner be found,
    Where they in soft sighs may their passions relieve.

Latin inscriptions were in various parts of the house. Over the clock in the kitchen might have been seen as late as 1731, ' *Si nocturna tibi noceat potatio, vini, hoc in mane bibis iterum, et erit medicina* '—an elegant rendering of the well-known phrase ' A hair of the dog that bit you.' Not only Ben Jonson but almost all the great poets of two centuries honoured this house with their presence. ' I dined today ', says Swift in the *Journal to Stella*, ' with Dr. Garth and Mr. Addison, at the *Devil Tavern*, near Temple Bar, and Garth treated.' Numerous similar quotations might be found show-ing the visits to this place of nearly all the great literary stars of the 17th and 18th cen-turies. Johnson frequently visited the house. He is said to have avoided it on occasions since he owed there a long score.

Simon Wadloe was one of the most famous landlords of this tavern. Pepys refers to him on 22 April 1661 as leading a fine company of soldiers all young comely men in white doublets (this was on Charles II's state progress from the Tower to Whitehall). Ben Jonson called Wadloe the king of skinkers, and there still exists a bust of him with this phrase engraved upon it. Among the verses on the door of the *Apollo* room occurred the lines :—

Hang up all the poor hop drinkers,
Cries old Sim, the king of skinkers.

In opposition to this *Old Devil* a *Young Devil* Tavern was opened also in Fleet St in 1707, and here the first meetings of the Society of Antiquaries were held, but the *Young Devil* was not a success and the house was soon closed. There was a third tavern named after the *Devil*, the *Little Devil*, Whitechapel. Ned Ward in 1703 highly commends the punch of this house, which he partook of in ' a room neat enough to entertain Venus and the graces '. It was a house entirely after Ned's fancy. ' My landlord was good company, my landlady good humoured, her daughter charmingly pretty, and her maid tolerably handsome, who can laugh, cry, say her prayers, sing a song, all in a breath, and can turn in a minute to all sublunary points of a female compass.'

The *Devil's House* was the name of a favourite Sunday resort in the 18th century in Hornsey Rd., Islington. It is said to have been the retreat of Claude Duval (? whence the sign Duval's house—Devil's house), who infested the lanes about Islington. However from a survey taken in 1611 it appears that the house bore already at that time the name of *Devil's House*. From its general appearance it seemed to date from Queen Elizabeth's reign. It was surrounded by a moat filled with water, and passed by a wooden bridge. Its attractions are held forth in a highly laudatory epistle disguised as a letter to the editor of the *Public Advertiser* in 1767. The landlord had had the gardens laid out afresh, had stocked the moat with tench and carp, and offered his patrons free fishing therein. He supplied tea, hot loaves and new milk as well as wines, and had refined the house's name from *Devil's House* to *Summer House*. The advertisement is designed to attract ' persons of both sexes of genteel taste to enjoy an innocent and delightful amusement '.

At Royston, Herts., there is a public-house known as the *Devil's Head*. There is no signboard, but a carved representation of the head formerly projected from the building, the name being underneath. The house is also associated with the highwayman, Claude Duval, and the sign is said (without much evidence for the theory) to be a corruption of *Duval's Head*. Probably the sign and the legend have both borrowed from the *Devil's House* at Islington, dealt with above.

St Patrick is almost exclusively an Irish sign. He is generally represented in the costume of a bishop, driving before him a flock of snakes, toads and other vermin, which he is said to have banished from Ireland. There is a house of this sign, however, at Standish, Glos.

In many instances no doubt before the Reformation the shopkeeper would choose his patron saint for his sign, to bring good fortune to his house. There are many instances of this among booksellers' signs.

Many saints have a local reputation and are perpetuated on the signboards in certain localities only, as for instance *St Thomas* at Canterbury, *St Edmund's Head*, at Bury St Edmunds, *St Cuthbert* at Monk's house, near Sunderland (this saint was the sixth Bishop of Northumberland), and at Scorton (Lancs. or Yorks.), Lindisfarne, and *St Wilfrid*, Ripon.

A 17th-century shopkeeper, William Ellis of Tooley St. had the sign of *St Clement*, perhaps on account of his being a native of the parish of St Clement's. Trades tokens of the house are extant. There is still a *St Clement's* (a licensed house) at Poole.

St Laurent was the sign of an inn in Lawrence Lane, Cheapside, but from a border of blossoms or flowers round the sign, the house was commonly called *Blossoms*, or by corruption, *Bosom's Inn*—such at least is the explanation of Stow. Flowers are said to have sprung up at the martyrdom of this saint, who was roasted alive on a gridiron. When in 1522 the Emperor Charles V honoured Henry VIII with a visit, bringing with him a retinue of 2,000 persons and 1,000 horses, to lodge the visitors various 'inns for horses' were 'seen and viewed'. Amongst these ' *St Laurance, otherwise called Bosoms Yn* ' is noted down to have ' XX beddes and a stable for IX horses '. In the 16th century the house seems already to have been famous as a carriers' inn (as it was for another three centuries). A satirical tract gives the names of its authors as ' John Dando the wiredrawer of Hadley, and Harrie Hunt, head ostler of *Besome's Inne* '. Another domestic of this establishment, Tom the Drawer of *Bosom's Inn*, presenting Misrule, is handed down to posterity in Ben Jonson's *Masque of Christmass*. The ancient connexion of this house with transport is preserved to this day in its modern use as a railway receiving office.

The *Catherine Wheel* found for example at Henley-on-Thames was formerly a very common sign, perhaps adopted from the badge of the order of the knights of St Catherine of Mount Sinai, created in 1063 for the protection of pilgrims on their way to and from the Holy Sepulchre. Hence it was perhaps a suggestive sign for an inn, as it intimated that the host was of the brotherhood although in a humble way, and would protect the travellers from robbery in his inn—in the shape of high charges and exactions. These knights wore a white habit embroidered with a Catherine Wheel (i.e. a wheel armed with spikes) and traversed with a sword stained with blood. There were also mysteries in which St Catherine played a favourite part, one of which was acted by young ladies on the entry of Queen Catherine of Aragon in London in 1501. Sometimes the sign has been put up in honour of this queen, or of the two or three other royal Catherines. The Catherine wheel was also a charge in the Turners' arms. Fleknoe says in his *Enigmatical Characters*, 1658, that the Puritans changed it into the *Cat & Wheel*, under which name it is still to be seen on a public-house at Bristol. In the 17th and 18th centuries, the *Catherine Wheel* was a famous carriers' inn in Southwark ; and in Larwood's time there was still an old house in Bishopsgate St. Without (now extinct) inscribed *Ye old Catherine Wheel*, 1594. The *Clock Wheel* near Eckington, Derbys., is no doubt another corruption of this sign. An old-fashioned Catherine wheel is not unlike that of a clock escapement.

Besides these there were other signs expressing a religious idea, or a Biblical phrase as the *Lion & Lamb*, which occurs on several 17th-century trades tokens of Snow Hill, Southwark, etc., and is still much in vogue. It is an emblematical representation of the Millennium, when the lion shall lie down by the kid. In the 18th century there was a *Lion & Lamb* on a signboard at Sheffield with the following verse :—

> If the Lyon show'd kill the Lamb,
> We'll kill the Lyon—if we can ;
> But if the Lamb show'd kill the Lyon,
> We'll kill the Lamb to make a Pye on.

There is still a *Lion & Lamb* at Ardleigh, Essex and there are two or three in the North country.

A variant (?) of this sign namely the *Wolf & Lamb* occurs occasionally, as formerly in Charles St., Leicester, and in a few other places. In Grosvenor St. it was probably once represented by a lion and a kid, but the public not minding the text called the sign the *Lion & Goat*, and that name it still bears. The *Lion & Adder* formerly at Nottingham and still at Newark and in various other places, and the *Lion & Snake* as at Lincoln, come from Psalm xci. 13. These two signs apparently came in use during the Commonwealth. They have a decided flavour of the time when Scripture language formed the common speech of everyday life. The *New Inn*, Gloucester, has in its courtyard a curious old wooden carving of a lion and snake. Presumably this has been a former sign either of the *New Inn* or of some other house.

The *Lamb & Flag* is another sign common all over England, representing originally the holy lamb with the nimbus and banner, but now so little understood by the publicans that on an alehouse at Swindon, Wilts., it is or was lately pictured with a spear, to which a red, white and blue streamer is appended. It may also be of heraldic origin, for it was the coat of arms of the Templars, and the crest of the Merchant Tailors. There is a well-known *Lamb & Flag* in St Ives, Oxford. The *Lamb & Anchor*, Milk St., Bristol, seems to be a mystical representation of hope in Christ. Both these last signs date from before the Reformation. From that period also dates the sign of the *Bleeding Heart*, the emblematical representation of the five sorrowful mysteries of the Rosary, viz., the heart of the Holy Virgin pierced with five swords. There was in Larwood's time an alehouse of this name, now no more, in Charles St., Hatton Garden. Bleeding Heart Yard adjoining the public-house is mentioned in *Little Dorrit*. The *Bleeding Heart* was, of course, the badge of the Douglases, who have some association with this part of London. The Heart was a constant emblem of Our Lady in the Middle Ages, thus on the clog almanacs all her feasts were indicated by a heart. This sign was lately changed to the *Kitchener's Arms*. The *Wounded Heart* one of the signs in Norwich in 1750 had the same meaning. The *Heart & Ball* appears on a trades token as the sign of a house in Little Britain, the Ball being simply some silk mercer's addition. The *Golden Heart* was a sign in Greenwich in 1737, next door to which Johnson used to live when he was newly come to town and wrote the Parliamentary articles for the *Gentleman's Magazine*. At present there are three public-houses with this sign in Bristol, and in other places it may be met with. There is an interesting example at Painswick, Glos. There was at Shrewsbury until 1820 a *Golden Heart & Trumpet*. The *Golden Heart* at Kingswood, Bristol, and a former house of this name in Shrewsbury had this sign corrupted into the *Golden Hart*.

Heaven was a house of entertainment near Westminster Hall: the committee rooms of the House of Commons were erected on its site. Butler alludes to this house in *Hudibras*:—

> False Heaven at the end of the Hall,

and Pepys records his dining at this house in the winter of 1660. *Paradise* was a messuage in the same neighbourhood, and *Hell & Purgatory* subterranean passages. In the reign of James I *Hell* was the sign of a low public-house frequented by lawyers' clerks.   There is still a *Paradise* at Liverpool.   *Heaven & Hell* are mentioned, together with a third house called *Purgatory*, in an old grant dated 1485.

The *Three Kings* is a sign representing the three Magi.   We find it used as early as the 16th century by Julyan Notary, in St Paul's Churchyard, one of the earliest London printers.   The *Three Kings* was formerly a constant mercer's sign.   Bagford gives as reason for this that the mercers dealt *inter alia* in linen girdles imported from Cologne, which city still has three crowns as its arms.   The Magi were called the three kings of Cologne because they were said to be buried in that city.   The Empress Helena brought their bones to Constantinople from whence they were removed to Milan, and thence in 1164 to Cologne, where they are still kept as sacred and miracle-working relics.   There was formerly a *Three Kings* sign carved in stone in front of a house in Bucklersbury, which street was once the headquarters of the mercers and perfumers.   The sign is now in the Guildhall Museum.   The three kings are in a row, all in the same garb and position, with their sceptres shouldered.   The history of the *Three Kings* was a favourite story in the Middle Ages.   They appeared in many of the ancient plays and mysteries.   In one of the Chester pageants, acted by the shearmen and tailors ; they are called St Kaspar of Tars ; Sir Melchior, king of Araby ; Sir Balthazar, king of Saba.   Melchior is usually represented as a bearded old man, Kaspar as a beardless youth, and Balthazar as a Moor with a large beard.   The trio may still be seen in effigy at Epiphany time round the Crib in any Roman Catholic or High Anglican church.   They survive as a sign in Clerkenwell Close, and they have been placed on a plaque on many houses of Messrs. Greene, King and Sons, brewers of Bury St Edmunds—they are the armorial bearings of the city of Bury, and the firm's trade mark.

Probably the sign of the *Kings & Keys* still remaining in Fleet St. is an abbreviation of the *Three Kings & Cross Keys.*   At Weston-super-Mare and at Chelmsford there is another sign which owes its origin to a somewhat mistaken analogy with the *Three Kings*, namely, the *Three Queens*.   When in 1764 the Paving Act for St James's was put into execution, the sign of the *Three Queens* in Clerkenwell Green was removed at a cost of upwards of £200 ; it extended not less than seven feet from the front of the house.

Though the legend of the *Man in the Moon* cannot strictly be styled a religious legend it may be included in this class, as the idea is said to have originated from the incident given in Numbers xv. 32–6.   Not content with having him stoned for his desecration of the day the legend transferred him to the moon.   It is however a pre-Christian tale, for the Jews had some Talmudical story about Jacob being in the Moon.   Almost every nation, whether ancient or modern, sees someone in the moon.   The *Man in the Moon* occurs on a 17th-century token of a tavern in Cheapside, represented by a half-naked man within a crescent, holding on by the horns.   There were formerly signs of this description in Little Vine St., Regent St. and in various other places, and there is still one in Chelsea.   On the site of the Vine St. House stands Vine St. Police Station.   Generally he is represented with a bundle of sticks, a lantern (which, one would think, he did not want in the moon) and frequently a dog. Thus Chaucer depicts him in *Cresseide*.★ Shakespeare also alludes to him in the *Tempest* † and the *Midsummer Night's Dream*.‡

It was a well-established fact with the old tobacconists that he could enjoy his pipe. Thus he is represented on some of the tobacconists' papers in the Banks Collection puffing like a steam-engine, and underneath the words, ' Who'll smoake with ye Man in ye moon ? '

★ Bk. V, l. 260.　　　　† Act II, Sc. 2.　　　　‡ Act III, Sc. 1.

Chapter XII

DIGNITIES, TRADES AND PROFESSIONS

TOOLS and utensils as emblems of trade were certainly placed outside the houses at an early period to inform the public as to the particular trade or occupation carried on within. Centuries ago the practice as a general rule fell into disuse, although a few trades still adhere to it with laudable perseverance. Thus a *broom* still informs us where to find a sweep ; an optician's shop still often has a huge pair of spectacles as its sign, the barber's pole may or may not represent a bandaged arm of the days of the barber surgeons.* In Larwood's time it was still usual to see a *gilt arm* wielding a hammer telling where the gold-beater lived, and a *last* or *gilt shoe* where to order a pair of boots. Those houses of refreshment and general resort which sought the custom of particular trades and professions also very frequently adopted the tools and emblems of those trades as their distinguishing signs. At other houses again signs were set up as tributes of respect to certain dignities and functions. Amongst these the *King's Head* and *Queen's Head* stand foremost, and no kings or queens were more favoured than Henry VIII and Queen Elizabeth, even for more than three centuries after their decease. Nearly a century and a half ago, there still remained a well-painted half-length portrait of King Henry VIII as a sign of the *King's Head* before a public-house in Southwark. His personal appearance doubtless was at the bottom of this popular favour. His plump and rubicund face with but little of the flattery required by painters in executing royal portraits made a merry, beery-looking Bacchus, eminently adapted for a public-house sign.

A very respectable folio might be filled with anecdotes connected with the various *King's Head* inns and taverns up and down the country and in London. Thus for instance it is said that when the Princess Elizabeth came forth from her confinement in the Tower in 1554, she went into the church of All Hallows, Staining, the first she found open, to return thanks for her deliverance from prison. As soon as this pious duty was performed the princess and her attendants went to the *King's Head* in Fenchurch St., now succeeded by the *London Tavern*, to take some refreshment, and there she dined on pork and peas. A monument of this visit is still preserved in the house in an engraving of the princess, from a picture by Holbein hung up in the coffee-room. The dish and cover from which she ate her dinner still remain and are shown there. There is a tradition that the bells of All Hallows were rung on this occasion with such energy that the queen presented the ringers with silken ropes. Actually it appears the legend rests on a shaky translation, for the princess took barge at the Tower and went direct to Richmond.

A more painful association is connected with another *King's Head*, which is or was

* See p. 207.

at Collins End, between Hardwicke House and Goring Heath. The inn has for its sign a well-executed portrait of Charles I. There is a tradition that the king while residing as a prisoner at Caversham rode one day, attended by an escort, into this part of the country. Hearing that there was at this inn a bowling-green frequented by the neighbouring gentry he struck down to the house, and endeavoured to forget his sorrows for a time in a game of bowls. This circumstance was recorded in these lines written beneath the signboard :—

> Stop, traveller, stop in yonder peaceful glade,
> His favourite game the royal martyr play'd.
> Here, stripp'd of honours, children, freedom, rank,
> Drank from the bowl, and bowl'd for what he drank ;
> Sought in a cheerful glass his cares to drown,
> And changed his guinea ere he lost his crown.

The sign seemed to be a copy from Van Dyck though much faded from exposure to the weather, and displayed an amount of artistic skill not usually met with on the signboard, but the only information the people of the house could give was that they believed it to have been painted in London. His son, Charles II, is also connected with an anecdote with a *King's Head* in the Poultry, for it is reported that he halted at this inn on the day of his entry at the Restoration, at the request of the landlady, who happened just then to be in labour and wished to salute his majesty. Mrs. King the lady so honoured was aunt to William Bowyer, the learned printer of the 18th century. In Ben Jonson's time there was a famous *King's Head* in New Fish St. ' where roysters did range '. It is this tavern probably that is alluded to in the ballad of *The Ranting Whore's Resolution* : in the *Roxburghe Ballads* :—

> I love a young Heir
> Whose fortune is fair,
> And frollick in *Fish Street dinners*,
> Who boldly does call,
> And in private paies all
> These boyes are the noble beginners.

At the *King's Head* by the corner of Chancery Lane Abraham Cowley was born in 1618 ; it was then a grocer's shop kept by his father. Subsequently it became a famous tavern of which tokens are extant. It was at this house that Titus Oates's party met, and trumped up their infamous stories against the Roman Catholics, trying to implicate James Duke of York in the murder of Sir Edmundbury Godfrey. In the reign of William III it was a violent Whig club. The distinction adopted by the members was a green ribbon worn in the hat. When these ribbons were shown, it was a sign that mischief was on foot, and that there were secret meetings to be held. North gives an amusing and lively description of this club :—

> The house was double balconied in front, as may be yet seen, for the clubsters to issue forth, *in fresco*, with hats and no perruques, pipes in their mouths, merry faces and diluted throat for vocal encouragement of the canaglia below, at bonfires, on unusual and usual occasions.

Here Pope-burning manifestations were organized, the Earl of Shaftesbury being president. In opposition to this Green Ribbon Club the Tories wore in their hats a scarlet ribbon with the words *Rex et Haeredes*. Ned Ward, with his usual humour, describes a breakfast consisting of a 415-lb. ox, roasted whole, given in 1706 by the master of this house to his customers. At the same time he takes the opportunity of praising the landlord as ' the honestest vintner in London, at whose house the best wine in England is to be drunk '. This was probably Ned's way of settling an old score. Another *King's Head* is mentioned by Pepys, 26 March 1664, in a reminiscence of his childhood when his father used to take him to the house for cakes and ale.

At the *King's Head*, Stutton, near Ipswich, which still exists, there was about eighty years ago the following inscription :—

> Good people, stop, and pray walk in,
> Here's foreign brandy, rum, and gin,
> And what is more, good purl and ale,
> Are both sold here by old Nat Dale.

Old Nat had lived for a period of eighty years under the shadow of the *King's Head*. The *King's Head* at Chichester has a charming sign with a portrait of Henry VIII on one side and one of the King of Hearts on the other. The *King's Head* at Sandwich has a grotesque 16th-century carving certainly not of a king's head, but probably the figurehead of some vessel.

Combinations with the *King's Head* are not very frequent. The *King's Head & Lamb* remaining in Upper Thames St. is evidently a quartering of two signs. The *Two Kings & Still*, sign of Henry Francis in Newmarket 1667, represented a still between two kings crowned holding their sceptres. It may have originated from the distillers' arms, the two wild men serving as supporters being refined into two kings, the garlands on their heads into crowns, and their clubs into sceptres.

Queen Elizabeth was for more than two centuries the almost unvarying type of the *Queen's Head*. This need not be wondered at when we consider her well-deserved popularity. A striking instance of the veneration and esteem in which she was held even through all the tribulations and changes of the Commonwealth is exhibited in the fact of the bells ringing on her birthday as late as the reign of Charles II. During the queen's lifetime, however, the sign-painters had to mind how they represented her, for Sir Walter Raleigh says in the Preface to his *History of the World*, 1614, that portraits of the queen ' made by unskilful and common painters ' were by her own order ' knocked in pieces and cast into the fire '. A proclamation to that effect had been issued in the year 1563. It appears worth printing in full :—

> Forasmuch as through the natural desire that all sorts of subjects and people, both noble and mean, have to procure the portrait and picture of the Queen's Magestie, great Nomber of Paynters, and some Printers and Gravers have already, and doe daily, attempt to make in divers manners portraictures of hir Majestie, in paynting, graving, and pryntyng, wherein is evidently shewn, that hytherto none hath sufficiently expressed the natural representation of hir Majesties person, favor, or grace, but for the most part

have also erred therein, as thereof daily complaints are made amongst hir Majesties loving subjects, in so much, that for redress hereof hir Majestie hath lately bene so instantly and so importunately sued by the Lords of hir Consell, and others of hir nobility, in respect of the great disorder herein used, not only to be content that some special coning paynter might be permitted by access to hir Majestie to take the naturall representation of hir Majestie, whereof she hath been allwise of hir own right disposition very unwillyng, but also to prohibit all manner of other persons to draw, paynt, grave, or pourtrayit hir Majesties personage or visage for a time, until by some perfect patron and example the same may be by others followed.

Therfor hir Majestie, being herein as it were overcome with the contynuall requests of so many of hir Nobility and Lords, whom she can not well deny, is pleased that for thir contentations, some coning persons, mete therefore, shall shortly make a pourtraict of hir person, or visage, to be participated to others, for satisfaction of hir loving subjects ; and furthermore commandeth all manner of persons in the mean tyme to forbear from payntyng, graving, printing, or making of any pourtraict of hir Majestie, until some speciall person that shall be by hir allowed, shall have first fynished a pourtraicture thereof, after which finished, hir Majestie will be content that all other painters, printers, or gravers that shall be known men of understanding, and so thereto licensed by the hed officers of the plaices where they shall dwell (as reason it is that every person should not without consideration attempt the same) shall and maye at their pleasures follow the sayd patron or first portraicture. And for that hir Majestie perceiveth that a grate nomber of hir loving subjects are much greved and take grete offence with the errors and deformities allready committed by sondry persons in this behalf, she straightly chargeth all her officers and ministers to see to the observation hereof, and as soon as may be, to reform the errors allredy committed, and in the mean tyme to forbydd and prohibit the shewing and publication of such as are apparently deformed, until they may be reformed which are reformable.

That there were signboards, however, representing her Majesty's ' person, favour, and grace ', during her lifetime, is evident from the fact that an ancestor of Pennant, the London topographer, made his fortune as a goldsmith at the sign of the *Queen's Head* in Smithfield during the reign of the great queen. In 1584 George Gower was appointed her sergeant-painter, and Nicholas Hilliard, the first English miniaturist, her miniature portrait painter. Similarly in the next reign, Hilliard was granted the sole right to paint miniatures of James I.

Of celebrated *Queen's Heads* we must begin with the highly respectable inn of that name, in which, before the reign of Queen Elizabeth, lived the canonists and professors of ecclesiastical law. It was situated in Paternoster Row, where its name is still preserved in Queen's Head Alley. From this place the lawyers removed to Doctors' Commons.

Nearly as ancient a building was the old *Queen's Head*, at the corner of Queen's Head Lane, Islington, a time-honoured building said to have been built by Sir Walter Raleigh, after he had obtained a ' lycense for keeping of taverns and retayling of wynes throughout Englande '. It was called by him the *Queen's Head* in compliment to his royal mistress. Essex and Burghley are also said to have resided there, and to have been visited by the queen. In the reign of George II it was used as a playhouse, and bills are still extant of plays acted there at that period. The ancient structure was pulled down in October 1829. There is a print of it in the *Gentleman's Magazine* for June 1794. There used to be a large pewter tankard in this house, with an inscription engraved on it, which is much too highly spiced to be given here. It was signed John Cranch, and bore the date of 1796.

In 1745 the landlady of the *Queen's Head*, Kingston, according to the *London Evening Post*

> was ordered by the Court to be ducked for scolding, and was accordingly placed in the chair and ducked in the river Thames, under Kingston Bridge, in the presence of 2000 or 3000 people.

In the beginning of the 19th century, when Marylebone consisted of green fields, babbling brooks, and pleasant suburban retreats there was a small but picturesque house of public entertainment, named the *Queen's Head & Artichoke* situated in Albany St. Its attractions chiefly consisted in a long skittle and ' bumble puppy' ground, shadowy bowers, and abundance of cream, tea, cakes, and other comforts. The only memorial now remaining of the original house is an engraving in the *Gentleman's Magazine* of November 1819, and the sign which still survives. The old sign was in 1772 a weather-beaten portrait of Queen Elizabeth. It is alleged that the second part of it was added by special request of Queen Elizabeth, who had enjoyed her dinner in the inn on a visit to Lord Burghley at Hatfield. The queen was Queen Elizabeth, and another story is that the house was reported to have been built by one of her gardeners, whence the strange combination on the sign.

Besides crowns * other emblems of royalty are occasionally used as signboard decorations. The sceptre is not uncommon ; the *Sceptre & Heart* was the sign of Samuel Grover, chirurgical instrument maker, on London Bridge, in the latter end of the 17th century. In all probability it is simply a quartering of two signs.

The *Royal Hand & Glove* was the loyal sign of a stationer at the corner of St Martin's Lane, in 1682. It doubtless refers to the royal hand holding the golden orb, surmounted by a cross. It is still the sign of an alehouse in Soho. The *Sword in Hand* may belong to this same class of signs, and represent the Sword of Justice or the Sword of State. The same orb or globe seems to be alluded to in the sign of the *Sword & Ball*, on Holborn Bridge, in the 17th century. What stands in the way of this explanation is that on the token of this house the sword is represented piercing the ball—but this may merely have been a fancy of the sign-painter, who did not understand its meaning. As for the *Sword & Mace*, the meaning is perfectly clear ; it was the sign of a house in Coventry.

The Church is almost as abundantly represented as royalty. Even long after the Reformation, the *Pope's Head* was still very common. Taylor the Water Poet in his *Travels through London*, 1636, mentions four *Pope's Heads*, but the most famous of all was a house of this name in Cornhill. According to Lydgate, *temp.* Henry VI :

> At that time the wine drawers at the Pope's Head tavern (standing without the door in the High Street), took the same man by the sleeve, and said ' Sir, will you drink a

* See p. 64.

pint of wine ? ' Whereunto, he answered, ' a penny spend I may,' and so drank his pint, for bread nothing did he pay, for that was allowed free.★ The Pope's Head tavern, with other houses adjoining, strongly built of stone, hath of old time been all in one, pertaining to some great estate, or rather to the king, as may be supposed both by the largeness thereof, and by the arms, to wit, three leopards passant gardant, which were the whole arms of England before the reign of Edward III, that quartered them with the arms of France three Fleur de lys.

This touting, or standing at the door inviting the passers-by to enter, was at one time a universal practice with all kind of shops, both at home and abroad. The regular phrase used to be ' What do ye lack ? ' This touting at tavern doors was still practised in the 18th century, as appears from Tom Brown :—' the sooty dog could do nothing but grin, and show his teeth and cry, *Coffee sir, tea, will you please walk in, sir ; a fresh pot, upon my word.*' Not only taverns but all sorts of shops kept these barking advertisements at the door. The ballad of *London Lyckpenny* enumerates a quantity of them. In Larwood's time there was ' Buy, buy, what'll you buy ? ' of the London butchers and the practice of touting at the doors of the small coffee-houses at Greenwich. Throughout the United States and Canada the custom of waiting at steamboat wharves and railway termini, to catch passengers, and worry them with recommendations to this or that hotel were among the last remains of the custom. It still survived in pre-war days in the touts of the tailoring shops in the Strand, and the barkers and runners of the restaurants in such popular seaside resorts as Blackpool, Cleethorpes and Skegness.

The *Pope's Head* tavern had a footway through from Cornhill into Lombard St. In this tavern, in 1464, a trial of skill was held between Oliver Davy, goldsmith of London, and White Johnson, ' Alicante Strangeour ', also of London. The trial consisted in making, in four pieces of steel the size of a penny, a cat's face in relief, and another cat's face engraved, a naked man in relief, and another engraved, which work was to be performed in five weeks. Oliver Davy, the native goldsmith, won the wager, as White Johnson, the foreign workman, after six weeks could only produce the two ' inward engraved' objects. The forfeit was a crown, and a dinner to the wardens, the umpires, and all those concerned in the wager. The works were kept in Goldsmith's Hall, ' to y^{at} intent that they be redy if any suche controursy hereafter falls to be shewede that suche traverse hathe be determyn'd aforetymes'. In Pepys's time this tavern like many others of that period and later had a painted room, as appears from a *Diary* entry of 18 January 1668. Here in 1718, James Quin, Garrick's rival, killed his brother actor Bowen. The jury brought in a verdict of manslaughter, and Quin for the offence was burned in the hand. The quarrel was a foolish one, arising out of a wager which of the two was the more honest man. This tavern seems to have continued in existence till the latter part of the 18th century.

The emblem of another class of dignitaries of the Roman Church, the *Cardinal's Hat or Cap*, was at one time common in England. Bagford says : ' you have not meney of them, they war set up by sume that had ben saruants to Tho. Wolsey'.

★ The imperfect tense shows that the excellent custom referred to had already fallen into disuse in Stow's time.

But we find the sign long before Wolsey's time, for in 1459 Simon Eyre gave to the Brotherhood of Our Lady in the church of St Mary Wolnoth ' the Tavern called the *Cardinal's Hat* in Lumbard Street ', and there was another trade sign of the *Cardinal's Cap* also in Lombard St. There is still a house of this name at Norwich. The two Lombard St. houses were still extant in the 17th century. The sign was also that of one of the Stairs on the Bankside, the name of which is still preserved to that locality in Cardinal's Cap Alley. (A brothel ?) of this sign is referred to by Skelton. The whole Bankside district was full of these houses. By proclamation of 1545 they were ' whited and painted with signes on the front for a token of the said houses ', and were under the jurisdiction of the Bishop of Winchester. An unkind critic in later years suggested that it was most convenient that the official residences of the Bishops of Rochester and Winchester, the Abbots of St Augustines, Canterbury, Battle and Hyde, and that of the Prior of Lewes, should be in the same neighbourhood.

The *Bishop's Head* was, in 1663, the sign of J. Thompson, a bookseller and publisher in St Paul's Churchyard. This seems rarely to occur as an inn sign.

A very general one however was the *Mitre*, which was the sign of several famous taverns in London in the 17th century. There was one in Great Wood St., Cheapside (called on the trades token of the house the *Mitre and Rose*), mentioned by Pepys in 1660 as ' a house of the greatest note in London '. Proctor, the landlord of this house, died at Islington of the plague in 1665 in an insolvent state, though he had been ' the greatest vintner for some time in London for great entertainments '. There was another *Mitre* near the west end of St Paul's, the first music-house in London, kept by Robert Herbert *alias* Forges. He was also a collector of natural curiosities and issued a catalogue of his ' rareties ' in 1664. A great part of this collection was bought by Sir Hans Sloane. It is conjectured that the *Mitre* was situated in London House Yard at the north-west end of St Paul's, on the spot where afterwards stood the house known by the sign of the *Goose & Gridiron*. Ned Ward describes the appearance of another music-house of the same name in Wapping, which he calls ' the Paradise of Wapping '. More probably it was in Shadwell where there is still a Music House Court, which seems to point to some such origin. The music consisting of fiddles, hautboys, and a humdrum organ he compares to the grunting of a hog added as a base to a concert of caterwauling cats in the height of their ecstasy. The music-room was richly decorated with paintings, carvings, and gilding ; the seats were like pews in church, and the orchestra railed in like a chancel. The musicians occasionally went round to collect contributions. The other rooms in the house were ' furnished for the entertainment for the best of companies ', all painted with humorous subjects. The kitchen used at that period by the customers in many taverns as a sitting-room was railed in and ornamented in the same gaudy style as the rest of the houses,—a number of canaries were suspended on the walls. Underground was a tippling sanctuary painted with drunken women tormenting the devil and other quaint subjects. The wine of the establishment was good. Houses of this kind were in a very real sense the ancestors of the modern music-hall.

Older than either of these was the *Mitre* in Cheap, which is mentioned in the vestry books of St Michael's Cheapside, before the year 1475. In a comedy *Your Five Gallants* by Thomas Middleton, about 1608, Goldstone prefers it to the *Mermaid*. But the most famous of the inns with this name, was the *Mitre* in Mitre Court, Fleet St., one of Johnson's favourite haunts 'where he loved to sit up late', and where Goldsmith and other celebrities and minor stars that moved about the great doctor used to meet him. This house is named in the play *Ram Alley, or Merry Tricks*, in 1611. It was one of those houses which, for more than two centuries, was the constant resort of all the wits about town. Even the name of Shakespeare throws (though somewhat dimly) its halo around the place. A manuscript song of five seven-line stanzas thus headed : *Shakespeare's Rime which he made at the Mytre in Fleete Street*, begins :—' From the rich Lavinian shore' and some few of the lines were published by Playford, and set as a catch. Another shorter piece is called in the margin : *Shakespeare's Rime* :—

> Give me a cup of rich Canary Wine,
> Which was the mitre's (drink) and now is mine ;
> Of which had Horace and Anacreon tasted
> Their lives as well as lines till now had lasted.

If the verses are genuine (which seems very doubtful—John Payne Collier said they were, but he was a somewhat biased witness in matters of literary forgery) they are however certainly not among Shakespeare's happiest efforts. In this same tavern Boswell supped for the first time with his idol, and the description of the biographer's delight on that grand occasion has a festive air about it.

There also took place the amusing scene with the young ladies from Staffordshire who wished to consult him on the subject of Methodism, ' which they did, and after dinner, he took one of them on his knees and fondled them for half an hour together '.

Hogarth, too, was an occasional visitor at this tavern. A card is still extant, wherein he requested the company of a friend to dine with him at the *Mitre*. The written part is contained within a circle (representing a plate) to which a knife and fork are the supporters. In the centre is drawn a pie with a mitre on the top of it, and the invitation :—

> Mr Hogarth's compliments to Mr King, and desires the honour of his company to dinner, on Thursday next η β π.

In this tavern the Society of Antiquaries used to meet before apartments were obtained in Somerset House.

In the bar of the *Mitre* in St James's Market, which was kept by her aunt (Mrs. Voss, formerly the mistress of Sir Godfrey Kneller), Farquhar overheard Miss Nancy Oldfield read *The Scornful Lady*, and was so struck with the proper emphasis and agreeable turn she gave to each character that he swore the girl was cut out for the stage. John Vanbrugh, a friend of the family, recommended her to Rich, and shortly she made her *début* at Covent Garden, with an allowance of fifteen shillings a week.

Though a dozen other famous *Mitre* taverns might be mentioned, especially the

Mitre in Ely Place, Hatton Garden, these are sufficient to show how general the sign was ; the partiality of tavern-keepers for it is perhaps accounted for in the following stanza of the *Quack Vintners*, 1712 :—

> May Smith, whose prosperous Mitre is his sign,
> *To shew the church no enemy to wine.*
> Still draw such Christian liquor none may think,
> Tho' e'er so pious, 'tis a sin to drink.

The *Mitre* also is found in a few combinations, as the *Mitre & Dove*, that is the Holy Ghost, now extinct, formerly in King St., Westminster ; the *Mitre & Keys*, in Leicester —evidently the *Cross Keys*, which are a charge in the arms of several bishoprics ; and the *Mitre & Rose*, which from trades tokens appears to have been the sign of a tavern in the Strand, as well as one in Wood St., Cheapside.

That the friars were also honoured on the signboard appears from a reference in 1708 to Fryar Lane, on the south side of Thames St. near Dowgate. 'It was formerly called Greenwich Lane, but of later years Fryar's Lane, from the sign of a Fryar sometime there.' There is still a *Black Friar* in Queen Victoria St. Probably this also was a Black Dominican Friar, for that order, above all others, had the reputation of being great topers, and therefore were not out of place on the signboard. Tokens are extant of a music-house, with the sign of the *Black-friar*, dated 1671.

Nuns also figured on the signboard as the *Three Nuns*, which was constantly used by drapers. Tom Brown says the sign was very dismally painted to keep up young women's antipathy to popery and single blessedness. Actually perhaps the sign was chosen because the sisterhoods were and are to this day generally very expert in making lace embroidery and other fancy work. In the 17th century, the *Three Nuns* was the sign of a well-known coaching and carriers' inn in Aldgate, which gave its name to Three Nuns Court close at hand. A modern tavern with the same sign still stands on the spot. Here the sign is said to relate to the neighbouring convent of Poor Clares or Minoresses who give their name to the Minories, not far away. Not improbably this sign after the Reformation was occasionally metamorphosed into the *Three Widows*. Peter Treveris, a foreigner, erected a press and continued printing until 1552 at the *Three Widows* in Southwark. The *Matrons*, also, may have originally represented Nuns ; this last hung, in the 17th century, at the door of John Bannister crutch and bandage maker near the hospital (the old Christ's Hospital) Newgate St.

At the present day the *Church* is a very common alehouse sign from the proximity of a church to the alehouse in question ; thus one inn in the town would be known as the *Market House*, whilst another might be known as the *Church* Inn. There is generally an alehouse close to every church (in Knightsbridge the chapel of the Holy Trinity was jammed in between two public-houses), whereby a good opportunity is offered to wash a dry sermon down. This church, now no more, was facetiously known as the *Heaven between Two Hells*. The entrance to the churchyard at Sonning, Berks., is to this day also the entrance to the famous local inn, the *Bull*. The *Fox &*

Goose at Fressingfield, Suff., is actually in the churchyard. It belongs to the incumbent and churchwardens, and is said to have been built in the 16th century to obviate the necessity of holding church ales in the church itself. In Bristol at the beginning of the last century, a Methodist meeting-room was immediately over a public-house, which gave rise to the following epigram :—

> There is a spirit above and a spirit below,
> A spirit of joy and a spirit of woe—
> The spirit above is the spirit divine ;
> But the spirit below is the spirit of wine.

Other signs connected with the Church are the *Chapel Bell* at Suton, in Norfolk, and the *Church Stile* at Knaresdale, Northumb., *Kirk Stile* at Loweswater, Cumb., or *Church Gates*, which are very common. The origin of this last comes from an old custom of drinking ale on the parish account on certain occasions at the church stile. Pepys mentions this when he was at Walthamstow, 14 April 1661. The custom may have been adopted as less unseemly than that of holding a Church Ale proper. At Warrington, Lancs., the vestry book records how the practice was observed on 5 November 1688, and how it was discontinued in 1732. There are said to be thirty-five occurrences of this sign in Lancashire alone. Often here and in Cumberland and Westmorland they are at the ends of the fell corpse-paths, by which the bearers carried bodies by bier to the lych gates of the parish churches.

Belonging to the Church was also the sign of the *Three Brushes*, or *Holy Water Sprinklers*, which was that of an old house near the *White Lion* prison, Southwark, in which there was a room with panelled wainscoting and ceiling ornamented with the royal arms of Queen Elizabeth. Probably it had been the court-room at the time the *White Lion* Inn was a prison. The house was certainly there before 1667.

Innumerable signs were borrowed from the army and navy ; thus by Larwood's time, every uniform in the service was represented near barracks or in other haunts of soldiers. The *Recruiting Sergeant* was generally the sign of the public-house where that worthy spread his nets, for example at Lincoln. The *Crossed Rifles* as at Bridgwater was used to attract riflemen, though sometimes the *Crossed Swords*, and usually the *Crossed Daggers* may be from the arms of the Hallamshire Cutlers Company. *Cross Guns* (Bristol), *Cross Lances*, *Cross Swords* (Grantham) and *Cross Pistols* are meant to allure respectively artillerymen, lancers, and various cavalry men. There is an *Old Recruiting Sergeant* in Garrett Lane, S.W., with a good painted sign. Above all the *Standard*, as at Ash Vale, Surrey, the *Banner*, or the *Waving Flag* was of common occurrence, not only in the neighbourhood of military quarters, but everywhere in towns and villages. At the *Standard* Tavern in the Strand, Edmund Curll the bookseller used to meet the mysterious Rev. Mr. Smith, who sold him Pope's correspondence. There is a *British Flag*, at Clapham, a *British Standard* at Liverpool, a *Flag* at Manningtree, Essex, a *Flagstaff* at Canning Town, a *Royal Standard* at Windsor, a *Standard of England* at Bristol, a *Standard of Freedom* at Northam and Southampton, a *Union Jack* at Roydon and one at Stretton-

under-Fosse, Warws., and a *Red, White, & Blue* at Ely.   The *Kettledrum* was the sign
of a house now extinct in St George St.   The *Drum*, formerly at Norwich and still at
Brentwood, and the *Trumpet* (York) are both of frequent occurrence, and the last is of
old standing.   One of the characters in Shirley's *The Ball*, 1633, commends the beer
of the *Trumpet*.   Possibly this was the *Trumpet* in Shire Lane, often referred to in the
Tatler, and one of the favourite haunts of Steele.   Bishop Hoadly was once present
at one of the meetings in this tavern, when Steele rather exposed himself in his efforts
to please.   He had a double duty devolving upon him, as well as to celebrate the
glorious memory of King William III, it being 4 November—as to drink up to conversation pitch his friend Addison, whose phlegmatic constitution was hardly warmed for
society by the time Steele was no longer fit for it.   One of the company, a red-hot
Whig, knelt down to drink the health with all honours.   This rather disconcerted the
bishop which, Steele seeing, whispered to him—' Do laugh, my lord, pray laugh ; it is
humanity to laugh.'   Shortly afterwards Steele was put into a chair and sent home.
Next morning he was much ashamed, and sent the Bishop this distich :—

> Virtue with so much ease on Bangor sits,
> All faults he pardons though he none commits.

There is an *Artilleryman* at Chelmsford, an *Artillery* at Great Warley, Essex, a *Dragoon*
at Bromsgrove, Worcs., a *Light Dragoon* at Cambridge, an *Engineers* in Gloucester Rd.
A *Grenadier* at Whitley, Hants, commemorates a local worthy who ' died of drinking
small beer '.   A *Life Guards* is to be seen at Rettendon, Essex, a *Royal Horseguardsman*
at Brentford, a *Jolly Guardsman* at Windsor, a *Light Horse* at Hounslow, a *Light Horseman* at Norwich, and a *Huzzar* at Hounslow.   The *Lancers* is at Yarmouth, the *Royal
Lancers* at Doncaster, the *Rifleman* at Ely, the *Thirteenth Rifleman* at Stalybridge, the
Rifle Volunteer at Reigate, the *Royal Rifleman* at Battersea, the *Rifle Volunteers* at Yarmouth, and the *Marksman* at Hackney, N.E. (?)   The *Valiant Trooper* was formerly at
Aldbury, Herts., the *Volunteer* is at Saxtead, Suff., the *Volunteers* at Weybridge, the
British Volunteer at Ponders End, the *Mounted Volunteer* at Norwich.   Finally (very
appropriately), the *Chelsea Pensioner* is in Chelsea.

The *Buckler* is a very old sign, and occurs in *Cocke Lorell's Bote*.   More general
was the sign of the *Sword & Buckler* which was frequently set up by haberdashers who,
according to Stow, first began to sell bucklers about 1570.   About this time the old-
fashioned buckler a foot broad, with a pike of four or five inches, began to give place
for a brief period to the improved article, half an ell broad, with a pike of ten or twelve
inches.

The great prevalence of this sign originated in the sword and buckler play once
very common in England.   Misson, who visited this country in 1698, says it was
growing a little out of date in his time.—

> Within these few years you should often see a sort of gladiators marching through
> the streets, in their shirts to the waste, their sleeves tucked up, sword in hand, and pro-
> ceeded by a drum to gather spectators.   They give so much a head to see the fight,
> which was with cutting swords and a kind of buckler for defence.   The edge of the

sword was a little blunted, and the care of the prizefighters was not so much to avoid wounding one another, as to avoid doing it dangerously ; nevertheless as they were obliged to fight until some blood was shed, without which nobody would give a farthing for the show, they were sometimes forced to play a little roughly. The fights are become very rare within these eight or ten years.

In the 17th century the ' play ' was very rough, which is evident from those matches at which Pepys was present, and which he describes at large. Jorevin, another Frenchman, who visited England in 1672 gives a detailed account of the sport. Another writer styles the fights a ' barbarous ' performance, by those whom necessity (occasioned by a scandalous laziness and indolence) induces to expose themselves to be horribly mangled for a little money, while the bloodily minded spectators satiate themselves with human gore to the great reproach of religion.

In the *Spectator*, No. 436, there is an amusing essay on these ' Hockley-in-the-Hole Gladiators ', and in No. 449 a letter appears in which the deceits of the champions are shown, and it is made clear that often the outcome of the matches was prearranged by the participants.

A few other instances of the *Sword* occur on signs, as the *Sword & Cross*, a sort of emblem of the Church militant, or perhaps an inversion of the *Cross Swords*. This was a sign ' next door to the Savoy Gate in 1711 '. The *Swordblade*, was a coffee-house in Birchin Lane in 1718. The *Sword & Dagger* is a combination reminiscent of the desperate duels amongst the ruffling gallants of the reign of James I. This sign of ill omen was, in the 17th century, in St Catherine Lane, Tower, as appears from the trades tokens issued there.

The *Dagger* was once common in London. The house of this sign in Holborn is referred to by Captain Face, in Ben Jonson's *Alchymyst* and various trades tokens testify the prevalence of the sign. Probably this arose from its being a charge in the city arms. It was supposed to represent the dagger Sir William Walworth used in slaying Wat Tyler. This at least was asserted in the inscription below the niche in which Sir William's statue was erected in Fishmonger's Hall. Actually, as Stow points out, this is erroneous, as when in 1381 a new seal was made for the city ' the armes of this city were not altered, but remayne as afore ; to witte, argent, a playne cross gules a *sword of Saint Paul* in the first quarter and no dagger of William Walworth as is fabuled '. The *Dagger & Pie* was in the 17th century the sign of a celebrated pie-shop in Cheapside, the Pie being added to the original sign. On the trades tokens of this house this was represented by a rebus of a dagger with a magpie on the point. Dagger-pies are frequently mentioned in the plays of the period ; for instance, in Dekker's *Satiromastix*, 1602, and in Prynne's *Histriomastix*, 1632. The London apprentices appear to have been good customers to this house. Whenever, for example, old Hobson, the merry haberdasher, went abroad, ' his prentices wold ether bee at the Taverne filling their heds with wine or at the *Dagger* in Cheapside cramming their bellies with minced pyes '. And in Haywood's comedy of *If you know not me you know Nobody* ★ the

★ Act I, Sc. i, 1606.

worthy citizen bitterly inveighs against the temptations held out to apprentices by the dainties of this house.

It is curious that booksellers, who flourished by the arts of peace, often chose the *Helmet* for their sign. Humphrey Joy, a bookseller and printer in St Paul's Churchyard in 1550, and another, celebrated in the reigns of Henry VIII, Edward VI, and Queen Mary, Rowland Hall by name, had both a *Helmet* for their sign. There was until lately, a stone carving of a helmet fixed in front of a house in Helmet Court on the south side of London Wall, with the date 1668 and the initials H. M. This was quite close to the Hall of the Armourers and Braziers in whose arms the helmet is a charge. Ned Ward mentions the *Helmet* in Bishopsgate not far away. He says that at the battles without bloodshed of the Trainbands in Moorfields the gallant warriors wished for beer from this house. Trades tokens are extant of the *Blue Helmet* in Tower St. From the same source we learn that there was in the 17th century, a sign of the *Plate*, that is the Breastplate, in Upper Shadwell; and a *Handgun* in Shadwell.

A few other old weapons remain to be mentioned, as the *Arrow*, once a great favourite when this weapon made the English name terrible whenever our troops took the field. In the 17th century there was a beer-house at Knockholt, Kent, under the *Arrow* sign, with these lines beneath :—

> Charles Collins liveth here,
> Sells rum, brandy, gin and beer;
> I make this board a little wider,
> To let you know I sell good cyder.

There is still an *Arrow* at Himbleton, Worcs., an *Archers* in Bathurst St., and a new house at Tunbridge Wells with a fine sign has the title of the *Long Bow*. The *Sheaf of Arrows* is recorded at Cranborne, Dorset, in 1634.

The *Cross-Bullets*, a name puzzling at first sight, was a sign in Thames St. in the 17th century, representing two bar-shot crossed, which the trades token elucidates by the equally puzzling legend, 'at the Cross bvlets'. The *Cross-Bullets* was an instrument of destruction formerly used in naval engagements, a kind of ancestor of shrapnel, and for that reason set up in the neighbourhood of shipping.

If we may believe a jocular article on a quack handbill in the *Spectator*, No. 444, there was a *Cannon Ball* in Drury Lane, next door to the *Surgeon's* Arms, the headquarters of a particularly brazen quack doctor.

The *Spear in Hand* is at the present day the sign of a public-house at Norwich, but this is undoubtedly a popular version of some family crest. In Jews' Row, or Royal Hospital Row, Chelsea, there was a very puzzling sign over a house which has now gone; this is the *Snowshoes*. It is the sign of a house of old standing, and was set up during the excitement of the American war of independence, when snow-shoes formed part of the equipment of the troops sent out to fight the battles of King George against 'Mr. Washington and his rebels'.

One of the low public-houses that stood on the outskirts of London, towards Hyde Park Corner, at the end of the 18th century, was called the *Triumphal Car*.   There were a great many other houses of the same description in that neighbourhood, the *Hercules Pillars*, the *Red Lion*, the *Swan*, the *Golden Lion*, the *Horse-shoe*, the *Running Horse*, the *Barleymow*, the *White Horse*, and the *Half Moon*, which two last have given names to two streets in Piccadilly.   The sign of the *Triumphal Car* was in all probability bestowed upon the house in honour of the soldiers who used to visit it and its neigh-bours about the middle of the 18th century.   The houses were much visited on Sun-days, particularly on review days, when there were long wooden seats fixed in the street before the houses for the accommodation of six or seven barbers.   These were em-ployed on field days in powdering those youths who were not adroit enough to dress each other's hair.   Twenty or thirty of the older soldiers would bestride a form in the open air, where each combed, soaped, powdered and tied the hair of his comrade, and afterwards underwent the same operation himself.   There was in Larwood's time a *Triumphant Chariot* public-house in Pembroke Mews, Chelsea.   This also has now disappeared.

The *Bombay Grab* an old house lately rebuilt in High St., Bow, belongs to military signs, as ' Grab ' or ' Crab ' is a slang expression for an infantry man in an Indian regi-ment ; perhaps the landlord at one time may have been in the Indian Army.   According to another authority a grab was a three-masted 18-gun sloop, such as sailed to India in 1734 with the first cargo of beer exported, brewed in the Bow Brewery.   Still another account has it that the grab was a privateer dhow which seized the cargo, and its turn was taken by a vessel of the Indian Marine, and that the house was built by one of the crew with his share of the prize-money.

Objects relating to the navy, or rather to shipping, are still more common in this seafaring nation than the attributes or emblems of any other trade or profession.   Ned Ward says of Deptford in 1703 that every house was distinguished by either the sign of the *Ship*, the *Anchor*, the *Three Mariners*, *Boatswain & Call*, or something relating to the sea.

> For as I suppose if they should hang up any other, the saltwater novices would be as much puzzled to know what the figure represented as the Irishman was, when he called the Globe the Golden Cabbage, and the Unicorn the White Horse with a barber's pole in his forehead.

There is scarcely a town in the kingdom that has not a *Ship* inn, tavern, or public-house.   Probably in most cases the derivation is the obvious one, but occasionally the sign may refer to the Constellation.   Tokens exist of ' the Ship without Templebar, 1649 ', probably the inn granted in 1571 to Sir Christopher Hatton.   The *Ship* in Lincoln's Inn Fields was established in 1549.   Here during the Gordon Riots of 1780 the plate from the Catholic Chapel, Mayfair, was kept and Mass was said by stealth. Here in 1798 a meeting of zealous friends to his Majesty subscribed for an engraving of Nelson's portrait to commemorate the Victory of the Nile.   William Faithorne the engraver (ob. 1691) seems to have occupied the same house afterwards, for Horace Walpole informs us that :—

> Faithorne now set up in a new shop at the sign of the *Ship*, next to the *Drake*, opposite to *Palsgrave Head*, without Temple Bar.

Among the trades tokens is one of ' Will Jonson at yᵉ *Drake*, Bell Yard, Temple Bar, 1667 '. It was doubtless a rebus, and alluded to the Admiral. He was deservedly popular, the mint-mark of the martlet on Queen Elizabeth's coins being termed by the vulgar a Drake. The situation of this sign near the *Ship* was appropriate enough.

At the *Ship* in the Old Bailey, kept by Mr. Thomas Amps, on Tuesday 14 February 1654, a plot against Cromwell was discovered. Carlyle in his *Cromwell* forcibly pictures the conspirators as eleven truculent, rather threadbare persons, sitting over small drink there on that Tuesday night, considering how the Protector might be assassinated. Poor broken Royalist men, payless old captains, and such like, with their steeple hats worn very brown, and jackboots slit, projecting there what they could not execute. The poor knaves were found guilty, but not worth hanging, and got off with being sent to the Tower for a while to ponder over their wickedness.

The *Ship*, Alverston, Glos., has a very pleasing pictorial sign. The *Ship* at Mere, Wilts., has a magnificent sign terminated by a bunch of grapes, and with a crown added in commemoration of a visit by Queen Victoria who slept there as a baby on her way to the *George* at Gloucester *en route* to Exeter.

The *Ship* at 22 Artillery Lane, generally known as *Williams*, was founded in 1682 under a free Vintners licence. For many years it has been managed ' in order to add to the comfort of persons purchasing at this establishment ' under very strict rules indeed. No smoking is allowed, and no second drinks are permitted, and no one is supplied with more than a gill of wine, half a gill of spirits, or a glass of beer. ' The proprietors reserve their right to conduct their business on their own lines, and respectfully request that persons who are not willing to act in conformity with their rules transfer their patronage to some other house.' ★ The *Ship* at Morecombelake has an unusual sign, showing not only the *Ship* itself, but also the refreshments of her complement, a glass of port for the skipper, and a tankard of beer for the seamen.

Names of famous men-of-war are often found on the signboard in seaports ; either in honour of some brilliant feat performed by them, or simply in compliment to the crew or in the hopes of obtaining their liberal patronage. Thus originated the *Albion*, the *Saucy Ajax*, the *Circe*, and *Arethusa*, formerly to be seen at Poplar, and innumerable others, may be met with in the vicinity of Plymouth, Portsmouth and other seaports. The naming of signboards in this way was an old custom : as two examples among the London trades tokens very sufficiently prove. Thus, for instance, the *Speaker's Frigate*, the sign of a shop in Shadwell in the 17th century. The frigate had been named after Sir Richard Stayner, speaker in the House of Commons in the

---

★ An excellent account of this house and a full copy of the rules are to be found in Mr. Topham's *Taverns in the Town*, pp. 198–9.

time of the Commonwealth, who had done good service under command of Admiral Blake in naval engagements with the Spaniards. In 1652, this ship was sent to ' Argier in Turkey' (Algiers) under command of Captain Thorowgood, with the sum of £30,000 to redeem English captives from slavery. After the Restoration the name of this ship was changed into the *Royal Charles* (which also occurs as a sign). This was the ill-fated ship taken by the Dutch in 1667, when, under Admiral de Ruyter, they made their descent on Chatham and Sheerness, and burnt or captured a great part of our fleet. The stern is still kept as a trophy in Rotterdam.

Other signs recalling famous ships are the *Shannon*, Bucklesham, Suff., the *Shannon and Chesapeake*, Todmorden, Yorks., the *Argo Frigate*, Sunderland, the *Tartar Frigate*, Broadstairs, the *Ship Argo*, Portsea, the *Ship Defiance*, Ipswich, the *Ship Isis*, Sunderland, the *Ship Lion*, Ropemaker Fields, the *Ship York*, Redriff St. The *Great Britain* and the *Great Eastern* are both in the by-no-means nautical town of Burslem, Stoke-on-Trent, and the *Llandoger Trow*, a fine old shipping tavern and a former headquarters of the local slavers and privateers, is at Bristol.

Ships occur in various conditions, as the *Full Ship*, Hull ; *Ship in Dock*, Dartmouth ; and the *Ship on Launch*, in every shipbuilding locality. The *Ship in Full Sail* was the sign of the first shop of Murray the publisher, Fleet St., probably in opposition to Longman, who had the *Ship at Anchor*. The *Ship in Distress* found, for example, in Marygold St., is a touching appeal to the good-natured wayfarer to assist in keeping the pump going, rather like the better known *Friend in Need* found, for example, at Dover. There was a *Ship in Distress* sign at Brighton in the 18th century on which the poet had assisted the painter to invoke the sympathy of the thirsty public :—

> With sorrows I am compass'd round,
> Pray lend a hand, my ship's aground.

There is still a house of this sign at Lea Bridge Rd. The *Ship* is to be met with in innumerable combinations : the *Ship & Pilot*, Bristol, the *Ship & Anchor* is not uncommon, and in one place at Chipping Norton, it is corrupted into the *Sheep & Anchor*.★ Ship is good English in many dialects for sheep. There is a token of William Eye ' at the Sheep' in Rye in 1652, representing a ship. The *Ship & Whale* in Derrick St. is no doubt in compliment to the Greenland Fishery. It occurs at South Shields. The *Ship & Notchblock* was a sailors' coffee-house now extinct in the Ratcliff Highway. All these explain themselves ; most of the other combinations seem to result from the quartering of two signs, as the *Ship & Bell*, Horndean, Hants ; the *Ship & Fox*, ' next door but one to the *Five Bells* tavern, near the *Maypole* in the Strand', in 1711. The *Ship & Star* on a trades token of Cornhill, may be the North Star by which ancient mariners used to navigate. The *Ship & Rainbow* is common to many places ; the *Ship & Shovel* near Guy's Hospital in Southwark, said to be a corruption of Sir Cloudesley Shovel, but more probably alludes to the *shovels* used in taking out ballast, coal, corn (when in bulk) and various other cargoes. This seems the likelier derivation for

★ Possibly this may be another version of the *Lamb & Anchor* (p. 182).

the *Ship & Shovel*, Craven St., Strand, presumably a house favoured by coal-heavers, as the *Coal-Hole* in the same region may have a similar derivation. (There is probably little substance in a recent writer's suggestion that it was so-called because of its murky reputation.) The original house stood to the east of the present one, and had many associations with Edmund Kean. The *Ship & Plough*, Hull, and the *Ship & Blue Coat Boy* now no more, formerly in Walworth Rd., although susceptible of explanation, are doubtless only but quarterings. The *Ship & Castle*, though of common occurrence, seemed to puzzle the public already in the 17th century. The *Search after Claret*, 1691, has :

> What resemblance the Ship and the Castle may bear
> To ships floating on clouds, or to castles in air,
> We know not ; but this we are sure of, 'tis plain
> Their clarets are perfectly Leger-de-Main.

If not a combination of two signs, it may have some reference to our national defences. It was a sign in Cornhill as early as 9 November 1716 : when a fowl was roasted there in a wonderful sun-kitchen in view of many gentlemen. ' The artist performer, who is a gentleman newly come from France, proposes to roast and boil meat, bake bread, prepare tea and coffee, and all kitchenwork done without common fire ; some particular thing to be seen every day that the sun shines out brightly. The machine is composed of about a hundred small looking or convex glasses.' There is a house of this sign at Congresbury, Som. Here the sign displays the arms of Bristol City.

Amongst all these ships there are a few sailor signs. The *Ship Friends* occur in Sunderland. The *Three Mariners* is an old sign, of which there are examples among the trades tokens, and which is still to be seen on two or three houses in London. There was formerly a tavern known by this sign in Vauxhall, and there is still a house of this name in Carland St., E. The Vauxhall house seems to have disappeared with a very remarkable chair which is said to have been used by King Charles II when he visited the tavern in disguise with his female associates ' to play chess, etc.'. Another house in Upper Fore St., Lambeth, with the sign ' *Three Merry Boys* ' may preserve the same in a corrupted form. In other places occurs the *Three Jolly Sailors*. At Castleford there used to be one representing the jolly sailors ' three sheets in the wind ', and under it the following professional invitation :—

> Coil up your ropes and anchor here,
> Till better weather does appear.

Probably the *Old Tumbling Sailors* near Kidderminster is a variant of this sign.

In North St., Hull, there is a sign of *Jack on a Cruise*, not on board H.M. ship, but on a spree. Larwood suggests that such cruises are generally confined to rather low latitudes. The peccadillos of Jack's betters are commemorated in the *Bedford in Chase*, Portsmouth. The story has it that the Captain put to sea hastily and all night chased an imaginary Frenchman only a few cables' length from his own ship. He had returned on board rather late and saw two foresails where there was only one. The *Boatswain* appears to have been a public-house in Wapping in the reign of Charles II, for Wycherly in the *Plain Dealer* refers to it.　The *Boatswain's Call* was a sign in Frederick St., Portsea, and there is a *Bo'sun & Call* at Chatham.　Larwood suggests that the sailors no doubt accept this invitation with much more pleasure than the boatswain's call of all hands on deck on a frosty winter morning.　Probably both houses were named after a patriotic sea song during one of the wars with France.　*Red, White & Blue,* and its synonym, the *Three Admirals,* both occur in more than one instance in Liverpool, and there is a *Red, White & Blue* at Ely and others at Stamford, Lincs., and East Retford, Notts.

　　The *Anchor* was, perhaps, set up rather as an emblem than as referring to its use in shipping.　It is frequently represented in the catacombs, typifying the words of St Paul. St Ambose says 'it is this which keeps the Christian from being carried away by the storm of life'.　Other earlier writers use it as a symbol of true faith, which one of them thus expressed :

> As an anchor cast into the sand will keep the ship in safety, even so hope, even amidst poverty and tribulation, remains firm, and is sufficient to sustain the soul ; though, in the eyes of the world, it may seem but a weak and frail support.

It was a favourite sign with the early printers, probably in imitation of Aldus whose anchor symbol is noted on p. 147.　Thus Thomas Vautrollier, a scholar and printer from Paris and Rouen, who came to England about the beginning of Queen Elizabeth's reign and established his printing-office in Blackfriars, had an anchor for his sign, with the motto 'Anchora Spei '.　At West Bromwich there is an alehouse having the sign of the *Anchor* with the following inscription :—

> O sweet ale, how sweet art thou,
> Thy cheering streams new life impart,
> Esteemed by all extremely good,
> To quench our thirst and do us good.

Sometimes a female figure in flowing garments is represented holding the anchor, in which case it is called the *Hope & Anchor.*　The *Blue Anchor* was painted of that colour as a ' difference' from other anchors : it is a common sign ; it was the trade emblem of Henry Herringman of the New Exchange, the principal London bookseller and publisher in the reign of King Charles II, the friend of Davenant, Dryden and Cowley. The *Anchor & Bollards* is to be seen at Exeter.　Other distinctions are the *Anchor & Hope* or *Hope & Anchor,*★ *Sheet Anchor* at Whitmore, Staffs. ;　the *Foul Anchor,* King's Lynn and at Yarmouth ;　the *Raffled Anchor,* Swan's Quay, North Shields ;　and the *Rope & Anchor,* which is very common, the anchor being generally represented with a piece of cable twined round the stem, but which may perhaps be a corruption of *Hope & Anchor.*
　　A few combinations also occur ; the *Anchor & Dolphin,* Chichester, seems plainly symbolic, as will be seen by reference to what has been said concerning the *Dolphin.* The *Anchor & Can* at Ross, and at Putson, Hereford, which seems to allude to the

★ See also p. 28.

Anker, a measure equalling 8⅛ gallons ; the *Anchor & Shuttle*, Luddendenfoot, Warley, Manchester, the shuttle being added in compliment to the weavers ; the *Anchor & Castle*, a quartering of two signs in Tooley St., the *Anchor & Vine* formerly at Charing Cross, etc.

Sometimes instead of a ship, some peculiar vessel is chosen, as, for instance, the *Sloop*, or the *Leigh Hoy*, a sort of smack. This last occurs amongst the trades tokens as a sign near St Catherine's Docks, and is still to be seen in Creek Rd. : the *Coble*, formerly to be seen at Newbiggin-by-Sea, was a sort of fishing boat common in Northumberland. The *Isle of Wight Hoy* and the *Llandoger Trow* (Llandogo is a village on the Wye, and a trow was a flat-bottomed barge) are both at Bristol. The *Tilt Boat*, Somers Quay, Thames St., is recorded in the 17th century, and was in Larwood's time still at Billingsgate. This last was an open passenger boat for Greenwich, Woolwich, Gravesend, and other places down the river. It took twelve hours to perform the voyage to Gravesend and much more if the wind was contrary, and the boat had not arrived before the tide turned. The tiltboats were not superseded by steamers before 1815. The *Dark House*, Billingsgate, was their starting-place, and passengers would probably patronize the tavern with this name in the immediate neighbourhood, as they go now for a glass of ale and a sandwich to the *Railway Hotel* or *Packet Boat* during the quarter of an hour preceding departure.

The *Fishing Smack* was a public-house formerly standing near St Nicholas's Church, Liverpool. The sign represented a man standing in a cart loaded with fish, and holding in his right hand what the artist intended to represent as a salmon. Underneath were the following lines :—

> This salmon has got a tail,
> It's very like a whale ;
> It's a fish that's very merry ;
> They say it's catch'd at Derry ;
> It's a fish that's got a heart,
> It's catch'd and put in Dugdale's cart.

A change in the occupant of the house induced a corresponding change of sign, and the following lines took the place of the preceding :—

> The cart and salmon has stray'd away,
> And left the fishing-boat to stay,
> When boisterous winds do drive you back,
> Come in and drink at the *Fishing Smack*.

There is another *Fishing Smack* at Deptford. The *Barking Smack* is at Norwich, the *Lobster Smack* at Canvey, the *Cutter* at Ely, the *Skiff* at Newcastle-on-Tyne. The *Schooner* is at Alnmouth, the *Pilot Boat* at New Brighton, the *Yacht* at Chester, and there is a *Galleons* by the Albert Dock. The *Spanish Galleon* at East Greenwich is dealt with above (p. 63.) There is a *Barge* at Shrewsbury, a *Barge Aground* at Brentford, a *City Barge* at Chiswick, there was an *Old Guildford Barge* at Lambeth, now extinct,

and there is a *Row Barge* at Woking. The *Old Barge* was a sign in Bucklersbury :
' When Walbrooke did lye open, barges were rowed out of the Thames, or towed
up so farre ; and therefore the place has ever since been called the *Old Barge*, of such a
sign hanging out over the date thereof.' The *Old Barge*, or the *Old Boat*, is still
frequently seen as a sign on the banks of some of the canals through which boats
and barges are towed. Sometimes along the canal (for example at East Retford,
Notts., by the Chesterfield Canal) is to be seen a *Packet*. Passengers as well as goods
were on occasion carried by canal boat in the days before the railways.

The *Boat*, an isolated tavern in the open fields at the back of the Foundling Hospital,
was the headquarters of the rioters and incendiaries, who, excited by the injudicious
zeal of Lord George Gordon, set London in a blaze during the ' No Popery ' riots in
1780. *Next Boat by Paul's* in Upper Thames St. may be seen on the trades token
of an alehouse, evidently kept by a waterman, who used to ply with his boat near
St Paul's. The token represents a boat containing three men, over it the legend,
Next Boat. *Next Oars* was the cry of the watermen waiting for a fare. Tom Brown
in his walk round London refers to the ' noisy multitude of grizly old Tritons, hollow-
ing and hooting out *Next Oars* '. *Next Boat* was also the sign of a public-house of
note adjoining Holland's Leaguer in Blackfriars, where Holland St. is now.

The Law is very badly represented on the signboard—the *Judge's Head* seems to
be the only sign in honour of the legal profession. A modern sign of this name
is to be seen over a law stationer's in Chancery Lane. It was the sign of Charles
King, a bookseller in Westminster Hall in 1718, and may be readily accounted for
in that locality. It was also the first sign of Jacob Tonson, the well-known bookseller and secretary of the Kit-Kat Club, when he lived near Inner Temple Gate,
Fleet St.

Lot Goodal, Beadle of St Martin's-in-the-Fields in 1680, had like other celebrities
taken his own goodly person for the sign of his house in Rupert St., as appears from
his advertisement, in which like a true Dogberry he informs the public that he has
taken in custody a silver watch with a studded case. The *Brown Bill* was another
constable's sign and is referred to as such in Middleton's early play *Blurt, Master
Constable*, 1602. The brown bill was a kind of battle-axe or hatchet affixed to a long
staff, used by constables. From this the men who carried it were called *Brown Bills*,
or as in Lyly's *Endymion*, 1591, *Billmen*.

Lawyers receive a somewhat backhanded compliment in the sign of the *Honest
Lawyer* (p. 267). One of the heads of this profession is commemorated in the *Rolls*,
a tavern kept by Ralph Massie, in Chancery Lane, in the reign of Charles II. In
various parts of the house and particularly in the great room upstairs the arms of the
Carew family spoke of its former possessors. Further back still it was a timber
tenement belonging to the knights of St John of Jerusalem, by whom it was sold to
Cardinal Wolsey, who for a time inhabited it. Behind this building was the house
and garden of Sir Walter Raleigh. All these remnants of bygone glory were swept
away in 1760. Then the house was rebuilt and the name changed into the *Crown &*

Rolls, adopted either from the Master of the Rolls or from the neighbouring Rolls House, where the rolls and records of Chancery were kept from the reign of Richard III.

Weavers signs are sometimes found. There is a *Weavers Arms* at Stoke Newington, a *Canterbury Weavers* at Canterbury, and a *Shuttle* at Norwich. The *Weavers* at Runcorn refers of course not to the craft but to the Cheshire River. The *Machine* at Ashbourne, Derbys., is no doubt a lace machine or a stocking frame.

The liberal arts are as badly represented on the signboard as the Bar. The *Poet's Head* was a sign in St James's St. in the 17th century ; who the poet was it is impossible to say now ; perhaps it was Dryden, since the trades tokens represent a head crowned with bays. The same sign had been used during the Commonwealth by Taylor the Water Poet, but in his case the poet was Taylor himself (p. 38).

The *Five Inkhorns* it is learned from the trades tokens was the sign of Walter Haddon, in Grub St., a very appropriate trade emblem in that locality. The sign still exists in Boundary St., Leicester Square. There was also a house with this sign in Petticoat Lane opposite which lived Strype's mother. Petticoat Lane in that time was the great manufacturing place for inkhorns. The *Hand & Pen* was a scrivener's sign which was adopted by Peter Bales, Queen Elizabeth's celebrated penman. He was the author of the *Writing Schoole Master*, and one of Walsingham's secret service staff much employed in dealing with intercepted letters. The sign of the *Hand & Pen* was also used by the Fleet St. marriage-mongers, to denote ' marriages performed without imposition '. The sign still appears over a house in Fleet St.

Music-shops always adhered to the primitive custom of using as their signs representations of the instruments they sold ; instance the *Harp & Hautboy* was according to the *London Gazette* the sign of John Walsh, ' servant of his Majesty ' in Catherine St., Strand, in 1700. The *Hautboy* was one of the most constant music-shop signs. It occurs as an inn sign at Oakham, Surrey. It was a reed instrument—a kind of prototype of the flute. There is still an inn sign of the *Hautboy & Fiddle* at Peterborough. Messrs. Novello, the well-known music publishers still adhere to the old tradition, and long carried on business in the Poultry under the sign of the *Golden Crotchet*. They now trade under the same sign in Wardour St. There is a *Crotchet* Inn at Witham, Essex.

The *French Horn* was once a very common sign, and is still of frequent occurrence ; as, for example, in Lambert Walk, at Henley, Stoke-on-Trent, and at Ware, Herts. There was once a *French Horn & Rose* in Wood St., Cheapside ; there is still a *French Horn & Half Moon* at Wandsworth, and a *Queen's Head & French Horn* in Little Britain, E.C. This last house was for many years kept by Peter Crawley, a noted member of the P.R., and there John Leech, the artist and a friend, used to study low life and boxiana under the tutelage of Black Sam. In the 17th century there was a *Horn & Three Tuns* in Leadenhall St. The trades tokens represent it as a French horn, though apparently a drinking horn would certainly have been a more useful instrument in the company of three tuns. It was evidently a corruption of the Bottlemakers' arms, which were *arg.* on a chevron *sa.* three bugle-horns of the first between three leather-bottles of the second.   These leather-bottles might easily be mistaken for tuns, and the bugle-horn be modernized into a musical instrument.

The *Bugle-horn* is fully as common ; it occurs on a trades token of 1667 as the sign of a house in Aldersgate St., and is still to be seen on many inns by the roadside, where the mail coach in coaching times used to announce its arrival by a cheerful tune from the guard's horn.   There is such a *Bugle Horn*, for example at Charlton, Kent.   Sometimes the *Horn* was used in a different sense.   It was the sign and badge of the cattle doctor and village gelder, and came to be exhibited as such either from its use in drenching animals, or from the fact of such an instrument being blown by the doctor, to give notice to the villagers of his approach.   At Massingham, Lincoln, the *Horn* Inn nearly two centuries ago, was kept by such a person.

The *Harp* in the beginning of the 18th century was the sign of a bird-fancier ' over against Somerset House in the Strand ', and is still used as a sign of many public-houses, generally denoting an Irish origin.   There is a *Harp* in Great Tower St., a *Harp of Erin* at Deptford, a *Welsh Harp* at Hendon, and a *Jew's Harp* in Redhill St. The famous friendly society the ' Antediluvian Order of Buffaloes ' is said to have been founded by an actor named Sinnet at the *Harp* near Drury Lane in 1822.   The *Jew's Harp* (an instrument formerly called *jeu trompe*, Jew's Trump, that is toy trumpet) was in former times the sign of a house with bowery tea-gardens and thickly foliated snuggeries in what was once Marylebone Park.   This was near the top of Portland Place and it was removed on the laying out of Regent's Park.   Speaker Onslow used to go there in plain attire, and sitting in the chimney corner join in the humours of the customers, until being recognized by the landlord one day as he was riding in his golden coach to the house in state, he found on going in the evening for his quiet pipe and glass that his incognito was betrayed.   This broke the charm and he never more returned.   At the end of the 18th century there was another *Jew's Harp* Tavern and Tea-garden in Islington.   It consisted of a large upper room, ascended by a staircase on the outside for the accommodation of company on ball nights, and in this room large parties dined.   Facing the south front of the premises was a large semi-circular enclosure with boxes for tea and ale drinkers, guarded by wooden soldiers painted in proper colours one between every two boxes.   In the centre of this opening were tables and seats placed for the smokers ; a trap-ball ground was on the eastern side of the house, whilst the western side served for a tennis court ; there were also public and private skittle grounds.   Both these houses are now no more.   We find a clue to this rather odd sign in Jonson's play *The Devil is an Ass.** from which it appears that it was formerly a custom to keep in some taverns a fool, who, sitting on a joint stool, used to play on a *Jew's Harp* for the edification of the customers.   The sign may indicate then a house where music and other entertainment were provided.   Another ' musical ' inn sign is that of the *Organ*, Stalybridge.

One of the signs originally used exclusively by apothecaries was the *Mortar &*

* Act I, Sc. i.

Pestle. Among the celebrities who sold medicines under this emblem was the noted John Moore, ' author of the celebrated *Worm Powder* ', to whom Pope addressed his rather unkind stanzas. There is a house with the sign *Pestle & Mortar* today at Wantage, Berks. The *Apothecary* leads us to the *Barber*, or rather *Barber Surgeon*, and the *Barber's Pole*, which is said to date from the time when barbers practised blood-letting. According to legend the patient undergoing this operation had to grasp the pole in order to make the blood flow more freely. Actually this use of the pole is illustrated in more than one illuminated manuscript. As the pole was of course liable to be stained with blood it was painted red ; when it was not in use barbers were in the habit of suspending it outside the door with the white linen swathing bands twisted round it. This in later times gave rise to the pole being painted red and white, or black and white, or even with red, white and blue lines winding round it. It was stated by Lord Thurlow in the House of Lords on 17 July 1707 when he opposed the Surgeon's Incorporation Bill that ' by a statute still in force the barbers and surgeons were each to use a pole. The barbers were to have theirs *blue and white* striped with no other appendage, but the surgeons were to have a gallipot and a red flag in addition, to denote the particular nature of their vocation.'

Besides the brass soap-basins appended to the pole, which still remained quite common in Larwood's time, the barbers in former times used to have other and more repulsive signs of their profession. In his time too some of the London dentists still followed the disgusting custom of exhibiting teeth as trophies in their windows, for in no less a thoroughfare than Sloane St. there was a certain chemist-dentist who exhibited in his window a whole bottleful of decayed teeth. The practice is now happily disused, but quack doctors at fairs still display ghastly collections of decayed teeth and shrivelled corns. Instead of cups ' lined with red rags to look like blood ' the genuine article was formerly exhibited in the windows, but this was already prohibited at an early period, since the *Liber Albus* enjoins ' that no barber be so bold or so daring as to put *blood in their windows* openly in view of folks, but let them have it carried privily unto the Thames, under pain of paying two shillings unto the use of the Sheriffs '.

Numerous more or less witty barber-publicans' inscriptions are recorded ; one of the best is that attributed to Dean Swift, penned by him for a barber, who also kept a public-house :—

> Rove not from *pole* to *pole*, but step in here,
> Where nought excels the shaving but the beer.

A variant often met was :—

> Rove not from pole to pole, but here turn in,
> Where nought excels the shaving but the gin.

Scott in the *Fortunes of Nigel* as a motto to Chapter IV, gives another version :—

> Rove not from pole to pole—the man lives here,
> Whose razor's only equall'd by his beer ;
> And where, in either sense, the Cockney put,
> May, if he pleases, get confounded cut.

The amalgamation of the two trades has led to some other rather feeble rhymes and jokes. A barber-publican in Dudley had the following joke, which Larwood stigmatizes as truly barbarous :—

> What do you think
> I'll shave you for nothing, and give you some drink ?

The point of the joke lies in the punctuation. A barber in Ratcliffe Highway, c. 1825, had the following *bona fide* invitation :—

> Hair cut with despatch,
> Shave well in a minute,
> And a glass in the bar-gain
> With a thimbleful in it.

> *Note*—Of gin and bitters, all for a penny ½d.
> Come in, Jolly Tars, and be scraped across the line.

Tools belonging to various handicrafts are common public-house signs at the present day. The *Hatchet* is an old house at Bristol, though probably the sign is relatively new. The place was formerly associated with Mace the pugilist. Recently it was preserved from destruction by the intervention of the Society for the Protection of Ancient Buildings. The *Axe* was a very old sign in Aldermanbury, now extinct, in the 17th century. It was one of the places visited *c.* 1608–38 by that thirsty tourist, Drunken Barnaby. From this inn the first regular line of stage wagons from London to Liverpool was established towards the middle of the 17th century. There is an *Old Axe* in Hackney Rd.

The *Cross Axes* is a sign at Preston, Bolton, etc. The *Axe* is also found combined with various other carpenter's tools, as the *Axe & Saw*, Carlton, Newmarket ; the *Axe & Compasses* at Aythorpe, Roding, Essex ; Leighton Buzzard, Beds. ; Newbury and Reading, Berks. ; Thrapston, Northants ; Ware, Herts., etc. ; and with butcher's implements as in the *Axe & Cleaver*, at Boston Spa, Yorks., and Much Birch, Herefs., the *Axe & Square*, Countesthorpe, Leics., the *Axe & Handsaw*, at Altrincham, Ches., and Heckington, Lincs. A house of this name was recently demolished at Burslem, Staffs. Another sign complimentary to the same class of workmen was the *Two Sawyers* which may still be seen near the garden wall of the archiepiscopal palace at Lambeth, and at North Somercotes ; not improbably this was the same house of which trades tokens are extant from the time of Charles II.

The *Chemical* Inn found at Leicester, and at Oldbury, refers in its sign to the local chemical industry, not of course to the content of the beer, and similarly the *Water Works* in North Staffordshire intends no unkind allusion to its gravity.

Signs referring to iron in its various states are very common on public-houses, as the smith was generally a good customer to them. There are a great number of *Miners Arms* in Staffordshire, Warwickshire, and the Black Country. The *Davy Lamp* is another sign intended to court the custom of miners, but though the lamp is used

The Swan, Clare

Cock and Bottle, Cannon Street

Three Kings, Lambeth Hill

The George & The Dragon, Snow Hill

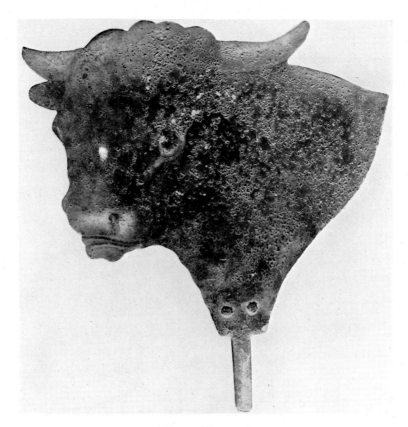

The Bull's Head

The Half Moon, Borough High Street

The Two Brewers (at Brewery)

6

The Man Loaded with Mischief (at Brewery)

The Load of Mischief, Blewbury

The Fox & Hounds, Barley, Herts.

The Scole Inn Sign, Scole, Norfolk

The White Hart

The Fox, Huntingdon

The Three Swans, Market Harborough

Shepherd and Dog, Brighton

Greyhound, Brighton

The Spread Eagle, Thame

The Griffin, Danbury

The Prince of Wales, Markstey

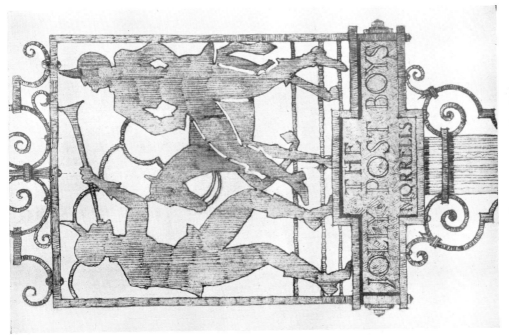

The Jolly Post Boys, Cockley

The Fox Inn, Bulmer

The Sultan, Waltham Abbey

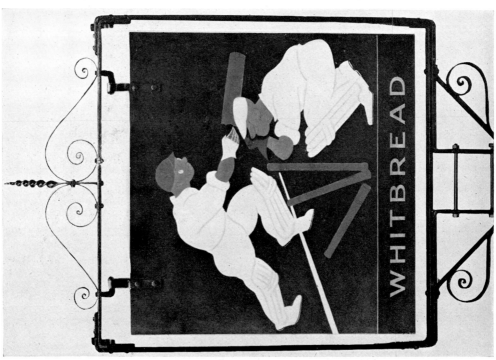

The Cricketers, Maidstone

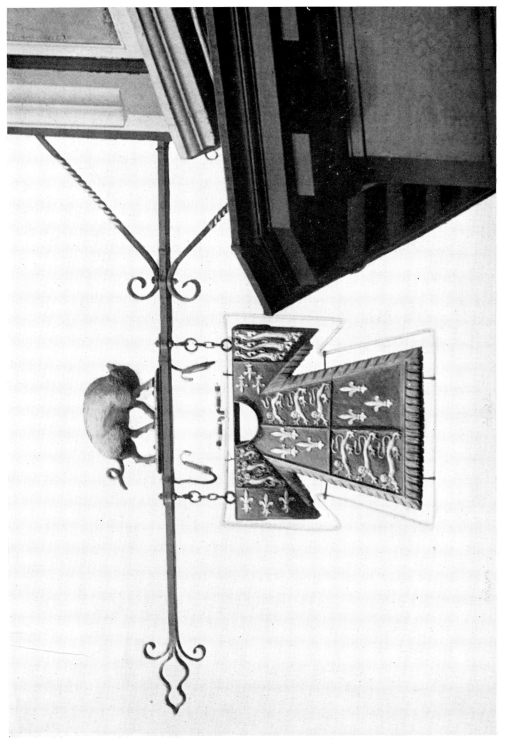

The Tabard, Gloucester

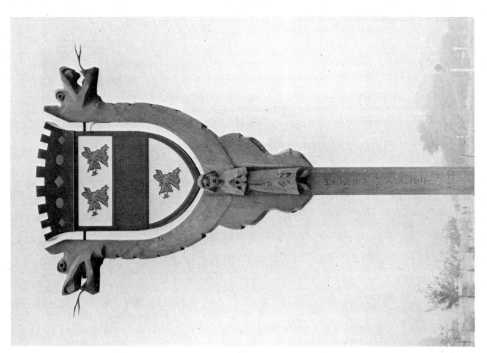

The Mylett Arms, Perivale

The Railway Hotel, Edgware

16

widely throughout the coalfields, the sign rarely occurs except in Northumberland, for example at Essington.   The *Forge* or the *Three Forges* is common in the Midland iron districts.   The *Dial* at Landport, Portsmouth, is an instrument used in mining. The *Anvil* as at Sheffield and at Saithery, Norf., the *Anvil & Blacksmith*, the *Anvil & Hammer*, the *Smith & Smithy*, etc., are all common about Sheffield.   So are *Hammers* combined with various instruments, as Pincers, Vice, Stithy, etc.   The *Two Smiths* was a sign in the Minories in 1655 ;   the trades tokens of the house represent two men working at the anvil.   *Hobnails* is a sign in Dudley, that town having been famous as early as the time of Henry VIII for the manufacture of nails of every description. There is another *Hobnails* at Washbourne, Glos. (?).   The *Cinder Oven* is a house at Norwich, the *Three Furnaces* is at Brierley Hill, Staffs.

The *Bag of Nails* was once a very common sign ;   there was in Larwood's time one still remaining in Arabella Row, Pimlico, and there is still one in Buckingham Palace Rd.   About 1770 or 1780 there might have been seen at the front of the house the original sign which depicted a satyr of the woods, and a group of jolly Bacchanals. The satyr having been painted black with cloven feet, it was by common consent called the *Devil*, while the Bacchanalians were transmuted into a *Bag of Nails*.   This was however only an old slang name for the house, for, in a conspiracy trial of 1765 one of the witnesses says ' He went into a public-house, the sign of the *Devil & Bag of Nails*, for so that gentry called it amongst themselves (though it was the *Blackamoor's Head & Woolpack*), by Buckingham Gate.'   This is presumably the *Bag o' Nails* still remaining in Buckingham Palace Rd.

A *bona fide* representation of a bag of nails was also used as a sign, as may be seen on the trades tokens of Henry Hurdam in Tuttle (Tothill) St., Westminster, 1663, where the bag of nails is combined with a hammer crowned.   And as it would be difficult to guess what the bag contained, and nobody cares to buy a ' pig in a poke ', the nails were sometimes represented protruding through it, as on the token of Samuel Hincks of Whitechapel, 1669.

Bakers and millers also are represented by a variety of signs.   The *Bushel* was a sign on the Bankside in the 17th century.   There is at the present day a *Bushel* at Grimstone, Dorset, and a *Bushel & Strike* at Royston, Herts.   Another at Ashwell near Baldock, Herts., has a fine pictorial sign, and there is another at Chesterfield.   The strike still survives as an archaic measure in some parts of the country-side—it is a ' struck ' bushel—the measure being filled level to the brim only, and any surplus being removed with a stick, as contrasted with a ' heaped ' bushel.   (The difference is that between a ' heaped ' teaspoonful and a ' level ' teaspoonful in the cookery books.)   It may be that the sign indicates a former use of the house by cornchandlers.   The *Mill* is found for example at Mirfield, Yorks., where we meet the *Dusty Miller*, a favourite sign in some parts of Yorkshire and Lancashire.   A reminiscence of childhood may have suggested the epithet in this sign, for there is the well-known nursery rhyme :—

> Millery, millery, Dusty Poll,
> How many sacks have you stole ?

P

Millers in the Army are invariably nicknamed 'Dusty'. The name is also applied ironically to a coal-miner. Houses of this sign at Chesterfield, Oldham, Rochdale, Whitehaven, etc., are in or near mining districts. There is an *Honest Miller* at Brook, Kent. The *Miller of Mansfield* is referred to above (p. 53). The *Millstone* may be seen at Burslem, Staffs.; Stamford, Stockport, and Macclesfield.

The *Windmill* itself is a very old sign. It was a tavern in Lothbury, Old Jewry, frequented by fast men in the reigns of Elizabeth, James I and Charles I. Jonson mentions it in *Every Man in his Humour*, 1598. The *Windmill*, Clerkenwell, is perhaps a successor to one named by Stow in 1528. The Middlesex magistrates held their sessions there *temp.* Edward VI, Mary and Elizabeth. There is also a *Windmill* at Bourne, Lincs., and another near Southwark Bridge; the *Mill* is found as a sign at Stamford, the *Water Mill* at Wivelsfield, Surrey.

The *Peel*, that is the long-handled wooden shovel used by bakers to place bread in the oven, was the sign of John Alder in Leadenhall St., 1668. The basket or *Panyer* to bring bread round still occurs as the *Paniers* at Yelvertoft, Northants, and gave its name to 'a passage out of Paternoster Row—called of such a sign Panyer Alley'. This is the highest spot in the City of London, as we are informed from an inscription under a stone figure of a boy sitting on a pannier, eating a very questionable bunch of grapes:

> When you have sought the City round,
> Yet still this is the highest ground.
> Aug. 26, 1688.

This figure has been temporarily removed. The *Pannier* is not an uncommon trade emblem. The *Baker & Basket*, the sign of a public-house in Leman St., and another in Worship St. and Appold St., occurs at Birmingham and at Coventry. The oldest sign showed a jug of beer, a drinking-horn and a bread loaf. Probably this is often the sign of a holder who has followed the two trades simultaneously. Later it developed suggestions of trade rivalry. In the house in Birmingham, both worthies appear on the sign, the Baker in a white cap, the Brewer in a red one. The baker's hand is resting on a substantial loaf: the brewer exhibits a foaming tankard, and the following dialogue ensues :—

> The Baker says, I've the Staff of Life,
>   And you're a silly elf;
> The Brewer replied, with artful pride,
>   Why, *this is life itself.*

The same jingle appears on a house in Ravenshurst St., Stratford Rd., E.

The *Two Brewers* or the *Two Jolly Brewers* used to be very common, but is now gradually becoming obsolete. There is an example of it at Windsor. It represented two brewer's men carrying a barrel of beer slung between them on a pole: it was also frequently called the *Two Draymen*. In the bar of the *Queen's Head*, Great Queen St. (which now has vanished), was preserved in Larwood's time a carved wooden sign, which formerly hung before this house, representing two men standing near a large tun.   There is a very pleasing example of this sign at Chipperfield, Herts.   The *Dray & Horses*, meaning of course the brewer's dray, has now in some instances superseded the *Two Jolly Brewers*.   It occurs for example at Tottenhill, Norf.   The *Still*, the chief implement in the manufacture of spirits, is very appropriately displayed before the houses where the produce of the still is sold.   There is a house of this sign at Sleaford.   Frequently it is combined with other objects, especially with the *Green Man* as in the instances given on p. 86.

The *Boy & Barrel*, formerly to be seen in Dagger Lane, London, and still to be found at Huddersfield, is all that remains of the little *Bacchus* on a tun, formerly found in almost every alehouse.   The *Compleat Vintner*, 1720, says :—

> A little Punch—
> Gut Bacchus dangling of a bunch,
> Sits loftily enthron'd upon
> What's called (in miniature) a Tun,

found for example at Thornbury, Glos.   The *Glass Barrel* at Birkenhead, etc., was a trick sign.   It consisted of a concave mirror attached to a board by hoops to imitate a barrel, and complete with bunghole.   Those looking at it saw their faces broaden (in anticipation of course of the good liquor to be found in the house).

The *Boy & Cup* at Norwich, in 1750, was a variant of this sign.   Other brewers and distillers' measures also are exhibited as the *Barrel*, formerly the *Porter Butt* (three in Bath), the *Brandy Cask* (three in Bristol), the *Rum Puncheon*, at Boston, Lincs., and formerly in Whitecross St., and such like.   Promises of fair dealing are held out in the sign of the *Full Measure* (four in Hull), the *Full Quart*, at Hewick, Som., the *Golden Measure*, Lowgate, Hull, whose sign was a gilt gallon can, and the *Foaming Tankard*.   An appeal is made to public joviality by such a sign as the *Parting Pot*, at Stamford, Lincs.   Some other signs of this class are dealt with on pp. 259–60.

Shoemakers generally confine themselves to the sign of the *Last*, which, for variety's sake, they paint red, blue and gold, etc.   But since ' coblers and tinkers are the best ale drinkers ', many alehouses have adopted this sign also.   One cobbler who kept an alehouse near Liscard, Ches., in Larwood's time traded under the sign of a *Wooden Last* with this distich :—

> All day long I have sought good beer,
> And, *at the last*, I have found it here.

The *Shears* was originally a tailor's sign, though like most other trade emblems it had become common in the 17th century.   A house of this sign at Wantage is illustrated in Mr. C. Harper's *Old Inns of England*.   There is one at Watledge, Glos., which apparently refers to sheep-shearing.   The *Hand & Shears* still existing in Cloth Fair, Smithfield, once played an important part at the opening of Bartholomew Fair. It was customary to make the proclamation for opening the fair late in the afternoon of 23 August, but actually the showmen and traders opened their booths early in the morning, the fair having been unofficially proclaimed half a day early by a number of tailors who met in this house.

The *Three Crowned Needles* looks also like a tailor's sign, and from the evidence of a trades token of 1669 we know that it was the sign of a shop in Aldersgate. Hatton thinks that a similar sign may have given its name to Threadneedle St. (Three Needle St.). *Three Crowned Needles* was a charge in the Needlemakers' Company arms. The *Tailors of Brentford*, Cholsey, Berks., may refer to the trade, or may have reference to some ballad so far not traced.

Among agricultural signs, the *Plough* leads the van, sometimes accompanied by the legend ' Speed the Plough'. Among the many that might be noted are that at Sutton, Suff., and the one at Higham Sobrion, Beds. Of two inscriptions on the sign of the *Plough* that have come under observation, both contain sound advice. That of the *Plough* at Filey says :—

> He who by the Plough would thrive,
> Himself must either hold or drive.

whilst on the *Plough Inn*, Alnwick, the following is cut in stone :—

> That which your father old
> Hath purchased and left you to possess,
>   Do you dearly hold
> To shew your worthiness.   1717.

Generally, no doubt, the meaning of the sign is the obvious one. Occasionally, however, it may refer to the constellation rather than the implement.

There is an *Agricultural Inn* at Penrith, Cumb., the *Plough & Horses* is a sign at Branston, Lincs., and there is another at Garvis Brook, Tunbridge Wells. An odd combination is the *Plough & Sail* at Snape Bridge, Suff. There is a *Fen Plough* at Chatteris, I. of Ely. The *Plough & Harrow* is very common, as, for example, at Littleport, Cambs., an inn with a good wooden sign. Two doors west from the *Harrow Inn* lived Isaac Walton, about 1624, carrying on the business of ' milliner and sempster', or what we should now call a linen-draper. Goldsmith's tailor, who lived at the sign of the *Harrow*, has gained immortality by the bad taste of poor Goldy and Johnson's snub to him upon it. There is another *Harrow* at Langley, Bucks. The *Horse & Harrow* is at West Hagbourne, Berks., the *Horse & Dorsers* at Cirencester, the *Horse & Chains* (? a chain horse or a corruption of *Horse & Chaise*) at Bushey, Herts., and a *Cart & Horses* at Shalford, Essex.

Signs relating to several crops are dealt with under trees and plants (pp. 151-60). Another which may well be recorded here is *Hemp Sheaf* at Stradbroke, Suff.

Near Bagshot, Surrey, there is a public-house called the *Jolly Farmer*, a corruption of the *Golden Farmer*, a nickname obtained by William Davis, 1627-90. He was a former possessor of the house so nicknamed on account of his wealth, and his custom of paying his rent always in guineas. These—so says the legend—he obtained as a footpad on Bagshot Heath. That some such thing happened is evident from the

Weekly Journal of 1718, which alludes to 'Bagshot Heath near the Gibbet where the *Golden Farmer* hanged in chains'. There is another *Jolly Farmers* at Benges, Herts. There is a *Ploughboy* at Lincoln, the *Farmer's Boy* at Brickendon, Herts., and a *Market Gardener* at Barnes, Surrey.

The use of the word *Jolly* on the signboard, formerly common, is now gradually dying away. Apparently workmen no longer desire to be advertised as *Jolly*; it is vulgar, and they prefer *Arms*—hence such heraldic anomalies as the *Chaff-Cutters' Arms*, the *Farmers' Arms*, the *Flint Millers' Arms*, the *Graziers' Arms*, the *Puddlers' Arms*, the *Paviors' Arms*, and so forth. The point is dealt with above (p. 80). There is, however, a *Jolly Gardener* at Rochdale, a *Jolly Gardeners* at Sohan, Cambs., and *Jolly Dealers* at Rochland All Saints, Norf. North Staffordshire is full of *Jolly Potters*.

There is a *Shepherd* at Doddinghurst, Essex, and a *Shepherd & Shepherdess* in Aldenham St., N.W. The *Shepherd & Shepherdess* calls up pictures of rouged shepherdesses with jaunty straw hats on the top of powdered hair a foot high, short quilted petticoats and high-heeled boots, courted in madrigals by shepherds dressed in the height of the elegance of the New Exchange gallants, with ribboned crooks and flowered-satin waistcoats. This was the sign of an 18th-century pleasure resort in City Rd., Islington. Cakes, cream, and furmety were its great attractions to invalids, who went thither for the pure country air of Islington :—

> To the *Shepherd & Shepherdess* then they go
> To tea with their wives for a constant rule,
> And next cross the road to the *Fountain* also,
> And there they sit so pleasant and cool,
> And see in and out
> The folks walk about
> And gentlemen angling in Peerless Pool.

More business-like is the sign of the *Shepherd & Dog*, found, for example, at Foxhall, Suff., and Fulling, Sussex (a fine picture sign—he too wears *patches*, but not on his face). So with the *Shepherd & Crook*, found, for example, at Burwash, Sussex, the *Crook* to be seen at Tondover, and the *Crook & Shears* which Larwood gives, but which has not been noted. All these may be found in many villages, and refer to the farm-labourer, to whom the care of the flock is entrusted, and not to the elegant Corydon, Daphnis or Strephon.

The *Fleece* occurs at Richmond, Yorks., the *Fold Gate* at Stradsett, Norf., the *Hurdle* at Horningtoft, Norf., and the *Sheep Shearers* at Knebworth, Herts.

There is a *Yeoman* at Poole, Dorset, and a *Kentish Yeoman* at Tunbridge Wells. An unusual sign is the *Labourers' Union* at Burton-on-Trent.

The merry, thirsty time of haymaking is commemorated in the usual signs of a *Load of Hay* and the *Cross Scythes*. There is a *Load of Hay* tavern on Haverstock Hill, formerly a favourite place for Sunday afternoon excursionists in the summer time, and another in Paddington near the station. Many years ago the eccentricity of Davies the landlord was one of the attractions of the place. Later the house was rebuilt and became a suburban gin-palace. The *Mattock & Spade* formerly at Coventry (but which disappeared in the bombing of the city) and the *Spade & Becket*, refer to spade labour ; the first is very general, the second less so, but an example occurs at Little Downham, I. of Ely. The becket is an instrument used for digging peat. There is a *Spade & Sprocket* at Stonea, Cambs. The sprocket is also an implement used in the Fen country. The *Peat Spade*, Longstock, Hants, tells its own tale.

The *Dairy Maid* was in great favour with the London cheesemongers of the 17th century. Akermann gives a trades token of such a sign in Catherine St. in 1653, a specimen of the liberties the token engravers took with the king's English, the country Phillis being transformed into a ' Deary Made '. This does not seem to survive as an inn sign. There is, however, a *Village Maid* at Lound, Suff., and a *Country Girl* at Selly Oak, Birmingham.

The *Harvest Home* at Plymouth, and at Oakington, Cambs., recalls the pleasant time of congratulation and feasting. The *Harvest Man* is found at Amber Hill, Lincs.

There is a *Hay Cutters* at Oxted, Surrey, and a *Hay Field* at Mile End. *Market* inns are too numerous to note. *Cattle Market* inns are found in many places, for example at King's Lynn, and at Retford, Notts.

One of the misfortunes of the countryman is pictured in the *Cart Overthrown*, which *is* a public-house sign at Lower Edmonton, though how it came to be such is difficult to guess. The *Jolly Carter*, the *Cart & Horses*, and the *Dray & Horses*, occur occasionally, and the *Jolly Waggoner, Jolly Waggoners*, and the *Waggon & Horses* are quite common, as for example at Ewell, Surrey, Horsham, Surrey, and Ipswich respectively. The *Kentish Waggoners* is in the Borough, the *Waggon* at Wix, Essex.

The *Woodman* is another very common sign, almost invariably representing the same woodman copied from Thomas Barker's picture, and evidently suggested by Cowper's charming description of a winter's morning in the *Task*. There is a *Drovers* at Darlington, and the *Drover's Call*, for example, at Gainsborough, Lincs., is still seen on many roadsides, though the profession that gave rise to it is wellnigh extinct. The herds of steaming, fierce-looking oxen formerly driven from all parts of the kingdom along the main roads leading to London, there to be devoured, are now nearly all sent by rail. A yet older practice produced the sign of the *String of Horses*, which may still be seen in the North and in Lincolnshire and dates from times before mail coaches and stage waggons existed, when all the goods-traffic inland had to be performed by strings of packhorses, who carried large baskets, hampers, and bales slung across their backs, and slowly wound their way through the uninhabited tracts, moors and fens which lay between the small towns and straggling villages.

Many signs still recall those days : the *Coach & Six* may yet be seen in some places. There was one in Westminster, and there is still one at Bustall, W.R. Yorks. The names of the coaches were often adopted by inns on the road ; for instance, the *Balloon*, the *Bang-Up*, the *Defiance* at Ipswich (though this may be a ship name), the *Express* at New Bridge, the *Hero*, the *Mail*, the *Royal Express* at Burslem, Stoke-on-Trent, the *Royal Mail* at Taunton, the *Sovereign*, the *Tally Ho* (at Eastbourne, with a good modern sign), the *Telegraph* at Putney Heath. Shrewsbury has a *Rainbow*, a *Telegraph*, and a *Comet*, all apparently named after coaches. Alas ! the railway has often swept away the signs as well as the coaches. Since in many cases the coaches were named after prominent persons royal or otherwise, it is not always easy to determine whether an inn bearing a personal name acquired its title direct, or at second hand from a coach.

In London there were in Larwood's time fifty-two public-houses known as the *Coach & Horses*, exclusive of beer-houses, coffee-houses, and similar establishments. (There is a fine modern sign of this name in Bruton St., Mayfair.) Stow says in his *Summary* that in 1555, Walter Ripon made a coach for the Earl of Rutland ' which was the first that was ever used in England '. But in his larger *Chronicle* he says coaches were introduced in 1564 by Guilliam Boonen, a Dutchman. Taylor the Water Poet who, as a waterman of course bore a grudge to coaches said ' it is a doubtful question whether the devil brought *tobacco* into England in a *coach*, for both appeared at the same time '. How common they became in a short time appears from all the satirists of that period ; not only the nobility, but even the citizens could no longer do without them, after they were once introduced. Not forty years after their first appearance Pierce Pennyless, speaking of merchants' wives, says : ' She will not go unto the field to cure on the green grasse, but she must have a coach for her convoy.' No wonder then that according to the *Coach & Sedan*, a pamphlet of 1636, there were then in London, the suburbs, and four miles compass without, coaches to the number of 6,000 odd. These were nearly all private carriages. Hackney coaches were established in 1625 by Captain Bailey. Their first stand was at the *Maypole* in the Strand. They numbered about twenty, and were attached to the principal inns. In 1636, the number of hackney coaches was confined to 50 ; in 1652, to 200 ; in 1654, to 300 ; in 1662, to 400 ; in 1694, to 700 ; in 1710, to 800 ; in 1771, to 1,000 ; in 1802, 1,100 ; but in 1833 all limitation of number ceased. The modern taxi is, of course, still legally recognized as a ' hackney carriage '.

At the *Coach & Horses*, Bartholomew Close, still remain some vestiges of the ancient buildings of St. Bartholomew's Hospital and Convent, viz., a clustered column in the beer cellar, walls of immense thickness, and an early English window in the taproom, etc. This building occupies the site of the north cloister. Another *Coach & Horses* in Ray St., Clerkenwell, is also built on classic ground, for it occupies the site of the once famous Hockley-in-the-Hole of bear-baiting memory. The sign once showed the lion attacking the mail at *Winterslow Hut* near Salisbury. This has lately been removed by Messrs. Whitbread, who own the house. An alehouse keeper in Oswestry travestied the *Coach & Horses* sign into the *Coach & Dogs*. There is a *Mail Coach* in Camomile St., W., with a good modern pictorial sign. The house was a coaching station, and adopted its name on this account. The *Phantom Coach* is at Coventry.

The *Wheel*, an object sometimes seen on signboards, may have been derived from the *Catherine Wheel* (the name of a favourite old coaching inn in Bishopsgate St.) or from the *Wheel of Fortune*. There is a *Wheel* at Ely, and a *Catherine Wheel* at Henley-on-Thames. The *Saddle* and the *Spur* are both very general on roadside inns, owing to the ancient mode of travelling on horseback. There is an interesting *Saddle* in—of all unlikely places—Blackpool. The *Whip* occurs at Briggate, Leeds.

In Norwich there is a curious combination, the *Whip & Egg*, which existed in that locality as early as the year 1750, and which is enumerated in London, under the name of the *Whip & Eggshell*, amongst the taverns in a black letter ballad, whilst a still earlier mention occurs in *Mother Bunch's Merriment* (1604). It has been explained as a corruption of the *Whip & Nag*, but the combination of these two would be so obvious that a corruption would scarcely be possible. The sign of the Norwich house has now been corrupted into *Whip & Nag*. In a ballad on the frost in 1685, when the Thames was frozen over, there are lines referring to the *Flying P——— Pot*, the *Whip & Eggshell*, and the *Broom*, so the sign is a fairly old one. The *Whip & Egg* therefore figures on the ice, and may have been brought together from the *whipping of eggs*, in making egg-punch, egg-flip, and similar beverages, much drunk on the ice in Holland. There were always crowds of Dutchmen on the ice, whenever the river was frozen over and they may have introduced their favourite drink and its sign. So at least argues Larwood, but the conclusion seems rather strained.

The *Three Jolly Butchers* used to be seen in the neighbourhood of markets and shambles, either in allusion to the three merry north-country butchers who according to the ballad killed nine highwaymen, or simply the favourite combination of three which is of frequent occurrence in heraldry and in folklore as well as in inn-sign nomenclature. The sign may be seen at Wood Green, N. 22. The *Cleaver* found at Darlington seems also to be in compliment to the trade as well as the *Marrowbones & Cleaver*. This last was in Larwood's time a sign in Fetter Lane, originating from a custom even then rapidly dying away, of the butcher boys serenading newly married couples with these professional instruments. Formerly, the band would consist of four or eight cleavers, each of a different tone, and by beating their marrowbones skilfully against these the performers obtained a sort of music somewhat after the fashion of indifferent bell-ringing. A largesse of half-a-crown or a crown was generally expected for this delicate attention. The butchers of Clare Market had the reputation of being the best performers. The last public appearance of this popular music is said to have been in 1863 at the marriage of the Prince of Wales, later Edward VII, when small bands of butchers perambulated the town playing 'God Save the Queen'. This music was once so common that Tom Killigrew called bones and cleavers the national instrument of England.

As the use of coaches gave rise to the sign of the *Coach & Horses*, so the sedan produced some signs, as the *Sedan Chair*, Broad Quay, Bristol and North Scarle, near Newark; the *Two Chairmen*, Warwick St. and Dartmouth. The *Three Chairs*, which has long since disappeared, was in the 17th century a famous tavern in the Little Piazza, Covent Garden. The *Sedan*, says Randle Holme, ' is a thing in which sick and crazy persons are carried abroad, which is borne up by the staves by two lusty men'. The first sedan chair used in England is said to have been one that the Duke of Buckingham had received as a gift from Charles I when Prince of Wales, on his return in 1623 from his romantic expedition to Spain. The use of it got the Duke into trouble, and he was accused of ' degrading Englishmen into slaves and beasts of burden'. According to another account, a Sir Saunders Duncombe introduced sedan chairs in 1634, when he procured a patent which vested in him and his heirs the sole right of carrying persons up and down in them for a certain time. Sir Saunders hereupon had forty or fifty sedans made, and sent them about town. Differences soon arose between the chairmen and coachmen. Pamphlets were written, ballads were sung on the occasion, and the public sided with one or the other, according to individual taste. Defoe in 1702 says, ' We are carried to these places (coffee-houses) in chairs, which are very cheap—a guinea a week, or a shilling per hour—and your chairmen serve you for porters to run on errands, as your gondoliers do at Venice.' The chairman of the aristocracy wore gaudy liveries and plumed hats, and their chairs were richly gilt and painted, and provided with velvet cushions. They used to be kept in the halls of their large mansions. We may infer from Gay's *Trivia* that the men were an insolent set of fellows :—

> Let not the chairman with assuming stride
> Press near the wall and rudely thrust thy side,
> The laws have set him bounds ; his servile feet .
> Should ne'er encroach where posts defend the street.
> Yet, who the footman's arrogance can quell,
> Whose flambeau gilds the sashes of Pall Mall,
> When in long rank a train of torches flame,
> To light the midnight visits of the same.

The extinguishers here referred to, used by link boys for putting out their torches when the chair had arrived at its destination, are still to be seen attached to the area railings of many of the houses in Grosvenor and St. James's Squares and other parts of the town fashionably inhabited at that period.

Another creature of this class, now completely extinct, was the *Running Footman*. There is one sign of him left in Charles St., Berkeley Square, representing a running man in gaudy attire with a long cane in his hand, and under it ' I am the only Running Footman'. It is said that the original sign is now in the bar parlour of a modern public-house in Maida Vale. The Running Footman was a class of servant used by the great in former days to run before the carriage to clear the way, to bear the torch at night, to pay turnpikes, but he served also to add to their pomp. Generally the livery was very rich, somewhat of the jockey fashion, with a silk sash round the waist. Sometimes instead of breeches he wore a sort of silk petticoat with a deep gold fringe. He carried a long stick with a silver head which has now descended to his successor the footman. The Duke of Queensberry, the notorious Old Q who died in 1810, was one of the last noblemen who kept running footmen. Whenever his grace wanted to engage one it was his custom to make the applicant put on his livery and run up and down Piccadilly, while he from his balcony watched his paces. It happened on a time that after one of those fellows had gone through all his evolutions and presented himself under the balcony, the Duke said ' That will do, you will suit me very well.' ' And so your livery does me ' was the answer, and off went the footman, running like a deer, and was never heard of afterwards. One of them ran for a wager to Windsor against the Duke of Marlborough in a phaeton with four horses, and lost only by a short distance, but it cost him his life, for he died very soon afterwards. Most of these running footmen were Irish, hence Dekker says : ' The Devil's footman was very nimble on his heeles, for no wild Irishman could outrunne him,' and Brathwaite has ' For see those thin-breech'd Irish lackies run.' St Patrick's Day was generally given to them as a holiday, which they invariably celebrated by purging themselves. In various country places the sign of the *Running Footman* has been corrupted into the *Running Man*.

Other signs dealing with transport of various kinds are the coach and canal signs dealt with elsewhere, the numerous railway signs, and in recent years such happy selections as the *Belisha Beacon* at Rainham, Kent, the *Bristol Bulldog* at Filton, Bristol, the *Canopus* (from the famous flying boat) at Rochester, the *Comet* (from another famous aeroplane) at Hatfield, Herts. (with a fine unusual modern sign by Eric Kennington), and the *Happy Landings* at Knowle, Bristol.

Another ' domestic ' sign is the *Trusty Servant* to be seen at Winchester College, and at Minstead, Hants. He has a pig's snout since he is not ' nice in diet ', a padlocked mouth so that he may not tell his master's secrets, an ass's ears (to show his patience), and a stag's feet for swiftness in doing his errands.

> A trusty servant's portrait would you see,
> This emblematic figure well survey ;
> The porkers snout not nice in diet shows,
> The padlock shut, no secret he'll disclose,
> Patient the ass his master's rage will bear,
> Swiftness in errand the stag's feet declare.
> Loaden his left hand apt to labour saith,
> The vest his neatness : open hand his faith.
> Girt with his sword, his shield upon his arm,
> Himself and master he'll protect from harm.

The origin of this sign is a picture on the wall of one of the rooms near the kitchen of Winchester College, where it is accompanied by the above verses in English and Latin.

There was formerly a *Stave Porter*, Dockhead, London, there is still a *Ticket Porter*, Arthur St., E.C. The *Porter's Lodge* was at Leicester, and there was a *Porter & Gentleman* in Larwood's time in three different places in London, but no example seems to have survived.

Blue Cap, the famous hound in 1763, gives his name to a sign at Sandiway, Ches., and (as the *Blue Cap Dog*) at Crewe. Among the Hunts mentioned are :—the *Bedale*

Hunt (Howe, N.R. Yorks.), the *Bramhill Hunt* at Arborfield, Berks., the *Brocklesby Hunt* at Goxhill, Lincs., the *Hampshire Hunt* at Cheriton, Hants, the *Old Berkeley Hunt* at Watford, Herts., the *Royal Hunt* at Ascot, the *Thornton Hunt* at Thornton Curtis, Lincs., and the *Surrey Hounds* at St John's Hill, London. There was formerly a *Chase* at Leamington. The *Tally Ho* is at Mettingham, Suff., and there is another house of this name at Trumpington, Norf., and a *Huntsman's Call* at Worcester Park. The *Huntsman* is a house with a good painted sign at Rochester, and there is a *Huntsman & Hounds* at Spexhall, Suff., and another at Walworth. The *Fox & Hounds* with a good gallows and pictorial sign is at Barley, Herts. Another instance of this sign is noted above ★ and still another is elsewhere.† The *Dog & Fox* is to be seen at Wimbledon. *Hark to Bounty* is at Slaidburn, N.R. Yorks., *Hark to Dandler* at Walmersley, Lancs., *Hark to Jowler* at Bury, Lancs., and *Hark to Lasher* at Edale, Derbys. This last sign is said by Mr. Monson Fitzjohn to refer to the surf on the Chinese coast, and he gives a very circumstantial account how the name came to be applied to this particular house. The more obvious derivation seems however much the likelier. *Hark up to Glory* was formerly at Rochdale, and *Hark to Melody* at Haverthwaite, Lancs. *Hark to Mopsey* is at Normanton, W.R. Yorks., and *Hark to Nudger* at Dobcross, Lancs. Larwood notes it as surprising that the *Brush* or *Foxe's Tail* is so rare as a sign, especially considering how many other hunting signs there are and the fact that the *Foxe's Tail* was one of the badges of the House of Lancaster. There is at least one occurrence of this sign, at Hopsley, Hants. The *Blue Fox* at Gunby, Lincs., is said to represent the electoral colours of the (Tollemache) Earls of Dysart, who purchased the manor in 1834. It is comparable with the curious 'blue' signs of Grantham, eight or nine miles away, described on p. 127.

The *Stag & Hounds* is at Bristol, the *Stag & Hunters* at Brendon, Devon, the *Queen's Staghounds* at Ascot. The *Hare & Hounds* is at Sheen, and the sign is generally quite common. The *Hare & Cats* at Norwich appears to be a travesty of it. An unusual sign is the *Hounds & Hare* at Loweswater, Cumb. The *Merry Harriers* is at Cowbeech, Suss., and there is another example of the sign at Cullompton, Devon. The *Holcombe Harriers* is at Tottington, Lancs. The *Greyhound* is, of course, very common, and is probably as often with reference to coursing as relating to heraldry. The *Greyhound* at Shrewsbury, now no more, is recorded from 1780 as the *Mason's Arms*. The sign was changed in the 1870's and the board depicted Master McGarth, winner of the Waterloo Cup in 1868, 1869, and 1871. Master McGarth was Lord Lurgan's famous hound, presented at Court by Queen Victoria's special request in 1871.

In Cambridge there is a sign of the *Birdbolt*, an implement formerly used to shoot birds. It appears to be a sign of some antiquity. In Nightingale Lane, East Smithfield, there was once an *Experienced Fowler*, now extinct : at Oldham and Rochdale there is a satirical sign, that of the *Trap*. The *Angler* is common enough in the neighbourhood of trout streams and other fishing resorts. There is an *Angler's* at Teddington.

Many professions are only represented by one or two objects relating to them.

★ P. 108.   † P. 109.

The *Tallow Chandler*, very common among the trades tokens, was always represented by a man dipping candles.

The *Scales* is a common sign referring to various trades : one of the engraved bill-heads in the Bagford Collection gives the *Hand & Scales*, viz. a hand holding a pair of scales. The *Spinning Wheel* was formerly much more common than now ; there is still a public-house with this sign at Hamsterley, near Darlington. The *Woolsack* was originally a wool-merchant's sign ; it is often accompanied by the *Black Boy*. Machyn mentions this sign ' the Volsake with-out Algatt ' in 1555. It seems to have been one of the leading taverns in Ben Jonson's time. He often alludes to it in his plays.* Like the *Dagger*, it was famous for its pies.

In the year 1682 the *Woolsack* in Newgate Market attracted great attention, owing to a wonderful phenomenon :

> An elm-board being touched with a hot iron, doth express itself, as if it was a man dying, with grones and trembling, to the great admiration of all the hearers.

Soon numerous other London taverns claimed public attention for similar wonders. The mantelpiece at the *Bowman Tavern*, Drury Lane, expressed its aversion of a red-hot poker as unequivocally as the elm-board at the *Woolsack*, and the dresser at the *Queen's Arms* in St Martin's Lane was evidently a chip of the same block. Indeed, boards were cauterized and groaned all over London.

The *Block* was a hatter's or Beaver Cutter's sign, the block being the mould on which the hat is formed. Beatrice refers to it in *Much Ado about Nothing* and Dekker, in the *Gull's Hornbook*. A similar performance is recorded at the *Chequers*, Oxford. This sign survives as that of a house in Shepherdess Walk, N.

The *Postboy* was the sign of a fishmonger's shop in Sherborne Lane in 1759. There is a *Jolly Postboy* at Cowley, Oxford. The *Up & Down Post* used to be a thriving inn on the highway between Birmingham and Coventry. The picture represented an erect and a prostrate pillar, either as a rebus or from a misunderstanding. Before the mail coaches were instituted the equestrian letter-carriers of the *up and down mail* used to meet at this house, exchange their bags and each return whence he came, thus effecting a considerable saving of time and trouble. Even washerwomen have been exalted to the signboard, for in Norwich there was the sign of the *Three Washerwomen* in 1750. The *Flat Iron* found in Liverpool and elsewhere is not a companion sign, but owes its origin to the position of the house, at a corner site where two roads intersected at a rather acute angle.

A few other signs remain, which cannot, strictly speaking, be called those of professions, yet are they—or at least they were—means of making a living, as the *Three Morris Dancers*, once a very common sign, but now, like the custom that gave rise to it, almost extinct. There is one still left, however, at Scarisbrook, Lancs., and in a few villages a remnant of the dance is also kept up on certain occasions. For details concerning morris dances and morris dancers, and the curious fashion in which the custom survived in London until relatively recent years in the May Day dance of

* For example, *The Devil is an Ass*, Act I, Sc. i ; *The Alchymyst*, Act V. Sc. 2.

the chimney sweeps with their Jack-in-the-Green, the reader is referred to any reputable work on folk dancing or on folk-lore generally.

In treating of games, we may advert to a rendering of the *Flying Horse* mentioned above (p. 52). Besides the mythological or heraldic origins there was another reason which sometimes prompted the choice of this sign. It was the name of a popular amusement, which consisted in a swing, the seat of which formed a wooden horse. This the ambitious youth mounted, and as he was swinging to and fro he had to take with a sword the ring off a quintain. If he succeeded, his adroitness was rewarded either with a number of swings gratis, or an allowance of beer. Such a *Flying Horse* served for a sign to an alehouse in Moorfields in the time of Queen Anne and there is still a house of this sign in that area. Swings, roundabouts, and such-like amusements were in those days the usual appendages of suburban alehouses, and to a very limited extent came down to Larwood's time. Lately several brewers have installed similar amusements in children's corners of the gardens of wayside hostelries, and probably many others would have done so but for opposition from some benches of licensing justices. These seem determined to put every possible hindrance in the way of the improvement of public-houses in the (quite vain) hope that by so doing they will be able all the more easily to abolish them.

Oil and colour shops generally, and some public-houses—mostly near theatres—adopt the sign of the *Harlequin*. One of the most noted amongst the latter was kept in the beginning of the 19th century in Drury Lane, by the eccentric John Richardson, the 'Prince of Showmen', as he called himself. In this tavern he saved some money, which enabled him to fit up a travelling theatre, by which he realized so much that when he died in 1836, he left £20,000. It used to be one of his boasts that he had brought out Edmund Kean, and several other eminent actors. He desired in his will to be buried at Marlow, Bucks. (where he was born in the workhouse), in the same grave with the 'Spotted Boy', a natural phenomenon which had been one of his luckiest hits, and brought him a considerable amount of money. A *Harlequin* sign is to be seen at the present day at Arlington Way, E.C.

For the sign of the *Green Man* there is a twofold explanation. The first is that it represents the green, wild, or wood men of the shows and pageants, such as described by Machyn in his *Diary* on Lord Mayor's Day, 1553, and in the account of the festivities when Queen Elizabeth was at Kenilworth Castle in 1575. Besides wielding sticks with crackers in pageants, these green men sometimes fought with each other, attacked castles and dragons, and were altogether a very popular character with the public. One of their duties seems to have been to clear the way for processions.

There is a good painted *Green Man* sign at Leytonstone. The *Wild Man* formerly on a sign at Quarry Hill, Ladybridge, Leeds, is the same as the *Green Man*. There is another *Wild Man* at Streethouses, N.R. Yorks., with a good sign which was shown at the inn sign exhibition of 1936. A pleasing story says that once when Queen Victoria was passing by the house the sign was veiled with a cloth, so that it should not shock her. A *Wild Man* at Norwich is said to commemorate Peter, the Wild

Boy of Herrenhausen, ? 1713. He is said to have been incarcerated for a time in Norwich Bridewell.

The second version of this sign is that it is intended for a forester, a verderer or ranger, and in that garb the Green Man is now almost invariably represented. There is however a good *Green Man* showing the likely origin of the name in the Jack-in-the-Green over a well-known house at 6–9 Bucklersbury. Even as far back as the 17th century it is evident from the trades tokens that the *Green Man* was generally a forester. Often he was Robin Hood himself, as may be inferred from the small figure frequently introduced beside him, and meant for Little John. The ballads and Michael Drayton in *Polyolbion* always describe Robin and his men as dressed in green—Lincoln green, or occasionally Kendal green. Green was, in fact, the ordinary dress of foresters and woodmen, and is referred to as such in the *Faery Queene*. It is unlikely in the extreme that as said by Monson Fitzjohn that ' a *Green Man* in the south of England' represents a Mohammedan who by his pilgrimage to Mecca has earned the right to wear the coveted green turban.

One of the most noted *Green Man* taverns was that on Stroud Green, Islington, formerly the residence of Sir Thomas Stapleton, of Gray's Court, Bart., whose initials, with those of his wife, and the date 1609, were to be seen on the façade. It was one of the suburban retreats frequented by the fashion in the days of Charles I, when it had been converted into a tavern. Two centuries ago the sign bore the following inscription :—

> Ye are wellcome all
> To Stapleton Hall.

A club used to meet annually at this place, the members styling themselves the Lord Mayor, Aldermen, and Corporation of Stroud Green. At Dulwich in the reign of George II, there was another *Green Man*, a place of amusement for the Londoners during the summer season ; it is enumerated, with other similar resorts, in this stanza from a ballad of 1745 :—

> That Vauxhall and Ruckholt and Ranelagh too,
> And Hoxton and Sadlers both Old and New,
> My Lord Cobham's Head and the Dulwich Green Man
> May make as much passtime as ever they can.
> > Derry Down, etc.

Ruckholt was a reputed mansion of Queen Elizabeth, at Leyton, in Essex. Being opened to the public in 1742 it became a fashionable summer drive during a couple of seasons : public breakfasts, weekly concerts, and occasional oratorios were numbered amongst its attractions. The house was pulled down in 1745. Old and New Sadlers Wells relates to the well-known place in Islington, at that period a music house. *Lord Cobham's Head* has been noticed on p. 62. The *Green Man*, 308 Edgware Rd., has a medicinal spring in its cellars and to this day customers desiring it are entitled to a phial of ' eye lotion' gratis. The *Coldbath* at Hereford apparently has no bath, but is named from a London house of this sign in Coldbath Fields.

To descend a little lower in the social scale of callings and professions, at Oswald-twistle, Accrington, we meet with the *Tinker's Budget*.   The budget is the tinker's bag of instruments ; we see the word thus used in Randle Holme :—' A Tinker with his *budget* on his back, having always in his mouth this merry cry :—" Have you any work for a Tinker ? " '   And Shakespeare in the *Winter's Tale* refers to the tinker with the sowskin budget.   *Tom of Bedlam* appears on signboards at Balsall, Warws., and at Redbourne, Herts. (?).   No doubt he was formerly not an uncommon sign, since he was such a favourite in ballads ; the *Merry Tom*, at Kirkcumbeck, Cumb., evidently refers to the same individual.   Notwithstanding all the fantastic ballads referring to Tom, he was but a sorry rogue.   Randle Holme has :—

> The Sow gelder and Tom of Bedlam are both wandering knaves alike, and such as are seldom or never out of their way, having their home in any place.   Tom of Bedlam is in the same garb as the Sow gelder, with a long staff, and a Cow or Ox Horn by his side, but his cloathing is more fantastic or ridiculous, for being a mad man he is madly decked all over with Rubins, Feathers, cuttings of cloth, and what not ; to make him seem a madman or one distracted, which he is no other but a dissembling knave.

The *Canting Academy*, 1674, gives him a similar attire and character.   Aubrey says much the same in his *Remains of Judaisme and Gentilisme*.

Tom's female counterpart was *Bess of Bedlam* which was formerly seen as a sign in Oak St., Norwich.   Bess was an old companion of poor Tom, for in *King Lear* Tom sings a snatch of a song with the words ' Come over the bourn, Bessy, to me ', and in the jollities of Plough Monday the fool and Bessy are two of the principal personages. There is a very unfavourable parallel between the Ladies and Besses of Bedlam in the *Muse's Recreation*, 1656, entitled :—' Upon the naked Bedlams and spotted Beasts we see in Covent Garden ', beginning :—

> When Besse ! she ne're was half so vainly clad,
> Besse ne're was half so naked, half so mad ;
> Again, this raves with lust, for love Besse ranted,
> Then Bess's skin is tanned—this is painted.

A third class of beggars called *Mumpers* is also found on the signboard under the name of the *Three Mumpers*.   After descending through all ranks of society we arrive at the great leveller Death, who also was represented on the signboard.   There was the *Three Death's Heads* in Wapping, of which house trades tokens are extant ; probably it was an apothecary's though as Larwood suggests the sign was a ghastly one for his customers.   Undertakers were strictly professional in their choice.   In the early 18th century, according to the advertisements in the original edition of the *Spectator*, No. CLXXXVI, there were *Four Coffins* over against Somerset House, and another in Fleet Street.

Another undertaker, James Maddox, clerk and coffin-maker of St Olave's, had for a sign the *Sugar-loaf & Three Coffins*.   The addition of the sugar-loaf had, of course, nothing to do with his profession.   It was simply the sign of a former tenant, suspended in front or fixed in the wall of the house.

Chapter XIII

THE HOUSE AND THE TABLE

INSTEAD of carved or painted signs hung above the doors, many shop and tavern keepers preferred to designate their houses after some external feature, such as the colour of the building—thus we find the *Red House*, the *White House*, the *Blue House*, etc. Others painted their doorposts a particular colour, whence the origin of the well-known *Blue Posts* of which there are one or two in West London, and one (? an imitation of these) in Portsmouth. In still older times painted posts or poles in front of the houses seem occasionally to have served as signs; Caxton's Reed Pale (Red Pole) seems to refer to some such distinction. Even in the 17th century such a distinction was still occasionally used, as with the *Green Pales* in Peter St., Westminster. Stukeley speaks of Mr. Brown's garden at the *Green Poles*, where was dug up an urn lined with lead and filled with earth and bones. In Sir George Etherege's play *She Would if she Could*, 1667,* the *Black Posts* in James St. are named. There are still seven *Blue Posts* in London, five of them in the West End. It seems likely that the origin of these signs is that given above, although it is suggested that perhaps some such houses may have been called from postboys' blue jackets. Provincial houses of this sign are generally called after the metropolitan ones. There is a *Red Post* at Peasedown St John, Som., and a *White Posts* in the Forest to the north of Nottingham. The newspapers in the beginning of the 18th century contain advertisements stating that the mineral water from Hampstead Wells might be obtained, at the rate of 3*d.* a flask, from the lessee of the wells, who lived at the *Black Posts* in King St., Guildhall.

A *Gate* inn such as may be seen at Dudley and at Hull was often so called from its proximity to a church lychgate or a toll gate, and in one case at any rate from its nearness to a prison gate. The sign is usually that of a five-barred gate with some such ditty under it as that of the *Gate Hangs Well* at Lyston :—

> The gate hangs well and hinders none,
> Drink hearty boys and travel on.

The roof and walls of a house are often referred to indirectly in such signs as the *Brick & Tile* at Retford, Notts. More primitive methods of roof covering are indicated in the *Sedge Sheaf* at Burnt Fen, Suff.

Garden-houses or summer-houses were also used as signs, as appears from a trades token ' at the garden-house in Blackfriars ', and also from a newspaper advertisement of 1679, where the garden-house in King St., St Giles, is mentioned. Frequent allusions to these garden-houses are found in old plays; they are severely attacked by Stubbs in his *Anatomy of Abuses*, that is as places ' wherein they may, and doubtless do, many of

---

* Act I, Sc. I.

them, play the filthy persons '. They are mentioned in the non-canonical Shakesperean play, *The London Prodigal*, 1604, and in Massinger's *Bondsman*,⋆ 1624, and *City Madam*, 1658. There is a *Garden House* at Hales, Norf.

The *Well & Bucket* is a sign in Bethnal Green Rd., not badly chosen, as it intimates an inexhaustible supply. It is of very old standing in London for it is mentioned in the *Paston Letters* in the year 1472 as the *Well with Two Buckets*, the sign of a grocer who sold goss hawks and soar hawks.

In old times the alehouse windows were generally open, so that the company within might enjoy the fresh air, and see all that was going on in the street ; but a trellis was sometimes put up in the open window. This trellis or lattice, was generally painted red. Thus Pistol says :—

> He called me even now by word through a red lattice, and I could see no part of his face from the window.

So common was this fixture that no alehouse was without it : according to Dekker's *English Villanies, Seven Times Pressed to Death*

> A whole street is in some places but a continuous alehouse, not a shop to be seen between red lattice and red lattice.

At last it became synonymous with alehouse :—

> Trusty Rachel was drinking burnt brandy with a couple of tinder-box cryers at the next red lattice.†

The lattices continued in use until the beginning of the 18th century, and after they disappeared from the windows were adopted as signs, and as such they continue to the present day. The *Green Lattice* occurs on a trades token of Cock Lane, and in Larwood's time figured at the door of an alehouse in Billingsgate, now extinct, whilst a century or so ago there was one in Brownlow St., Holborn, which had been corrupted into the *Green Lettuce*. The *Green Lettuce* sign still survives at King's Lynn.

When balconies were newly introduced, they were also used in the place of signs. Lord Arundel was the inventor of them, and Covent Garden the first place where they became general. ' Every house here has one of 'em,' says Richard Broome, in 1659. Trades tokens 'of the *Bellconey*' in Bedford St., are still extant, and also tokens of 'John Williams, the king's chairman, at yᵉ lower end of St Martin's Lane, at yᵉ Balconey, 1667 '. The first house that adopted a balcony was situated at the corner of Chandos St. 'which country people were wont much to gaze on ' ; soon, however, they became so common that further distinctions had to be added, as the *Iron Balcony* (St James's St., 1699), the *Blue & Gilt Balcony* (Hatton St., 1673). Lamps have also, for two or three centuries, frequently done duty as signs, and still occasionally act as beacons to those who want the assistance of the doctor, the chemist, or (in Larwood's time) the sweep.

⋆ Act I, Sc. III. † Tom Brown's *Works*, Vol. III, p. 243.

Ale- and coffee-houses a century ago were frequently decorated with gorgeous lamps : this was already the custom in Tom Brown's time :—

> Every coffee-house is illuminated both without and within doors ; without by a *fine glass Lanthorn*, and within by a woman so light and splendid you may see through her without the help of a Perspective.

The quacks in Moorfields had always lamps at their doors at night, with round glasses having the same colours as the balls in their signs, and this custom was passed down to Victorian days by the chemists, who had circular red, green or yellow bull's-eye glasses in their lamps.

The *Brass Knocker* in the Great Gardens, Bristol, is another sign taken from the exterior of the house, so is the *Flower-Pot*, which was very common in old London. One of the last remaining stood at the corner of Bishopsgate St. and Leadenhall St. It dated from an early period, and was, in the heyday of its fame, a celebrated coaching inn. The introduction of railroads, however, gave it a death-blow ; for some time it continued to languish as a starting-point for omnibuses, and was finally demolished to make room for merchants' offices in 1863. Trades tokens of this inn are extant in the Beaufoy Collection. Burn, the compiler of the catalogue, suggested that the *Flower-Pot* was originally the vase of lilies, always represented in the old pictures of the Salutation or Annunciation. The Angel and the Virgin had been omitted and nothing but the vase left. The theory elaborated by later writers suggests that the figures of the *Virgin* and the *Angel* were omitted for the sake of economy, or sometimes that they were obliterated by the Puritans from notions of religious bigotry, so that only the Flower-Pot remained. This, however, seems somewhat improbable. There is no apparent reason why it should not have been a real flower-pot, or rather vase, which our ancestors frequently had on the top of the pent-houses above their shops. In order to distinguish them from ordinary flower-pots some painted theirs blue, hence the sign of the *Blue Flower-Pot* as appears from the advertisement of Cornelius a Tilborgh, who styles himself ' sworn chirurgeon in ordinary to King Charles II, to our late sovereign King William, as also to her present majesty Queen Anne '. This worthy lived in Great Lincoln's Inn Fields, Holborn Row, and besides the *Blue Flower-pot* at his front door, his customers might recognize the house, by ' a light at night over the door ', and a *Blue Ball* at the back-door. There is still a *Flower Pot* at Stowmarket, Suff. The *Two Blue Flower Pots* used to be a sign in Dean St., Soho ; and the *Two Flower-Pots & Sun Dial* in 1700 was in Parker's Lane, near Drury Lane. The *Blue Pot* still survives at Boston.

Innumerable objects from the interior of the house were likewise adopted as signs. The upholsterers, for instance, generally selected pieces of furniture. At the end of the last century the *Royal Bed* was a great favourite. The *Board* or *Table* is still a great favourite in the north—in Durham alone at least sixty public-houses with that sign could be named. According to Monson Fitzjohn, there were in 1838, 280 *Boards* in the (six ?) northern counties alone. The *Board* is not to be confused with *A' Board*, which in Cumberland and presumably elsewhere means 'to board intoxicating liquor'. Probably many of these *Boards* were originally *A'Boards*. Others again seem to be a (blank sign) board—the mark of a house having no proper sign of its own.

The *Salt Horn* * at Bradford and Leeds, and the *Saltbox*, at Hatton, Derbys., may be domestic in origin or may possibly be 'musical'. The Saltbox was a musical instrument of a sort—it was beaten like a drum, a rolling-pin being used as drumstick.

In Dudley we find a very substantial and tempting *Round of Beef* with the following rhymes :—

> If you are hungry or a-dry,
> Or your stomach out of order,
> There's sure relief at the *Round of Beef*,
> For both these two disorders.

There was a *Baron of Beef* formerly at Cambridge, the *Round of Beef* at Ely, and the *Ribs of Beef* at Norwich, which has now been re-named the *Fye Bridge Tavern*. The *Flank of Beef* was at Spalding, the much less tempting *Cow Roast* at Hampstead, and there is one at Tring, Herts., besides a couple of unpretending *Beef-Steaks* at Bath. There is a *Shoulder of Mutton* at Kirkby Malzeard, W.R. Yorks, and another at Old Newton, Suff., and there was at Hackney in the 18th century *The Shoulder of Mutton & Cat*, now known as the *Cat & Mutton*, which had the following rhyme :—

> Pray Puss, don't tear,
> For the Mutton is so dear ;
> Pray Puss, don't claw,
> For the Mutton yet is raw.

On the sign a terrier was in close pursuit of the thieving cat. It is sometimes supposed that the sign was a warning to dishonest customers. It was there in Larwood's time, but the verses were gone. This sign suggested to another innkeeper on the common at Horsham the sign of the *Dog & Bacon*. An epicurean publican at Yapton, Arundel, had a more gastronomic combination, viz. the *Shoulder of Mutton & Cucumbers*. It was at the *Shoulder of Mutton* in Brecknock that Mrs. Siddons, England's greatest tragic actress, was born, 14 July 1755. *Legs of Mutton* on the signboard do not appear to be so common as Shoulders. There is a *Leg of Mutton & Cauliflower* at Ashtead, Surrey (p. 243). The *Rump & Dozen* formerly at Norwich is said to refer to a rump of beef and a dozen of claret. But by far the finest of all dishes represented on the signboard was the *Boar's Head* as in Eastcheap. The first mention of this inn occurs in the reign of Richard II, in the testament of William Warden, who gave ' all that tenement called the *Boar's Head* in Eastcheap ' to a college of priests, or chaplains, founded by Sir W. Walworth, the Lord Mayor, in the adjoining church of St Michael, Crooked Lane. The presence of Prince Hal in this house was not entirely an invention of Shakespeare. No wonder, then, at the proud inscription on the sign, which still existed in Maitland's

---

* This is the salt horn which formerly at dinner marked the line of demarcation ; for whether a guest was to be placed above or below the salt was a matter of etiquette strictly to be attended to.

time :—*This is the chief tavern in London*.   At one time the portal was decorated with carved oak figures of Falstaff and Prince Henry.   In 1834 the former was in the possession of a brazier of Eastcheap, whose ancestors had lived since the Great Fire in the shop he then occupied.   The last great Shakesperean dinner-party at the *Boar's Head* took place about 1784, on which occasion Wilberforce and Pitt were present.

On the removal of a mound of rubbish at Whitechapel brought there after the Great Fire a carved box-wood bas-relief boar's head was found, set in a circular frame formed by two boar's tusks, mounted and united with silver.   An inscription was pricked in the back :—' Wm. Brooke, Landlord of the Bore's Hedde, Estchepe, 1566 '. This object, formerly in the possession of Stamford, the publisher, was sold at Christie and Manson's on 27 January 1855.

The original inn having been destroyed by the fire was rebuilt and continued in existence until 1831, when it was finally demolished to make way for the streets leading to new London Bridge.   Its site was between Small Alley and St Michael's Lane.   The ancient sign, carved in stone, with the initials I.T. and the date 1668 is now preserved in the Guildhall Museum.   The *Boar's Head* had many associations other than its Shakesperean ones.

In the month of May 1718, one James Austin, ' inventor of the Persian ink powder ', desiring to give his customers a substantial proof of his gratitude, invited them to the *Boar's Head* to partake of an immense plum-pudding, of 1,000 lbs., a baked pudding of a foot square, and the best piece of an ox roasted.   The principal dish was put in the copper on Monday May 12, at the *Red Lion* inn by the Mint in Southwark, and had to boil fourteen days.   From there it was to be brought to the *Swan Tavern*, in Fish St. Hill, accompanied by a band of music playing *What lumps of pudding my mother gave me*.   One of the instruments was a drum in proportion to the pudding, being 18 feet 2 inches in length, and 4 feet diameter, which was drawn by ' a device fixt on six asses '.   Finally the monstrous pudding was to be divided in St George's Fields, but apparently its smell was too much for the gluttony of the Londoners, the escort was routed, the pudding taken and devoured, and the whole ceremony brought to an end before Mr. Austin had a chance to regale his customers.

The back windows of the *Boar's Head* looked out upon the burial-ground of St Michael's Church, also demolished *c.* 1831 to make room for the streets leading to London Bridge.   There rested the remains of one of the waiters of this tavern.   His tomb, in Purbeck stone, had the following epitaph :—

HERE LIETH THE BODYE of Robert Preston, late Drawer at the Boar's Head Tavern, Great Eastcheap, who departed this life, March 16, Anno Domini, 1730, aged 27 years.

> Bacchus, to give the topeing world surprize,
> Produc'd one sober son, and here he lies.
> Tho' nurs'd among full Hogsheads, he defy'd
> The charm of wine and ev'ry vice beside.
> O Reader, if to Justice thou'rt inclin'd,
> Keep Honest Preston daily in thy Mind.

> He drew good wine, took care to fill his pots,
> Had sundry virtues that outweighed his fauts (*sic*),
> You that on Bacchus have the like dependance,
> Pray, copy Bob, in measure and attendance.

Amongst other *Boar's Head* inns are to be noted one in Southwark, the property of Sir John Falstolf of Caistor Castle, Norf., who died in 1460, and whose name Shakespeare adopted in the play. There was another one without Aldgate, the resort of certain 'lewd players' in 1557.

At the beginning of the 19th century there was a noted tavern in Bond St. called *The Brawn's Head*, and the general opinion was that at one time it had a brawn or boar's head for its sign. This however was a mistake, the house was named after the head of a noted cook whose name was Theophilus Brawn. He had formerly been the landlord of the *Rummer* Tavern in Great Queen St., and the article (as the letters THE were usually supposed to be) was simply an abbreviation of the man's Christian name.

Most gastronomic signs doubtless originated in the old custom of landlords selling eatables :—

> 'You brave-minded and most joviall Sardanapalitans,' says Taylor the Water Poet, addressing the country tavern-keepers, 'have power and prerogative (cum privilegio) to receive, lodge, feast, and feed, both man and beast. You have the happiness to Boyle, Roast, Broyle, and Bake, Fish, Flesh, and Foule, whilst we in London have scarce the command of a *Gull*, a *widgeon*, or a *woodcock*.'

In a volume of 1685, entitled *The Praise of Yorkshire Ale*, we are told that Bacchus held a parliament in the *Sun*, behind the Exchange in York, to consider the adulteration of wine, the various drinking-vessels and other matters sold in alehouses, as :—

> Papers of sugar, with such like knacks,
> Biskets, Luke olives, Anchoves, Caveare,
> Neats' tongues, Westphalia Hambs, and
> Such-like cheat, Crabs, Lobsters, Collar Beef,
> Cold puddings, oysters, and such like stuff.

Hence, the once common sign of the *Three Neats' Tongues*, one of which existed in Larwood's time in Spitalfields but which is now extinct. Another one in the 18th century was very appropriately situated in Bull and Mouth St. The *Ham* is the usual porkman's sign, though at a house now extinct at Walmyth, Yorks., there was once a public-house sign of the *Ham & Firkin*. There is a *Ham & Chef* at Scagglethorpe, E.R. Yorks. At St Ives, Hunts., is a *Spare Rib*. The *Crab* Inn occurs at Shanklin, the *Crab & Lobster* at Ventnor, the *Cod & Lobster* at Staithes, N.R. Yorks. The *Lobster* is a sign on trades tokens of a shop in Bearbinder (now St Swithin's) Lane, and also near the *Maypole* in the Strand. There is an inn of this name at Coatham, N.R. Yorks. There is a *Crawfish* at Thursford Guist, Norf., and the *Butt & Oyster* at Chelmondiston, Suff., and an *Oyster* at Butley, Suff. Those eatables, all more or less salt, were sold as incitements to drink, and went by the cant term of shoeing horns, gloves or pullers-on. They are often alluded to by ancient authors.

The *Pie* was a sign in very early times, and, says Stow, gave its name to Pie Corner

' a place so called from such a sign, sometimes a fair inn for receipt of travellers '. A famous inn with the sign was the *Pie* in Aldgate. Defoe in his *History of the Plague* tells of ' a dreadful set of fellows ' who used to revel and roar nightly in that inn during the time the plague was at its height, but within a fortnight all of them were buried.

The *Cock & Pie* was once common. At a (still existing) inn of this name at Ipswich there used to be a rude representation of a cock perched on a pie, which was discovered whilst the house was undergoing some repairs. This was also, about the middle of the 18th century the sign of a house famed for conviviality which stood on the site of the present Rathbone Place, Oxford St., and was the resort of the ' fancy ' of those days. A variety of romantic but not very convincing explanations are given as to the origin of the sign. The ancient Catholic oath, to swear by *Cock & Pie* (by God and the Pie, or Catholic service book or alternatively by Cross and Pyx) and the fable of the magpie (Old English *pie* or *pye*) and the peacocks, have been duly considered, but the sign is probably only an abbreviation of the *Peacock & Pie*. In ancient times the peacock was a favourite dish, and was introduced on the table in a pie, the head with gilt beak, being elevated above the crust, and the beautiful feathers of the tail expanded. As a dainty dish, then, it may have been put up as a trap to hungry or epicurean passers-by. At last the dish went out of fashion, and even the name became a mystery and was rendered by the sign-painters according to their own understanding, by a *Cock & Magpie* which is still very common. There used to be a public-house with such a sign in Drury Lane, which was already in existence some three centuries ago, when the rest of Drury Lane was still occupied by farms and gardens and the mansions of the Drury family. Hither on May Day the youths and maidens of the metropolis who danced round the Maypole in the Strand were accustomed to resort for cakes and ale and other refreshments. This house gave its name to the *Cock & Pye* Fields, between Drury Lane and St Giles' Hospital. A house of this name still survives in Wilson St., Finsbury, E.C. At Whittington, Derbys., the original name was mutilated by a provincialism into the *Cock & Pynot*. In this alehouse, later a private house and now invested in Chesterfield Corporation, the Revolution of 1688 was plotted between Thomas Osborne first Earl of Danby and afterwards first Duke of Leeds, William Cavendish Earl and first Duke of Devonshire, and Mr. John d'Arcy. They met by appointment on a heath adjoining the house, but a shower of rain coming on, they adjourned to the inn. The ' plotting parlour ' is still shown in which the conspirators met, with Cavendish in the Chair. In Hone's *Table Book* there is a woodcut of the inn and its gallows sign. There is a *Pigeon Pie* at Sherburn.

The *Pickled Egg* formerly existing in Clerkenwell is now extinct. It is said that Charles II here once partook of the dish and this so flattered the landlord that he adopted it as his sign, and so it has remained for more than two centuries. It gave its name to a lane called Pickled Egg Walk, in which there was a notorious cock-fighting house, frequently mentioned in advertisements *c.* 1775. The lane too has now been renamed. The *Cheshire Cheese* is still very common ; there is a famous tavern of this name in Wine Office Court, Fleet St., and numerous public-houses in the country have adopted it as a sign. The Wine Office Court house is said to have been Johnson's favourite place of resort, and ' his ' chair is still to be seen there. Boswell however says little or nothing of the house.

Drinkables are not frequent as signs if we except such signs as those of the *Rhenish Wine House* and the *Canary House*, two taverns of old London, named after the wines they sold. *Barley Broth, Beeswing,* and *Yorkshire Stingo* (as in the New Rd., now Marylebone Rd.) are all fairly common. The first applies either to whisky or beer, the second is the delicate crust formed on good port after long keeping in bottle. Two houses of this name at Wellingborough and at York were noted for their port in 1790. There was however a celebrated race-horse named *Beeswing* mentioned on p. 114. Yorkshire Stingo is the well-known name of a kind of ale. From the house last named the first pair of London omnibuses were started running to the Bank and back on 4 July 1829. They were constructed to carry twenty-two passengers all inside. The return fare was one shilling or sixpence for half the distance, together with the luxury of a newspaper. George Shillibeer was the owner of these carriages, and it was said that the first conductors were the sons of naval officers. They wore uniforms rather like that of midshipmen. Certainly they had been in Paris with Shillibeer who had organized a similar service there. It was alleged that the young ladies of Paddington used to ride to King's Cross ' to improve their French '. Eventually Shillibeer was ruined by railway competition. A service of ' Shillibeers ' was run from this house in 1929 in commemoration of the centenary of the introduction of the service.

Drinking vessels are very appropriate alehouse signs. Apart from those already dealt with on p. 211, amongst the oldest certainly ranks the *Black Jack*. This is common even in the present day, although the vessel that it represented has long since fallen into disuse. It was a leather bottle sometimes lined with silver or other metal, and perhaps took its name from a part of the soldiers' armour. Sometimes it was ornamented with little silver bells ' to ring peales of drunkeness ', in which case it was called a ' gyngle boy '. This primitive bottle has been celebrated in the ballad :—

> God above that made all things,
> The heaven, and earth, and all therein,
> The ships that on the sea do swim
> For to keepe the enemies out that none come in,
> And let them all do what they can,
> It is for the use and pains of man ;
> And I wish in heaven his soul may dwell,
> Who first devized the leather bottle.

Its various good qualities are next explained, and finally :—

> Then when this bottle doth grow old,
> And will no longer good liquor hold,
> Out of its side you may take a clout,
> Will mend your shoes when they are worn out,
> Else take it and hang it upon a pin,
> It will serve to put odd trifles in,
> As hinges, awls, and candle ends,
> For young beginners must have such things.

Another Roxburghe ballad entitled *Time's Alternation, or the Old Man's Rehearsal* speaks of disuse of the black jack as a sign of the degeneracy of the times :—

> Black jacks to euery man
> Were filled with wine and Beere,
> No pewter Pot nor Canne
> In those days did appeare :
>
> .   .   .   .
>
> We took not such delight
> In cups of silver fine ;
> No pewter Pot nor Canne
> In those days did appeare.
>
> .   .   .   .
>
> None under the degree of a knight
> In Plate drunk Beere or Wine.

In Thomas Heywood's *Philocothonista, or Drunkard Opened Dissected and Anatomized*, 1635, there is an interesting detailed inventory of all the various drinking-vessels of the day :—

> Of drinking Cups divers and sundry sorts we have ; some of elme, some of box, some of maple, some of holly, etc.   Mazers, broad mouthed dishes, naggins, whiskins, piggins, creuzes, alebowles, wassel bowles, court dishes, tankards, kannes, from a pottle to a pint, from a pint to a gill.   Other bottles we have of leather, but they are most used amongst the shepheards and harvest people of the countrey : small jacks wee have in many alehouses of the citie and suburbs lipt with silver : blackjacks and bombards at the Court ; which when the Frenchmen first saw, they reported at their return into their countrey that the Englishmen used to drink out of their bootes.   We have besides cups made of hornes of beastes, of cockernuts, of goords, of eggs of estriches ; others made of the shells of divers fishes brought from the Indies and other places, and shining like mother of pearle.   Come to plate, every taverne can afford you flat bowles, french bowles, prounet cups, beare bowles, beakers ; and private householders in the citie, when they make a feaste to entertain their friends, can furnish their cupboards with flaggons, tankards, beere cups, wine bowles, some white, some percell guilt, some guilt all over, some with covers, others without, of sundry shapes and qualities.

The *Leather Bottle* is a common alehouse emblem at the present day.   In Larwood's time there was one still to be seen, carved in wood, suspended in front of an old ale-house at the corner of Charles St., Hatton Garden.   The *Black-jack* Tavern, in Clare Market, which was in Larwood's time still in existence, but is now no more, acquired some celebrity from being the favourite haunt of Joe Miller, the reputed author of the famous *Jest Book*.   The house was also for a long time known by the cant name of the *Jump*, which it had received when Jack Sheppard one day escaped the clutches of Jonathan Wild's emissaries by jumping from a window into the street.   There is still a *Black Jack* in Lincoln's Inn Fields.   The *Black Joke* at King's Lynn may be a corruption of the same name.   From the *Leather Bottle* to the *Golden Bottle* is not so great a step as would appear at first sight, the golden bottle being simply the leather bottle gilt.   It may be seen above the door of Messrs. Hoare the bankers in Fleet St., a firm established for centuries under the same sign, although not always occupying the same premises. There is a *Golden Bottle* Inn at York. That the *Golden Can* was also an old sign may be concluded from a mention in the nursery rhyme :—

> Little Brown Betty lived at the *Golden Can*,
> Where she brewed good ale for gentlemen.

The *Golden Can* is still to be seen on two public-houses in Norwich. The *Guilded Cup* in Houndsditch is mentioned in a quaint little pamphlet of 1641 on the virtues of ' Warme Beere '. The *Toby Jug* exists as a sign at 507 Hackney Rd. and on the Kingston-by-pass-road. The *Flask* was the sign of an old-established tavern in Ebury Square, Pimlico. In the 18th century there were two famous *Flask* taverns in Hampstead : the one called the *Lower Flask* was an inn at the foot of the hill, and is mentioned in an advertisement on the cover of the *Spectator*, No. 428. The *Upper Flask* was a place of public entertainment near the summit of Hampstead Hill, and is now a private residence. The well-known Kit-Kat Club used to meet at this tavern in the summer months. Another house in Hampstead still preserves the *Flask* name. It is situated in Flask Walk, N.W. There is still a *Flask* at Highgate, and there are others at Robin Hood's Bay and in Pimlico. Concerning the Hampstead houses, it is asserted that the *Flask* is a powder-flask, a necessary provision for the guards and passengers of coaches, so that they might deal with the highwaymen who infested Hampstead Heath, but probably the origin is rather as suggested above.

Besides these there occur as publicans' signs at the present day more homely vessels such as the *Pitcher & Glass*, the *Brown Jug*, the *Jug & Glass*, the *Bottle & Glass*, the *Foaming Quart*, etc. The last named is particularly common in North Staffordshire. There is a *Quart* at Runwell, Essex, and a *Two Quarts* at Norwich, a *Pot & Glass* at Eaglescliffe, Durh., a *Bottle & Glass* at Lincoln, and a *Bottles* at Occold, Suff. It may be as Monson Fitzjohn suggests that the signs date from the time when glass drinking-vessels were just coming into general use, and that the landlords adopted them in order to show they were supplying all the latest modern conveniences. At Newark the *Bottle* is accompanied by the following inscription :

> From this Bottle I am sure
> You'll get a glass both good and pure,
> In opposition to a many,
> I'm striving hard to get a penny.

The *Gallon Can* still remains at Yarmouth. The *Pewter Pot*, an old sign, is thus alluded to by Randle Holme :—

> This should be looked upon by all good artists to be the most ignoble and dishonourable bearing ; but as the custom takes away the sense of dislike, so the frequent use takes away the dishonour, which is seen by those multitudes that have it for their cognizance, in so much that it is painted over their doors by the wayside.

The *Pewter Pot* in Leadenhall St. was a famous carriers' and coaching inn in 1681.

The *Six Cans* was in Holborn (a sign evidently suggested by the *Three Tuns*), and in the same locality, the *Six Cans & Punchbowl*.

This last object, the *Punchbowl*, was introduced on the signboard at the end of the 17th century when punch became the fashionable drink. It survives here and there, for example at Low Row, Cumb. In one instance at Penelewey, Cornwall, we have the *Punchbowl & Ladle*, but most generally the *Punchbowl* is found in combination with other very heterogeneous objects. The reason for this is that punch, like music, had a sort of political prestige. It was the Whig drink, whilst the Tories adhered to sack, claret and canary, connected in their memory with bygone things and times, including perhaps the French alliance. It followed that the punchbowl was added as a kind of party-badge to many of the Whig tavern signs, and hence such combinations as the following all of which survived until Larwood's time and some of which remain at the present day : the *Crown & Punchbowl*, Horningsea, Cambs., the *Magpie & Punchbowl*, Bishopsgate Within, the *Rose & Punchbowl*, Redman's Row, Stepney, and elsewhere, the *Red Lion & Punchbowl* (now only the *Red Lion*), St John's St., Clerkenwell, the *Half Moon & Punchbowl*, Buckle St., E., the *Parrot & Punchbowl*, Aldringham, Suff. ; still extant. The *Fox & Punchbowl* was at Old Windsor (the first element in the sign is perhaps meant for the politician who had a taste for the beverage). The *Ship & Punchbowl* and the *Union Flag & Punchbowl*, both in Wapping, are now no more, and the *Dog & Punchbowl*, Lynn, Ches., also seems to have disappeared. The *Punch Bowl*, Hindhead, Surrey, however takes its name from the Devil's Punch Bowl, a famous depression in the neighbouring hills. In other cases perhaps the sign may indicate an inn used for the meet of hounds, when punch was (and is still on occasion) handed round.

The *Two Pots* was the sign of a public-house at Boxworth, St Ives, accompanied by the following verses :—

> Rest, traveller, rest ; Cooper's hand
> Obedient brings two pots at thy command.
> Rest, traveller, rest ; and banish thoughts of care,
> Drink to thy friends and recommend them here.

The celebrated *Two Pots* at Leatherhead could boast a most venerable antiquity, for it is believed to be the very alehouse where the notorious Eleanor Rummynge tunned her ' noppy ale ', and made

> thereof fast sale
> To travellers, to tinkers,
> To sweaters, to swinkers,
> And all good ale-drinkers.

There was at the end of the 18th century, a painted sign still remaining, which under a coating of summer's dust and winter's mud, faintly showed two pots of beer placed in the same position as they are on the title-page of the original edition of Skelton's poem. The house has disappeared since Larwood's time. The sign of the *Two Pots* still exists at Haddenham, I. of Ely, and there is a *Three Pots*, at Horseway Bridge, Chatteris in the same county, and at Burbage, near Hinckley, Leics.

The *Rummer*, another drinking-vessel, is also common : there is one in Old Fish St., and there are three *Rummer* public-houses in Bristol alone.   A tavern of that name was kept by Samuel Prior, uncle of Matthew Prior, who took his nephew as an apprentice to learn the business and be his successor.   Prior alludes to this uncle and his little professional tricks in the lines :—

> My uncle, rest his soul, when living,
> Might have contrived me ways of thriving ;
> Taught me with cider to replenish
> My vats or ebbing tide of Rhenish ;
> So, when for Hock I drew pricked white Wine,
> Swear't had the flavour and was right wine.

To his stay in this tavern also alludes the bitter Whig satire in *State Poems* :

> A vintner's boy the wretch was first preferr'd
> To wait at vice's gates and pimp for bread ;
> To hold the candle, and sometimes the door,
> Let in the drunkard, and let out the whore.

In 1709 there was another *Rummer* tavern ' over against Bow Lane, in Cheapside ', where ' the surprizing Mr. Higgins, the posture master, that lately performed at the Queen's Theatre Royal in the Haymarket ', was to be seen every evening at six.

A near relative of the *Rummer* was the *Bumper*, a tavern in St James's St., Covent Garden, kept by Richard Estcourt the actor.   According to an advertisement in the *Spectator* of 1711, his drawer was ' his old servant Trusty Anthony, who has so often adorned both the theatres in England and Ireland ; and as he is a person altogether unknown in the Wine Trade, it cannot be doubted but that he will deliver the wine in the same natural purity as he receives it from the said merchants '.

Finally the *Tankard* is still of frequent occurrence.   There is a public-house at Ipswich with this sign, which was formerly part of the house of Sir Anthony Wingfield, one of the legal executors of Henry VIII.   It is in Tankard St., now renamed Tacket St. There is another *Tankard* at Bentley.   The hanap or tankard was generally of silver, and was formerly one of the most valuable properties of an alehouse, for in an Act of 13 Edw. I, it says that ' if a tavern-keeper keep his house open after curfew he shall be put on his surety the first time by the *hanap* of the tavern or by some other good pledge therein found '.   Silver tankards were more or less common in all the London taverns. In some houses they were reserved for the more distinguished visitors ; in others, as at the *Bull's Head* in Leadenhall St., ' every poor mechanic drank in plate '.   They were of different sizes, and an experienced toper well knew for which name to call when ordering a tankard proportionate to his thirst.   From the curious old tippler's handbook of *c.* 1714 *A Vade Mecum for Maltworms*, we gather that the names of the tankards at the *Sweet Apple*, in Sweet Apple Yard, were the *Lamb*, the *Lion*, the *Peacock* (in honour of the brewer), *Sacheverell* (in memory of the notorious divine of St Andrew's, Holborn) and *Nan Elton* (a lady whose fame seems to have perished).   The same work also relates a curious instance of enthusiasm in a publican. His house, the *Raven* in Fetter Lane, was famous for :—

> Massy tankards form'd of silver plate,
> That walk throughout his noted house in state ;
> Ever since Eaglesfield in Anna's reign,
> To compliment each fortunate campaign,
> Made one be hammer'd out for every town was ta'en.

We may suppose each tankard named after a victory—the greater the victory, the greater the tankard ; and can imagine the gratifying display of loyalty in emptying these tankards to the perdition of Popery, French money and wooden shoes.

Besides the tankard for drinking beer or wine, there was also the *Water Tankard*, though this is not recorded as a tavern sign. In Ben Jonson's comedy *Every Man in his Humour*, 1598, Cob, the water-carrier of the Old Jewry, says :—' I dwell, sir, at the sign of the *Water Tankard* hard by the *Green Lattice*.' These water-tankards were used for carrying water from the conduits to the houses, and were therefore a professional sign of the water-carriers. In Wilkinson's *Londina Illustrata*, there is an engraving of Westcheap as it appeared in the year 1585, copied from a drawing of the period, in which the Little Conduit is seen with a quantity of water-tankards ranged round it.

Amongst the other articles of furniture which are represented on the signboard we must first of all notice that useful article the *Looking Glass*, which was the favourite sign of the booksellers on London Bridge.

Other pieces of furniture include the *Cabinet*, a common upholsterer's sign in the 17th and 18th centuries. There is a public-house of this sign at Reed, Herts. The *Three Crickets* or little stools we gather from a 17th-century trades token was in Crooked Lane. The *Cradle* occurs in Taylor's *Carrier's Cosmography*, 1637, where he gives a rather curious insight into the postal arrangements of that time :—

> Those that will send any letter to Edinburgh, that so they may be conveyed to and fro to any parts of the kingdom of Scotland, the poste doth lodge at the signe of the *kings armes* or the *Cradle* at the upper end of Cheapside, from whence every Monday any that have occasion may send.

Generally, however, it did not designate so respectable a business ; the *Compleat Vintner*, 1720, explains the secret implications of that sign :—

> The pregnant Madam drawn aside,
> By promise to be made a bride,
> If near her time and in distress
> For some obscure convenient place
> Let her but take the pains to waddle
> About till she observe a *Cradle*
> With the foot hanging towards the door,
> And there she may be made secure
> From all the parish plagues and terrors,
> That wait on poor weak woman's errors.

But if the head hang tow'rds the house,
As very often we see it does,
Avaunt, for she's a cautious bawd
Whose business only lies abroad.

It is but a step from the last interpretation of this sign to the *Colt & Cradle* (see p. 32).

A publican in Tamworth, Staffs., took the *Coffee-Pot* for a sign, probably on the strength of the derivation of *lucus a non lucendo*, because he sold no coffee. The *Coffee-Pot* at Tamworth apparently disappeared some years ago, but a house of the same name in Warwick Lane remained until air-raids on London. The *Sugar-loaf* was a common grocer's sign of former times, the selection of which, says Larwood, showed great disinterestedness on their part, the article being that on which the least profit was made.

At 44 Fenchurch St. a very old-established grocery firm still carried on business in Larwood's time under the sign of the *Three Sugar Loaves*. Presumably he refers to the business of Messrs. Davison and Newman, now at 14 Creechurch Lane. The *Sugar-loaf* was not always exclusively a grocer's sign, nor the *Three Balls* a pawnbroker's as appears from an advertisement in the *Postman*, 3–6 February 1711. There was a house with a *Sugar-loaf* sign in Pall Mall. Of compound *Sugar-loaf* signs the *Swan & Sugarloaf* has already been mentioned (p. 140), and the *Crown & Sugarloaf* (p. 65). The *Sugar-loaf* is also a public-house sign, though not a very appropriate one. The *Blue Bowl* suggestive of punch-making occurs on (three) public-houses in Bristol. One of the signs is said to have been painted originally by David Cox who much admired a blue bowl, an heirloom of the landlord, and painted the sign as an agreeable variation from the common *Punch Bowl*.

Foremost amongst kitchen utensils ranks the *Gridiron*, which was very common in the 16th century and may perhaps have been a jocular rendering of the *Portcullis*. The *Frying Pan* is still a constant ironmonger's sign—thus in Highcross St., Leicester, there is or was a gigantic gilt specimen with the inscription *Family Frying Pan*. This also occurs as an inn sign at Brick Lane, E.

The *Pewter Platter* was famous as a carriers' inn in St John St., Clerkenwell, in 1681. At this inn Curll's translators were lodged and had to sleep three in a bed, and there according to *Lloyd's Evening Post* 9–12 January 1767 'he and they were for ever at work to deceive the publick'. Probably this was a very early sign for eating-houses. It still survives as the sign of a house in Leather Lane, E.

The *Pump* is a fairly common alehouse sign, and occurs as such on a token of Tooley St. with the following lines :—

The Pump runs cleer
Wh. Ale and Beer,

which may be a travesty of a verse in *Histrio-mastix* 1610 :—

Yet a verse may run cleare,
That is tapt out of Beere.

In Larwood's time a publican in Old Swinford, Staffs. and Worcs., who combined engineering with his trade had a similar sign with the words 'Hands to the Pump'. A house of this name survives at Handsworth, Birmingham, not far away. In the reign of Charles I there was a public-house, the *Blue Pump* in Blackfriars, near the famous Hollands Leaguer. It represented a man, evidently a sailor, pumping with all his might with the legend which ran :—' Poor Tom's last refuge '. Of compound *Pump* signs the best known is the *Bull & Pump*, which has been dealt with above (p. 122).

With the *Pump* we may place the *Bucket*, though this was apparently only the sign of a shop in Aldersgate St., of which there are trades tokens extant. The *Tub* was the name of a tavern in Jermyn St. in the reign of Charles II, as appears from a letter sent by Nell Gwynn from Windsor in 1684 to her milliner and factotum, addressed to ' Madam Jennings, over against the *Tub* tavern in Jermyn St., London '. Another utensil, the *Dust-Pan*, is common with hardware shops but does not seem to be recorded as an inn sign. There is one in Islington, at a shop next to the house in which Charles Lamb lived, at night it was illuminated and hence called the *Illuminated Dust-Pan*. There formerly existed a colossal specimen of the *Hour-Glass* sign carved in wood in Upper Thames St., near All Hallows Church. This was formerly the tap-house of the City of London Brewery. The *Golden Jar* which was the sign of a china shop in Tavistock St., and this also does not seem to be recorded over inns or alehouses. Even in Larwood's time *jars* painted red and green were the usual oilman's sign, representing those vessels in which oil is kept in Eastern countries, and in which Ali Baba's forty thieves came to an untimely end. Formerly oil used to be imported in this country in similar jars, hence their adoption as trade emblems.

The *Key* was a sign once largely used not only by locksmiths as at present but also by all manner of shops. Thus there was a celebrated tavern of this sign at the corner of Henrietta St., Covent Garden, *c.* 1690. The *Golden Key* in Fleet St. is named in an advertisement in *Mercurius Publicus* of 1660 concerning a lost hawk. There is still a *Golden Key* at Ipswich. The *Lock & Key* was a sign of a public-house in West Smithfield. It was during the Commonwealth, that of a house in the parish of St Dunstan's, belonging to Praise God Barebones citizen and leather-seller of London. The sign of the Smithfield *Lock & Key*—not painted on a board but a metal padlock with its key—was dislodged by a German bomb in the War of 1914–18. It is now in the London Museum. The house was recently de-licensed. The *Key & Castle* is an unusual sign which occurs in Norwich. This was the badge of the 12th Suffolk Regiment, and was no doubt put up by a veteran of the regiment. The *Cross Keys* is dealt with above (p. 178).

Chapter XIV

DRESS: PLAIN AND ORNAMENTAL

OF signs relating to dress only a few are to be found. One of the most common is the *Hat*, the usual hatter's sign which may also be found before taverns and public-houses. In such cases however it is probably that it was the previous sign of the house which the publicans on entering left unaltered. Alternatively it may have been used to suggest 'a house of call' to the trade. The age of each individual hat-sign might formerly sometimes be gathered from its shape. Thus in Larwood's time there was one in Whitechapel made out of tin, and representing the cocked hat worn at the end of the 18th century so probably a relic of that time. There is still a *Hat* sign at Ealing, and a *Cocked Hat* at Aspley, Nottingham.

The *Hat & Feathers* may date back to late Tudor or to Stuart times. The puritanical Philip Stubbes in his *Anatomie of Abuses*, 1585, is very hard upon the fashion of wearing 'cockes combes . . . ensignes of vanite . . . and feathered flagges of defiaunce to virtue', Dekker calls the swell of his day 'our feathered ostrich', and in the *Sun's Darling*, not published until 1656, he mentions 'some alderman's son wondrous, giddy, and light-headed, one that blew his patrimony away in *feathers* and tobacco'. There is a publican's sign of the *Hat & Feathers* still in existence at Grantchester, Cambs., another at Clerkenwell Rd., and it occurs also at Manchester, Norwich, etc. Another old hatter's sign is the *Hat & Beaver*, which at present may be seen at the door of a publican's in Leicester. Shopbills of this once common sign occur amongst the Banks Collection, representing a beaver seated on the edge of a stream, with a hat above him. The relation between the two is evident, presumably about as gratifying to the beaver as the mention of mint sauce to a spring lamb.

Felt hats for a long time were exclusively worn by the aristocracy. Stow says that 'about the beginning of Henry VIII began the making of Spanish feltes in England, by Spaniardes and Dutchmen, before which time, and long since the English used to ride, and goe winter and sommer in knitcapps, cloth hoods, and the best sort of silk throm'd Hatts'. These caps, termed statute caps, are frequently alluded to by the dramatists and authors of that period. Rosalind, for instance, in *Love's Labour's Lost* taunts her lover with the words : 'Well, better wits have worn plain statute caps.' The sign of the *Cap & Stocking* still in Leicester refers to the still-flourishing trade of that town in those articles. In St John St., Clerkenwell, there was an old-established public-house and place of resort, called the *Three Hats*. It is mentioned by Isaac Bickerstaffe in his comedy *The Hypocrite*, where Mawworm thus alludes to it :—

> Till I went after him (Dr. Cantwell,) I was little better than the Devil ; my conscience was tanned with sin, like a piece of neat's leather, and had no more feeling than the sole of my shoe ; always a roving after fantastical delights ; I used to go every Sunday evening to the *Three Hats* at Islington ; it's a public-house . . . mayhap your Ladyship may know it. I was a great lover of skittles, too, but now I cannot bear them.

At this house the earliest equestrian performers used to give displays in 1758. There was Thomas, an Irishman, surnamed Tartar ; then came Johnson, Sampson, Price, and Cunningham. Dr. Johnson went here to see his namesake. His remarks upon the show are unusually inane :—

> His performances show the extent of human powers in one instance, and thus tend to raise our opinion of the faculties of man. He shows what may be obtained by persevering application : so that every man may hope, by giving as much application, although, perhaps, he may never ride three horses at a time, or dance upon a wire, yet he may be equally expert in whatever profession he has chosen to pursue.

The *Three Hats* occurs also amongst the trades tokens of the 17th century. There is one of the *Three Hats & Nag's Head* in Southwark.

The *Wig* survived until lately as an inn sign at Redisham, Suff., but disappeared in recent years.

The *Anodyne Necklace* was as notorious in the 18th century as *Yadil*, or Iodine Lockets are in our day. Advertisements concerning it were continually appearing in the papers, for example in 1718.

> The Anodyne Necklace for children's teeth, women in labour, and distempers of the head ; price 5s. Recommended by Dr. Chamberlain. Sold up one pair of stairs at the sign of the *Anodyne Necklace*, without Temple Bar ; at the *Spanish Lady* at the Royal Exchange, next Threadneedle Street ; at the *Indian Handkerchief*, facing the New Stairs in Wapping. etc.

To attract attention, there was frequently some book of not very delicate character, advertised as ' given away gratis ' at this house. To whet the appetite still further, a restriction was sometimes added that ' this curious book will not be given away to any boys or girls, or any paultry person '.

At the present time there is in Sheffield a public-house called the *Blue Stoops* : Larwood thought this referred to an ancient garment, worn in the beginning of the 17th century, and also named by Ben Jonson in *The Alchymyst*,* but it is likelier that this is a variant of the *Blue Posts*. Stoup is still used provincially for a gatepost, and the first suggestion seems as unlikely as that advanced by another writer, that an ancient (holy water) stoup in blue stone stood for many years before the House and gave it its name.

The *Bonny Cravat*, at Woodchurch, Kent, to judge from the adjective, seems rather

---

* Act IV, Sc. II.

Eight Bells, Watford

The Cross Keys, Sherborne

Dolphin, Worthing

Archery Tavern, Eastbourne

The Ham Hotel, Worthing

The Shelley Arms, Nutley

The Spon Croft, Oldbury Road,
Smethwick

The Court Oak, Harborne, Birmingham

The Deer's Leap, Perry Barr,
Birmingham

The Toll Gate, Holyhead Road,
Coventry

The Red Lion, Grantchester

The White Hart, St Albans

The White Swan, Fleet Street, E.C.

Butcher's Arms, Sheepscombe, Nr. Stroud

The Grey Goat, Penrith

The Greyhound

White Hart, Littlehampton

White Hart

Cock Inn, Hingham, Norfolk

Swan Inn, Worthing, Norfolk

The Old Cock, Harpenden

Bedford Arms, Bedford Street, Norwich

Raven, St Giles Street, Norwich

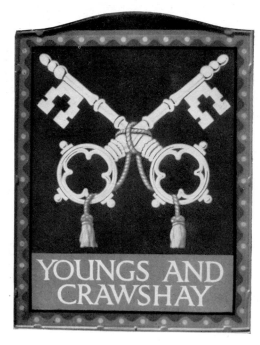

Cross Keys, Wymondham, Norfolk

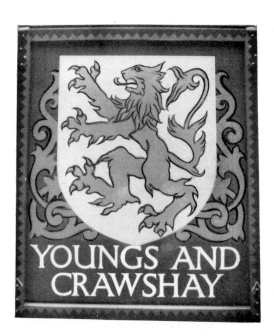

Red Lion, Aldborough, Norfolk

Red Lion, Eye, Suffolk

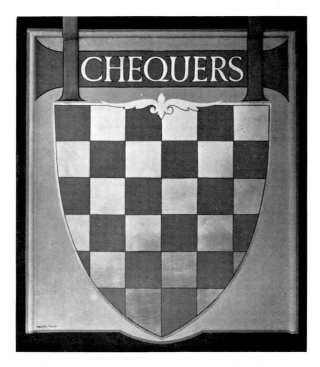

Chequers, Fareham

Blue Anchor, Trotton

Licensee B. Rowe

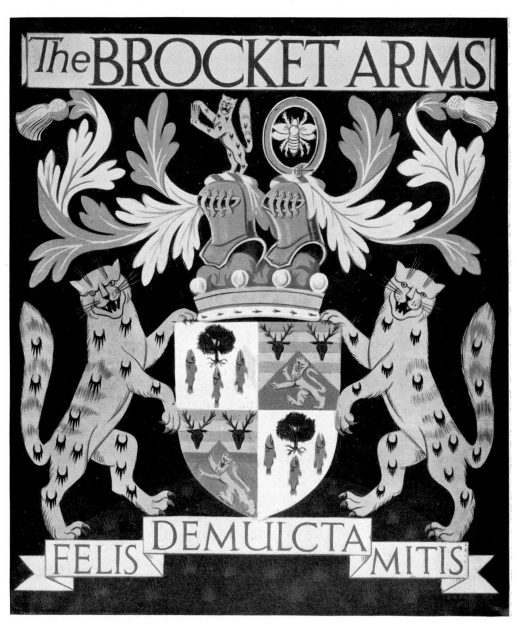

The Brocket Arms, Ayot St Lawrence

Tankerville Arms, Hounslow

Bedford Arms Hotel, Woburn

The Grafton Arms, Barnham, Suffolk

The Crawshay Arms, Philadelphia Lane, Norwich

Buck, Earsham

to have been suggested by the old song ' *Jenny, come tie my bonny cravat* ', than by the introduction of the cravat as an article of dress. According to another account the second word is really carvet, a close-cropped yew hedge. According to still another the sign is really the *Bonny-Corvette*.

The *Tabard* was of course the well-known inn in High St., Southwark, whence Chaucer and the other pilgrims started on their way to Canterbury. It has a literature of its own. Originally it was the property of the Abbot of Hyde near Winchester, who had his town residence within the inn-yard. The earliest record relating to this property is in 1304 when the Abbot and convent of Hyde purchased of William of Lategareshall two houses in Southwark, held by the Archbishop of Canterbury at the annual rent of 5s. 1½d., and suit to his court in Southwark, and 1d. a year for a purpresture of one foot wide on the king's highway . . . etc. It is a fact on record that Henry Bayley, the hosteller of the *Tabard*, was one of the burgesses who represented the borough of Southwark in the Parliament held in Westminster in 1376, and he was again returned to the Parliament held at Gloucester in 1378. The tavern itself is named, at the very period when Chaucer's poem is supposed to have been written, in one of the rolls of Parliament. In 1381 in a list of malefactors who had participated in the rebellion of Jack Cade, occurs the name ' Joh'es Brewersman, manens apud le Tabbard, London '. Stow thus notices the *Tabard* among the fair inns of Southwark :—

> Amongst the which the most ancient is the *Tabard* ; so called of the sign, which as we now term it, is a jacket or sleeveless coat, whole before, open on both sides, with a square collar, winged at the shoulders, a stately garment of old time, commonly worn of noblemen and others, both at home and abroad in the wars, but then, (to wit, in the wars,) their arms embroidered or otherwise depict upon them, that any man by his coat of arms might be known from others ; but now these tabardes are only worn by the heralds, and be called their coate of armes in service.

Formerly there stood in the road, in front of the *Tabard*, a gallows sign with an inscription concerning Chaucer and his nine and twenty pilgrims. Gallows, inscription and sign all disappeared in 1766. Speght who described the *Tabard* in his second edition of Chaucer 1602 does not mention it. Perhaps it was put up after the fire of 1676, when the *Tabard* changed its name into the *Talbot*.

In Larwood's time the inn was known by the name of the *Talbot*, and it was full of traditional lore concerning Chaucer and his merry pilgrims. In the centre of the gallery there was a well-painted picture, said to be by Blake, representing the Canterbury Pilgrimage, but much defaced from dirt, age and smoke. Behind this picture was a door opening into a lofty passage with rooms on either side, one of which on the right hand was still designated the Pilgrims' Room. The house was repaired in the reign of Queen Elizabeth, and from that period probably dated the fireplace, carved oak panels and other parts spared by the fire of 1676, which were still to be seen in the beginning of the 19th century. The house was pulled down in 1875 and a modern public-house now stands on or near the spot. It retains the old name, but

R

that is all.   Talbot Yard also preserves the name in a mutilated form.   Mr. Popham
may well style the story of the *Tabard* in the last century or so a major tragedy.

As leather breeches were much used for riding in the 17th and 18th centuries,
the occupations of breeches-maker and glover were frequently combined, hence the sign
of the *Breeches & Glove* on old London Bridge, the shop of ' Walter Watkins, Breeches-
maker, Leather-seller, and Glover '.   A Cornish publican of Larwood's time at Camel-
ford chose the sign of the *Cotton Breeches*.   The *Leather Gaiters* is at Hauxton, Cambs.
Cockers is good Lancashire for old footless stockings worn in lieu of gaiters, and the
Doff Cockers at Bolton indicates a house where a man may take off his wet leg-wear
and drink his beer in peace, while his cockers dry before the fire.   Stockings or legs
are of constant occurrence in the 17th-century trades tokens but they are generally
as the signs of hosiers not of publicans.

Boots and shoes occur in greater variety and abundance than any other article of
dress.   The *Boot* is a very common inn sign, perhaps owing to the thirsty reputation
of the cobblers, or from the premises having been at one time occupied by shoemakers.
Houses of this sign are found at Great Beallings, Suff., Bracknell, Didcot and Wallingford, Berks., and there are at least five in Buckinghamshire.   Monson Fitzjohn suggests
that sometimes the sign is armorial (a boot is the crest of the Husseys), sometimes convivial (a jack-boot is a more capacious receptacle than a black jack), sometimes it
merely suggests that the landlord will care for the personal appearance of travellers
who have made a long journey.   The *Boot & Slipper* might formerly be seen at Smethwick and at Benwick, I. of Ely, the *Golden Slipper* at York, the *Hand & Slippers* was a
sign in Long Lane, Smithfield, in 1750.   There is a *Shoe* at Wroxall, Warws., and the
Boot & Shoe is quite common, for example at March, I. of Ely, at York, and at Doncaster and Darlington.   It is sometimes supposed to indicate a welcome to all comers,
whether they wear the horseman's jackboot, or the labourer's or artisan's clouted shoe.
At York the sign was a man's boot and a horseshoe, suggesting, it appears, a welcome
to pedestrians as well as to riders, whether by coach or on horse-back.   The *Boot &
Clog* at Penrith is no doubt a variant of the boot and shoe.   The *Slipper* at Shrewsbury,
at any rate if its recently erected sign may be relied on, relates not to footwear but
to coursing.   The sign shows a ' slipper ' releasing greyhounds from the leash.   The
Sole & Heel is found at Hauxton, Cambs.   The *Shoe & Slap* occurs in a handbill of
1667 concerning a freak show.   A slap was a kind of ' ladies' shoe, with a loose sole '
the origin probably of the present word *slipper*.   Another kind of shoe (? an inn sign)
is also mentioned in an advertisement in the 17th century—the *Laced Shoe* in Chancery
Lane.   The *Clog* is often used as a shoemaker's sign in Lancashire and the midland
counties, the *Five Clogs* was that of a quack, and the *Patten* was the sign of a toy-shop
in the Haymarket ' Over against Great Suffolk Street, and by Pall Mall '.   In Larwood's
time this last remained over a fishmonger's shop in Whitecross St. near the prison.

The very common sign of the *Star & Garter* refers to the insignia of the Order of
the Garter.   Anciently it was simply called the *Garter*, and it is so styled in the *Merry
Wives of Windsor*.   Charles I added the star to the insignia, and his example was

followed on the signboard.   Soon after that time the Garter was treated with a great deal more respect than at present, for Sandford in the *Lancaster Herald* in 1686 complained that several coffee-houses had the sign of the *Garter* with coffee-pots, etc., painted inside, which he considered downright desecration.   Hence order was given to those offenders ' to amend the same, or else they should be pulled down '.

The *Garter* at Windsor where Falstaff lived in grand style ' as an emperor in his expense ' was not a creation of Shakespeare's fancy but did really exist, and was most probably on the same site as that at present occupied by the *Star & Garter*.   The first *Star & Garter* at Richmond was built in 1739, on what was then a portion of the waste of Petersham Common ; it was rented at 40s. a year.   A drawing by Thomas Hearne of the comparatively insignificant tenement then raised is still preserved at the hotel.

The *Star & Garter* was also the sign of a famous ordinary in Pall Mall, now extinct. Here the Duke of Ormonde in the reign of Queen Anne gave a dinner to a few friends, and was charged £21 6s. 8d. for the two courses, each of four dishes, without any wine or dessert.   In this house in 1765, Lord Byron, the poet's grandfather, killed Mr. Chaworth in an irregular duel, the result of a dispute whether Mr. Chaworth who preserved his game or Lord Byron who did not had more game on his estate.   About the same time there was another *Star & Garter* tavern at the end of Burton St., near the famous Five Fields in Chelsea, which the *Tatler* styles ' a place where robbers lie in wait '.   The site is now occupied by Eaton Square and Belgrave Square.   At this tavern, Johnson the equestrian rode in July 1762 for the gratification of the Cherokee king, when on a visit to this country.   Often the sign has been corrupted—an attractive though not very plausible theory attributes the *Leg of Mutton & Cauliflower* at Ashtead, Surrey, to a perversion of this sign.

The *Pincushion* is the sign of a public-house at Wyberton, Lincs., but why chosen it is difficult to say ; and the *Purse* occurs amongst the trades tokens of West Smithfield, with the date 1669.   This last sign was also that of one of the taverns visited by Drunken Barnaby at Barnet, where he had his misfortune with the bears.

Chapter XV

GEOGRAPHY AND TOPOGRAPHY

FOREMOST in this division stands the *Globe*—'the great Globe itself', a trade emblem common to publicans, outfitters and others who rely upon cosmopolitan customers. It may sometimes be from Portugal whose emblem it is, suggesting that Port, etc., are obtainable within. Shakespeare's famous theatre was called the *Globe*, from its sign representing Atlas supporting the world. It is said to have been named originally from a neighbouring tavern of this sign. Often it appears that the *Struggler* (p. 265), and the *World turned upside down* (p. 270), may be debased forms of this sign.

One of the most famous *Globes* stood in Fleet St. till the beginning of the 19th century. It had been one of the favourite haunts of Oliver Goldsmith, who was never tired of hearing a certain 'tun of a man' sing there *Nottingham Ale*. Several actors also used the house—amongst others the centenarian Charles Macklin and Tom King, the associates of Garrick and Sheridan. Many amusing anecdotes concerning the place have been preserved in Joseph Brasbridge's *Fruits of Experience*, 1824. At Aldborough, W.R. Yorks., there is a *Globe* public-house in which may be seen a tessellated pavement, part of a Roman villa. The publican informs passers-by of this by the following inscription on his signboard :—

> This is the ancient manor-house, and in it you may see
> The Romans work a great curiositee.

And the absence of the apostrophe certainly makes it so. The *Globe* exists as an inn sign at King's Lynn.

Of all the signs which may be termed Geographical, those referring to our own island are, of course, the most common in this country. *Britannia* is very general. Hone, in his *Everyday Book* mentions a public-house in the country where London porter was sold, and the figure of Britannia was represented in a languishing reclining posture, with the motto ' *Pray, sup-porter* '. Sometimes no doubt the *Britannia* sign refers to a famous ship, the first Cunarder, 1840.

Some early inhabitants seem to be commemorated by the sign of the *Ancient Briton* found, for example, at St Albans and at Tunstall, Stoke-on-Trent. This does not bear the obvious meaning, but refers simply to a true Tory patriot. Thus Boswell uses the expression of himself in one of his letters to Dr. Johnson. Many inns still exist with such names—the *North Briton* at Aycliffe, Durh., the *Generous Briton* at Newark, the *True Briton* at 42 Stewarts Rd., S.W. That this is the meaning attached to the word is evident from other signs of the same family, as *Generous Briton*, etc., all common signatures to political letters in the newspapers of the *Junius* period.

The modern *John Bull* found, for example, at Ipswich, and still later *Old English Gentleman* to be seen, for example, at Cheshunt, Herts., descend from the same stock, and are all equally common. *Old England* is a sign in Delamore Crescent. The *Ordinary Fellow* at Chatham is said to be named after his late majesty, King George V.

Formerly signs representing buildings or localities in London were common, though generally they bore very little resemblance to the places intended. Among the trades tokens we find the *Exchange*, a tavern in the Poultry in 1651, the *East India House*, in Leadenhall St., like most of this description of signs, prompted by the vicinity of the building represented. Perhaps the *Old India House* at Gloucester was named after this. *Charing Cross* was the sign of a shop in that locality where canaries were sold in 1699, and also an (? inn) sign at Norwich in 1750. The *Old Prison* was in Whitechapel—this Old Prison was intended for King's Cross. *Camden House* in Maiden Lane 1668—this must have been named in honour of Baptist Hicks the wealthy mercer of the *White Bear* in Cheapside, who died as Viscount Camden in 1628. He built Hicks Hall on Clerkenwell Green, and presented it to the county magistrates as their session-house.

About 1700 *Hyde Park* was the sign of a shop or tavern in Gray's Inn Lane. A public-house in Bridge Row, Chelsea, mentioned before 1750, and existing in Larwood's time but now no more, bore the name of the *Chelsea Waterworks*. The Waterworks after which it was named were constructed *c.* 1724. A canal was dug from the Thames near Ranelagh to Pimlico, where a pump was placed for the raising of water into pipes which conveyed it to Chelsea, Westminster and various parts of western London. There is another *Waterworks* Inn in Staffordshire, and a *Watering Trough* at Walsall.

The *Lancashire Witch*, a sign of an exhibition of shell-work and petrifactions in Shoreditch, 1754, can hardly be named as Larwood suggests from Mother Shipton, a very distinguished Yorkshire woman, but may be from one of the ladies later made famous by Harrison Ainsworth.

York figures more frequently on the signboard than any other place in England, as one might expect of a city

> . . . for my monie,
> Of all the cities that ever I see,
> For merry pastime and companie,
> Except the cittie of London.

From the trades tokens we see that the *City of York* was a sign in Middle Row, Holborn, in the 17th century. *York Minster* is one of the few cathedrals ever seen represented out of its own city. Larwood, clearly no Yorkshireman, rather unkindly suggests that this is because it stands in the capital of the county from whence came Yorkshire stingo.

The *Castle* being such a general sign, many traders adopted some particular castle. *Dover Castle* and *Walmer Castle* are found most frequently among these. The first is mentioned in an amusing advertisement of 1759, announcing the foundation of a lodge of female Freemasons at the *Angel*, Southwark, in opposition to the spurious *Dover Castle* (Lambeth) lodge.   Larwood suggests gallantly that the *Angel* sign was well chosen for the purpose, though the *Silent Woman* might have been equally appropriate. *Llangollen Castle* was formerly painted on a sign in Deansgate, Manchester : under it is the following rhyme :—

> Near the above place in a vault,
> There is such liquor fixed,
> You'll say that water, hops and malt,
> Were never better mixed.

Many other castles occur, such as *Jersey Castle*, on the token of Philip Crosse in Finch Lane in the 17th century, *Denbigh Castle*, Stoke-on-Trent, *Dover Castle*, Westminster Bridge Rd., *Edinburgh Castle*, very appropriately situated in Caledonian Rd. (there is another fine pictorial sign of *Edinburgh Castle* over the Edinburgh Stores in Milford Lane, Strand, W.C.), *Milford Castle* and *Morpeth Castle* both in Cadogan Terrace, *Rochester Castle*, High St., N.16, *Stirling Castle*, London Wall, *Walmer Castle*, Peckham Rd., and *Warwick Castle*, Portobello Rd.   *Jack Straw's Castle* has already been referred to (p. 45).   *Rats Castle*, a term used for a disused house, is at St Albans.

Towns were often adopted for signs if the landlord hoped to attract the custom of the natives of such places.   The *City of Norwich* was the sign of a house in Bishopsgate St. in the 17th century, either for the reason just alleged, or because ' *the fall of Niniveh with Norwich built in an hour* ' was one of the penny sights of that period.   *Chiltern Hundred*, a house at Boxley, Kent, doubtless refers to the district the acceptance of whose stewardship serves as a means of resigning from the House of Commons.   The *Wiltshire Shepherd* was a sign in St Martin's Lane in the 17th century.   The Wiltshire downs were famous for their flocks of sheep.   At Whitley, Hants, near Basingstoke, there is a public-house sign representing a grenadier in full uniform, holding in his hand a foaming pot of ale ; it is called the *Whitley Grenadier*, and bears the verses :—

> This is the *Whitley Grenadier*,
> A noted house for famous beer,
> My friend, if you should chance to call,
> Beware and get not drunk withal ;
> Let moderation be your guide,
> It answers well whene'er 'tis try'd.
> Then use, but not abuse, *strong beer*,
> And don't forget the Grenadier.

This sign seems to have been suggested by the tragical death of a grenadier, which is thus recorded on a tombstone in the churchyard of Winchester Cathedral :—

> Here sleeps in peace a Hampshire Grenadeer,
> Who caught his death by drinking cold *small beer*.
> Soldiers be warned by his untimely fall,
> And when you're hot, drink *strong*, or none at all.

There is another *Grenadier* (an imitation) at the present day at Colchester. The appended lines are said to have been written by Joseph Warton :—

> An honest soldier never is forgot,
> Whether he die by musket or by pot.

The *Flitch of Bacon*, Little Dunmow, Essex, is a fairly common sign in this county and is sometimes seen in others. The custom of giving a flitch of bacon is not peculiar to Dunmow. In the reign of Edward III a manor in Staffordshire was granted upon much the same conditions. At Wansford Bridge which crosses the river Nen in Northampton, is the *Haycock Inn*, deriving its name from a curious incident : the river overflowed its banks and carried away a haycock with a man upon it. Drunken Barnaby says of the circumstance :—

> On a Haycock sleeping soundly,
> Th' river rose, and took me roundly
> Down the current ; people cryed,
> Sleeping, down the streame I hyed ;
> *Where away !* quoth they, *from Greenland !*
> *No : from Wansford Bridge in England.*

The stone bridge of thirteen arches carries the Great North Rd. across the river. The *Haycock Inn*, at one end of the bridge has on the signboard a pictorial representation of the scene. Monson Fitzjohn explains the not very subtle joke by saying that Wansford, Northants, only just escaped being in 'Holland' (i.e. the Holland Division of Lincolnshire). As a matter of fact the nearest part of Holland is a good nine miles away so probably the joke is less subtle than he had supposed. This is an example of a house which after a long existence as an inn fell into decay with the disuse of the roads and became a private house—in fact the hunting-lodge of a local family. From the 1880's to 1928 it served this purpose, but it again reverted to its old use in 1928.

Scotland which produces Edinburgh ales and Highland whisky is honoured by numberless signs. *Land o'cakes* the name given by Burns is a sign at Middle Hill Gate near Stockport. Burns is quite rightly very popular among the publicans ; not only are the poet himself and several of his heroes exalted in innumerable places, but at Kirby Moor some of his verses are even introduced on the sign :—

> When Neebors anger at a plea,
> An' just as wud as wud can be,
> How easy can the barley bree
>   Cement the quarrel ?
> It's aye the cheapest lawyer's fee,
>   To taste the barrel.

Since the Highlander's love for snuff and whisky was such that he wished to have 'a Benlomond of snuff, and a Loch Lomond of whisky', nobody could make a better public-house sign than the *Highland Laddie*, nor a better snuff-shop sign than the kilted

Highlander who stood generally at the door of these establishments. Many of these wooden Highlanders still survive in our older towns. A good London example is *Phineas* the sign of Messrs. Catesby the linoleum dealers in Tottenham Court Rd., who has been adopted as a mascot by the medical students of University College not far away. The *Highland Laddie* is a quite common sign and occurs for example at Hyde, Ches., at Kidsgrove, Staffs., and at Hanley, Stoke-on-Trent. There is a *Highland Chief* at Hertford. The *Highland Tavern* is at Handsworth, Birmingham. The ubiquity of the Scotch packman produced the sign of the *Scotchman & his Pack*, St Michael's Hill, Bristol, and in some other places. The house is said, however, to commemorate not so much the Scotchman as his robber, a certain William Curtis who was hanged in 1741. There is a *Scotch Piper* at Lydcote, Lancs. *Gretna Green* used at one time to be a not very uncommon sign on the Border ; there is one at Aycliffe, Durh.

Of the colonies, dependencies and Dominions, *Gibraltar* is found for example at Chatham, as the *Gibraltar Gardens* at Norwich, and as the *Rock of Gibraltar* at Tynemouth. The *Cape of Good Hope* is also considered worthy the honour of the signboard. The frequency of this sign all over England seems to render it probable that it was not so much adopted in honour of the colony as to express the landlord's *hope* of success, and therefore as a sort of equivalent to the *Hope & Anchor*, or the *Hope*. The sign is found for example in Albany St., N.W., and at Bridgwater, Broseley, Salop. Many such supposedly humorous signs came into fashion at the beginning of the 19th century. Probably a few *Hope* inns have the same origin. One at Camberley, Surrey, however, is named after Gen. Sir Alexander Hope, a former Governor of the Royal Military Colleges at Marlow and Sandhurst. The *Jamaica* tavern may have been christened in compliment to the birthplace of rum. There is a house with this name in Southwark Park Rd., Bermondsey, which is one of the many houses stated in its time to have been a residence of Oliver Cromwell. After the Restoration this house seems to have become a tavern, and here according to the custom of the times Pepys on Saturday 14 April 1667 took his wife and her maids to give them a day's pleasure. Subsequently, he frequently returned to this place, which seems to have been the same he elsewhere calls the *Halfway House*. Besides this, there is the *Jamaica &Madeira* coffee-house, now usually known simply as the *Jamaica Coffee-House*, a well-known business tavern in St Michael's Alley, Cornhill. An *Australia* is to be found at Tydd St Giles, I. of Ely, and an *Australian* in Milner St.

Only a few European nations and towns are represented. The *Algarva* in Chancery Lane takes its name from an emirate of Portugal. In the time of Charles II it was the town residence of Sir Richard Fanshawe, formerly ambassador to the Court of Portugal, the diplomat who negotiated the marriage of Charles with Catherine of Braganza.

In the reign of Charles II there was a house of indifferent fame in Moorfields called the *Russia House*, perhaps opened during the time that the Russian ambassadors visited the king. The house became notorious in 1667 through the trial of Gabriel

Holmes and his band of youthful incendiaries. *Russia House* was one of the places where they planned their expeditions and spent their money : the object of their incendiarism being simply that they might steal the goods which would be flung into the streets by the terrified inmates of the burning houses.

Copenhagen House until relatively recently stood isolated in the fields north of London, near the old road to Highgate. It was said to have derived its name from the fact of a Danish prince or ambassador having residence in it during a great plague in London. Another tradition is to the effect that early in the 17th century upon some political occasion great numbers of Danes left that kingdom and came to London, whereupon the house was opened by an emigrant from Copenhagen as a place of resort for his countrymen. This tradition probably refers to the reign of James I, who was visited in London by his brother-in-law, the King of Denmark, at which time it is very probable that there was a considerable influx of persons from the Danish capital. *Coopen-Hagen* is the name given to the place in the map accompanying Camden's *Britannia* 1695. For many years previous to its demolition the house had a great reputation amongst Cockney excursionists, and its tea-gardens, skittle-ground, Dutch pins, and particularly Five Play were great attractions. The Metropolitan Cattle Market now occupies its site, and a modern public-house in York Rd., N., only perpetuates its name.

The *Antwerp Tavern* was a famous house behind the Exchange in the 17th century. Tokens of it are extant, representing a view of Antwerp from the river. The extensive trade of Flanders, in the Middle Ages and long after made Antwerp a favourite subject for signboards, it having the best harbour in Flanders. There is a house of this sign still at Dover.

Dutchmen in some instances have been appointed to preside over public-houses on account of their reputed love for drink, thus we have the *Two Dutchmen* at Marsden, W.R. Yorks., and the *Jovial Dutchman* at Crich, Derbys.

Besides drinking, the Dutchman has long had a reputation for smoking, whence the tobacconists of the 18th century used frequently to have on their sign, a Scotchman, a Dutchman, and a Sailor, with the following rhyme :—

> We three are engaged in one cause,
> I snuffs, I smokes, and I chaws.

A tobacconist in Kingsland Rd. had the same men, but a different reading of the text :—

> This Indian weed is good indeed,
> Puff on, keep up the joke,
> Tis the best, 'twill stand the test,
> Either to chew or smoke.

The introduction of coffee produced signs of various sultans, but the *Turk's Head* may perhaps date from earlier times, and have an origin similar to that of the *Saracen's*

Head. The Turks throughout the 15th, 16th and 17th centuries were a common topic of conversation, and the bugbear of the European nations. This is well exemplified in old churchwardens' accounts where one finds frequent entries of the purchase of special forms of prayer against invasion by the Turks, and notes of briefs for raising funds to ransom various Christian captives held in slavery. The first prototypes of newspapers were the printed despatches of the 1530's concerning the battles of the emperor with the Turks, and even at the end of the 17th century no newspaper was complete without its news from the Danube and movements of the Turks. One of the earliest patents granted for pistols contains a clause that square balls are not to be used 'except against the Turks'. The number of *Turk's Heads* in London in the 17th century was considerable ; not less than eight trades tokens of different houses with this sign are known to exist.

Dr. Johnson used often to take supper at the *Turk's Head* in the Strand : 'I encourage this house (said he) for the mistress of it is a good civil woman, and has not much business.' At another *Turk's Head*, Gerrard St., Soho, Johnson formed, in 1763, that well-known club, which was long without a name, but which after Garrick's funeral became distinguished by the name of the Literary Club. After the death of the landlord of this house, the club removed to the *Prince* in Sackville St., and after two or three more changes it finally settled down at the *Thatched House*, St James's. The original portrait of Sir Joshua Reynolds presented to the club by the painter himself is still preserved, one of its peculiarities is that the artist has represented himself wearing spectacles. The club is (?) still in existence, under the name of the *Dilettanti Club*. Moser's *Memorandum Book* of 1799 says the house ' was, more than fifty years since, removed from a tavern of the same sign, the corner of Greek and Compton Streets. This place was a kind of headquarters for the Loyal Association during the rebellion of 1745.'

The *Turk's Head* is still a fairly common sign. Instances of it have been noted at Derby, Hosketon, Suff., Leeds, Leicester, Nottingham, Retford, Notts., Ryde, Twickenham, Weymouth, Yarmouth, etc. The inn of this name at Leeds is now a popular restaurant. The *Turk's Head*, York, recently demolished, is said to have been a favourite haunt of Dick Turpin.

The *Three Turks* was a sign at Norwich in 1750, and even now there are other signs of *Turks* to be found, though both Larwood's further instances are now extinct —the *Turk & Slave*, Brick Lane, Spitalfields, and the *Great Turk* (i.e. the *Sultan*) at Wolverhampton. This last sign was of considerable antiquity, for in 1600 it was the sign of John Barnes, a bookseller in Fleet St. The *Sultan* at Waltham Abbey, Herts., has a fine modern pictorial sign after L. S. Lee. One or two other *Sultan* and similar signs are dealt with on p. 40.

One of the most prosperous Turkish towns was commemorated by the *Smyrna* coffee-house in Pall Mall, fashionable in the reign of Queen Anne. The wits and beaux used to take their constitutionals in St James's Park, and then go to the *Smyrna*, where, sitting before the open windows, they could see the ladies carried past in their sedans or coaches, on their return from the Mall. This coffee-house seems to have had a reputation for politics. In the *Tatler* (No. 10) a ' cluster of wise heads ' is said to sit every evening from the left side of the fire at the *Smyrna* to the door, and in No. 78, the public is informed that ' the seat of learning is now removed from the corner of the chimney in the left hand towards the window, to the round table in the middle of the floor, over against the fire, a revolution much lamented by the porters, and chairmen, who were greatly edified through a pane of glass that remained broken all the last summer '. Prior, Swift, and Pope were constant visitors to this house.

There was a *Grecian* coffee-house in Devereux Court, Strand, which was equally well frequented for nearly two centuries. It derived its name probably from having been opened by a Greek, the natives of that country having been among the first to open coffee-houses in London. It was a very fashionable house in the time of the *Spectators* and *Tatlers* : ' My face is likewise very well known at the Grecian ', says Addison in *Spectator*, No. 1. It seems generally to have been frequented by literati and savants, some of them rather hot-headed. According to King's *Anecdotes* :—

> Two gentlemen, constant companions, disputing one evening concerning the accent of a Greek word, the two friends thought proper to determine the question with their swords. For this purpose they stepped into Devereux Court where one of them named Fitzgerald, was run through the body and died on the spot.

In this coffee-house Mrs. Mapp, the famous bone-setter, performed her cures before Sir Hans Sloane in 1736. The coffee-house was closed in 1843 ; a bust of Essex is in front of the house it formerly occupied with the inscription ' This is Devereux Court, 1676 '.

Various reasons are given to account for the sign of the *Saracen's Head*. Selden says in *Table Talk* :—' When our countrymen came home from fighting with the Sarasens, and were beaten by them, they pictured them with huge, big, terrible faces (as you will see the sign of the *Saracen's Head* is,) when, in truth, they were like other men. But this they did to save their own credit.' Actually the sign may have been adopted by those who had visited the Holy Land, either as pilgrims or when fighting the Saracens. An old story has it that it was first set up in compliment to the mother of Thomas à Becket, who was the daughter of a Saracen ; formerly the sign was very general. During the time of the Commonwealth, the *Saracen's Head* in Islington was a place of resort for the Londoners. In the *Walks of Islington and Hogsden, with the Humours of Wood Street Compter*, a comedy by Thomas Jordan (the ' poet to the Corporation of London ') 1648, the scene is laid at this tavern. The *Saracen's Head*, Snow Hill, was one of the last remaining in Larwood's time (it is now extinct), and at the same time one of the oldest, being named in *Tarlton's Jests*. Stow says, ' next to this church (St Sepulchre's in the Bailey) is a fair and large inn for receipt of travellers, and hath to sign the *Sarazen's Head* '. The courtyard had many of the characteristics of an old English inn with galleries all round leading to the bedrooms, and a spacious gate through which the dusty mail-coaches used to rumble in, the tired passengers creeping forth and thanking their stars in having escaped the highwaymen and the holes and sloughs of the road. It was at this inn that Nicholas Nickleby and his uncle waited upon Squeers, the Yorkshire schoolmaster. Dickens describes the old tavern as it was in the last years of mail-coaching, when it was one of the most important places for arrivals and departures in London, and describes in detail the signs over the gateposts of the coach yard, ' two Saracens' heads and shoulders, which it was once the pride and glory of the choice spirits of this metropolis to pull down at night'. There are numerous provincial occurrences of this sign, for example at Lincoln and at Towcester. The famous *Saracen's Head* at Southwell is the house where Charles I surrendered to the Scottish Army in 1646. There are also several *Blackamoors* and *Blackamoor's Heads* in London and the Provinces.

Blackamoors and other dark-skinned foreigners have always possessed considerable attraction as signs for tobacconists, and sometimes also for coffee-houses, and public-houses. Pipe-smoking negroes, with feathered head-dresses and kilts are to be seen outside tobacco-shops on the Continent as well as in England. In the 17th and 18th centuries the *Virginian* sign was common in England owing to the first tobacco having been imported from Virginia. The *Virginia Plant* and the *Virginia Planter* have been dealt with above (p. 160).

Publicans have a strange fancy for Indian Kings, Queens and Chiefs. An *Indian Queen* at Boston is Princess Pocahontas who in 1613 married John Rolfe, a local man. There was in Larwood's time a sculptured sign of an *Indian Chief* at Shoreditch, having all the appearance of an old ship's figurehead. It has now disappeared. The *Indian Chief* sign still survives however at Chesterton, Cambs. In Dolphin Lane, Boston (Lincs.), there used formerly to be a sign with some fanciful, masked-ball dressed figures on it which were meant to represent the *Three Kings of Cologne*, but they conveyed so little the idea of those holy personages that the public called them the *Three Merry Devils*. Eventually by a strange metamorphosis these three merry devils were transformed into one very strangely dressed female called the *Indian Queen*. There is another *Indian Queen* still at Bodmin (but see p. 41). The *African Chief*, formerly in Ossulton St., but recently swept away in street improvements, is evidently a variant upon these Indian chiefs.

Another sign of venerable antiquity is the *Black Boy*. Machyn's *Diary* has an entry concerning the murder of a person dwelling at the *Black Boy* in the Cheap in 1562. This *Black Boy* seems to have been a tobacconists sign from the first; for in Ben Jonson's *Bartholomew Fair* * we find :—' I thought he would have run mad o' the Black Boy in Bucklersbury, that takes the scurvy roguy tobacco there.' In the 17th century, the *Black Boy* was the sign of a celebrated ordinary in Southwark. At the *Black Boy* in Newgate St., the Calves' Head Club was sometimes held. It was not restricted to any particular house, but moved yearly from one place to another, as it was found most convenient. An axe was hung up in the club-room crowned

---

* Act I, Sc. 1.

with laurel : the bill of fare consisted of calves' heads, dressed in various ways ; a large pike, with a small one in his mouth (an emblem of tyranny) ; a large cod's head ; a boar's head, to indicate stupidity and bestiality. There is a *Black Boy* at Retford, Notts., and there are numerous others in the provinces. A very pleasing sign of this name is at Bosham, Sussex. It belongs to Messrs. Henty and Constable of Chichester, and has the good painting which their houses usually display. The distinction between *Black Boy* and *Blackamoor* is said to be that the former is a negro, and the latter a Moor or Arab.

The *Black Girl* is a variety of this sign at Clarborough, Notts. So, too, appears to be the *Arab Boy*, an alehouse on the road between Putney and East Sheen. The *Two Black Boys* occurs on one of the London trades tokens, where the two are represented as shaking hands.

The *Black Boy & Camel* (doubtless a black boy leading a camel) was not many years ago the sign of a tavern in Leadenhall St., where it was already in existence in the year 1700. Tickets for the ' Annual feast for the Parish of St. Dunstan, in Stepney, being revived ', to be kept at the *King's Head* in Stepney in 1700 were advertised in the *London Gazette* as obtainable at this house. There is a *Black Boy & Still* at Brentford, Mx. A very odd sign which seems to defy all attempts at a rational explanation is the *Black Boy & Stomach-ache*.

Jerusalem was sure to figure early on signboards of those inns favoured by pilgrims on their way to the Holy Land. Long after pilgrimages were discontinued it was still retained as a sign. In 1657 we find it in Fleet St. What the sign was like it is impossible now to say, but on the trades token of the house the Holy City is represented by one single building. There is another token extant of a house also in Fleet St., without date or name of the shop, on which there is a view of a town with the usual conventional representation of the temple of Solomon. A similar idea seems to be conveyed by the sign of the *Gates of Jerusalem*, Bishopsgate St., E.C., commonly known as *Dirty Dick's*. There is also a *Trip to Jerusalem* at Nottingham and a *Pilgrim* at Coventry. There was in Larwood's time an *Old Jerusalem* tavern in Clerkenwell, now no more, so called after the Knights of St John. This house was situated in the principal gateway of the Hospital, which was handed over to the ' modern ' Order of St John in 1873.

Mount Pleasant is a name frequently bestowed upon public-houses, not always with any allusion to such a locality but simply on account of its being an alluring name of the same maudlin class as *Cottage of Content*, found at Betchworth, Surrey, Birmingham, Mersham, Kent, Redhill, Surrey, and in Wells Rd., S.E.16, and the *Bank of Friendship*, still to be seen at Hartford St., Mile End, etc. There is said to be a mountain of that name in America, which obtained some celebrity from being the locality on which was gathered the sassafras (*Orchis mascula*), the plant which produces the saloop. This drink came in vogue at the beginning of the 18th century. Reide's coffee-house in Fleet St. was the first respectable house where it was sold. When it was opened in 1719, the following lines painted on a board hung in front of the house.

In later times until the closing of the establishment in 1833, they were preserved in the coffee-room :—

> Come all degrees now passing by,
> My charming liquor taste and try ;
> To Lockyer come and drink your fill,
> *Mount Pleasant* has no kind of ill.
> The fumes of wines, punch, drams, or beer,
> It will expel ; your spirits cheer ;
> From drowsiness your spirits free ;
> Sweet as a rose your breath shall be,
> Come taste and try, and speak your mind,
> Such rare ingredients here are joined.
> *Mount Pleasant* pleases all mankind.

Lockyer had begun life with half-a-crown, and by selling saloop at Fleet-ditch, amassed sufficient capital to open the place in Fleet St., where he died worth £1,000, in March 1739.

Pepys mentions going to *China Hall*, but gives no further particulars. It is not unlikely that this was the same place which in the summer of 1777, was opened as a theatre. Whatever its use in former times it was at that period the warehouse of a paper manufacturer.

Besides the above-mentioned geographical signs, we have others of more modern introduction, such as the *South Australian* in Cadogan St., Chelsea, and the *North Pole*, in New North Rd., which last, presumably like a former house of the same name mentioned by Larwood as in Oxford St., commemorates one of the expeditions that have taken place every now and then since Frobisher first began on the discovery of *Meta Incognita*. There are *Market* inns, *Market* taverns, *Market* vaults, etc., innumerable, and often such titles veil the identities of ancient houses whose original signs were much more picturesque. Sometimes an adjective has been compounded with the noun so that a house appears to be called the *Newmarket* Inn, whereas its proper title is and always has been the *New Market* Inn. This is the case for example with the well-known house at Islington. There are numerous *Half-Way Houses*, generally on old roads and having as a rule the obvious origin. The *Halfpenny House* in Richmond, Yorks., is a corruption of this. To justify its title a halfpenny toll was quite illegally exacted there, which in later years went to swell the funds of Richmond Hospital.

There exists a class of signs in some respects geographical yet from their indefinite character perhaps more adapted for insertion in the following chapter than here. Such are the *Four Counties* situated at No Man's Heath where the four shires of Warwick, Stafford, Leicester, and Derby meet, and a picture of the fiery sun going down behind a hill, called the *World's End*, at St George's, near Bristol, and at Chelsea, S.W. The *First & Last* (inn in England) may be seen in many other localities besides at Sennen, Cornwall. The *First In, Last Out* refers as a rule to the position of a house on the outskirts of a town. Probably the name was popularized also by its applicability to the habits of a regular customer.   The sign is found at Bideford, Dunstable, Luton, and in many other places.   *No Place* Inn is a public-house in the suburbs of Plymouth, the sign representing an old woman standing at the door accosting her husband who has just returned home—' Where have you been ? '   ' No place.'   There are many other signs of an equally indefinite character which might be given here, but probably few of them are worth special mention.

Chapter XVI

HUMOROUS AND COMIC

ANIMALS performing human actions, or dressed in human garments, are great items in signboard humour. This is a kind of comicality undoubtedly dating from the first development of human wit. Numerous Egyptian, Greek and Roman caricatures of animals personating men have come down to us. From these this conceit was borrowed by the mediaeval artists. Their manuscripts teem with such subjects, and so much was this kind of humour relished at that period that even in church decoration the caricatures of animals were liberally mixed with the subjects from biblical history. Thus the well-known sign of the *Pig & Whistle* is seen in more than one church, for example in a stall carving at Winchester Cathedral a sow is represented sitting on her haunches playing on a whistle the companion carving of which is a pig playing on a violin, in accompaniment to which another pig appears to be singing. In one of the Harleian MSS. a sow is represented dressed in 15th-century fashion with horned headdress and stilted heels and playing on a harp.

In old towns, such as Chester, Macclesfield, Coventry, the *Pig & Whistle* is still found on signboards. A house of the same name mentioned by Larwood was in Oxford St. There is another house of this name in Liverpool, others at Burnt Fen, Suff., and Newport Pagnall, Bucks., and there is a *Peg & Whistle* at Helion Bumpstead, Essex. Many different learned and pseudo-learned explanations have been given for its origin, some saying it was a corruption of the *piggin and wassail bowl*, or of the *pix and housel*, others that it is a facetious rendering of the *Bear & Ragged Staff*. Theorists in Larwood's time claimed for it a Danish-Saxon descent, as *pige-washail*, our *Ladies' Salutation*. The Scots also claim it as their own ; *pig* being a pot or potsherd, *whistle*, small change, and ' to go to *pigs and whistle* ' a free translation of ' *going to pot* '. Since Larwood wrote, any amount of ink and paper have been devoted to theorizing as to the origin of this very interesting sign, but there is little to add to his conclusion that a pig with a whistle is still but a pig. Probably the sign does not relate in any way to the Virgin, and there is nothing in the *Pig & Whistle* but a freak of the mediaeval artist.

As little hidden meaning is there in the *Cat & Fiddle*, still a great favourite in Hampshire. The only apparent connexion between the animal and the instrument is that the strings are or were made from the cat's entrails, and that a small fiddle is called a *kit*, and a small cat a *kitten*. Besides, they have been united from time immemorial in the nursery rhyme :—

Heigh diddle diddle,
The cat and the fiddle.

Among other explanations offered is the one that the sign may have originated with the sign of a certain *Caton fidele*, a staunch Protestant (or by other accounts a loyal Governor of Calais) in the reign of Queen Mary, and only changed into the cat and fiddle by corruption. If so, it must have lost its original appellation very soon, for as early as 1589 we find ' Henry Carr, signe of the *Catte & Fidle* in the Old Chaunge '. Formerly there was a *Cat & Fiddle*, at Norwich, the cat being represented playing upon a fiddle, and a number of mice dancing round her. Beverley Minster contains an old carving of a cat playing a fiddle. An anonymous Frenchman is said to have named the house after his faithful cat Mignonnette—La Chatte Fidele. Or Caton-Cato is used by French authors (e.g. Molière in *Tartuffe* and Racine in *Les Plaideurs*) for a man of strict probity. The reader may take his choice from these explanations. There is still a house of this sign at Hinton Admiral, Hants, and another very picturesque inn of this sign, much admired by Americans visiting the West Country, lies four miles out of Exeter on the Sidmouth road. The bagpipes being the national instrument of the Irish, the sign is there frequently changed into the *Cat & Bagpipes*. This was, about a century ago, the sign of a public- and chop-house at the corner of Downing St., Westminster, where the clerks of the Foreign Office used to lunch.

The *Ape & Bagpipes* occurs on trades tokens as the sign of John Tayler, in St Ann's Lane. The sign at East Harlesey, N.R. Yorks., is said to be a skit upon the Highland cattle drovers who passed through the place on their way to London. The *Cat & Custard Pot*, Paddleworth, Kent, is apparently merely a local nickname for the *Red Lion*. A new sign of the same name at Shipton Moyne, Glos., is taken from that of the inn in Surtees' *Handley Cross*. The sign shows a scene from the book with Mr. Jorrocks in the centre. We have one modern sign in London of this class, namely, the *Whistling Oyster*, the name of an oyster-shop in Drury Lane. An inn of this name remained until 1889. According to the story the proprietor of the shop *c.* 1840, discovered among his stock an oyster which really did make a hissing sound such as might fairly be styled a whistle—why, it is difficult to say. Perhaps the creature whistled with apprehension when it realized it was at a shop in Vinegar Yard. The subject was much debated, the curiosity was exhibited and a fancy portrait of it appeared in an early number of *Punch*. According to another account the proprietor announced he had whistling oysters to display to his customers and secured much trade in this way. When any visitor (after a drink for the good of the house) demanded to see the rarity, he was told it had just been eaten, but there would be another tomorrow.

The *Jackanapes on Horseback* was unfortunately for the monkeys reference to a painful truth. A jackanapes or monkey on horseback was generally the winding-up of a bear- or bull-baiting at Paris Garden. Holinshed in his *Chronicles* 1562 relates how, at the reception of the Danish ambassadors at Greenwich—

> For the diversion of the populace, there was a horse with an ape on his back which highly pleased them, so that they expressed their inward conceived joy and delight with shrill shouts and variety of gestures.

S

The ' inward conceived joy' one may safely suppose, was not expressed by either the monkey or the horse, particularly since dogs were often let in the ring to frighten both the horse and its jockey.   Thomas Cartwright in 1572 refers to the sight of a jackanapes on horseback as entertaining both to the parson and his parishioners, so that the service was gabbled through, in order that all might be present at the sport.   The *Grenning Iackanapes* is a sign mentioned by Eliot in his *Fruits for the French*, or *Parlement of Pratlers* 1593, ' ouer against the Vnicorne in the Iewrie'.   The *Hog in Armour*, in Hanging Sword Court, Fleet St., is mentioned in an advertisement in 1678.   It is named among the absurd London signs in the *Spectator* 2 April 1711, and is still occasionally seen, though the sign no longer exists in London.   In Larwood's time this was a favourite term applied to rifle volunteers by costermongers, street fishmongers, and such like.   A jocular name for this sign is the *pig in misery*.   In this second form especially it is still used for anyone unsuitably and uncomfortably clad or employed. There is also a *Goat in Armour* on the Narrow Quay, Bristol, a *Goat in Boots* on the Fulham Palace Rd., and one at Chester.

In 1663 this house was called the *Goat*, and enjoyed the right of commonage for two cows and one heifer upon Chelsea Heath.   The sign is an interesting one.   The original one was painted by le Blond, then it was repainted by Morland.   Unfortunately it has been often repainted again since.   A vast deal has been written on the origin of the sign—how it may once have been the *Mercury*, a fairly common sign denoting that post-horses were to be obtained, and how the Dutch inscription, *Mercuruis ist der Goden Boode* (Mercury is the messenger of the Gods), became corrupted into its present form.   However, the house was called by its present name at least as early as 1663, there is no evidence that it was ever called *Mercury*, and no obvious reason why an English inn should carry a Dutch sign.   Moreover by 1738 some other *Goats-in-Boots* had already appeared, not the result of any mythological metamorphosis. The *Craftsman* for 17 June 1738, in ridiculing some lenient measures taken by Government, blames the signs for putting a martial spirit in the nation, and proposes that ' no lion should be drawn *rampant* but *couchant* ' ;   and none of his teeth ought to be seen without the inscription, ' Though he shows his teeth he won't bite.' ' All bucks, bulls, rams, stags, unicorns, and all other warlike animals ought to be drawn without horns. Let no general be drawn in armour, and instead of truncheons let them have musterrolls in their hands.   In like manner, I would have all admirals painted in a frock and jockey cap, like landed gentlemen.   The common sign of the two *Fighting Cocks* might be better changed to a *Cock & Hen*, and that of the *Valiant Trooper* to a *Hog in Armour*, or a *Goat in Jackboots*, as some Hampshire and Welsh publicans have done already for the honour of their respective countries.'   The sign then, seems to be a sort of caricature of a Welshman, the goat having always been considered the emblem of that nation, and the jackboots an indispensable article of Taffy's costume.   Grose mentions a Welshman with his goat, leek, hayboots, and long pedigree, as a standard joke.   Not improbably then the switch carried by the goat on this sign was originally a leek. The *Goat & Boot* found at Colchester is not to be confused with the sign last dealt with.

The goat here developed from the crest of the local Dighton family, an antelope, and the boot was added by the landlord about 1790, either being sea boots to induce sailors to use the house, or jackboots, to suggest that the house (like a jackboot) was often filled with beer.

There is a *Goat* at Deeping St James's, Lincs., and there are numerous examples of the *Goat & Compasses*. This is often alleged to be a corruption of the God encompasseth us, or of the joiners' arms. Another story makes the God encompasseth us a Puritan version of the original sign. Still another story has it that the *Goat* was a sign favoured by Welsh innkeepers, and that it was charged with the (Masonic) emblem when the landlord was a Freemason, in much the same fashion as nowadays licensees exhibit plaques with the initials R.A.O.B., etc.

Of similar origin to the *Goat in Boots* is the well-known *Welsh Trooper*, representing a man with a leek in his hat riding on a goat. This sign may still be seen in London. In the Roxburghe ballads the Welshman with his jackboots and leek occurs in an old woodcut ; in other places he is drawn riding a goat, and similarly dressed. *Puss in Boots* occurs at Windley, Derbys. The *Goat in Boots* may have suggested the idea of making a sign of this nursery-tale hero.

The *Dog* also appears dressed as the *Dog in Doublet*, a sign which may be seen at Pyebridge, Derbys., at Northbank, Cambs., and in a few other out-of-the-way places. Dr. Johnson used the phrase as a metaphor. Speaking of an old idea newly expressed, he said : ' It is an old coat with a new facing,' then laughing heartily, ' it is the old dog in a new doublet ! ' The sign may be either a symbol of impropriety—a dog pretending to be a man, or merely an indication that the house has changed hands—the old dog has a new doublet.

The *Dog* occurs in various other humorous combinations. Ned Ward in 1703 mentions a famous inn, the *Devil's Lapdog* in Petty Cury, Cambridge. The *Dog & Pot* is said to be often an ironmonger's sign. If so, it may conceivably have originated in a (fire) dog and cooking-pot. The *Dog's Head in the Pot* is mentioned in *Cocke Lorell's Bote*, a pamphlet issued by Wynkyn de Worde. The sign is depicted in very early times however as a real dog with a real pot. It was that of an inn in Great or Little Horemead, Herts., in 1563 ; it occurs, says Mr. Norman, in some ' lately discovered Tudor carvings from an old house in Gloucester, and on a couple of 17th century tokens from Red Cross St., and from Old St., St Luke's respectively '. It was probably then originally a mocking sign to indicate a dirty, sluttish housewife. A woodcut above the second part of the Roxburghe ballad, *The Coaches Overthrow*, represents various dirty practices. From the upper windows of one of the houses a woman is emptying the contents of a chamber pot almost on the heads of the people underneath, and the sign of the house is the *Dog's Head in the Pot*, representing a dog licking out a pot. A coarse woodcut sheet of the commencement of the 18th century, evidently to judge by the costume copied from a much older original, represents two ancient beldames with high-crowned hats, starched ruffs and collars, and high-heeled boots in a very disorderly room or kitchen. One of the women wipes a plate with the bushy tail of a

large dog, whose head is completely buried in a capacious pot, which he is licking clean.
Under is :—

> All sluts behold, take view of me,
> Your own good housewifry to see.
> It is (methinks) a cleanly care,
> My dishclout in this sort to spare,
> Whilst Dog, you see, doth lick the pot,
> His taile for dishclout I have got, etc.

There is a *Dog & Pot* at Windsor, and there is a *Dog's Head in the Pot* at Bishop's Stortford, and another at Slough. The original *Dog's Head in the Pot* sign from the iron-
mongery warehouse at the corner of Charlotte St. and Blackfriars Rd. is now in the
Cuming Museum, Walworth Rd. The sign is also called the *Dog & Crock*, as in the
Blackfriars Rd., at Michelmerch, Hants, and elsewhere. In the western counties the
word ' crock ' is indiscriminately applied to iron and earthern pots. Probably the *Dog
(Shepherd's) & Crook*, found at Braishfield, Hants, is a corruption of this sign.

The *Dancing Dogs* was a sign at Battlebridge, Northants, in 1668, as appears from
the trades tokens. This kind of canine entertainment was one of the attractions of
Bartholomew Fair, where Ben Jonson mentions ' dogs that dance the Morris '. Other
quaint animal signs include *Two Sneezing Cats*, said to have been formerly somewhere
in London ; the *Flying Monkey*, Lambeth, the *Monkey Island* at Bray, Berks., the
Gaping Goose at Gosforth, Leeds, at Oldham, and in various parts of Yorkshire ; and
the *Loving Lamb* (two in Dudley). On the *Gaping Goose* sign was depicted a gander
with his mouth wide open after the manner of geese and ganders, with perhaps a suggestion that the mouth was open because the bird was thirsty.

Equally absurd is the *Cow & Snuffers*, at Llandaff, Glam. In a play of George Colman, entitled *The Review, or The Wags of Windsor*, the following lines occur :—

> Judy's a darling ; my kisses she suffers,
> She's an heiress, that's clear,
> For her father sells beer,
> He keeps the sign of the *Cow & the Snuffers*.

The same song also occurs in the *Irishman in London, or the Happy African*. The
sign represents a red cow standing near a ditch full of reeds and grasses, with a gigantic
pair of snuffers, placed as if they had fallen from the cow's mouth. The oddity of the
combination in all probability pleased a publican who had heard the song, and he
adopted it forthwith as his sign, leaving the arrangements of the objects to the taste
of the sign-painter. According to another account the sign was deliberately adopted
from a bet of 1770 as to who could think of the two most incongruous objects to appear
together on an inn sign. I have not traced any occurrence of this sign in England.

The *Colt & Cradle* might have been seen in St Martin's Lane in 1667. It was lately
a common sign for houses of evil repute in Holland, where the cradle was carved above

the door, with the colt in it lying on his back : the inscription is, ' Het paard in de Wieg ' (the horse in the cradle).   According to Stow in ancient times ' English people disdayned to be bawdes, froes of Flaunders were women for that purpose ', it is probable that these ' froes ' introduced this sign from their own country.   In Dutch *paar* means ' a couple ', either united by the bands of lawful marriage or otherwise.   The original form of the sign, then, we suppose was ' the couple in the cradle ' (' *het paar in de wieg* '). With the adding of the usual Dutch diminutive *paar* became *paartje*.   From *paartje* to *paardje*, a small horse, the transition was easy enough, and, covered with that transparent veil, the indelicate sign has come down to the present day.   This seems so much the more probable meaning, since the *Cradle* in London also was a ' bad sign ' (see p. 236).

The *Goose & Gridiron* occurs at Woodhall, Lincs., in Birmingham and in a few other localities.   It is said to owe its origin to the following circumstances :—The *Mitre* (see p. 191) was a celebrated music house in London House Yard at the north west end of St Paul's.   When it ceased to be a music house, the succeeding landlord, to ridicule its former associations, chose for his sign a goose stroking the bars of a gridiron with his foot, in ridicule of the *Swan & Harp*, a common sign for early music houses.   This is the origin given by the *Tatler*.   The sign may be a vernacular reading of the coat of arms of the Company of Musicians, probably suspended at the door of the *Mitre* when it was a music-house.   These arms are : a swan with his wings expanded, within a double tressure counter flory *argent*.   The double tressure might have suggested a grid-iron to unlearned passers-by.   The original sign was in a kind of vane at the top of the building.   After the rebuilding of the house it appeared upon the conventional sign-board.

Paddy's Goose is, at the present day a nickname for a public-house in Shadwell properly called the *White Swan*.   In former years this tavern was notorious.   According to one account it was a camping house for the Navy.   According to another the landlord made a habit of befriending the victims of the press-gang.   A not very convincing account of the origin of the sign says that a fugitive from the press-gang was on occasion hidden away behind a secret door in front of which the landlord stood, cooking a goose, when the officers visited the house.   It is likelier that the sign refers to a tailor's goose, or to the traditional Irishman who (as in the old nursery rhyme *Three Men Went a-Hunting*) is always making comical errors.   An ' Irish ' anything is much inferior to the English variety.   An ' Irish Beauty ' has two black eyes, ' Irish legs ' are thick and clumsy ones (the Irish women by special dispensation from the Pope wearing their legs with the thick ends downwards), an ' Irishman's Rise ' is a demotion, and ' an Irish Wedding ' is one where the guests have black eyes instead of white favours. Of this house it is said that a burly Irishman insisted that the swan was a goose, and offered to fight anyone of a contrary opinion.   So a goose it became, and is to this day.

Not a few signs represent proverbs or proverbial expressions, the *Bird in Hand*, for instance, with occasionally the *Book in Hand* as in Long Acre and at Alford, Lincs.   The latter sign is probably in general heraldic.   A book in hand is the crest of the Apple-whaites, Crewes, Salthouses, etc.   The former denotes the landlord's full appreciation of the truth of the proverb, ' One bird in the hand is worth two in the bush '. It is frequently accompanied by the following distich :—

> A bird in hand is better far
> Than two that in the bushes are.

This sign occurs among the trades tokens, being literally rendered by a hand holding a bird. Sometimes the sign is heraldic, and represents a falcon and gauntlet, no doubt a family crest. More often it seems to be a dig at a rival house the *Bush*—a bird in hand being worth two in the bush. There are said to be 174 houses in England with the *Bird in Hand* sign. They seem particularly common in North Staffordshire. There are examples also at Shrewsbury, Bridgnorth, High Wycombe, etc., etc.

Innumerable are the jokes resorted to by landlords to intimate the hard truth that no credit is given. Sometimes the hint is conveyed in an ingenious manner by a watch face without pointers displayed in the bar accompanied by the significant words *No Tick*. Frequently the pill is gilt in the most agreeable manner. A deceptive hope of ' better luck tomorrow ' is frequently held out as :—

> Drink here, and drown all sorrow,
> Pay today, I'll trust tomorrow.

Or :—

> Pay today and trust tomorrow,
> And so endeth all our sorrow.

The idea was ingeniously expressed at Smethwick :—

> Sacred to the memory of Poor Trust, who fought hard at the battle of Deception, but fell under General Bad Pay.

A print formerly hung up in a public-house in Nottingham, depicting a black tombstone (or signboard,—it is difficult to say which) spotted with briny white tears and giving the inscription with still greater force :—

> This monument is erected to the memory of Mr. Trust, who was some time since most shamefully and cruelly murdered by a villain called Credit, who is prowling about, both in town and country, seeking whom he may devour.

Others have the picture of a dead dog, and under him :—

> Died last night, Poor Trust ! Who killed him ? Bad Pay !

A very general inscription is a jingle sometimes accorded to (Hudibras) Butler, sometimes to the Earl of Rochester :—

> This is a good world to live in,
> To lend, or to spend, or to give in ;
> But to beg or to borrow, or to get a man's own,
> It is such a world as never was known.

Or :—

> The rule of this house, and it can't be unjust,
> Is to pay on delivery, and not to give trust ;
> I've trusted many to my sorrow,
> Pay today, I'll trust tomorrow.

Stuck up in the bars and tap-rooms of a few old-fashioned country inns may be seen :—

> All you that bring tobacco here
> Must pay for pipes as well as beer ;
> And you that stand before the fire,
> I pray sit down by good desire,
> That other folks as well as you
> May see the fire, and feel it too.
> Since man to man is so unjust,
> I cannot tell what man to trust.
> My liquor's good, 'tis no man's sorrow,
> Pay today, I'll trust tomorrow.

At an alehouse in Ranston, Norf., the usual information was conveyed in the following manner (to be read upwards, beginning from the bottom of the last column) :—

More	beer	score	clerk
for	my	my	their
do	trust	pay	sent
I	I	must	have
shall	if	I	brewers
what	and	and	my

At other places it comes in a still more questionable shape, reminiscent of the curious literary conceits of the old monkish rhymesters. In the following, the letters must be connected into words, thus—*The brewer*, etc.

> Th   ebr :   Ewe   !   Rh   eH.   Ass ?
>   en.   THIS.   cLEr
> k a N d ! IM.   ustp, A   YM   Ys
>   cO.r.ef,   O
> r   IFIT r US ?   tandam, No   tpA.
>   iD wha. ts ;   Ha :
> LLiD ,   O ? Fo   Rm.   Or   .e.

A little wayside inn, between Pateley Bridge and Ripon, has this plaintive appeal to a stiffnecked race :—

> The Malster doth crave
> His money to have,
> The exciseman says have I must.
> By that you can see
> How the case stands with me ;
> So I pray you don't ask me for trust.

A small beer-house, the *Lengdon* Inn at Werrington, Devon, had :—

> Gentlemen, walk in, and sit at your ease,
> Pay what you call for, and call what you please ;
> As trusting of late has been to my sorrow,
> Pay me to-day, and I'll trust ee to-morrow.

The *Maypole* near Hainault Forest has :—

> My liquor's good,
> My measures just ;
> Excuse me, sirs !
> I cannot trust.

At Preston in Lancashire :—

> Greadley Bob, he does live here,
> And sells a pot of good strong beer ;
> His liquor's good, his measures just,
> But Bob's so poor he cannot trust.

The *Green Man* on Finchley Common, under a trophy composed of two pipes crossed and a pot of beer, presents us with the following :—

> Call . Softly
> Drink . Moderate
> Pay . *Honourably*
> Be Good . *Company*
> Part . FRIENDLY
> Go . **HOME** . quietly.
> Let those lines be no MANS Sorrow
> Pay to **DAY** and I'll **TRUST** to Morrow.

Even in the ruined city of Pompeii a similar caution is found. Above the door of a house, once inhabited by a surgeon occurs the intimation :—' EME ET HABEBIS '. One publican however at Littletown, Durham, seems to have taken a somewhat opposite view to his fellows, putting up for a sign the *Bird in the Bush*. It seems hardly likely however that this was a hint that tick was available.

Another proverb illustrated is the *Cow & Hare* at Stafford, Bottisham, Cambs., and other places, evidently suggested by the adage, ' A cow may catch a hare '. There was formerly another example of this sign in Norwich. A manuscript note of c. 1708 in the hand of Partridge the almanac-maker refers to a house of this sign by White-chapel Church. Perhaps the sign may be connected with witchcraft. Witches of course habitually took the shape of hares, and in this form would pay off an old score against a farmer by robbing his cows of their milk. In Camden's time care was taken to kill any hare found near the cattle on May-Day. Of the same class as the *Cow & Hare* is *Who'd ha' thought it !* which sometimes is seen on an alehouse sign, as for instance, at Fulham. It is said to have been used sometimes when the licensee had been so successful in the Trade as to be able to buy the freehold of the house. The understood second line of the couplet is :

> Malt and Hops had bought it.

The sign of the *Jolly Brewer*—*Who'd ha' thought it*, occurs in Jersey Rd., Hounslow, and at Nine Mile Ride, Berks. *Who'd Have Thought It* is at Barking, Essex. A house of this name at Lockeridge, Wilts., is said to be so called from its position. Originally, it seems to have implied that, after a hard struggle in some other walk of life, the landlord had succeeded in opening the long-wished-for alehouse.

Why Not, the name of a public-house at Windsor, at Essington, Staffs., and at Dover, seems to imply quite the reverse, and to have been adopted as the motto of a more sanguine landlord ; unless it may be considered as a ready answer to the understood question ' Shall we go and have one ? '

The *Lame Dog* is very common, but was particularly appropriate at Brierley Hill, Staffs., the establishment being formerly kept by a collier, rendered lame in a pit accident. Under a pictorial representation of a lame dog trying to get over a stile, the following appeal is or was made to the thirsty and benevolent public :—

> Stop, my friends, and stay awhile
> To help the Lame Dog over the stile.

There is another *Lame Dog* at Norwich. Sometimes, as formerly at Bulmer, Essex, and at Codicote, Herts., we see a somewhat similar idea expressed by a man struggling through a globe—head and arms protruding on one side, his legs on the other—with the inscription ' Help Me Through This World '. The sign is also called the *Struggler*, or the *Struggling Man* as at Dudley, the *Struggler in the Globe*, as at Lincoln and at Hampton, where the house, kept by a widow, was the *Widow's Struggle*. In Salop St., Dudley, the struggle was represented by a man with a dog beside him walking against a strong head wind. The *Live & Let Live* has a somewhat similar meaning ; it occurs at North End, Fulham, at Little Downham, I. of Ely, at Coddenham, Suff., and in many other places. Sometimes it is said to be a road inn's remark upon railway competition. To this class, also, the *Shirt* seems to refer—' A witty, though unfortunate, fellow having tryed all trades, but thriving by none, took the pot for his last refuge, and set up an alehouse with the sign of the *Shirt*, inscribed under it " This is my last shift ". Much company was brought him thereby, and much profit.'

Another widow's sign is that of the *Widow's Son*, Devon's Rd. The legend of this house and the Good Friday currant buns is so well known as to need no repetition.

The uncertainty of success in trade is expressed by the sign of the *Two Chances* and *Hit or Miss* found at Watford and at Keysoe, Beds. They refer to the good and the bad chance which innkeepers have to run. This sign formerly also occurred at Hannington, Northants, and at Clun, Salop. At Openshaw, Manchester, a similar idea is expressed by a sign representing two men running a race which seems to promise a dead heat, with the inscription *Luck's All*.

Other signs have in them a sort of satirical humour, such as the well-known *Four Alls*, seen at Rokeby, Yorks., representing a king who says, ' I rule all ; ' a priest who says, ' I pray for all ; ' a soldier who says, ' I fight for all ; ' and John Bull, or a farmer, who says, ' I pay for all.'   Sometimes as at Cheltenham, Chepstow, Chippenham, Lechdale, Marlborough, Salisbury and (? formerly) at Dover, a fifth is added in the shape of a lawyer, who says, ' I plead for all.'   A good example at Ovington has the punning signboard.   Often in such signs the pictures are portraits—George IV, the bishop of the diocese, a well-known barrister who has won a local *cause célèbre*, etc.

The author of *Tavern Anecdotes* observes that he used to notice in Rosemary St. the sign of the *Four Alls*, but passing that way some time after, he found it altered into *Four Awls* ;   the sign-painter who had renewed the picture had probably found himself not equal to the representation of the four human figures.   Certainly three and four awls constitute the charges in the shoemakers' arms of some of the continental trade societies or guilds.   Sometimes the *Alls* sign may be connected with the fact that ' alls ' was a cant term for the remainders of various beverages.   *Four & Five Alls* was a mixture of these, and in some of the signs each of the ' Alls ' has in his hand a glass (? of this mixture).   A rather similar sign, less often found, is the *Triple Plea*, to be seen for example at Halesworth, Suff.   The sign depicts a man on his death-bed. Around him are ranged the parson pleading for his soul, the doctor for his body, and the lawyer for his estate.   In the background stands the Devil, presumably as the remainder-man of all four.

The *Naked Boy* was a satirical sign reflecting upon the constant changes of the fashion of our ancestors.

> So fickle is our English nation,
> I wou'd be clothed if I knew the fashion.

The same idea is expressed in the *Introduction to Knowledge*, by Andrew Borde, 1542, where a *naked man* is introduced undecided (on account of the continual changes in the fashions) the style of dress he should adopt :—

> Now am I a frysker, all men doth on me looke,
> What should I do but set cocke on the hoope,
> What do I care yf all the worlde me fayle,
> I will get a garment shall reche to my tayle.

Thomas Coryate also reflects upon this ever-varying change in his *Crudities* :—' It hath given occasion to the Venetians and other Italians to brand the Englishmen with a notable mark of levity by painting him stark naked with a pair of shears in his hand, making his fashion of attire according to the conception of his brain sick head, not to comeliness and decorum.'

Thomas Heywood, in the *Rape of Lucrece*,★ 1638, has a very similar passage.

Shakespeare seems to allude to the sign of the *Naked Boy* in the *Comedy of Errors*,†

★ Epigr. XXVI.   † Act IV, Sc. 3.

where Dromio says, ' What, have you got the picture of old Adam new apparell'd.'
At Skipton-in-Craven there is still a stone bas-relief of the *Naked Boy*, fixed in the front
of a house, with the date 1633.

The *Good Woman* is at Leek, Staffs., Buxton, Derbys., and at Necton, Norf., the
Headless Woman at Duddon, Ches., the *Quiet Woman* is rare. She was formerly at
Pershore, Worcs., and may still be seen at Earl Sterndale, Derbys. The *Silent Woman*
is apparently quite extinct now. There were formerly houses so called at Widford,
Essex, and at Pershore, Worcs. Such signs represent a woman carrying her head in her
hands.

Where is your head? is still a question addressed to forgetful people and a careless
child is told he would ' lose his head if it were loose '. Probably the origin of the sign
is rather as Larwood, quoting Brady of the *Clavis Calendaria*, suggests, ' The martyrs
who had been decapitated were, therefore, usually represented with headless trunks,
and the head on some adjoining table, or in their hands ; and it was easy for ignorance
and credulity to be led into the belief that those holy persons had actually carried their
heads about for the benefit of believers.' The sign of the *Good Woman* preserved in
Larwood's time, particularly by the oil-shops, although originally meant as expressive
of some female saint who had met death by decapitation, has been converted into a
satirical suggestion against womankind. It is now commonly called the *Silent Woman*.
The fact, however, of its being particularly an oilman's sign, makes it possible that
it may have some reference to the heedless (corrupted into headless) virgins of the
parable.

There is a very curious example of this sign at Widford, Essex, representing on
one side a half-length portrait of Henry VIII, on the reverse, a woman without a head,
dressed in the costume of the latter half of the 18th century, and with the inscription
Forte Bonne. The addition of the portrait of Henry VIII has led to the popular belief
that the headless woman is meant for Anne Boleyn, though probably the sign is simply
a combination of the *King's Head* and *Good Woman*. At Ripponden, W.R. Yorks.,
the licensee has laboured the point, and an inscription reads :—

> Here is a woman who has lost her head.
> She's quiet now—because, d'ye see, she's dead.

Lawyers, priests, and women have, at all times and in all countries, received a liberal
share of abuse and slander. In a sign (? derived from the *Good Woman*), the *Honest
Lawyer*, found for example at Folkestone and King's Lynn, is represented with his head
in his hand. Another similar sign is the *Man loaded with Mischief*, the sign of an alehouse in Oxford St. The original, said to be painted by Hogarth, was fastened to the
front of the house, and had the honour of being specified in the lease of the premises as
one of the fixtures. An engraving of it was exhibited in the window. This sign
has been imitated in other places. Sometimes it is called the *Mischief*, as at Blewbury,
Berks., which has a good painted sign, or the *Load of Mischief* as at Norwich. A
century ago there was one to be seen in Madingley Rd., Cambridge.

At present there is a house in Plymouth called *No Place* Inn ; and formerly there was at Norwich a public-house called *Nowhere*, a name which suggests the ready answer of a truant husband returning home in the small hours of the night to his wife's enquiry where he has been.   Another sign to which constant allusions are made in the old writers, is the *Three Loggerheads*.   Perhaps it originated in a corruption of the *Three Leopards' Heads* (Libber Heads—Logger Heads) of the Goldsmiths' arms, since the three Leopards Heads of the Shrewsbury borough are still usually known as the Logger-heads.   By corruption this gives rise to a joke which old and stale as it is has not yet lost its charm.   It represents two silly-looking faces, with the inscription—

We three
Loggerheads be

—the unsuspecting spectator being, of course, the third.   Thus in James Shirley's *Bird in Cage*, 1633, Morrello, who counterfeits a fool, says, ' *We be three of old*, without exception to your lordship, only with this difference, I am the wisest fool.'   In John Day's *Comedy of Law Tricks*, 1608, Julia says, ' Appoint the place prest', to which the answer is, ' *At the three fools*.'   Sometimes it was two asses, and it is thus in Beaumont and Fletcher's *Queen of Corinth*.★   In this form it was still seen on valentines, etc., in Larwood's time.   Shakespeare too, alludes to this sign in *Twelfth Night*.†   Dekker in the *Gull's Hornbook*, ridiculing the manners and customs of his day, speaks of the bloods sitting on the stage at the theatres ' but assure yourself, by continual residence, you are the first and principal man in election, to begin the number of *We three* '.   In a pamphlet of 1642, the Loggerheads are thus mentioned :—

A Loggerhead alone cannot well be,
At scriveners' windows many time hang three.
A country lobcocke, as I once did heare,
Upon a penman put a grievous jeare.
If I had been in place, as this man was,
I should have called this country coxcomb asse.

This alludes to one of the jokes in *Mother Bunch's Merriments*, 1604, where a country fellow asks a poor scrivener, sitting in his shop, ' I pray you, master, what might you sell in your shop, that you have so many ding-dongs hang at your door ? '   ' Why, my friend,' quoth the obligation-maker, ' I sell nothing but loggerheads.'   ' By my fay, master,' quoth the countryman, ' you have a fair market with them, for you have left but one in your shop, that I see ' ; and so, laughing, went his way, leaving much good sport to them that heard him.   This old anecdote may have given rise to scriveners using the Loggerheads as their sign.   In the 17th century the sign might have been seen in London.   There was one in Tooley St. in 1665, having on its trades token the inscription, ' We are 3 ' ; another variety had ' We three Logerheads ' underneath the usual heads.   In the ballad of the *Arraigning and Indicting of Sir John Barleycorn, Knt.*,

★ Act III, Sc. 1.   † Act II, Sc. 2.

the trial takes place at the *Three Loggerheads*, by the Justices Oliver and Old Nick. The witnesses are cited at the sign of the *Three Merry Companions in Bedlam*—namely Poor Robin, Merry Tom, and Jack Lackwit. The inn-sign has given rise to one or two place-names, in Mold and in Staffordshire.

The *Labour in Vain* occurs among the trades tokens, and such a sign gave its name to Old Fish St., to which Hatton in his *New View of London*, 1708, gives as an alternative name *Labour in Vain Hill*. The sign represented two women scrubbing a negro ; hence it was called by the lower classes, the *Devil in a Tub*. ' To wash an Æthiop ' is a proverbial expression, often met with in ancient dramatists, for labour in vain. The *Labour in Vain* survives at Tarnfield, Staffs., and at Old Swinford, Worcs., and at Easter- gate, Sussex. All these have good pictorial signs. *Labour Lost* formerly at Daventry was a variation on the same theme.

The *Case is Altered* generally alludes to some alteration in the affairs of the landlord, either ' for better or for worse '. A public-house near Banbury was so called on account of being built on the site of a mere hovel. Another house still surviving of the same name was erected in 1805 on the road between Woodbridge and Ipswich, to meet the demand of the soldiery then quartered in those two towns. Its sign in those days was the *Duke of York*, or some such name. But when, after the downfall of the Corsican tyrant, and the subsequent declaration of peace, the barracks were pulled down, the soldiers disbanded, and the benches of the alehouse remained empty, the old sign was removed, and in its place put up the sad truth—*The Case is Altered*. In another instance at Oxford the sign is said to have been adopted as a quiet hint by a sharp business man, who succeeded as landlord to an easy-going fellow whose customers had been allowed to run up debts. A correspondent of *Notes and Queries* says :—

' I saw this sign in the West of England :—A parson, with a large wig and gown, and seated at a table ; another dressed like a farmer stood talking to him. In the distance, seen through the open door, was a bull. The story, of course, is that related of Plowden, the celebrated lawyer, and which is now in most books of fables. The farmer told Plowden that his (the farmer's) bull had gored and killed the latter's cow. " Well," said the lawyer, " the case is clear, you must pay me her value." " Oh ! " said the farmer, " I have made a mistake. It is *your* bull which has killed my cow." " Ah ! the case is altered," quoth Plowden. The expression had passed into a proverb in Fuller's time.'

In another instance the inscription accompanies the former sign of the *Dove* with a branch of olive in its beak, the original sign being later improved by the conversion of the bird into a *Raven*. It is so found for example in Massinger's *Parliament of Love*,★ and the *Roman Actor*.† Probably the sign originated in a biblical text, perhaps Psalm cxxvii. or Galatians iv. 11. This sign occurs in some London localities, as at Willesden, and elsewhere. It is found also at Banbury, Wealdstone, Boston, at Wellow, Notts., and there are or were examples at Ipswich, at Bentley, Suff. (as the *Cause is Altered*) at Dover, and as *Now the Case is Altered* at Hatton, Warws. In some

★ Act II, Sc. 2.   † Act III, Sc. 2.

cases it is said to refer to disputed ownership of the property, legal decisions on the point being several times reversed.

The sign of the last house in a row on the outskirts of a town used frequently to be the *World's End*. This sign is also mentioned above (p. 254). This was represented in various punning ways, sometimes by a globe in the clouds, as on the trades token of Margaret Tuttlesham, of Golden Lane, Barbican, in 1666. Others rendered it by a fractured globe on a dark background, with fire and smoke bursting through the rents, and thus it was represented at the *World's End* in King's Rd., Chelsea, in 1825. At Ecton, Northants, it is depicted as a horseman whose steed is rearing over an abyss, on the edge of a world terminated perpendicularly. A fourth and more homely way of representing it was by depicting a man and a woman walking together on the margin of a landscape, with this distich:

> I'll go with my friend
> To the world's end.

The out-of-the-way sites of such houses were the causes of their not enjoying the best of reputations. Those at least of the *World's End* at Chelsea and at Knightsbridge were of evil repute, and were much patronized by the gallants of the reign of Charles II. Congreve's play *Love for Love* refers to them in this connexion. Pepys also honoured with an occasional visit a *World's End*, the 'drinking house by the Park'. On Sundays 9 and 28 May 1669, for instance, he went to church at St Margaret's, Westminster, 'and there eat and drank at the *World's End*'. In 1708 Tom Brown alludes to its equivocal reputation. There is still a *World's End* at Tilbury.

The *World Turned Upside Down* is still common, being generally represented by a man walking at the South Pole; in that guise it was to be seen some century ago on Greenwich Rd. But the meaning of the sign is a state of things the opposite of what is natural and usual. This is a conceit in which the artists of former ages took great delight, and which they represented by animals chasing men, horses riding in carriages, and similar pleasantries. An inn of this sign still remains in the Old Kent Rd. One, now extinct, near Reading, represented a hare shooting a man, and a man pulling a cart.

An instance of the *Moonrakers* has already been noted as the name of a fair booth. The sign occurs over an inn in Great Suffolk St., Southwark, where it has been for well over a century. The origin of this is no doubt in one of the ancient tales of the *Wise Men of Gotham*. A *Moonraker* is a nickname for a native of Wiltshire, and a not very convincing story told there has its origin in a ruse of some Wiltshire smugglers. A sign with a rather similar origin is the *Cuckoo Bush* at Gotham, Notts. The Wise Men of Gotham were very much enamoured of the melodious song of the cuckoo. They therefore set about the building of a wall around the bush where he performed, thinking that by so doing they would be able to retain him always on the spot.

The *Cradle & the Coffin*, or *First & Last*, was formerly a sign at Norwich, and one can still be seen on the South Quay, Yarmouth. This combination may have its moral. Not so the equally serious *Mortal Man*, in the little village of Troubeck, Westmd., for

there the denomination is simply borrowed from the beginning of the inscription which
has nothing of the *memento mori* about it :—

> Thou mortal man that liv'st by bread,
> What is it makes thy nose so red ?
>
> Thou silly elf with nose so pale,
> It is with drinking Burkett's ale.

This imaginary dialogue is supposed to be held by the two figures formerly on the
signboard, the one a poor miserable-looking object, the other, who indulged in Burkett's ale, the chubby picture of health, with a nose like that of Bardolph. This sign
was the work of Ibbetson ; the picture is now gone, but the verses remain.

At Hedenham, Norf., there is a sign called *Tumble-down Dick*, representing on one
side Diogenes, on the other, a drunken man, with the following distich:

> Now Diogenes is dead and laid in his tomb,
> Tumble-down Dick is come in his room.

There is another house of this sign at Woodton, Norf., said to have been so named
by a royalist landlord in 1660, and to refer of course to Richard Cromwell. The sign
actually represents a jolly old farmer in a red coat, with bottle and glass in his hand,
falling from his chair in a state of intoxication. The allusion is very common in the
satires published after the Restoration, amongst others, Hudibras.*

The same idea, and almost the identical words, occur again in Butler's *Remains*,
in the tale of the Cobbler and the Vicar of Bray.

We meet it also in the ballad, ' Old England is now a brave Barbary ', that is
horse, from a *Collection of Loyal Songs*.†

Dick's bacchic propensities are also sung in many an old song. Two of the
Luttrell Ballads ‡ allude to his weakness in this respect :—

> Dick loved a cup of nectar.

and

> Drunken Dick was a lame Protector.

At Alton, Hants, a drunken man is represented upsetting a table covered with cups and
glasses. The verses underneath this picture are the same as at Hedenham, except that
it is Barnaby who is said to be defunct, and not Diogenes. The earliest certain mention
of the sign is in the *Original Weekly Journal* for April 26–May 3, 1718, where a murder
is reported to have been committed at the *Tumble-down Dick* in Brentford. ' Tumble-
down Dick, in the borough of Southwark,' says the *Adventurer*, No. 9, 1752, ' is a fine
moral on the instability of greatness, and the consequences of ambition.'

Perhaps to the same origin may be referred the sign of *Soldier Dick*, which occurs

* Pt. III, Canto II, l. 231.
† Reprinted in 1731, Vol. II, p. 231.   ‡ Vol. II, pp. 11 and 36.

at Furness Vale, Ches., and *Happy Dick* at Abingdon. *Tumble-down Dick* was also the name of an 18th-century dance, a fact which gives additional strength to the supposition that Richard Cromwell was intended.

The *Jolly Toper* is a common public-house sign, probably put up as a good example to the customers ; in London there used to be a *Tippling Philosopher*, now extinct, in Liquor Pond St., opposite Reid's great brewery in Gray's Inn Rd. Which philosopher was intended is not certain (it would be more or less appropriate to several of them). There is or was another house of the same sign at Caldecot, Mon. Theophrastus, in his *Treatise on Drunkenness* says that the seven sages of Greece often met together to indulge in a cheerful glass. Plato not only excuses a drop too much occasionally, but even orders it. Heraclitus, the weeping philosopher, never laughed but when he was half-seas-over, Xenocrates gained a golden crown, awarded by Dionysius the tyrant to the deepest drinker, and Socrates carried off the palm from his contemporaries by his drinking capacities.

A very curious and rare sign was formerly to be seen at Nidd, W.R. Yorks. This was the *Ass in the Band-Box*, now extinct. We find it mentioned in October 1712 in Partridge's manuscript *Book of Celestial Motions*. ' At the end of this month the villains made the Band-box plot, to blow up Robin and his family with a couple of inkhorns, and that rogue Swift was at the opening of the band-box and the discovery of the plot. The truth of it all was : "—— in a Band-box ".' This alludes to the well-known plot of a band-box sent to the Lord Treasurer containing a very poor infernal machine, made of inkhorns. The affair, however, has never been satisfactorily cleared up. The sign seems to have originated from a somewhat coarse joke called ' selling bargains ' with which the maids of honour amused themselves in Swift's time, and which is mentioned in his *Polite Conversation*. Possibly, however, it may be a vernacular reading of some crest, such as an antelope or a unicorn issuing out of a mural crown. When the original sign was repainted about 1800 the original figure was replaced by Napoleon, sitting on an ass, and sailing in a bandbox (to the invasion of England). Lord Mountgarvel at Nidd Hall has the sign now. Perhaps the *Roaring Donkey*, Holland-on-Sea, Essex, may have originated from a sign of this kind. There is a *Kicking Donkey* also at Oving-ton in Essex.

In the borough of Southwark is a sign on which is inscribed the *Old Pick-My-Toe*, which, in the absence of any better origin, we may suppose to be a vulgar representa-tion of the Roman slave who, being sent on some message of importance would not stay to pick a thorn from his foot, until he had completed his mission. *Jack of Both Sides*, at Reading, is so named because the house stands at a point where two roads meet in the form of a Y, and the house being wedge-shaped, has an entry at each side. Such a house in London is often vulgarly called a *Flat-Iron*. The *Old Smugs* is a sign on the trades token of Joseph Hall, at Newington Butts, 1667, representing a smith and an anvil ; but whether Joseph Hall himself was ' old Smvgs ', or whether he kept a tavern frequented by blacksmiths is not known. This last is also the name of one of the characters in the *Merry Devil at Edmonton*. The *Battered Naggin* (*sic* for Noggin) is an

The Griffin

Buck, Thorpe, Norwich

The Golden Hind, Plymouth

The Ship Inn, Thursby

The Royal George, Worthing

36

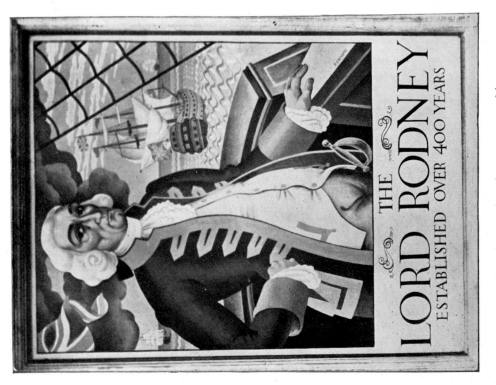

The Lord Nelson

The Lord Rodney, Church Green, Keighley

The Nelson, Birmingham

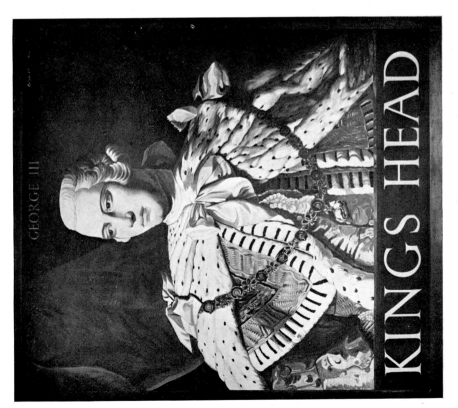

King's Head, Drayton

King's Head, Davey Place, Norwich

Somerset Tavern, Luton

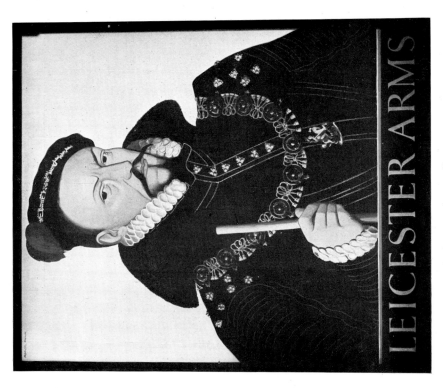

Leicester Arms, Luton

The King's Head, Richmond, Yorks.

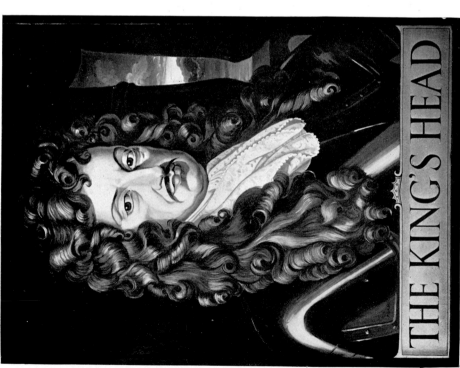

The King's Head, Gravesend

The Spotted Cow, Littlehampton

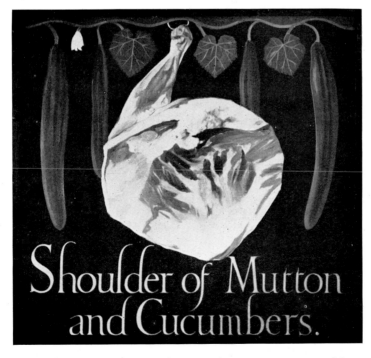

Shoulder of Mutton and Cucumbers, Yapton, Arundel

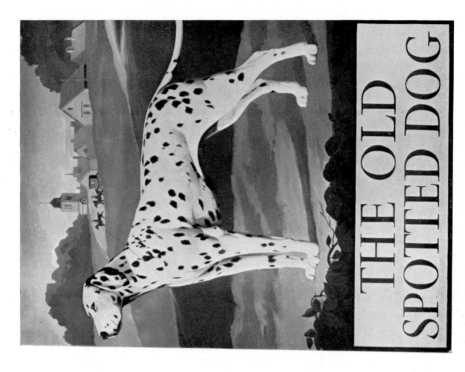

The Old Spotted Dog, Neasdon

The Greyhound

The Greyhound Inn, Reepham, Norfolk

The Blue Boys, Kipping's Cross, Kent (two sides)

The Swan, Tingrith

The Peacock, Bourneville

46

The Squirrel, Battle, Sussex

The Hampshire Hog, Hammersmith

The Bear Inn, Amberley, Glos.

The Red Cow Hotel, Hammersmith

Wagon & Horses, Ridge Hill, Nr. St Albans (two sides)

Irish sign, being a figurative expression for a man who has had more than is good for him,—'he has got a lick of a battered naggin'. The *Noggin*, without the adjective, occurs at a few places in Lancashire and Yorkshire. The *Tumbling Sailors*, representing three seamen half-seas-over and reeling arm-in-arm down a street, might formerly be seen at Broseley, Salop, and is still found near Kidderminster. The *Cripple's* Inn, formerly at Stockingfield, Warws., was doubtless nothing more than a very lame attempt at comicality. The *Hat in Hand* at Boxhill, promises a polite host ; and contrasts rather with *Old Careless*, the ominous name of a public-house at Stapleford, Notts., the *Spite Hall* at Brandon, Durh., or with *Old No*, which occurs in Silver St., Sheffield ! *Slow & Easy* is the unpromising name of an alehouse at Lostock, Ches. It may be meant for a version of the Italian proverb, meaning that the landlord will be content with fair and small profits, and acquire fortune by slow and easy steps.

T

Chapter XVII

PUNS AND REBUSES

PUNNING on names or a figurative rendering of them is a very old practice on inn —and other signs. It was probably at first adopted not so much with any intent at joking as to assist the memory by giving the name a visible token. This would take the place of writing at a time when but few persons could either read or write. From the 12th to the 16th century punning was at its greatest height. Throughout the 17th century it is frequently found in the sermons, some of which form continuous displays of verbal fireworks. Like other diseases, punning broke out again subsequently with redoubled virulence and made great havoc in the reign of Queen Anne. 'Several worthy gentlemen and critics', says the *Tatler* for 23 June 1709, 'have applied to me to give my censure of an enormity, which has been revived after being long suppressed, and is called Punning. I have several arguments ready to prove that he cannot be a man of honour who is guilty of this abuse of human society.' Bagford makes this remark on the subject :—

> As for rebuses or name devices, thei ware brought into use heare in England after King Edward ye 3 had conquered France, and this was taken up by most people heare in this nation, especially by them which had none armes ; and if their names ended in *ton*, as Haton ; Boulton ; Luton ; Grafton ; Middellton ; Seton ; Norton ; they must presently have for their signes or devises a hat and a tun ; a boult and a tun ; a lute and a tun ; and so on, which signifies nothing to ye name, for all names ending in *Ton* signifieth a toune from whence they tooke their name. It would make one very merry to loke ouer ye learned Camden in his *Remaines*, and to consider ye titles of our ould books printed by Haryson, Kingston, Islip, Woodcooke, Payer, Bushell, . . .

Camden in his *Remains* mentions these punning signs, and gives a similar statement to Bagford, that they were introduced from France, where they are still much in fashion.

> Morton, Archbishop of Canterbury, a man of great wisdome, and borne to the universall good of this realme, was content to use *mor* upon a ton, and sometimes a mulberry-tree, called *Morus* in Latine, out of a ton. So *Luton, Thornton, Ashton*, did note their names with a Lute, a Thorn, and an Ash upon a Ton. So an *Hare* on a bottle for *Harebottle*, a Maggot-pie upon a Goat for *Pigot, Med* written on a Calf for *Medcalfe* : *Chester*, a chest with a starre over it ; *Allet*, a Lot ; *Lionel Ducket*, a Lion with L on his head, where it should have beene in his tayle ; if the lion had been eating a ducke it had been a rare device,—worth a Duckat or a duck-egge. And if you require more, I refer you to the wittie inventions of some Londoners ; but that for Garret Dewes is most memorable : two in a garret casting dews at dice. This for rebus may suffice, and yet if there were more, I think some lips would like such kind of Lettice.

How punning signboards were concocted we may gather from another reference in Ben Jonson's *Alchymyst*,⋆ where a rebus sign is to be found for Abel Drugger.   The Alchemist provides him with *a bell* for Abel, ' one standing by whose name is *Dee*, in a *rug* gown, . . .

> And right anenst him a dog snarling *er*,
> There's *Drugger*, Abel Drugger . . .'

The Cockneys have at all times been celebrated for this kind of pleasantry.   The birdbolt through a tun, or *Bolt in Tun*, for Bolton, the device of the priors of St Bartholomew, is still in existence in Fleet St., though now over a railway receiving office. On some of the 17th-century trades tokens we meet with a tun pierced by three arrows. This variant of the *Bolt in Tun* was called the *Tun & Arrows* (or *harrows* as the Cockney tokens have it).   In the reign of Charles II there was one in Bishopsgate St. Within and another in Bishopsgate St. Without.   The *Moon & Sun*, Aldersgate and in Lincolnshire and Hertfordshire, where the Monsons had estates, is, of course, a rebus on the family name.

The *Hand & Cock* was the punning sign of John Hancock in Whitefriars.   George Cox, tallow-chandler, in the Minories, had *Two Cocks* for his sign.   Thomas Cockayne, a distiller in Southwark, had the same sign as a feeble pun on part of his name.   Christopher Bostock, not seeing any possibility of hammering a rebus out of his own name, fortunately for him lived at Cock's Key, and so could make up for this misfortune by punning on the name of that place, whence his sign triumphantly exhibited the *Cock & Key*.

John Hive, St Mary's Hill 1667, had the sign of the *Beehive*, Grace Pestell, in Figtree Yard, Ratcliffe, the *Pestle & Mortar*, John Atwood in Rose Lane, the *Man in the Wood*, Andrew Hind, over against the Mews, Charing Cross, a *Hind*.   Taylor the Water Poet mentions in his *Pennilesse Pilgrimage*, 1630, a similar sign at Preston, that of ' Master Hinde, host of the *Hinde* '.   Jane Keye, Bloomsbury Market 1653, had a *Key*. The *Lion & Key* was in 1651 a sign in Thames St., punning perhaps on the neighbouring Lion's Quay.   This is still the sign of a public-house in Hull, whilst the *Red Lion & Key*, now extinct, still occurred in Larwood's time in Mill Lane, Tooley St.   The *Lion & Key* found at Hull and elsewhere is said to refer to the capture by Wellington in 1812 of the *Key to Spain*, Ciudad Rodrigo.   The lion then would be a British Lion holding in his paws the key to Spain.   This explanation seems very far-fetched, and is rendered still less likely by the existence of some lion and key signs in the 17th century.

The *Hat & Tun*, a pun on the name of Hatton, is still preserved on a public-house sign in Hatton Wall.   A man named Nobis, at the beginning of the 19th century opened an inn on the road to Happisburgh, Norf., which he called *Nobis Inn* and made free with grammar in order to find a punning motto, ' *Si Deus Pro Nobis Quis Contra Nobis* '.   Bells have been used by innumerable persons of the name of *Bell*.   The *Salmon* was the sign of Mrs. Salmon, the Madame Tussaud of the 18th century.   Her gallery was first in St Martin's-le-Grand, near Aldersgate, whence she removed to Fleet

⋆ Act II, Sc. 1.

St. opposite what was Anderton's Hotel, then called the *Horns*. The *Brace* in Queen's Bench Prison was so called on account of its being kept by two brothers of the name of Partridge.

The *Black Swan* in Bartholomew Lane, nicknamed *Cobwebb Hall*, a tavern of great resort for the musical wits in the 17th century, was kept by Owen Swan, parish clerk (whence its name) of St Michael's, Cornhill.

A few punning signs still remain. At Oswaldtwistle, Lancs., at Warbleton, Sussex, an old public-house had the sign of a war-bill in a tun, which sign of the *Axe & Tun* is further intended as an intimation to axe for beer ! Another innkeeper named Abraham Lowe who lived halfway up Richmond Hill, near Douglas, I. of M., had the following innocent attempt at punning on his name :—

> I'm Abraham Lowe, and half way up the Hill,
> If I were higher up, what's funnier still,
> I should be *lowe*. Come in and take your fill,
> Of porter, ale, wine, spirits, what you will,
> Step in, my friend, I pray, no further go ;
> My prices, like myself, are always low.

A boxer named Belthorn in the early part of the 18th century is said to have given his name to the *Bell & Horns* at Brompton and to have removed thence to the *Bell & Thorn*. There are numerous examples of *Dewdrop Inn* (Do drop in !) for example at Hathern, Leics., New Cross, S.E., Luton. The *Magnet & Dewdrop* is at Millwall. Presumably there is a reference here to the not very good pun, also to the drawing power of the magnet. Or perhaps the original sign was a Magnet with a bright steel ball. The *Pure Drop* inn in Cornwall, and at Wareham (Dorset), is probably a variation of the same sign. Probably many of these supposedly humorous punning signs developed rather less than a century and a half ago, when the old signs were going out of favour and when landlords were trying to move with the times. The *Fair Flora* formerly at Norwich is said to have referred to the game of skittles—a ' fair floorer ' occurring when a skilful player swept the board with one throw of the ' cheese '. A modern punning sign is that of Messrs. Barclay and Perkins houses, the *Fellowship*, Catford, S.E.6, painted by Sir Arthur Cope. This shows a fine picture of H.M.S. ' Victory '. Another *Fellowship* at Bristol shows the ' Herzogen Cecile ', which went ashore a few years ago. Similarly the *Wellington*, Newmarket, a fine modern sign by Mr. H. G. Theaker, has a picture of the Duke on horseback in the background, but in the foreground a Wellington-boot. A similar sign is that of the *Gnu* (New) Inn at Stedham, Sussex, which has a fine modern sign by Ralph Ellis, still another that of the *Tired Tyre* near Bristol, Glos. A modern punning sign referring to broadcasting is the *Listen Inn* at Cann, Dorset.

Chapter XVIII

CHANGES OF SIGN

IN some towns it is quite unsafe to assume that a house of any particular sign even if it is known to have been licensed for several centuries, is necessarily identical with another house of the same sign mentioned even a century ago. Inns have changed and even exchanged signs in a very confusing fashion. The first series of instances noted below are from the single town of Shrewsbury and are based wholly on Mr. Lloyd's admirable work elsewhere noted.

Here as usual ' Old ' in an inn sign is usually meaningless, and licensees omit or include the adjective at their fancy. *Bush* is used synonymously with *Hawthorn Bush*, and the *George* is the *George & Dragon*. One *Plough* appears also as the *Old Plough* and the *Speed the Plough*, another is sometimes called the *Plough & Harrow*. The *Plume of Feathers* appears also as the *Feathers*, and the *Queen's Head*, the *Old Queen's Head*, and the *Queen's Hotel* are identical.

The *Albion* was formerly the *Fighting Cocks*, one *Barley Mow* the *Lord Hill*, another the *Cross Guns*, one *Britannia* the *Engine & Tender*, another the *Welsh Harp*. The *Crown* was at one time the *Crow*. The extra letter cannot have been added to avoid confusion, since there was already one other *Crow* in the town, but there were two *Crowns*. The *Eagle* was renamed the *Black Horse* when the old *Black Horse* was closed, the *Golden Cross* was *c.* 1780, the *Sextry*, that is the Sacristy of St Chad's Church (p. 171) and the *New Market Vaults*, a very uninspiring sign, was formerly the *Golden Heart*, a sign of great interest and antiquity. Other instances in this single town are : the *Barge*, earlier the *Bridge*, and earlier still the *Barge*, the *Bird in Hand* formerly the *Hit & Miss*, the *Bowling Green* once the *Beacon*, the *Bridge* called the *New* Inn until the 1880's, the *Bugle* formerly the *French Horn*, and before that again the *Bugle*. The *Castle* was formerly the *Bull & Pump*, another *Castle* formerly the *Hare & Hounds*. The *Case is Altered* was originally the *Sun & Ball*, then the *Live & Let Live*, and is said to have taken its present sign when the landlord was prosecuted and fined. The *Clarendon* was once the *Market Tavern*, the *Cross Keys*, 1820, was called the *Globe* in 1780, the *Eagle* was once the *Eagle & Sun*, the *Greyhound* until the 1870's was called the *Masons' Arms*, the *Hero of Moultan* is the same building as the old *Red Lion* which disappeared *ante* 1780. The house was revived in the 1850's under this title. The *Hog in Armour* is probably equivalent to the *Rifle Volunteer*. The *Horseshoe, fl.* 1861, appears from 1879 onwards as the *Three Horseshoes*, and reverts to its old title *c.* 1906. The *Jones Arms* was formerly the *Horseshoe*, and was renamed in honour of the winner in an electoral contest in 1807, the *Nelson's Arms*, previously the *Fleece*, was earlier still the *Crown & Glove*. The *New Sun* was formerly the *Crow*, the *Old Gullet* (actually several centuries newer than the *Gullet*) was formerly known as first the *Seven Stars*, then the *Little Gullet*, the *Pheasant* was at one time called the *Reaper*, the *Shrewsbury Arms* was first the *Greyhound*, then the *Horse & Jockey*, then the *General Hill*, the *Old Slipper* has been successively the *Slipper*, the *Hope & Anchor*, the *Odd-fellows Arms*, and the *Old Slipper*. The *Smithfield Hotel* was formerly the *Globe*, the *Station Hotel* until 1916 the *Grapes* (and still having a good carved *Grapes* sign), and the *String of Horses* had this title from 1828, but was previously known successively as the *Royal Oak* and the *Cross Keys*. Clearly if Shrewsbury is a typical town in this matter, I think it is not, a good many historical theories as to the persistence of signs through the centuries will rest upon a very insecure foundation.

A casual glance at the list given above will indicate some of the main reasons for such changes of sign as have occurred here or elsewhere. Sometimes they originate in a corruption of the original sign (either the name itself perverted upon the provincial tongue, corrupted or refined by the licensee or his landlord, or affectionately nicknamed by his patrons). Sometimes the cause must be sought in the sign itself, battered by the winds, and blistered by the sun, and repainted much at the fancy of the sign painter. Often too a change of sign was due to a change of circumstances which made the old one no longer appropriate. A former hero was dead and buried, and a Pharaoh arose which knew not Joseph, or a local land-owning family parted with its estates, so in due course its arms disappeared from the signboard. Often too, when one well-known house closed down a neighbouring one adopted its sign, presumably in order to allure its customers. Finally a great many changes occurred simply at the fancy of the landlord. In the '60's, '70's and '80's, those days of atrocious taste, many charming and picturesque old names were replaced by spiritless abominations like *Jones's Stores* or *Smith's Vaults*. Indeed such changes as have occurred have rarely been for the better, as a glance at the list below will indicate. It is gratifying that in recent years many brewery companies and private persons proprietors of licensed houses have restored the original attractive names in place of the trite and tame abominations which usurped their places in the days of our grandfathers. One house crying out for the restoration of its original title is the *George & Thirteen Cantons* in Soho, quite recently ' modernized ' into the ' *Scots Hoose* '. An instance of the replacing of a trite name by a good one occurred recently at Finsbury Park where on rebuilding the *Station Hotel* was rechristened the *Silver Bullet*. Similarly only a few months ago (1944) the *White Heart*, Gainsborough, has reverted to its proper title of the *White Hart*, and a white heart with a fearsome dagger in it on the signboard has been replaced by a hart rampant *arg*. A witty teetotaller is so rare a phenomenon that I cannot but record a teetotal change of sign of a house in Hertfordshire. Here the *Old Fox* was converted into a teetotalarian by a son-in-law of Sir Wilfred Lawson, the ' temperance ' enthusiast, and rechristened the *Old Fox with his Teeth Drawn*.

The list below does not profess, of course, to be a complete one. It comprises merely the instances noted in the author's somewhat desultory reading of houses where marked changes of sign are elsewhere referred to in the text. Even so it brings out very clearly what a great number of changes have occurred, and how very unsafe it is to equate an existing house with another of the same name existing even a century ago.

Conversely it indicates how an inn with a very unattractive title may perhaps on investigation be found to have had a long history and once to have displayed an attractive and interesting sign. It is not suggested that in every instance the premises have been in continuous use as a licensed house, though in most they have. In many of the cases noted the premises have of course been entirely rebuilt, but the house has retained its identity though not its name. I have only occasionally given cross-references to other mentions of the same house in the text. These will all be found in the general index.

INDEX OF CHANGED SIGNS

(Not including the Shrewsbury instances noted above.)   ('e' signifies houses now extinct.)

Now :—		Sometime :—
e *Black Swan,*	York,	*Bricklayers' Arms,*
		Eclipse.
Black Swan,	Melton Mowbray,	*Flying Childers.*
Boar's Head,	Norwich,	*Greyhound* until 1792. (Present sign from crest of Norgate family.)
Bowling Green Hotel,	Cellarhead, Staffs.,	*Spotted Cow.*
British Tar,	York,	*Fortunate Tar.*
Brunswick,	York,	*Fishergate Tavern.*
e *Buck,*	York,	*Horse & Groom.*
Burton Stone,	Clifton, York,	*Plough.*
Cabin of Content,	Upper Gorwall, Staffs.,	*Cottage of Content.*
Cambridge,	Norwich,	*Barley Mow.*
Cameron Hotel,	Darlington,	*Anchor.*
Cannon,	York,	*Black Boy.*
Carrs,	Strand,	*King's Head.*

Case is Altered.—(Many different origins, for which see p. 269. A common one was the substitution of a *Raven* for a *Dove*.)

Castle,	York,	*Wheatsheaf.*
Castle,	West Lulworth, Dorset,	*Jolly Sailor,*
		Traveller's Rest,
		Green Man.
Caveac,	Finch Lane,	*Spread Eagle.*

(Change made to commemorate landlord's name, or a masonic lodge.)

Chapter House,	Paternoster Row,	*Chapter Coffee House.*
City Arms,	Hereford,	*Hotel.*
City Arms,	York,	*Chapter* (Coffee House),
		Grapes.
Clarendon,	Oxford,	*Star.*
Clinton Arms,	Newark,	*Cardinal's Hat,*
		Kingston Arms.
Coach & Horses,	Bristol,	*Hole in the Wall* ('Spyglass' of *Treasure Island*).
Cock,	Fleet St.,	*Cock & Bottle.*
Cock & Tabard,	Tothill St.,	*Cock* until c. 1850.
e *Cotherstone,*	York,	*Bay Horse.*
County,	Taunton,	*London.*
Coventry Arms,	Corfe Mullen, Dorset,	*Cock & Wheatsheaf.*
Craven Arms,	Craven Court, Strand,	*Cloudesley Shovel.*
Cricketer's Arms,	Norwich (? successor to)	*Red Lion.*
Cricketer's Arms,	York,	*Earl of Dublin,*
		Three Arrows.
Criterion,	Camberley, Surrey,	*Golden Fleece.*
Cross Keys,	Saffron Walden,	*Whalebone* until 1754.
Crown,	Market Place, Bristol,	*Guilder.*

(Evidently the sign has been translated, though actually a guilder is a florin rather than a crown.)

Crown,	Camberley, Surrey,	*Bricklayers' Arms.*

Now :—		Sometime :—
Crown,	Hungate, York,	*Whale Fishery,*
		Oddfellows' Arms.
Crown,	Micklegate, York,	*Rose & Crown,*
		Grapes,
		Cup.
Crown,	North St., York,	*Tiger,*
		Leopard.
Crown,	Walmgate, York,	*Crown & Cushion.*
Crown & Anchor,	Ipswich,	*Chequers,*
		Rampant Horse.
e *Crown & Anchor,*	York,	*Bay Horse,*
		Manchester Tavern,
		Market Street Tavern.
Crown & Harp,	York,	*Hudson's Arms.*
Crown Posada,	Newcastle,	*Crown* (see p. 77).
Cups,	Colchester,	*Three Cups.*
Daniel Lambert,	Stationers' Hall Court,	*King's Head.*
Devereux Tavern,	Strand,	*Grecian Coffee House.*
Dorset Arms,	Withyham, Sussex,	*Ale House.*
Duke's Head,	Thetford, Suff.,	*Griffin.*
Duke's Head,	York,	rebuilding of *Duke of York.*
Dun Cow,	Darlington,	*Low Fleece.*
e *Eagle,*	York,	*Glovers' Arms,*
		Gardeners' Arms.
Eagle & Child,	York,	*Ruben's Head.*
Ebor Vaults,	York,	*Three Jolly Butchers.*
Eugene Aram,	Knaresborough,	*White Horse.*

(Aram was of course a local man.)

Exhibition Hotel,	York,	*Bird in Hand.*
Five Miles from Any-		
where,	Upware, Cambs.,	*Lord Nelson.*
e *Flying Dutchman,*	York,	*Bloomsbury.*
e *Foresters' Arms,*	York,	*Three Tuns.*
Fountain & Star,	Cheapside,	*Les Trois Frères.*
e *Fox,*	York,	*Beech Tree,* in 1850,
		Lord Byron.
Full Moon,	York,	*Barleycorn,* until 1843.
Fye Bridge Tavern,	Norwich,	*Ribs of Beef.*
Garden Gate,	York,	*Whale Fishery,*
		Slip.
George,	York,	*Bull alias Rose* (until 1868),
		? *Bull* 1459, 1497.

King George, in many places originally *George & Dragon.* Converse change happened with :

George & Dragon,	Hull,	*George.*
George & Dragon,	Norwich,	*Abraham Hall.*
G.I.,	Hastings,	*Central Hotel.*
e *Gibson's Vaults,*	York,	*Board.*
Glassblowers' Arms,	York,	*Glasshouse.*

Now :—		Sometime :—
Globe and Seven Stars,	Norwich,	*Hell Cellar.*
Golden Hart,	Shrewsbury,	*Golden Heart.*
Golden Lion,	Weymouth,	*Feathers* (1643),
		Lion (1664).
Grapes,	Limehouse,	*Bunch of Grapes.*
Grapes,	York,	*Black Boy.*
Great Mogul,	Quayside, Newcastle,	*Crown.*
e *Green Tree,*	Lawrence Row, York,	*Yew Tree.*
e *Green Tree,*	Water Lane, York,	*Gate.*
Greyhound,	York,	*Pig & Whistle.*
e *Griffin,*	York,	*Marquis of Granby.*
Grosvenor Hotel,	Stockbridge, Hants,	*King's Head.*
Grove,	Dulwich,	*Green Man.*
Grunting Hog,	St. Ives,	*Pig & Whip.*
Guildhall Stores,	Norwich,	*Labour in Vain.*
Half Moon,	York,	successively *Square & Compass* and *Seven Stars* since 1822.
Halfpenny House,	Richmond, Yorks.,	*Halfway House.*
Hand & Heart,	York,	*Reindeer.*
Hand of Providence,	Dudley,	*Red Hand of Ulster.*
Hare & Hounds,	Southwark,	*Beggar's Bush* (for *Badger's Bush*).
Haymarket Inn,	York,	*Shoulder of Mutton,*
		Gifford's Tower,
		Tower of London.
e *Hibernian,*	York,	*Harp,*
		Lincoln Arms.
Holland Arms,	Kensington,	*White Horse.*
Ironmongers' Arms,	Norwich,	*Sun & Anchor.*
Jack Straw's Castle,	Hampstead,	*Castle* (in Clarissa Harlowe *c.* 1740).
Jolly Farmer,	Bagshot, Surrey,	(successor of *Golden Farmer* (p. 212) existing certainly since 1729 and changed *c.* 1823, because of cheerful expression of portrait of Davis on signboard).
Jolly Sailor,	Margate, York,	*Waterman's Arms.*
Jump,	Clare Market,	*Black Jack* (p. 232).
King of Bohemia,	High St., Hampstead,	the original sign was a portrait of the *Elector Palatine*—see *Palatine Head*—the present sign shows that of *Good King Wenceslas.*
King of Denmark,	Ludgate Hill,	*Magpie & Stump.*
King of Prussia,	Islington,	(if Goldsmith may be depended upon as an historian).
		French King,
		Queen of Hungary.
King of Russia,	Abergavenny,	*King of Prussia.*
King William IV,	York,	*Golden Ball.*
King George V,	High Wycombe,	*Old King of Prussia.*

Now :—		Sometime :—
King's Head,	Exchange Alley,	*Swan* (until *c.* 1740).
King's Head,	Paternoster Row,	*Queen's Arms.*
King's Head,	Sutton Bonnington, Notts.	*Spread Eagle.*
Kitchener's Arms,	Norwich,	*Wounded Hart* (until *c.* 1914–15).
Kitchener's Arms,	Windsor,	*Prince of Prussia.*
Lamb,	Norwich,	*Holy Lamb.*
Lamb,	Wallingford,	*King's Head,* 1550, then *Bell.* *Lamb* since 1669.
Langport Arms,	Langford, Som.,	*Swan.*
Lansdowne Arms,	Calne, Wilts.,	*Catherine Wheel.*
Lendal Bridge Hotel,	York,	*Railway Tavern.*
Lion,	Bedford,	*Red Lion.*
Lion,	Buckden, Hunts.,	successively *Lamb, Lamb & Flag, Lion & Lamb.*
Listen Inn,	Cann, Dorset,	*New Inn.*
Little John,	York,	*Robin Hood.*
London Hotel,	York,	*Turf Coffee House, Cricketers' Arms.*
London Tavern,	Fenchurch St.,	successor of *King's Head.*
e *Lord Nelson,*	York,	*Crystal Palace.*
Lord Raglan,		*Bush,* then *Mourning Bush.*
Lord Warden,	Dover,	on site of *Ship.*
Lowther Hotel,	Old Ouse Bridge, York,	*Labour in Vain, Keel.*
Luttrell Arms,	Dunster,	*Ship* until *c.* 1779.
Magpie,	York,	*Magpie & Stump.*
Mail Coach,	York,	*Barrel.*
Market Tavern,	York,	*Leopard.*
Markham Moor Inn,	Markham Moor, Notts.,	*Black Horse.*
Marquis of Granby,	Chandos St.,	*Hole in the Wall.*
e *Masons' Arms,*	Shrewsbury,	*Greyhound.*
Masons' Arms,	York,	*Quiet Woman.*
Methuen Arms,	Corsham, Wilts.,	*Red Lion.*
Minster Inn,	York,	*Gardeners' Arms.*
Mitre & Clarence,	Chatham,	*Mitre.*
Moorgate,	Moorfields,	*Swan on Hoop.*
Mount,	York,	*Saddle.*
Mourning Cross,	Phoenix Alley, Long Acre,	*Crown.* See *Poet's Head.*
Newcastle Arms,	George St., York,	*Craven Ox.*
Newcastle Arms,	North St., York,	*Sawyers' Arms, Grey Horse.*
New Clown,	Islington,	*King of Prussia, Joey Grimaldi, Clown.*
New Crown,	Newcastle,	*Kouli Khan.*
Newdegate Arms,	Nuneaton,	(George Eliot's *Oldenport Arms*), *Black Bull* until 1816.

	Now :—		Sometime :—
Nell Gwynn's Tavern,	(Winter Garden Theatre —Part of),		Mogul.
North Eastern Hotel,	York,		George.
Old Curiosity Shop,	Liverpool,		Curiosity, i.e. Museum (p. 297).
Old Grey Mare,	Clifton, York,		Grey Horse.
Old London,	Ludgate Hill,		London Coffee House.
Old Number 5,	York,		New Bridge St. Hotel, Board.
Ostrich,	Colnbrook, Beds.,		Crane, but earlier Ostrich.
Ouse Bridge Inn,	York,		King's Arms.
Parson & Clerk,	Streatley, Warws.,		Royal Oak.
Phoenix,	York,		Labour in Vain.
Plough & Sail,	nr. Arundel, Sussex,		New Inn.
Plumbers' Arms,	York,		alias Cock & Bottle, originally Mansion, Duke's Place.
Poet's Head,	Phoenix Alley, Long Acre,		Crown, Mourning Crown (p. 39).
e Pontack's Head,	Abchurch Lane,		White Bear.
Post Boys,	Frimley, Surrey,		Harrow.
Prince of Windsor,	Old Kent Rd.,		Prince of Saxe-Cobourg.
Queen Inn,	York,		Princess Victoria, Queen Victoria, Queen's Head.
Queen's Head,	Bootham Square, York,		Princess Victoria.
Red Rose,	Bow St.,		Red Cow.
Reindeer,	York,		Highland Red Deer.
e Rifleman,	York,		Light Horseman.
Robin Hood,			frequently should be Green Man, for which see p. 222.
Royal Clarence,	Bridgwater,		rebuilding of houses, the Angel and the Crown, then the Royal Hotel.
Rover Arms,	Newnham, Northants,		Bakers' Arms.

(Here the 'squire asked for the change of sign, and offered to present an armorial window if the change were made. ' The sign ' of the house is this window.)

Royal Fountain,	Canterbury,		Fountain.
Royal Fountain,	Sheerness,		Fountain.
Royal Hotel,	Bideford,		including a mansion, the Colonial house built on site of New London Inn.
Royal Hotel,	Burslem, Stoke-on-Trent,		Castle & Falcon.
Royal Hotel,	Purfleet,		successively Bricklayers' Arms, Purfleet Hotel, Wingroves.
Royal Oak,	Rising Brook, Stafford,		Why Not.
Rummer,	Bristol,		mediævally : le Ropeseld, Greene Salters, Abyndon's Inn, later : Jonas, New Inn, New Sun Inn.

Now :—		Sometime :—
Same Yet,	Prestwich, Lancs.,	*Seven Stars.*

(Change said to be due to painter's literal interpretation of landlord's orders.)

St. Peter's Vaults,	York,	*Spotted Dog.*
e *Shakespeare,*	York,	*Barrel.*
Ship,	Charing Cross,	(? on site of or successor to *Rummer*).
e *Ship,*	York,	*Labourer,*
		Labouring Man.
Ship & Shovel,	Bermondsey,	*Pig & Whistle.*

(Renaming said to be in honour of Sir Cloudesley Shovell.)

Short's,	Pope's Head Alley,	*Pope's Head,* then
		Reaves Chop House.
Short's,	Strand,	*Strand Hotel.*
Slipper,	York,	*Boot & Shoe.*
Speech House,	Forest of Dean,	*King's Lodge.*
Spiller's Head,	Clare Market,	*Bull & Butcher.*
Sportsman,	York,	*Dog & Gun.*
Spread Eagle,	York,	*Bricklayers' Arms,*
		Malt Shovel.
Square & Compass,	Wesley Place, York,	*Joiners' Arms.*
Suffolk Hotel,	Long Melford, Suff.,	*Greyhound.*
Sun,	York,	*Sir Sidney Smith.*
Suspension Bridge,	Hammersmith,	*Goat.*
Sycamore,	Minster Yard, York,	*Green Tree.*
Talbot,	Ripley, Surrey,	*Dog* (in 1636).
e *Talbot,*	Southwark,	*Tabard.*
Talbot,	York,	*Blacksmith's Arms,*
		Harcourt Arms (until 1865).
Tam o' Shanter,	York,	*St. Nicholas,*
		Burns.
Thomases Hotel,	York,	incorporates part of *Etridge's Royal Hotel.*
Three Crowns,	Stoke Newington,	*Cock & Harp.*

(Said to have been changed in honour of a visit by James I, 1603.)

Three Tuns,	Windsor,	*Guildhall.*
Tivoli,	Hull,	*Bull,* changed to *Bull & Sun* in 1751 on a new landlord coming from the *Sun.* Then changed again apparently for no reason at all.
Trumpet,	York,	*Free Gardeners' Arms.*
Turk's Head,	York,	*Saracen's Head.*
Unicorn,	Tanner Row, York,	*Oddfellows' Arms.*
Upholsterers' Arms,	York,	*Greyhound.*
Welbeck,	Mansfield,	*Salmon & Lobster.*
Wells,	Hampshire,	replaced *Green Man.*
Whalebone,	Netherton, Ches.,	*Fishbone.*
Whateley Hall Hotel,	Banbury,	*Three Tuns.*
Wheatsheaf,	Nursery Lane, York,	*Crown,*
		Golden Ball,
		Barley Sheaf.

Now :—		Sometime :—
Whitehead's,	Bishopsgate,	*White Hart.*
White Horse,	Dorking,	*(Maltese) Cross House.*
White Swan,	Stratford-on-Avon,	*King's Head.*
William IV,	Romsey, Hants,	*(but established 1768).*
Wynnstay Hotel,	Oswestry,	*Wynnstay Arms,*
		Bowling Green,
		Cross Foxes (see p. 83).
York Arms,	York,	*Chapter Coffee House.*
Yorkshire Hussar,	York,	*Yorkshire Tavern.*
Yorkshireman,	York,	*Yorkshireman's Arms.*

Chapter XIX

MISCELLANEOUS SIGNS

THIS chapter deals with signs which could not well be classed under any of the former divisions.

About 1825 there was a public-house in Clare Market called the *A B C*, where the alphabet from A to Z was painted over the door. Even at the present day many public-houses are called the *Letters*; thus there are two in Shrewsbury, there was formerly one, now extinct, at Aspatria, Cumb., and there is still one at Carlisle, one in Oldham, and others in various places. *Great A* was a public-house at Yaxham, Norf. (now extinct). *Letter A* is at Whittlesey, I. of Ely, *Alpha* is found in York Rd., S.W., *Letter B* is found at Probus, Corn., and (a rival house to *Letter A*?) at Whittlesey, I. of Ely. *B♯* (Be sharp) a not very suitable sign, is found at Birmingham, Hull and Lincoln. Perhaps one or more of these houses may have been formerly a musician's or a music-seller's. *Grand B* may be seen at Long Framlington, Northumb. The *C.B.* at Artengarthdale, N.R. Yorks., is supposed to be named from Charles Bathurst, Lord of the manor, who insisted upon his initials being stamped upon each pig of lead produced by the local works. The *E.U.R.* (colloquially 'Ere you are) at Ipswich represents the Eastern Union Railway, one of the constituent concerns of the Great Eastern Railway, absorbed into the L.N.E.R. and now, of course British Railways. *Q* is at Stalybridge, Ches., and *Q in the Corner* in Sheffield. *Z* was formerly a grocer's sign in this country, and was said to stand for Zingiber (ginger), but this was perhaps only a corruption of the figure 4, a constant grocer's sign in some parts of Scotland (for example at Stirling), implying that the provisions came from the four quarters of the world. *Number IV* is still the sign of an alehouse at 74 Hope St., Salford. *Number Three* is to be seen at Great Layton, Lancs. *No Seven*, Ledbury, Herefs., and *No Five* and *No Ten*, Hereford, are the street numbers of the houses concerned in the days before they were licensed. The last two, for example, were Nos. 5 and 10 Widemarsh St. 'Old' in inn signs, as explained elsewhere, is in general quite meaningless. It is appropriate to such a typically English institution as the inn that the *New Inn* sign should be almost the oldest in the country. The *New Inn*, Gloucester, has a well-recorded history from 1450, the *New Inn*, Dorchester, from 1398. At Harbury, Warws., is a house with the charming sign of the *Old New Inn*.

The *Bell* is one of the commonest signs in England, and was used as early as the 14th century, for Chaucer says that the 'gentil hostelrie that heighte the Tabard', was 'faste by the Belle'. Most probably bells were set up as signs on account of our national fondness for bell-ringing, which procured for our country the name of the 'ringing island', and made Handel say that the bell was our national musical instrument. A recent author reckons 483 houses of this name in England, excluding all

Blue Bells, Ring o' Bells, etc. Paul Hentzer, a German traveller, who visited this country 1596–1600, says ' the English are vastly fond of noises that fill the air, such as firing of cannon, beating of drums, and *ringing of bells* ; so that it is common for a number of them to go up into some belfry, and ring bells for hours together for the sake of exercise'. Aubrey makes a similar remark. A peal of bells usually consists of eight, hence the frequency of the *Eight Bells* ; besides these there are *One Bell* at Hatfield, Herts., at Crayford, Kent, and Watford. There was formerly a *Two Bells* at Whitechapel Rd., E., a *Three Bells* at Hordle, Som., a *Four Bells* at Woodborough, Notts., *Five Bells* at Burnham, Norf., and at Salisbury, *Six Bells* at Stoke Poges, Bucks., and at Barton Miles and at Preston, Suff., *Eight Bells* at Kelsale, Suff., *Ten Bells* at Stonham, Suff., and at Norwich. There is a *Ring o' Bells* at Wolverhampton, Taunton, Stoke-on-Trent, Birmingham, etc., and there was a *Three Swans & Peal* formerly at Walsall, Staffs., a *Nelson & Peal* in Warwickshire, and many others mentioned in a previous chapter. There is still a *Five Ringers* at Deal, and there was formerly an *Eight Ringers* at Norwich. One of the oldest *Bell* taverns in Middlesex stood in King St., Westminster ; it is named in 1466 in the expense book of Sir John Howard (Jockey of Norfolk), later first Howard Duke of Norfolk. Pepys dined at this house, 1 July 1660. In November of the same year he was there again ' to see the 7 flanders mares that my Lord has bought lately'. In Queen Anne's reign the October Club, consisting of about one hundred and fifty Tory county members of Parliament, used to meet at this tavern. The *Bell* in Warwick Lane, Newgate St., was in Larwood's time another example of the old London coaching inns, still in its original condition, the galleries being propped up to prevent their falling down. Everything about the place had a 17th-century look—the country carts, the chickens here in the very heart of the city, the inn kitchen with its old black clock, its settles and white benches. The very smell of the cookery going on seemed more homely and old English than the hot greasy vapours emanating from the areas of modern taverns. Coming into this yard from the adjacent crowded streets was like entering a latter-day Pompeii. It was at this inn that Archbishop Leighton, the honest, steady advocate of peace and forbearance, died in 1684. According to Burnet :—

> He often used to say that if he were to choose a place to die in, it should be an Inn ; it looks like a pilgrim's going home, to whom this world was all as an Inn, and who was weary of the noise and confusion in it. He added, that the officious tenderness and care of friends was an entanglement to a dying man ; and that the unconcerned attendance of those that could be procured in such a place would give less disturbance. And he obtained what he desired.

At the *Bell* in the Poultry lived in the reign of King William and Queen Anne, Nathaniel Crouch the famous bookseller who was the first to condense great and learned works into a small and popular form. He generally wrote under the name of ' John Burton'. The *Bell* in Holborn is said to have been named after the crest of Sir Ralph Grigge who resided there. The *Bell* at Tewkesbury is the scene of *John*

Halifax, Gentleman. The *Bell* at Edmonton was the rendezvous of John Gilpin and his wife in Cowper's famous poem.

At Finedon, Northants, there is a fine old half-timbered inn called the *Bell*, alleged to have been founded A.D. 1042 (!). It has for a sign the portrait of a female with the following lines beneath :—

> Queen Edith, lady once of Finedon,
> Where at the *Bell* good fare is dined on.

The *Bell* Inn at Oxford kept by John Good, had :—

> My name, likewise my ale, is good,
> Walk in and taste my own home brew'd ;
> For all that know John Good can tell,
> That, like my sign, it bears the *Bell*.

There was a *Golden Bell* in St Bride's Lane, Fleet St., in the reign of Queen Anne. There is still a house of this name—the *Golden Bells*—at Lower Assendon, Oxon. The *Black Bell* is mentioned by Stow :—

> Above the lane's (Crooked Lane) end upon Fish Hill Street, is one great house, for the most part built of stone, which pertained some time to Edward the Black Prince, son of Edward III, who was in his lifetime lodged there. It is now altered to a common hostelry, having the *Black Bell* for a sign.

The monument now stands on the site of this house. The *Bow Bells* is in Bow Rd.

The *Bells of Ouseley*, Old Windsor, displays four bells on a blue ground. The sign is said to represent a famous peal of bells at Oxeney Abbey, Oxford. Another *Bells of Oseney* is to be seen in Oxford. This house was a notorious haunt of footpads in coaching days. There is a *Village Bell* (? Village Belle ?) at Eling, Hants.

The *Bell* occurs in innumerable combinations, most of which seem to have no particular meaning, but simply to arise from the old custom of 'quartering' signs. Among them are the *Bell & Anchor*, still remaining in Hammersmith Rd., which was much visited by persons of fashion in the beginning of the reign of George III. Representations of the place and its visitors may be seen in several of the caricatures of that period, published by Bowles and Carver of St Paul's Churchyard. In Larwood's time there was a *Bell & Lion* at Crewe, Ches.—a house of this name still survives at Tarporley, Ches. The *Bell & Bullock*, Netherem, Cumb., probably contains two signs united on account of the alliteration ; there was a *Bell & Cuckoo* formerly at Erdington, Birmingham, and a *Bell & Candlestick* also formerly in Birmingham. There is a *Bell & Bowl* at Whaplode, Lincs.

The *Bell & Crown* is very common and occurs for example at Winchester. This is a reasonable combination, for the bell has from time immemorial been rung to express the public feeling on royal entries, whether into the world or into a town, on the occasion of royal marriages or deaths, at times of great victories and declarations of peace, and in other loyal celebrations. Hence many bells are inscribed with the

U

words FEAR GOD, HONOUR THE KING, which in the beginning of the 18th century seems also to have been a common inscription on the sign of the *Bell*. This sentiment was thus versified by a sign-painter, who evidently had more loyalty than poetical genius :—

> Let the King
> Live long.
> Dong Ding,
> Ding Dong.

Few signs have so often been wrongly explained as the *Bell Savage*, on Ludgate Hill, now the publishing office of Messrs. Cassell who do business under the sign of *la Belle Sauvage*. Stow says it received its name from one Isabella Savage, who had given the house to the company of cutlers. He was certainly much nearer the truth than the *Spectator*, who states that it was called after a French play of *la Belle Sauvage*. Another writer following Stow asserts that the inn was once the property of Lady Arabella Savage, familiarly called 'Bell Savage' which name was represented in a rebus by a wild man and a bell, and so it was always drawn on the panels of the coaches that used to run to and from it, until the railways changed our style of travelling. The true origin of the name is manifest from a document in the Close Roll of 1453 concerning Savage's Inn *alias* the Bell on the Hoop. It has no connexion whatever with Princess Pocahontas, as is often asserted. In the 16th century the *Bell Savage* appears to have been a place of amusement. By the gate of the *Bell Savage* Sir Thomas Wyatt rested for a time when his ill-advised rebellion had collapsed. One of the attractions about that period was Bank's wonderful horse, Marocco, which here performed his tricks before a half-admiring, half-awestricken audience, many of whom considered the animal a wizard, if not a devil. To mine host of the *Bel Savage* and all his honest guests, was dedicated the satirical tract of *Marocco Extaticus*, in which this horse is introduced. During the civil wars this inn is mentioned apparently as a Royalist house in 1642. Upon search at *Bell Savage* (by order of Parliament) great quantities of plate were found, intended for York, but stayed by order. Grinling Gibbons lived at one time in Bell Savage Yard, and in his house there had a carved pot of flowers ' which shook surprisingly with the motion of the coaches that passed by'—or so says Horace Walpole. A very odd accident happened in this inn during the terrific storm of 26 November 1703. A Mr. Hempson, we are told, was blown in his sleep out of an upper room window, and knew nothing of the storm nor of his aerial voyage, till awaking, he found himself lying in his bed on Ludgate Hill. The house was for centuries a coaching inn, so its name spread to the provinces and some innkeepers copied its sign, whence there was formerly a *La Belle Sauvage* at Macclesfield, and others in one or two other places. There are still several examples of the sign along the Holyhead road.

Balls were extremely common in former times, frequently in combination with other objects ; this arose from the custom of the silk mercers in hanging out a *Golden Ball*. Constantine the Great adopted a golden globe as the emblem of his imperial dignity, on which, after he embraced Christianity, he placed a cross, and with this addition it continues as one of the insignia of royalty at the present day. The early silk-mercers adopted the golden globe, or ball, as their sign, perhaps because in the Middle Ages, all silk was brought from the East, and more particularly from Byzantium and the imperial manufactories there. The *Golden Ball* continued as a silk-mercer's sign until the end of the last century, when it gradually fell to the Berlin wool shops, and with some few of them it has continued until the present day.

Balls of various colours were invariably the signs of quacks and fortune-tellers in the 18th century ; the Bagford Bills are full of *Red*, *Blue*, *Black*, *White*, and *Green Balls*, all signs of those gentry who profess to cure all the evils flesh is heir to. How they came to choose this sign is hard to say—we can scarcely imagine that they were intended to represent magnified pills. Moorfields was the headquarters of this trade. The *Compleat Vintner* in 1720 has :—

> If in Moorfields a Lady stroles
> Among the *Globes* and *Golden Balls*,
> Where ere they hang she may be certain
> Of knowing what shall be her fortune.
> Her husband too, I dare to say,
> But that she better knows than they.

There is still a *Golden Ball* at Norwich, and another with a good pictorial sign at Bridgwater. The *Two Golden Balls* at the upper end of Bow St., Covent Garden, was a place famous for concerts, balls and other amusements at the end of the 17th and the beginning of the 18th century.

The *Plough & Ball* survives to this day at Nuneaton, Warws., and innumerable other combinations with the ball might be mentioned.

The *Three Blue Balls*, generally a pawnbroker's sign, was also in old times used for taverns and other houses, while pawnbrokers used at pleasure such signs as the *Blacka-moor's Head*, the *Black Dog & Still*, etc., both named as pawnbrokers' signs in the *Daily Courant* for 1718. On 26 March 1668 Pepys tells us that coming from the theatre in Lincoln's Inn Fields he and his party went to the *Blue Balls* Tavern in the same locality, where they met some of their friends, including Mrs. Knipp and had very good value for their reckoning of ' almost £4 '. There is still a public-house sign of the *Blue Balls* at Newport, I. of W., and another *Blue Ball* at Pottersbury, Wilts. The latter had formerly as its sign a terrestrial globe with over it a heart, and the motto *Cor supra Mundum*. The *Ring & Ball*, Fenchurch St., seems suggested by the game of pall mall, revived in Victorian times under the name of croquet, in which a ball was struck by a mallet through an iron ring. This sign is mentioned in an advertise-ment in the *London Gazette* of 18–21 November 1700.

The *Bat & Ball* is a common sign for public-houses frequented by cricketers, as at Hambledon, Hants, Oxford, Horndean, Salisbury, etc. It occurs in four places in Kent. Bat and ball was a game played more or less like rounders. It developed into cricket, *c.* 1750–91, and the Hambledon house claims to be the original home of cricket. The *Bat & Ball* on Broadhalfpenny Down shows on its signboard Richard (or John)

Wyven inside the tables at which sat the fathers of modern cricket. The tables themselves are still preserved in the Hambledon *Bat & Ball's* one public room. The *Cricketers' Arms* is found at Norwich, Oakmoor, Staffs., etc., and there are examples of the *Five Cricketers*, and many others. The *Eleven Cricketers* as at Dartford, Kent, is commonly found in one form or another throughout Kent and Surrey. There is a good *Cricketers* sign at Putney Common, and another fine one designed by Ralph Ellis was lately erected by Messrs. Watney over their house at Hale, Surrey. The *Umpire* is at Sheffield, the *Test Match* at Nottingham. The *Wrestlers* obtains its name from a sport formerly in great favour in this country, and still cultivated in some parts. An inn of that name at Yarmouth is more celebrated for the *jeu d'esprit* of Nelson than for anything else. When the fleet was riding in the Yarmouth roads, the landlord, desirous of the patronage of the bluejackets, requested permission to call his house the *Nelson Arms*. His lordship gave him full power to do so, but at the same time reminded him that his *arms* were only in the singular number. There is a good *Wrestlers* sign at Hatfield, Herts., and a *Hurdler*, with a portrait of Lord Burghley, at Stamford.

The old national antipathy betwixt this country and our neighbours across the channel, is recorded in the *Antigallican* (the name assumed by a London association in the middle of the 18th century). This could not fail to be a favourite sign. At the beginning of the 19th century there was a tavern of this name in Shire Lane, Temple Bar, kept by Harry Lee, of sporting notoriety and father of Alexander Lee, the first and ' original ' *tiger* in which capacity he was produced by the notorious Lord Barrymore. There were formerly three public-houses with that sign in London, besides some in the country, there is still an *Antigallican* in Tooley St., and an *Antigallican Arms* at Charlton, Kent. The *Three Frogs* dealt with elsewhere (p. 78) is a similar manifestation of anti-French feeling. Other political signs will be found as the Heads or Arms of prominent politicians, especially for example such men as Wilkes and Sheridan in the 18th century, and George Canning, Lord Liverpool, Russell, Grey, Cobden, Peel and Gladstone in the 19th century. Sometimes they are more cryptically expressed as the *Three Lords*, or the *Three Johns*, *q.v.* The *Ballot Box* at Harrow may date not from the Ballot Act of 1872 but from the People's Charter of 1838, when election by ballot was the fourth point of the Chartists' demands.

On 29 September 1783 the first balloon—or air-balloon as it was then called— was let off at Versailles in the presence of Louis XVI and the Royal Family. A sheep was the first aeronaut and with this freight in a cage the balloon rose to a height of about 200 yards, floated over a part of Paris, and came down in the Carrefour Maréchal. The novelty was at once taken hold of by caricaturists, ballad-mongers, writers of comic articles, and also by the sign-painters. As those primitive balloons were in the opinion of the vulgar filled with smoke, the tobacconists considered them as within their province, and thus the *Balloon* became a favourite device with this class of shops. Several of their tobacco papers are preserved in the Banks Collection. As a sign the *Balloon* or *Air-balloon*, not uncommon in Larwood's time, though it rarely remains now, might formerly be seen at Kingston, Hants, and still survives at Bilston, Staffs., and Birdlip, Glos., etc. In this latter place it may be connected with a certain Walter Powell who made a balloon ascent at Malmesbury, and was never heard of again.

The *Blue Pudding* at Hull had formerly as its sign a plum pudding on fire, surrounded by brilliant blue (brandy) flames. The *Bo-Peep* at St Leonards is said to owe its sign to the fact that its liquor is better than one might once have supposed from the outside appearance of the house.

At the castles of the nobility the weary traveller formerly found food and shelter. The lower hall was always open to the adventurer, the tramp, the minstrel, and the pilgrim ; the upper hall to the nobleman, the squire, the wealthy abbot, and the ladies. It was natural then that the *Castle* should at an early period have been adopted as a sign of good entertainment for man and beast. Such a sign became historical in the Wars of the Roses ; for according to *King Henry VI* (Pt. II),* the Duke of Somerset, who had been warned to ' shun castles ', was killed by Richard Duke of York, at an alehouse, the sign of the *Castle*, in St Albans.

According to Hatton's *New View of London*, in 1708 the *Castle* Tavern in Fleet St. had the largest sign in London ; next to it came the *White Hart* Inn, in Southwark.

In the reign of George I the *Castle* near Covent Garden was a famous eating-house, kept by John Pierce, a leading chef of his day. Here the feat was performed of a young blood taking one of the shoes from the foot of a noted toast, filling it with wine and drinking her health. After this the shoe was consigned to the cook, who prepared from it an excellent *ragoût*, which was eaten with great relish by the lady's admirers.

The *Castle & Falcon* (probably a combination of two signs, as there is a Falcon Court close by) is the sign of an inn in Aldersgate. This house in the reign of Queen Elizabeth was opposite to Aldersgate, which was occupied by John Day, the most considerable printer and publisher of his time. In after years the house became a famous coaching-inn, and its reputation spread to all parts of England, whence we meet at present with *Castle & Falcons* in various towns, as at Birmingham, Chester, Newarkon-Trent, and formerly at Burslem, Staffs. Probably the sign arose from a combination, still it is worthy of remark that the crest of Queen Catherine Parr was a crowned falcon perched on a castle, and the bird of course being as large as the castle.

The *Three Old Castles* occurs at Mandeville, near Somerton, the *Castle & Banner* at Hunny Hill, I. of W., perhaps originating in the banner floating from the castle turret, when the lord of the manor was residing there. *Castles-in-the-Air* is to be seen at Lower Quay, Fareham, Hants, where the origin seems to be an allusion to the ordinary sign swinging in mid-air—a piece of humour on the part of the landlord. The *Castle & Wheelbarrow*, at Rouse Lench, Worcs., was doubtless another innkeeper's notion of suggestive humour. There is a *Castle of Comfort* at Midstead, Som.

Perhaps the most patriarchal of all signs is the *Chequers*, which may be seen even on houses in exhumed Pompeii. Originally it is said to have indicated that draughts

* Act 5, Sc. 2.

and backgammon were played within. Brand, ignorant of any existence of the sign in so remote a period as that mentioned, says that it represented the coat of arms of the Earls of Warenne and Surrey, who bore checky *or* and *az*, and in the reign of Edward IV possessed the privilege of licensing alehouses. Another account has it that the nobleman was the Earl of Arundel, and the reign that of Philip and Mary. A more plausible explanation, and one which is not set aside by the existence of the sign in Pompeii, is that the chequers represent a merchant's or money-changer's abacus. This sign afterwards came to indicate an inn or house of entertainment, probably from the circumstance of the innkeeper also following the trade of money-changer—a coincidence still very common in seaport towns. The *Chequers* at Tonbridge is said to date from 1264.

Chaucer's Pilgrims put up in Canterbury, at the sign of the *Chequer of the Hope* (i.e. the *Chequers on the Hoop*).

This inn is still pointed out in Canterbury, at the corner of High St. and Mercery Lane, and is often mentioned in the Corporation records, under the title of the *Chequer*. It is situated in the immediate vicinity of the Cathedral, and was therefore appropriate for the reception of the pilgrims. There is another fine *Chequers* at Horley, Surrey.

In or near Calcot's Alley, Lambeth, was formerly situated an inn or house of entertainment called the *Chequers*. In the year 1454 a license was granted to its landlord, John Calcot, to have an oratory in the house and a chaplain for the use of his family and guests as long as his house should continue orderly and respectable, and adapted to the celebration of divine service.

When the inn had another sign besides the *Chequers*, these last were invariably painted on the doorpost. An example of this might formerly be seen at the *Swiss Cottage*, Chelsea, now extinct as an inn sign. Apparently the sole surviving example of this nowadays is at the *Methuen Arms*, Corsham, Wilts.

The *Black Chequers*, formerly in Cowgate, Norwich, was so called on account of the chequers being black and white, whilst others are red and white, blue and white, or in such other contrast as may be fancied by the publican.

The *Criterion* is an interesting sign, found for example at East Retford, Notts., and at Shrewsbury. Presumably it suggests that it is so good as to form a standard by which other inns are to be judged. According to Monson Fitzjohn there are altogether about 270 houses of this sign in England.

The *Crooked Billet* found at Wych St., W.C., Ash, Kent, Doncaster, Holbeach, Maidenhead, Ryehill, Wokingham, etc. etc., is a sign for which no likely general origin has been discovered ; it may have been originally a ragged staff, or a pastoral staff, or a *bâton cornu*—the ancient name for a battle-axe. It may signify then a house catering for men at arms (? a good *billet*). On the other hand the billet may be a trunk or tree branch, a serf's weapon or ox or other yoke, a shepherd's crook, a bishop's crozier, a wheel felloe, or the wood rind of a stone quern. It may be heraldic (the cross being a saltire, the symbol of St Julian, patron of travellers, and the arms of the Nevilles), or a maunch, the arms of the Whartons. It is also the name for a part of a tankard. Frequently the sign is represented by an untrimmed stick suspended above the door, as at Wold Newton, E.R. Yorks., where it is accompanied by this poetical effusion on one side of the signboard :—

> When this comical stick grew in the wood,
> Our ale was fresh and very good ;
> Step in and taste, O do make haste,
> For if you don't 'twill surely waste,

On the other side :—

> When you have viewed the other side,
> Come read this too before you ride,
> And now to end we'll let it pass ;
> Step in, kind friends, and take a glass.

This house is also known as the *Anvil Arms*. A briefer poem occurred formerly on the sign of the *Crooked Billet* at Wotton, Bucks. :—

> May Uff
> She sells good stuff
> And that's enough.

Much has been written on the *Crooked Billet* sign, probably because almost every occurrence of it differs from every other instance. It may be that the curious cluster of *Crooked Billet* signs in Essex near the Thames Estuary have a common origin.

Taylor the Water Poet mentions two taverns with the sign of the *Mouth*, the one without Bishopsgate, the other within Aldersgate. Trades tokens of the first house are extant, representing a human head with a huge mouth wide open. The names of the rooms in the house were ' the Pomegranate ', ' the Portcullis ', ' Three Tuns ', ' Cross Keys ', ' Vine ', ' King's Head ', ' Crown ', ' Dolphin ', and ' Bell ', all of them favourite tavern signs, and usual names for tavern rooms. (Four of the room names still survive at the *Royal Fountain*, Sheerness ; the *Rose*, the *Crown*, the *Star* and the *Sun*. Sometimes rooms are named after flowers, after virtues, or after English kings. At the *Shakespeare* at Stratford they are named after Shakesperean plays.) The *Merry Mouth* is still a sign at Fifield, Berks., but this is said to be named after a local landowner called Murimuth.

The *Gullet* is an unusual sign formerly found at Shrewsbury but recently destroyed. Probably the old inn was in Gullet Passage, and the sign may have taken its name from the street, not *vice versa*. It is known to have existed at any rate from 1527. There is also an *Old Gullet* in the town.

The *Hand* was a sign of a victualler near the Marshalsea in Southwark in 1680. Hands occur in many combinations, owing to the custom of the draughtsmen and sign-painters representing a hand issuing from the clouds to perform some action or hold some object ; thus a hand holding a coffee-pot was a very general coffee-house sign. The *Hand* seems to have had unpleasant associations. According to Tom Brown :

> Where the sign is painted with a *Woman's Hand* in it, 'tis a bawdy house, where a man's it has another qualification ; but where it has a star in the sign 'tis calculated for every lewd purpose.

A few combinations of the hand refer to games, as the *Hand & Ball*, Barking, which appears on a trades token of 1650. This seems to be derived from some of the innumerable games at ball in which our ancestors delighted. The *Hand & Raquet*, Whitcombe St., Haymarket, is so called from the adjoining tennis court, erected in 1678. The *Old Hand & Tankard* is a public-house sign at Wheatley, Halifax. The *Hand & Tench* seems to point to a connexion with fishing. It was a mug-house in Seven Dials in 1717. The mugs displayed the features of the Whig heroes and were something like modern Toby jugs. The mugs used to be suspended above the door, or on the sign-iron, not only in this, but in all the other mug-houses. The mug might be considered as much a badge of King George's friends as the white cockade was that of the Jacobites. The last of the mug-houses to be suppressed was the *Barley Mow* in Salisbury Square, Fleet St. Here in the year 1716 such a disturbance arose through a Tory mob bursting in to wreck the house that the landlord threatened to shoot the first man to lay hands on his property. He carried out his threat, the mob duly wrecked the house, and the military had to be called out to suppress the riot. The landlord was tried for murder, but found guilty only of manslaughter and five of the ringleaders of the mob were duly hanged in Salisbury Court a few weeks later. The house was associated with the ' Society of Cogers '. The present house on the same site, rebuilt in 1937, was named the *Cogers* to mark the association.

The *Hand & Heart* was, in 1711, the very appropriate sign of a marriage insurance office in East Harding St., Shoe Lane. Two right hands holding a heart was a very old symbol of concord. Aubrey in *Remains of Gentilisme & Judaisme* gives quotations from Tacitus, by which he derives it from the Romans.

The *Heart in Hand* is still a common alehouse sign. It is found as the *Hand & Heart* at Peterborough, and at Ilkeston, Derbys., and as the *Heart & Hand* at Grantham. A similar meaning is conveyed by the equally common *Hand-in-Hand*, found for example at Ipswich, or *Cross Hands* as at Salford, Oxon. At Turnditch, Derbys., this sign was called the *Cross o' the Hands*, and a corruption of this again is the *Cross in Hand*, at Waldron, Sussex. The *Hand in Hand* was also one of the usual signs of the marriage mongers in Fleet St. Pennant says :

> In walking along the streets in my youth, on the side next this prison (the Fleet) I have often been tempted by the question, ' Sir, will you be pleased to walk in and be married.' Along this most lawless space was most frequently hung up the sign of a

male and female hand conjoined, with, 'Marriages performed within' written beneath. A dirty fellow invited you in ; the parson was seen walking before his shop, a squalid profligate figure, clad in tattered plaid nightgown, with a fiery face, and ready to couple you for a dram of gin or a roll of tobacco.

We have elsewhere referred to famous museums in inns (pp. 60–1). There are one or two *Museum* inns or hotels still to be found, for example at Farnham, Dorset. Formerly there were other houses of this name, especially in the Midlands, at Birmingham, Wednesbury and Sutton Coldfield. These had fairly good exhibitions of stuffed birds, coins and curios generally. The *Black Horse*, Birdlip, Glos., had a really good collection of this kind, quite recently dispersed. Probably other *Museums* gained their signs in this way in the days when licensing justices were not so much inclined as they are nowadays to frown upon the development of side-shows at licensed houses.

The *Hole-in-the-Wall*, Southwark, has a Museum containing *inter alia* a key reputed to be that of the condemned cell in Newgate. There is another curious museum at the *Tiger* on Tower Hill, and still another at the *Wheatsheaf*, Leman St. The famous collection at Charlie Brown's is dealt with elsewhere. Other more specialized shows are to be seen in many riverside fishing inns, for example the *Ferry Boat*, Tottenham.

A few other houses still have general collections of curiosities, for example the *Borough Inn*, Hanley, Stoke-on-Trent, and the *Curiosity*, locally known as the *Old Curiosity Shop*, Liverpool. There is also a museum of a sort in the *Bull & Bear*, Shelton, Stoke-on-Trent, though it consists mainly of stuffed fish. The *Headless Woman* at Duddon, Ches., has a good museum. This is an interesting house mentioned in *Lavengro*. The licensee publishes this not very convincing account of the derivation of the name (see p. 267) :

> A party of Cromwell's soldiers, engaged in hunting down the Royalists in the Chester district, visited Hockenhall Hall, but found that the family being warned of their coming had buried all the silver and other valuables and then fled for safety, leaving only a faithful old housekeeper in charge of the Hall, thinking it unlikely that the soldiers would do her any harm.
>
> The soldiers, being incensed at finding nothing of value, locked up the housekeeper in a top room and proceeded to torture her to make her tell them where the valuables were hidden. She remained faithful and was finally murdered by the soldiers cutting off her head. Tradition says that afterwards, on numerous occasions she was seen carrying her head under her arm, walking along the old bridle path between Hockenhall Hall and the spot where it comes out on the Tarporley Road near to the public-house.

It is not known whether the *Observatory* at Hanley, Stoke-on-Trent, derived its name from the provision of a telescope for the customers' benefit. Probably the *Exhibition* at Shelton and the *Crystal Palace* at Tunstall in the same city are named in honour of the great Exhibition of 1851. The inns of this city have a high cultural standard, and one of them, the *Gordon* in Kingsway, Stoke, has a church organ which was brought to the house on the closing down of a local music hall, the Hippodrome. Recitals are regularly given on it.

The *Leg* used formerly to be at the door of every hosier. It was also the sign of a tavern in King St., Westminster, frequented by Pepys. Trades tokens are extant of the *Leg & Star*, kept by Richard Finch, in Aldersgate in the 17th century. It may have represented a leg with the garter round it, and the star of that order ; but more probably it was a combination of two signs.

The *Legs of Man* is found at Burslem, Stoke-on-Trent, Redmire, N.R. Yorks., Sandbach, Ches., Leeds, Bolton and Wigan, Lancs., etc. It is rarely found except in north-west England. It may be either a sign adopted to attract Manxmen, or possibly one adopted like the *Eagle & Child* in compliment to the (Stanley) Earls of Derby, formerly Kings of Man. A popular tradition has it that the three legs ' kneel to England, kick at Scotland, and spurn Ireland'. The house at Leeds is known locally as the *Three Kettle Spouts*. The Redmire House was formerly called *Nobody*, q.v., and the legs sign is supposed to be a play upon the phrase ' No body'.

The *Cunning Man* is at Burghfield, Berks., the *Smiling Man* at Dudley. The *Old Man*, Market Place, Westminster, was probably intended for Old Parr, who was celebrated in ballads as ' The Olde, Olde, Very Olde Manne'. The token represents a bearded bust in profile, with a bare head. In the reign of James I it was the name of a tavern in the Strand, otherwise called the *Hercules* Tavern, and in the 18th century there were two coffee-houses, the one called the *Old Man's*, the other the *Young Man's* Coffee-house.

The *Fountain* was a favourite sign with the Londoners before the Reformation, perhaps on account of its connexion with the martyrdom of St Paul. When his head was struck off it rebounded three times, and a fountain gushed up at each spot where the head had touched the ground. During the Plague of 1665 a quack medicine advertisement used to figure constantly in the papers from ' Mr Drinkwater at the *Fountain* in Fleet St.' Evidently Drinkwater intended a pun by selecting the fountain as his sign. The *Fountain* in the Strand was famous as the meeting-place of the high Tory party of 1685, who here talked over public affairs before the meeting of Parliament. The pamphleteer Roger l'Estrange who had been recently knighted by the king took a leading part in these consultations. In the reign of George II this same house became a great resort for the Whigs, who sometimes used to meet here as many as two hundred at a time, making speeches and passing resolutions. For this reason it was proposed that Jepson the landlord should write under his sign :—

> From this fam'd Fountain freedom flow'd,
> For Britain's and the People's good.

In this tavern in 1694 Edward Law of Lauriston, subsequently famous as the Mississippi schemer, quarrelled with the magnificent and mysterious Beau Wilson ; they left the house, adjourned to Bloomsbury Square, and fought a duel, in which Beau was killed. The Kit Kat Club, in winter, used to meet at this house. The Club was first established in an obscure house in Shire Lane ; it consisted of thirty-nine distinguished noblemen and writers, gentlemen zealously attached to the Protestant succession of the house of Hanover.   The name of the club is said to have been derived from the first landlord, who was called Christopher Cat ; he excelled in the making of mutton pies, which were named after him Kit Kat, and were the standard dish of the club.

> Here did th' assembly's title first arise,
> And Kit Kat's wits sprung first from Kit Kat's pies.

There is a well-known *Fountain* with a good pictorial sign at Cambridge, and another good one at Chichester.

The *Saltwell*, near Dudley, Worcs., is so called from a medicinal brine bath which is found on the premises and which is in occasional use to this day.   The *Fountain &* *Bear* was a publisher's sign in Cheapside in 1663.   The *Rock & Fountain* is a (? unique) sign at Shrewsbury.   Probably it refers to Exodus xvii. 1–7.

The *Sun* and the *Moon* have been considered as signs of pagan origin, typifying Apollo and Diana.   Whether or no this conjecture be true would be difficult to prove, but certain it is that they rank among the oldest and most common signs, not only in England but on the Continent.

Like the *Star* (see p. 280), the *Sun* did not enjoy a good reputation.   Henry Peacham thus cautions young men from the country :—

> Let a monyed man or gentleman especially beware in the city *ab istis calidis et callidis solis filiabus* as Lipsius : these overhot and crafty daughters of the *Sunne*, your silken and gold laced harlots, everywhere (especially in the suburbs) to be found.

The reason of this sign having been especially adopted by houses of ill fame may be the one Tom D'Urfey gives in his *Art of Living in London*, 1642, in ' Collin's Walk Through London ', where speaking of a frail and fair one, he says :—

> And like the *Sun*, was understood
> To all mankind a common good.

Taylor the Water Poet mentions three *Sun* taverns.   Being compelled one day on his ' pennylesse pilgrimage ' of 1630, to dine out of doors, he says :—' I made virtue of necessity, and went to breakefast in the *Sunne* : I have fared better at three *Sunnes* many a time before now ; in Aldersgate Street, Criplegate, and New Fish Street ; but here is the oddes : at those *Sunnes* they will come vpon a man with a tauerne bill as sharp cutting as a taylor's bill of items : a watchman's bill or a watch hooke falls not halfe so heauy vpon a man.'   The *Sun* on Fish St. Hill is also named by Pepys, 22 December 1660.   The finest of all the *Suns* did not exist in Taylor's time ; it was built behind the Exchange after the fire of 1666 :—

> Behind ! I'll ne'er believe it ; you may soon
> Persuade me that the sun stands behind the moon,

are the opening lines of a ballad of 1672 entitled *The Glory of the Sun Tavern, behind the Exchange.* From this ballad it is evident that the tavern was splendidly furnished, and offered comforts not generally to be met with at that time.

> There every chamber has an aquaeduct,
> As if the sun had fire for water truckt,
> Water as't were exhal'd up to heavens sprouds,
> To cool your cups and glasses in the clouds.

Pepys was a frequent visitor at this house, and in fact, all the pleasure-seekers of the period patronized it. The profligate Duke of Buckingham in particular was a constant customer. Simon Wadloe, the landlord, had made his fortune at the *Devil & St Dunstan*, whereupon he went to live in the country and spent his money in a couple of years. He then cheated Nick Colbourn out of the *Sun*, and Nick, who had amassed a handsome competence in the house, was easily persuaded to retire, and left it ' to live like a prince in the country ', says Pepys. During the reign of Charles II, the house appears to have had an excellent custom, and was from morning till night full of the best company. The *Sun* in Clare St. was one of the haunts of Joe Miller, and is often given as the locality of his jokes :—

> Joe Miller sitting one day in the window of the Sun Tavern, Clare Street, a fish woman and her maid passing by, the woman cried, ' Buy my soals, buy my maids ! ' ' Ah ! you wicked old creature,' cry'd honest Joe, ' what, are you not content to sell your own soul, but you must sell your maid's too ? '

A well-known provincial *Sun* is that at Hitchin, known to have existed since 1575 and probably established as a rival to the local *Angel c.* 1523.

A stereotyped joke of the publican connected with the *Sun* is the motto ' the best liquor (generally beer) under the *Sun* '. Sometimes the sign is called the *Sun in Splendour*, as at Notting Hill, the ' splendour ' having reference simply to the golden beams or rays usually drawn by the painter. The *Sun in Splendour* is one of the badges of Richard II, it is also a charge in the arms of the Distillers' Company. There was formerly a carved gilt stone sign of the *Sun*, dating from 1668, walled in the front of a house in the Poultry, a district once very rich in astronomical signs. Another *Sun* was at Oxford in the Cornmarket. The full title of the place was the *Sun Vaults*. It is said to have originated as a licensed house from the meeting of the portmannimote in Carfax churchyard.

The sign of the *Sun* occurs in endless combinations, often capricious, without any other reason than a whim, or from an alliteration, as the *Sun & Sawyers*, Poplar High St., and the *Sun & Sword*, now extinct, formerly in Cable St. ; or quartered with other signs, as the *Sun & Anchor*, *Sun & Dover*, Coldharbour Lane, *Sun & Horseshoes*, Mortimer St. (p. 118), *Sun & Whalebone*, Latton, Essex. The *Sun & Thirteen Cantons* has already been mentioned on p. 176. Innumerable other signs of the same sort occur among the London public-houses of the present day. The *Sun & Hare* was a stone carved sign walled up in the façade of a house in the High St. Southwark. But for the initials H. N. A., it might be taken for a rebus on the name of Harrison, with these it may be a jocular corruption of the *Sun & the Hart*, the badges of Richard II (see p. 97).

The *Rising Sun* is nearly as common as the *Sun* in his meridian ; perhaps on account of the favourable omen it presents for a man commencing business.   In 1726 it was the sign of a noted tavern in Islington Rd., notable for oxen roasted whole and hogs barbecued whole.

The *Rising Moon*, found for example at Matley, Lancs., is presumably merely an eccentric variation upon the *Rising Sun*.

One of the learned questions propounded by Hudibras to that cunning man Sidrophel the Rosicrucian, was :—

> Tell me but what's the natural cause
> Why on a sign no painter draws
> The *full moon* ever, but the *half*.*

This might be true in Butler's time, but is no longer so ; at Leicester, for instance, there are two signs of the *Full Moon*, and it occurs in many other places, as for example at Taunton.   There is a *Moon* at Spondon, Derbys., and a *New Moon* at Carcroft, W.R. Yorks.   The *Crescent* or *Half Moon*, found for example at Oundle, was the emblem of the temporal power, as the *Sun* was that of the spirituality.   This is Larwood's explanation.   However here for once it is possible to agree with Mr. Block.†   Probably very often the sign is a symbol of Our Lady.   ' To this day throughout the Christian world the Virgin stands upon the Crescent.'   There are a few *Crescents*, but many *Half Moons*.   A pleasing sign of this name may be seen at Croydon.

Ben Jonson once desiring a glass of sack went to the *Half Moon* in Aldersgate St., but found it closed, so he adjourned to the *Sun* in Long Acre, and wrote this epigram :—

> Since the *Half Moon* is so unkind,
>   To make me go about,
> The *Sun* my money now shall have,
>   And the *Moon* shall go without.

The *Half Moon* still surviving in Holloway Rd. was famous in the 18th century for excellent cheese cakes, which were hawked about the streets of London by a man on horseback, and formed one of the London cries.   This circumstance is noted in a poem in the *Gentleman's Magazine* for 1743, entitled *A Journey to Nottingham*.   In April 1747 this advertisement appeared in the same magazine :—

> Half Moon Tavern, Cheapside, April 13.
> His Royal Highness the *Duke of Cumberland* having restored peace to Britain, by the ever memorable Battle of Culloden, fought on the 16th April 1745, the *choice spirits* have agreed to celebrate that day annually by a Grand Jubilee in the *Moon*, of which the Stars are hereby acquainted and summoned to shine with their brightest lustre by 6 o'clock on Thursday next in the Evening.

The *Crescent & Anchor* is a sign at Norton-in-Hales, Salop, the *Half Moon & Seven*

* *Hudibras*, Pt. III, c. 3.   † *Op. cit.*, p. 30.

Stars at Aston Clinton, near Tring, Herts., and in Gt. George St., a *Moon & Stars* at Norwich, (and) the *Half Moon & Star* at Ipswich, and the *Sun, Moon & Seven Stars* at Blisworth, Northants.

These *Seven Stars* have always been great favourites, they seem to be the same pleiad which is used as a Masonic emblem—a circle of six stars, with one in the centre : possibly the seven stars is the *Plough*, or more probably the ancient seven planets. As a change upon the *Seven Stars*, a publican at Counterslip, Bristol, has put up the *Fourteen Stars*.

We have seen (p. 299) that the sign of the *Star* was 'calculated for every lewd purpose'. This was a great change certainly from mediaeval times, when a star was that which appeared in the East to announce the birth of Our Lord, the emblem of Our Lady, who was thus styled (star of the sea), the signification of the name Miriam in Hebrew—or *Stella Jacobi* (Star of Jacob), *Stella Matutina* (morning star), *Stella non erratico* (fixed star, unerring star), etc. A star was always painted either on her right shoulder or on her veil, as may be readily observed in the works of early Italian masters in the National Gallery.

A star of sixteen rays is the crest of the Innholders' Company. The usual inn star is the heraldic *estoile*, so should have six waved points. A similar figure is the *mullet* which has five plain points. The *Morning Star*, Bristol, is named after a once famous ship. The *North Star* or the *Polar Star* is a general symbol of constancy. Married couples used to gaze at it as soon as possible after their nuptials. The sign occurs occasionally as for example at Portsmouth. An odd mixture is the *Seven Stars & Naked Boy*. The original sign was the *Seven Stars*. After the Fire of 1666 the (fat) *Naked Boy* was used as a neighbouring sign, of the *Fortune of War*. From this it was adopted by the Host of the *Seven Stars* two doors away. The original is now in the Guildhall Museum. Oliver Cromwell used to meet some of his party at the *Star* in Coleman St. as was deposed by one of the witnesses in the trial of Hugh Peters in 1660.

The *Star* at Alfriston, Sussex, is a very good house of *c.* 1450, now in the possession of Messrs. Trust Houses. There are several other religious emblems carved on the front of the house and there is some plausibility in the suggestion that the inn was built as a shelter for pilgrims on their way to the shrine of St Richard of Chichester, and that it belonged to a local Religious House, perhaps the great Abbey of Battle. The house is mentioned in Harrison Ainsworth's once famous novel, *Ovingdean Grange*.

The *Star & Crown* was the sign of a haberdasher in Princes St., Coventry St., 1785, who among other things, sold 'dress and undress hoops'. It occurs as an inn sign at Broadway, S.W.

The signs of the Zodiac appear occasionally to have been adopted by conjurors and astrologers. Ned Ward describes them as figuring, in his time, at the door of a 'star-peeper' in Prescot St.

Other houses of these signs seem often to be named after coaches (pp. 214–15).

The *Rainbow*, Fleet St., opposite Chancery Lane, is the oldest coffee-house in London. The proprietor, one James Farr, a barber, was in the year 1657 presented by the inquest of St Dunstan's in the West for making and selling a sort of liquor called Coffee, as a great nuisance and prejudice to the neighbourhood, etc.

The presentment is preserved among the records of St Sepulchre's Church.

A very odd sign is the *Rent Day* in Cambridge St., near the Edgware Rd.

The *Thunder Storm* is the sign of a public-house at Fremwellgate Moor, Durh., and the *Hailstone*, formerly at Knowle End, Staffs., and at Dudley, Worcs. These houses may have taken their names from a severe storm, which visited the neighbourhood at or about the time of their opening, just as the *Haycock* at Wansford, Northants (see p. 247), is said to owe its origin to the fact of Drunken Barnaby floating a long way down the river on a haycock during an inundation, and landing near that place.

The *Hole-in-the-Wall* is believed to have originated from the hole made in the wall of the debtors' or other prison, through which the poor prisoners received the money, broken meat, or other donations of the charitably inclined. Perhaps sometimes it may refer to a house where liquor was sold illicitly. It has been suggested that the reference is to Ezekiel viii. 7–10. The old sign of the *Hole-in-the-Wall* shows such an opening in a square piece of brickwork. Generally it is believed to refer to some snug corner, perhaps near the town walls. At the old public-house in Chancery Lane the legend is as given. Hard by, in Cursitor St., prisoners for debt found a temporary lodging up to a relatively recent date.

Trades tokens are extant of this house. Thomas Moore, in the time of George IV when pugilism and gin drinking were fashionable accomplishments, used to visit the parlour of Jack Randall the proprietor *c.* 1820. It was here that he picked up his materials for his now almost forgotten rhyming satires on the politics and general topics of his time.

At the *Hole-in-the-Wall* in Chandos St. Claude Duval the highwayman was taken prisoner ; whilst the *Hole-in-the-Wall* in Baldwin's Gardens was the citadel in which Tom Brown used to entrench himself from duns and bailiffs, with Henry Purcell as his companion in revelry and merriment. Tom Brown's introductory verses, prefixed to Playford's *Musical Companion*, 1698, are dated ' from Mr. Stewart's at the *Hole-in-the-Wall* in Baldwin's Gardens '. Another *Hole-in-the-Wall* still existed in Larwood's time in Kirby St., Hatton Garden. There are others at Sherborne, Dorset, at Hull and at Spalding. Some of them are so called merely as having a narrow entrance from a comparatively wide handsome street.

Anciently, instead of being a painted board, the object of the sign sometimes was carved and hung within a hoop, hence many of the ancient signs are called the ' —— *on the Hoop* '. In the close roll 1370, we find the *George on the Hoop* ; 1443, *Hart on the Hoop* ; 1447, the *Swan on the Hoop*, the *Cock on the Hoop*, and the *Hen on the Hoop*. Besides these we find mentioned the *Crown on the Hoop*, the *Bunch of Grapes on the Hoop*, the *Mitre on the Hoop*, the *Angel on the Hoop*, the *Falcon on the Hoop*, etc. In 1795, two of these signs were still extant. A *Bunch of Grapes within a Hoop* is still preserved in Newport St., and a *Cock on the Hoop* in Holborn. These hoops seem to have originated in the highly ornamented bush or crown which latterly was made of hoops and covered with evergreens.

The *Hoop & Bunch of Grapes* was the sign of a public-house in St Alban St. (now part of Waterloo Place) kept at the beginning of the 19th century by a once famous Matthew Skeggs who obtained his renown from playing in the character of Signor Bumbasto a concerto on a broomstick at the Haymarket Theatre adjoining. There is another *Hoop & Grapes* at Farringdon St., and still another—a Trust house—an interesting old house in Harrow Alley off Aldgate. The *Hoop & Griffin* was a coffee-house in Leadenhall St. *c.* 1700.

The *Hoop & Toy* is a public-house in Thurloe Place, South Kensington. Here the original meaning of the hoop seems entirely lost, as its combination with the toy seems to allude to the hoop trundled by children. The *Toy* at Hampton used to be a favourite resort with the Londoners till 1837, when it was pulled down to make room for private houses. Seventeenth-century trades tokens of this house are extant. According to Lysons, in the survey of 1653 mention is made of a piece of pasture ground near the river called the *Toying* place, the site, probably, of a well-known inn near the bridge now called the *Toy*.

Cardmakers usually took a card for their sign, as the *Queen of Hearts & King's Arms* which was the sign of a cardmaker in Jermyn St. in 1803. One of the Bagford bills has : ' At the *Old Knave of Clubs* at the Bridgefoot, in Southwark, lived Edward Butling, who maketh and selleth all sorts of hangings for rooms.' Possibly he sold also playing cards. These knaves, however, seem at one time to have been a badge, for at the creation of seventeen knights of the Bath by Richard III, the Duke of Buckingham was ' richely appareled, and his horse trapped in blue velvet embroudered with the *knaves of cartes* burnyng of golde, which trapper was borne by foteman from the grounde '. The *Queen of Trumps* is a sign at West Walton, Lincs. The *Pack of Cards*, Combe Martin, Devon, is said to have been built by a 17th-century squire from the proceeds of a change in his luck when he had staked his all upon a last rubber.

Other games have produced the sign of the *Golden Quoit* in Whitehaven, and the *Corner Pin* which figures in a Seven Dials ballad :—

> When first I saw Miss Bailey,
> Twas on a Saturday,
> At the *Corner Pin* she was drinking gin,
> And smoking a yard of clay, etc.

Those devoted to the ancient game of skittles, recently happily revived, know that the corner pins are the most difficult to strike, and that from their fall with the rest depends whether the throw counts double or not. Houses of this sign are found in St John St., at Hull, Erith, and elsewhere. The *Middle Pin* is no doubt a rival house to the local *Corner Pin*.

Of the merry festivities of May-Day scarcely a trace was left in Larwood's time

The White Horse Hotel, Dorking, Surrey

The Plough, Redford

The Falcon, Eltham, S.E.9

The Pied Horse, Slough, Bucks,

The Black Boy, Sudbury

The Rose & Crown, Low Hesket

The Jack of Trumps, Barnham, Suffolk

The Queen, Corby

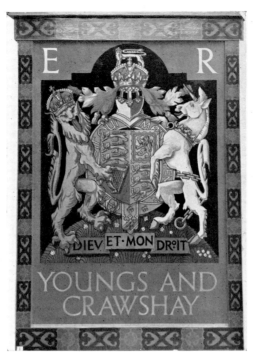

King's Arms, Ludham, Norfolk

Ship Inn, Foulsham, Norfolk

Ship Inn, King St., Norwich

The Comet, Hatfield

The Saracen's Head, Margate

The New Wellington, Newmarket

The Highland Laddie, Glasson

Rifleman, St George's, Norwich

The Cogers, Salisbury Court, E.C.4 (two sides)

The Tally-ho, Barnet

Dick Turpin, Gadshill (two sides)

The Brewery Tap, Ferneaux Pelham, Herts.

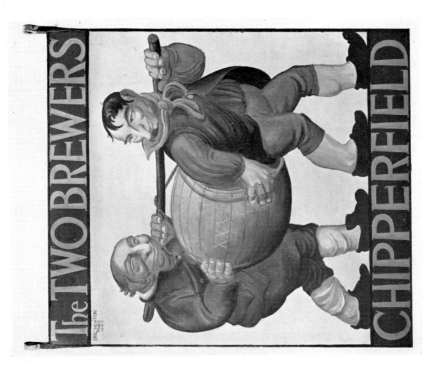

The Two Brewers, Chipperfield

The Three Magpies, Sells Green, Send

The Black Swan, Abingdon

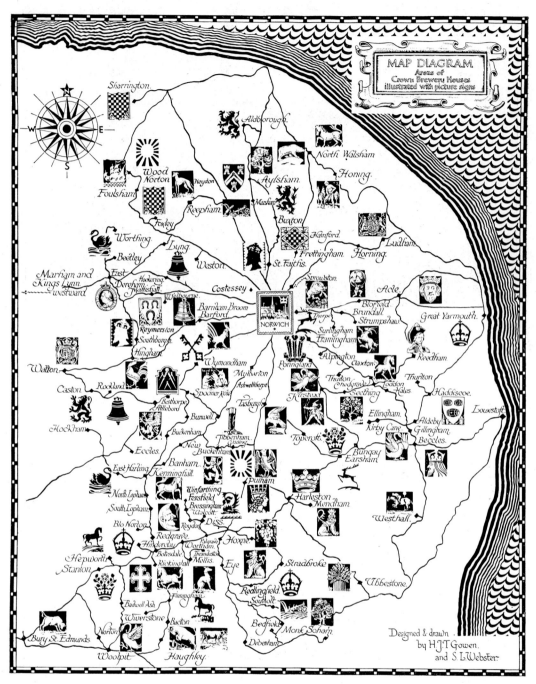

Map Diagram

Greene King Trade Sign

The Jolly Caulkers, Rotherhithe

except the dance of the sweeps and the sign of the *Maypole*. The latter is the only one surviving still. Stubbs with puritanical horror thus describes the *Maypole* :—

> . . . these oxen draw home this Maie pole (this stinckying Idoll rather) which is coured all ouer with flowers and hearbes bounde rounde aboute with stringes, from the toppe to the bottome, and sometyme painted with variable colours with two or three hundred men, women, and children following it with great devotion. And thus being reared up with handkerchiefs and flagges streaming on the toppe they strawe the ground aboute, binde green boughes aboute it, sett up sommer houses, Bowers and Arbours hard by it. And then fall they to banquet and feast, to leape and daunce aboute it, as the Heathen people did at the dedication of their Idolles, whereof this is a perfect pattern, or rather the thing itself.

According to Featherstone, another sulky Puritan, ' of tenne maydens which went to fetch May, nine of them came home with childe'. The consequence of all this grumbling was that the Maypole was abolished in the godly times of the Commonwealth, and as a matter of course, revived at the Restoration—but its prestige was gone. At present it is however commemorated on a few signboards. There is one mentioned in *Barnaby Rudge*, on the outskirts of Hainault Forest, where all the regulations of the house were laid down in rhyme. There is on the stable door :—

> Whosoever smokes tobacco here
> Shall forfeit sixpence to spend in beer,
> Your pipes lay by when you come here,
> Or fire to me may prove severe.

An old, and rather uncommon sign, is the *Wheel of Fortune*, which may be seen at Alpington, Norf., and in other places. This wheel is sometimes represented with four kings, one on each quadrant. In the Middle Ages it was a very common symbol being frequently painted in churches, as among the half-obliterated frescoes of Catfield church, Norf., and in domestic dwellings, as in the early Tudor mansion Little Morton Hall, Ches.

The *Monster* was at one period an inn of some resort in Willow Walk, Chelsea, later a starting-point for the Pimlico omnibuses. Its name is perhaps a corruption of Monastery. The whole of the manor of Chelsea was leased (in 1368) to the abbot and convent of Westminster. At this period, or shortly after, the sign of the *Monastery* may have been set up to be handed from generation to generation, until the meaning and proper pronunciation were forgotten. This sign, it is believed, is unique. The sign is still carried by a modern public-house on the site of the old one. Ned Ward mentions a *Green Monster* Tavern in Prescott St., but this may have been one of his jokes on the very common *Green Dragon*. The tavern in question was a very unlucky house and not less than three or four landlords had failed in it, which was not to be wondered at, for the street appears at that time to have been one of the soberest in London. According to Ned, one ' would walk by forty or fifty houses and not an alehouse '.

x

The *Million Gardens* in 1718 was a house in Strutton Ground, Westminster, where tickets might be obtained for a lottery of plate in 1718. The name in reality was *Melon Gardens*. Probably the lottery association may have helped in the corruption of the original name.

The *Norwich a Port* of which there were formerly two examples in Norwich city refers to a scheme of 1814 for giving Norwich direct communication with the sea at Lowestoft. A canal was duly opened, much to the indignation of Yarmouth, but nothing much came of it, although indirectly it made Lowestoft a port and a watering-place too.

Pepys on 3 August 1660 dined at an ordinary called the *Quaker*, after a somewhat unusual godfather for a tavern. This house was situated in the Great Sanctuary, Westminster, and was only pulled down in the early 19th century to make way for a market-place, which in its turn made room for a new sessions-house. This in its turn has been replaced by the Middlesex Guildhall. The last landlord opened a new house in Thieving Lane, and adorned the doorway of this house with twisted pillars decorated with vine-leaves brought from the old *Quaker*. John Thomas Smith gives a view of this house in the additional plates to his *Antiquities of Westminster*.

The *Pilgrim* has been mentioned incidentally (on p. 253) as a sign at Coventry. There is another public-house of this name in Kennington Lane. In 1833 a figure of a pilgrim was placed upon the roof of this house, which by concealed mechanism moved to and fro like the Wandering Jew, doomed to wander up and down until the end of the world. It was however of contemptible workmanship and very soon got out of order.

The *Gypsy's Tent* occurs at Hagley, Worcs., the *Gypsy Queen* formerly at High-bury, and still in High St., S.E.27. The queen alluded to was Margaret Finch who died at Norwood in 1760 at the age of 109. Norwood was her residence during her last years, and there she told fortunes to the credulous. The woman, when a girl of seventeen, may have been one of the dusky gang pretty Mrs. Pepys and her companions went to consult, 11 August 1638. A granddaughter of Margaret Finch, also a so-styled queen, was living in an adjoining cottage in the year 1800.

The *True Lover's Knot* is a sign at Northwood, Mx., the only example of it met with. In the north of England and in Scotland there still survived in Larwood's time the custom of betrothed working-class lovers presenting each other with a curious kind of knot called 'a true lover's knot'. This was formerly a common present between lovers of all stations of life in England.

The *Folly* is not unusual; it is generally applied to a very ambitious, extravagantly furnished or highly ornamented house. In such a sense it was already used in Queen Elizabeth's reign. One of the most notorious 'Follies' was a vessel of timber divided into sundry rooms with a platform and balustrade on the top, which in the reign of Charles II was moored above London Bridge. When the moored coffee-house was broken up the name was taken by one on dry land. A still surviving house at Thames Ditton is apparently called after this one. *Trouble House* at Tetbury is said by some to commemorate two successive landlords, both of whom committed suicide. More probably it was named in reference to Luddite outrages which were particularly rife in the district. Still another explanation is that its builder and its two past owners all were ruined financially by it.

The sign of the *Blue Coat Boy*, usually chosen by toy-shops, printsellers, and colour-men, was either in compliment to the scholars of Christ's Hospital, or was named after the Bridewell Boys, that is foundlings and deserted children, who wore a blue coat and trousers, with a white hat. There was a *Blue Coat* coffee-house in Sweeting's Alley, near the Exchange, in 1711. At present it is generally called the *Blue Boy* as in the houses formerly existing at Old Swinford, Worcs., Minchinhampton, Glos., and in a few other places, and at Hertford, or the *Blue Boys* as at Kippings. In Islington there are still two such signs.

The *Weary Traveller* occurs at 204 Sutton Rd., Kidderminster, the *Traveller's Rest* in a great many places, sometimes accompanied by the phrase *Rest & be Thankful*, which last advice served as a sign to two public-houses at Whitehaven, and one at Cutcombe, Som. The *Traveller's Rest* at Flash Bar is one of the highest inns in England, more than 1,500 feet above sea-level. There is a *Traveller's Call* at Hazel Grove, Stockport, a *Traveller's Joy* with a good pictorial sign at Emsworth, Hants, and a *Traveller's Welcome* at Hagbourne, Berks. The *Moderation* is a sign at Reading.

Finish was the sign of a notorious night-house in Covent Garden, kept at the beginning of the 19th century by a Mrs. Butler. Here, according to *Tom Crib's Memorial to Congress* the gentlemen of the road used to divide their spoil in the grey dawn of the morning, when it was time for the night-birds to fly to their roost. Until shortly before Larwood's time this was a gloomy, disreputable coffee-house where beer and spirits could be obtained when all the public-houses were closed. This house was originally named the *Queen's Head*, but was nicknamed the *Finish* from its being the place where the fast men of the day generally 'finished off'. There is a *Final* in King William St., another at Bermondsey, and a *Farewell* at Castleton.

Farewell then, it is a traveller's word. Farewell to the next inn and beyond, farewell to countless inns of comfort and good cheer, in countless taverns of deep drinking, until nightfall and we together may enter the final inn.

EXPLICIT EXPLICEAT
AUCTOR BIBERE EAT

Chapter XX

SOME NOTES ON THE MODERN INN SIGN

BY GERALD MILLAR

A sign, being the introduction to an inn, should attract by its appropriate character. The subject of signs has been favoured by generations of poets, writers and artists; it has enriched English literature besides forming the basis of decent advertising. It has been observed that ordinary people are familiar with the quips, profound sentiments and political allusions of the myriad signs which embellish the inns of the English countryside. . . . You conclude that a sign should be a jovial impertinent sort of affair, eloquent of the broad humour of the English who continue to find something to laugh at.

So Professor A. E. Richardson wrote in his preface to the catalogue of the Exhibition of Inn Signs which was held in 1936 at the Building Centre, then in Bond Street, and which celebrated the renewed recognition of the inn sign as a separate and not inglorious art. Owners unhooked their signs and sent them to town; a committee was formed under the chairmanship of the late Sir Guy Dawber, Vice-President of the Council for the Preservation of Rural England, and included Sir Edwin Lutyens, Professor Richardson and the chairman of the Brewers' Society; an illustrious poster artist spent an entire fortnight hanging the signs, a unique undertaking; the President of the Royal Academy opened the Exhibition; the public flocked; and the Press of this and other countries opened its columns to a bit of fun in that sombre autumn. The last exhibition of its kind had been held in 1762, when Hogarth helped to make it a success; it came into rivalry with a more serious exhibition of easel pictures, and there was an orgy of pamphleteering and back-chat in scurrilously precise language. The 1936 Exhibition suffered no such disadvantage; one critic described it as 'a minor National Gallery', another as a 'nursery rhyme for grown-ups'. Something of the English genius, something from *The Beggar's Opera* and Dickens and the ballads and the broadsheets, something spontaneously low-brow, came startlingly to life. The aim of this Exhibition was to insist that each public-house had its own sign, painted or otherwise, but not a mere lettered board (at Brancaster Staithe on the north Norfolk coast-road you will see the *Hero*, but only in lettering, so that you will need to know that Nelson was born a mile or two inland). Above all, not merely the intimation, often in unlovely lettering, that here is the *Pig & Whistle*, subordinated to Messrs. So-and-so's Sparkling Ales and Stouts. A register of sign artists was started, with details and samples of their work in miniature, and then the war came.

In the spring of 1948 an Inn Crafts Exhibition was held in the Royal Institute of British Artists' Galleries in Suffolk St., London. It was the joint venture of the Brewers' Society and the Central Institute of Art and Design, who acted with the four craft societies concerned and with Sir Eric Maclagan as chairman of the Selection Committee. It too was novel. Sir Charles Tennyson wrote in the preface :

> It is to the crafts that industry must look for the maintenance of the highest standards of quality and design. Nowadays, in the struggle to reduce costs, only a relatively small percentage of industrial workers are taught the skilled use of tools and the percentage of unskilled and semi-skilled labour seems steadily to increase. . . . Moreover, the industrial designer too often has an inadequate knowledge of the material for which he has to design, and of the basic principles applicable.

The success of the Exhibition was assured by some seventy brewers commissioning work, in all the classes, which was for actual use or display in their public-houses. And since the inn sign is an affair of individual craftsmanship, or at least workmanship, it was not surprising that it formed the biggest class. The signs stole the picture ; they hung from the ceiling in the largest room like the banners of an order of chivalry, and many of them were enhanced by fine brackets and frames and cresting in wrought iron. Moreover, there were several three-dimensional essays, some of them indicating a successful future.

There have of late years been several other small exhibitions of inn signs or competitions for their design. Enough has been done to show that the art is alive and back again ; the trouble at the moment is that no new public-houses are being built, or seem likely to be. And a house is seldom rechristened. So that new sign-work must be devoted to replacement of inferior work or to the embellishment of houses possessing no signs to themselves. It is not easy work but, rather, highly specialized and individual, whether in the round or on the flat. The vast majority of signs have been, and probably will remain, painted boards ; their ratio in both London exhibitions was nineteen out of every twenty. Here the most accomplished painter of easel pictures may be an inferior inn sign artist. The wheel has come full circle : early signs were painted because people could not read ; the modern sign must attract people who haven't time to read, who pass it at thirty miles an hour if in a built-up area or faster if not. At the same time it must find its way into the hearts of regular customers. Its appeal must be thus both static and dynamic. Design is all-important. A sign must be well balanced and sturdy, a firmly defined and happy arrangement of coloured shapes. Robust is the right adjective and gusto the right noun. A well-defined silhouette in few colours is a well-founded opinion of the ideal. Perspectives and light and shade, unless indicated in the most poster-like way, are best avoided. There is no room for subtlety, for intellectualism or irony except in its broadest form. That is why heraldry, properly treated, is bound to succeed. It has a stark simplicity and the decorative value of an Italian primitive. The older the arms the simpler, for at least one of their first purposes was that a man might quickly recognize his friends or enemies in battle. Yet heraldry needs skill and instinct for balance and decoration, notably when intricacy is unavoidable. Many heraldic signs of the past years are flat and lifeless—you have only to compare a Victorian royal coat of arms with one of the time of Charles II or Queen Anne to see how drab and formalized it had become.

A quickened sense of style has improved heraldry and the modern signs reflect the change. Perhaps the secret of successful work is to go back to the nursery and try to pluck the heart out of the subject. A good example of this process is the simplification of the acknowledged masterpiece. You have a *King's Head* and you choose Charles I, and that means van Dyck; or Henry VIII, and that means Holbein. You have therefore to produce the essentials of van Dyck or Holbein on a board, larger than life and more simply than according to the master's hand. Not so easy, yet far from impossible. The good poster artist and the good inn sign artist achieve it.

The decisive disadvantage of the painted sign is its quick deterioration from exposure to the English climate. A few treasured signs exist whose owners ascribe them to the old masters. But weather has paid no more respect to a Hogarth or Stubbs or Morland than to the local sign-painter; and if Crome painted a *Man Loaded with Mischief* a succession of later hands must have touched him up. Mr. Ralph Ellis, a distinguished 'full-time' painter of inn signs who has peopled Sussex with first-rate work of a wide range of subject and manner, writes:

> The inn sign is a very different matter to any form of painting which is protected from the weather. I think it is fairly safe to say that one year outside is equivalent to 50 years inside, and is the main drawback to inn sign painting, a factor which can be very discouraging to the painter, and I presume to the owner too. Whatever kinds of paints and varnishes are used, or however much care is taken year by year to preserve the painting, it may be said that 20 years, slightly more or less according to degree of exposure, is the limit of its life. A picture may not require restoring for a hundred years or more, a sign may and probably will require some retouching at the end of its first twelve months of exposure, especially the side most exposed to the sun. If when first painted the work was allowed to harden for three months before varnishing and hanging, many of these troubles would be postponed, but this is not encouraged. The care of the sign is, or should be, part and parcel of the sign painter's work, and it is advisable to take down, inspect and clean them every year. If only someone would discover a varnish which would permanently protect!

Glass is mainly rejected, both as inartistic and as too great a temptation to small boys with air-guns or catapults or well-aimed stones. A few years before the war Messrs. Greene King, brewers at Bury St. Edmunds, commissioned a series of painted signs by Mr. E. M. Dinkel, whose range is also wide and whose heraldic work is notably successful. They were done on quarter-inch copper 'plymax' (26 gauge copper, with edges sealed) 3 feet 2 inches by 2 feet 4 inches wide, a suitable and pleasing size. They were framed in strong and heavy teak, fortified with angle-irons, and were glazed with quarter-inch unbreakable armour-plate glass, with an air space between the plate and both sheets of glass, obtained by stout rubber slips. The current of air between painting and glass was gained by ventilating holes at the top and the bottom of the frame, so placed (with small channels laid to falls) to act as outlets for condensation. This process was expensive but successful. It might be added that this firm likes to add the name of the village at the bottom of the sign, an agreeable addition which had to be ruthlessly blacked out in the war because of the threat of invasion.

The hand-painted sign will go on, long may it, but for durability's sake good work is being done with chemical-industrial processes. We have travelled some way since Professor Richardson, in the catalogue of the Inn Signs Exhibition, dismissed 'essays in Olde Englysshe' with the words: 'But even such lapses count as nought by comparison with those enamelled signs which are supposed to be proof against water.' Mechanical reproduction of 'enamelled signs' is one thing; here we are interested in mechanical reproduction of individual work. A firm of experts writes:

> Signs in vitreous enamel, frequently used for advertising, stand up to weather conditions and the sun's rays extremely well, and the life of such signs often exceeds 20 years. Nevertheless they seem to be in disfavour partly because of the recent restrictions in the use of steel for such purposes, and partly because such signs are usually in the form of flat panels fixed to walls with ugly screws, and rust spreads from the exposed edges of the sign where the enamel coating is thin.
>
> Considerable interest has been shewn recently in the development of signs for outside use in vitreous enamel which are of a novel construction and frameless, with no exposed edges and no fixing screws on the face of the sign. The general construction is attractive in appearance, and artists' designs can be faithfully copied.
>
> The vitreous enamelled sign requires practically no maintenance other than the painting of external supporting ironwork, and occasional cleaning of the surface with soap and water or other cleaning material generally used for cleaning the household bath.
>
> The cost of the sign compares favourably with a hand-painted sign when durability and cost of maintenance are taken into account.

This firm has, in the manner described above, executed a successful sign, designed by Mr. M. C. Farrar Bell for Trust Houses Ltd., for their *Parrot* inn at Forest Green in Surrey.

Another most effective treatment, which combined durability and fidelity to the original design with consistency of size and shape and series, has been evolved by Messrs. Frederick Leney, brewers, of Wateringbury in Kent, a subsidiary company of Messrs. Whitbread. The process is briefly described in *Inn-Signia*, the third volume of the Whitbread Library:

> An original design is painted by one of the skilled artists who specialize in this work. The outlines of this design are enlarged and then engraved on a metal sheet, which is painted in accordance with the original design. When, after two or three years, the sign needs repainting to restore its pristine freshness of colour, the work can be carried out without difficulty by a comparatively unskilled painter following the colour guide and the easily traced etched lines on the metal.

In spite of this centralized method, the signs belong each to its house; the frame and simple wrought-iron cresting are uniform; and thus both individuality and uniformity are gained, a very sound result whether artistically or commercially. Moreover, this firm and its parent have done some bold and engaging rechristening, so that many of these Kentish signs, in a series now nearly 350 strong, are modern in subject as well as treatment. Messrs. Whitbread have even made little facsimiles of them, rather like cigarette cards in metal, which can be collected in series of fifties, and which admirably publicize an essay in sound and original workmanship.

Lettering is vastly important, but it does not do to dogmatize. Readability and fitness are what is wanted. There is the Roman model and its evolutions, which may go very well on a sign. Or, it may look mannered and precious and over-refined. An inn sign is a hearty and rather theatrical affair, and must reflect the nature and atmosphere of the house, inside and outside, which it advertises. The subject has been well put in a recent note on the external and internal decoration of public-houses, by Mr. R. Y. Goodden and Mr. Kenneth Rowntree. The passage embraces more than the sign, yet is appropriate here :

> As in the use of colour, so in the choice of lettering quiet refinement is not altogether the appropriate standard for use in public houses. There is room for something more decorative and adventurous than the faultless roman and sanserif types so much in use today. Shaded and decorated 'Egyptian' types, cut-out marbled letters and even the white cut-out letters stuck to (and now fast falling off) the outside of windows, deserve a second thought, as does the personal and highly decorative work in cursive scripts and flourishes of an able and imaginative signwriter. The richness and variety of lettering on old tombstones will surely excuse the brewer or the publican of any charge of excessive boisterousness in the use of lettering, provided that the styles of letter chosen are really decorative and not merely bizarre. A good piece of signwriting can be the making of a simple exterior.

I have heard it said that, the inn sign being specialized, it should be given for design and execution only to those specially qualified. That is true enough. But the qualification is wider and odder than might be supposed. Mr. Ralph Ellis and Mr. E. M. Dinkel have been mentioned ; there have been other leading artists too. Mr. Cosmo Clark, Mr. Keith Henderson and Mr. Eric Newton, to name only three others, have painted admirable signs. Miss Gertrude Hermes' carving in low relief on the sign bracket of the *Myllet Arms* at Perivale, and Mr. Eric Kennington's sculptured signs of the *Comet* at Hatfield and the *Nag's Head* at Bishop's Stortford are successful examples of contemporary success. But a name is not everything : a great deal of almost anonymous work of the highest standard has been done, often through a marriage of local talent. Messrs. Youngs, Crawshay & Youngs' (Norwich) surveyor and a local artist have between them designed and executed signs of great merit, so good that they occupied the end wall of the principal room at the 1936 Exhibition and Mr. Fred Taylor, who hung the show, insisted that another sign should be specially painted and sent from Norwich to ensure a balance of colour and design. A director of the Newcastle Breweries has designed and made some very unusual signs in metal ; and one of the most striking exhibits in 1936, a pair of crossed keys in wrought iron, gilded and acetylene-welded (and weighing three-quarters of a ton), was made by a Dorchester blacksmith. The biggest firms do not necessarily have the best signs. Payment has varied, and indeed it is something of an act of faith for the owner of a little house doing little business to provide it with an expensive sign ; there is the artist to pay and perhaps a frame and cresting of wrought iron into the bargain. A fair price for designing and painting a two-sided sign by an artist of repute might be between £25 and £50, according to the design and size and to the artist's position.

The scope and opportunities of the rarer three-dimensional sign are endless. 'There would seem', writes Mr. M. C. Farrar Bell in an article * about them, 'to be several reasons for their rarity. First, their initial cost is usually greater than that of the painted board, although they are much easier to maintain and in the long run may very well be more economical. Secondly, they are not as a rule such good " eye-catchers " as painted signs because they dispense with the advantage of a large area of brightly coloured background. Thirdly, there are fewer craftsmen who work " in the round ".' Nevertheless, the most memorable and best loved signs of the past seem to have been in the round : the hounds chasing their fox across the wooden gantry at Barley in Hertfordshire ; the hive of live bees at Grantham ; the white hart on his roof at Salisbury ; or that legendary triumphal arch of the *White Hart* at Diss, which from 1655 until about 1800 spanned the Norwich road, 'supporting two White Harts and a multitude of allegorical figures and illustrating the story of Diana and Actaeon with attendant angels, lions, Justices and other figures, all carved with the greatest richness and detail', and costing £1,057 in the austere period of the Commonwealth. What a tragedy that this flowering of the eccentric English genius is only to be seen in a rather dim engraving. The few old City signs in the Guildhall Museum show a range of invention and material ; and materials are more various nowadays. Then, people get fonder of things ' in the round ' ; Mr. Bell tells how, at the *Bear* in Wantage, American soldiers in the war finally insisted on riding on the bear himself, to his utter destruction ; and one remembers mild riots when London undergraduates took a tobacconist's Highlander around with them. The feeling goes back to the nursery.

The three-dimensional sign offers the same problem as the painted board, one of fitness and simplicity of design. An example of good siting is Mr. Eric Kennington's sign (to Mr. E. B. Musman's design) of the *Comet* at Hatfield. It stands well to the front of this striking house in a large parking space ; it is a stone monolith column carved in low relief, ancient in style, with a stark and streamlined chromium-plated ' Comet' aircraft on top—a challenging combination. One or two of the big Birmingham outer-ring houses have fine signs in stone applied, indeed formalized, on the façade. Another happy example is the *Henry VIII* at Hever Castle in Kent, where the king, after Holbein, stands in coloured semi-relief in a frame, so that you see him front and back in a very human and recognizable way. Elsewhere and indeed every-where the customary two dimensions can be turned into three ; beehives or bunches of grapes or animals galore. At the 1948 Inn Crafts Exhibition there were one or two very successful attempts : an open-worked cock in brightly coloured metals wired for illumination, for example, and nothing more nor less than a straw ' dolly' in the form of an anchor, a charming use of that most decorative yet simplest and cheapest of all rural arts, but needing some form of cover or protection from the weather. Again, fitness is all.

Another successful type of sign, with the illusion rather than the reality of three

* *A Monthly Bulletin*, January, 1950.

dimensions, is in cut-out metal, usually framed. A good example is at the *White Hart* Royal Hotel, at Moreton-in-Marsh, Gloucestershire, made by Mr. C. A. Purbrook for Trust Houses, Ltd ; here the metal is coloured. The sign of the *King's Head* at Halstead in Essex, designed by the late Basil Oliver for Messrs. Greene King, relies for its admirable effect purely on silhouette. Wrought iron is secondary rather than primary to the sign itself, and mainly serves as frames, with scroll-work and cresting, or as the supporting bracket. The pity about this lovely craft is its expense, because any capable smith can make a satisfactory job to a design. We have never aspired to the lace-like delicacy of the work in the Tyrol, where whole scenes are depicted in gilded and painted metal. The projection, too, of the Tyrolese signs is enormous, and in many parts of the country—in the area ruled by the L.C.C., for instance— by-laws frown on projection. (For an entirely new sign, by the way, permission must be got from the Ministry of Town and Country Planning through the local council, who require to see a design. This rule does not apply to repainting or to the replacement of an existing sign.) In an article * ' Wrought Iron and the Inn Sign ', Mr. Marcus Whiffen wrote :

> Few media allow such freedom within the range of their technical limitations. There could be no more perfect foil for the intricacy of wrought-iron work than the clean surface of a modern building, and no more suitable employment for it than the sign-bracket of a modern inn. Perhaps we might even take a hint from the Huntingdon Fox [now in the Victoria and Albert Museum] and from time to time use iron for the sign itself. Among contemporary sculptors there is a new interest in the possibilities of metal, and the English inn might well become the field in which that much-discussed union of all the arts—architecture, painting and sculpture—was at last achieved. But in any case the use of wrought iron is a vital part of its tradition and one which we should not easily abandon.

An unworthy practice is to hang lesser and usually undistinguished signs and notices from the main sign or its supports ; or to plaster the front of a house with them. These may be neon-lit. Supplementary signs are necessary enough to graduate for better design, at least to be grouped in some comelier way. So we come to the owners'—that is, almost everywhere, the brewers'—names. Here again it is wrong to dogmatize ; a useful passage on lettering has already been quoted. Some of the brewers' coloured boards and lettering are pleasant enough ; they signify that owner and him only, they advertise both his beer and his style. Others are less happy and some are worse ; one owner subjects the front of even the smallest house to an enormous enamelled metal sheet which qualifies for Professor Richardson's stricture. Moreover you cannot expect a brewer recklessly to abandon a sign or device or style which, however deplorable æsthetically, has come to stand for much goodwill. Nevertheless owners are taking to the house mark, which has a clear field and a good tradition. An early example has been the glazed plaque, measuring 1 foot 11 inches by 1 foot 3 inches wide, which the late Mr. Kruger Gray designed, as a play on the owners' name, and which Messrs. Doulton & Co. have manufactured for Messrs.

---

* *A Monthly Bulletin*, October, 1949.

Greene King [plate 63]; this little plaque adorns the front of all their public-houses, whether of brick or in lime-washed East Anglian plaster. There were sixteen designs for new house marks at the 1948 Inn Crafts Exhibition, all for glazed earthen-ware except for one in glass and another in perspex and aluminium; some of these are being manufactured and will be distributed. A good sign for the house itself and a good house mark to denote its owner: what could be better?

The revised text of Larwood and Hotten's standard book contains the history and lore of the sign from its birth centuries ago. These few notes are added to argue that the craft still offers great opportunity for good work and perhaps for good fun too. We can do with them both.

Appendix

A BRIEF BOOK-LIST OF WORKS ON INNS AND INN SIGNS

History of Signboards by Jacob Larwood and John Camden Hotten. Chatto & Windus. 1907. 3s. 6d.

Quaint Signs of Olde Inns by C. J. Monson-Fitzjohn. Herbert Jenkins. 1926. 7s. 6d.

The English Inn : Past and Present by A. E. Richardson, A.R.A., and H. Donaldson Eberlein, B.A. H. T. Batsford Ltd. 1925. 21s.

Catalogue of the Inn Signs Exhibition. Preface by A. E. Richardson, A.R.A. ' A Monthly Bulletin.' 1936. 1s.

The Renaissance of the English Public House by Basil Oliver, F.S.A., F.R.I.B.A. Faber & Faber. 1947. 21s.

Inn Signs—Their History and Meaning by Sir Gurney Benham, F.S.A. The Brewers' Society. 1939.

Inns and Inn Signs in and near Burton by W. E. Tate, F.R.Hist.S. Warwick Savage. 1944. 2s.

Inn-Signia. The Whitbread Library. 1948. 5s.

The Spotted Dog by Reginald Turner. Sylvan Press. 1948. 12s. 6d.

What Inn Signs Tell by W. Block. Published in France. 1929. 5s.

Inns and Inn Signs : Sacred and Secular by C. R. Swift. Published privately by the Author. 1947. 10s. 6d.

Index

Note : *CAPITALS* denote general references ; otherwise references are to specific inn signs

Printed in Great Britain by Butler & Tanner Ltd., Frome and London